The Battle of Marathon
in Scholarship

The Battle of Marathon in Scholarship

Research, Theories and Controversies Since 1850

DENNIS L. FINK

McFarland & Company, Inc., Publishers
Jefferson, North Carolina

LIBRARY OF CONGRESS CATALOGUING-IN-PUBLICATION DATA

Fink, Dennis L., 1942–
The Battle of Marathon in scholarship : research, theories and controversies since 1850 / Dennis L. Fink.
    p.   cm.
Includes bibliographical references and index.

ISBN 978-0-7864-7973-3 (softcover : acid free paper) ∞
ISBN 978-1-4766-1534-9 (ebook)

1. Marathon, Battle of, Greece, 490 B.C.   2. Greece—History—Persian Wars, 500–449 B.C.—Historiography.   I. Title.
DF225.4.F56 2014   938'.03—dc23   2014013615

BRITISH LIBRARY CATALOGUING DATA ARE AVAILABLE

© 2014 Dennis L. Fink. All rights reserved

No part of this book may be reproduced or transmitted in any form or by any means, electronic or mechanical, including photocopying or recording, or by any information storage and retrieval system, without permission in writing from the publisher.

On the cover: Battle of Marathon © 2014 Clipart.com

Printed in the United States of America

*McFarland & Company, Inc., Publishers
Box 611, Jefferson, North Carolina 28640
www.mcfarlandpub.com*

To my grandson, Logan Kap,
who daily battles against cystic fibrosis.

Acknowledgments

First I want thank my wife, Pat, who suggested that I write this book, put up with my obsessive need to work on it and never complained about the cost of books that I needed. I cannot give enough thanks to Kara Kohn and the other reference librarians and staff at the Plainfield Public Library as they made it possible for me to do research from home as they procured books for me from all over the country.

Thanks also go to Bill Siavelis, Denny Schillings and Myras Osman, fellow history teachers who read parts of my manuscript and gave me encouragement throughout the writing process. Also, thanks to Mark Herr, who read sections and gave suggestions and support, and finally to Rob Combs whose constant enthusiasm and encouragement really helped me when my confidence waned.

Table of Contents

Acknowledgments	vi
Preface	1
1—The Major Ancient Sources Evaluated	3
2—The Persian Military	14
3—The Greek Military	30
4—The Rise of Persia	62
5—The Ionian Revolt	79
6—Greece and Persia, 492–490 BCE	109
7—The Battle	116
8—The Importance of the Battle of Marathon	188
Chapter Notes	191
Bibliography	217
Index	227

Preface

This book was born in 1963 when as an undergraduate I completed an independent study paper on the Battle of Marathon at Illinois State University. The research instilled in me a lifelong interest in ancient Greek history and especially the Greco-Persian Wars. During my 35-year career teaching the history of Western civilization at Homewood-Flossmoor high school in Illinois, I thought about the Battle of Marathon and taught about it, but further research was put on the back burner. After my retirement from teaching high school, I continued to read and talk about the Battle of Marathon until my wife, Pat, suggested that I write a book about it. After thinking about it, I took it as a personal challenge and began to do research.

During my initial research in 1964 I had spent a great deal of time in the Classics Library at the University of Illinois in Champaign. As I began my new research, I found the computer revolution had made it much easier to access sources. Through my part-time employment at Northern Illinois University, as a supervisor of history student teachers, I have been able to utilize JSTOR which gave me access to all the research published in the major scholarly journals throughout the world. My local public library in Plainfield Illinois gave me immeasurable help in acquiring books from major academic libraries throughout the United States through interlibrary loan. The computer also gave me access to important websites such as the ones on the Trireme Project, the Persian military and military reenactments. In addition, a blog on hoplite warfare exposed me to interesting new theories and views on the topic.

As I pursued my research it quickly became apparent to me that my lack of specialized training in ancient history, lack of Greek and Latin language skills, and my lack of academic experience at the university level prevented me from presenting any new or unique perspectives on the topic; however, as I read through the vast literature that exists, I began to think I could write a book that would be of use to a substantial audience.

During my career of 35 years teaching high school history and 44 years of serving as a university supervisor of history student teachers, I became convinced that content knowledge is one of the most important characteristics of good teaching. At the same time, I also recognized the difficulty that teachers in middle school and high school face in trying to keep up to date with the latest scholarship in their fields due to the heavy demands of their teaching schedule, large class sizes, grading demands, extracurricular demands and the other time-consuming demands of teaching. I believe this problem could be helped if university teachers would provide books that made the latest research and developments in their field available to teachers and other interested readers in some summary form.

I believe my book can help in this area. It makes available in one source most of the major scholarship available in English from the past 162 years on the Battle of Marathon.

It also includes chapters on source evaluation, the rise of the Persian Empire, the Persian and Greek military, the Ionian Revolt and an in-depth examination of the battle itself, including reasons for the unexpected Greek victory. While it provides a fairly comprehensive overview of the above topics, it also includes resources for those wanting to look at any of the topics in more depth with comprehensive endnotes and a bibliography of 400 sources.

Rather than needing to be read cover to cover, the book's organization allows readers to zero in on their particular areas of interest, which could be as broad as the battle itself, more detailed such as hoplite warfare, or even more limited such as the conflicting viewpoints on *othismos* or the conflict over the weight of the hoplite's panoply. I also felt that based upon my career in education I would be able to present the material in a manner using appropriate language that would make it accessible and understandable and useful for high school students, college students, graduate students, perhaps even general European history teachers in colleges and universities and finally the general public, some of whom have a great interest in ancient Greek history. At the same time, my endnotes and bibliography will provide a vast amount of information and sources for those interested in doing more research on any of the covered topics.

A major problem for any person writing about the Battle of Marathon is the lack of primary sources. There are no Persian narrative histories that cover the topic, and *The Histories* by Herodotus, which presents our most complete version of the battle, evokes great controversy. Thus I felt the first chapter would have to cover the ancient sources that are available and examine the controversy surrounding Herodotus. Next it became clear to me that in order to understand the Battle of Marathon a reader would need a great deal of information concerning the Persian military, the Greek military, the rise of the Persian Empire, the Ionian Revolt and Greco-Persian relations prior to 490. In the chapter on the actual Battle of Marathon I have followed the example of Peter Krentz and have broken down the Battle of Marathon and the questions about it into separate sections and examined how various historians have dealt with each section and the theories that they have advanced over the past 162 years.

The 2,500-year anniversary of the Battle of Marathon was in 2010, and major new books were published and events took place in celebration of the battle. Marathon is one of the best-known battles in ancient history, but was it really an important battle that saved Western civilization, or was it simply a minor skirmish and defeat as the Persians viewed it? The final chapter deals with this issue.

1

The Major Ancient Sources Evaluated

As one approaches the study of the Achaemenid military, the Athenian military and the Battle of Marathon, it is essential to examine the primary sources and ancient secondary sources that apply. We immediately face difficulties in studying the Achaemenid military as the Persians have not left behind written archives, a native Persian literature or historical writings.[1] Most official Persian correspondence was done using parchment or papyrus, which has not survived. We have at our disposal Babylonian Akkadian clay tablets, but they deal primarily with business transactions and contracts, so they are of little help on political or military matters. In addition, large numbers of tablets dating from 509 to 497 BCE and 492 to 457 BCE have been found in Persepolis, but they primarily are records of supply centers and treasury building operations. They are useful for a social and economic history but not very useful for political or military purposes. Some papyrus sources have survived in Egypt, and they have been of some help as they refer to garrison affairs in Egypt.[2] For information on dress and armament, the relief structures at Persepolis and the glazed tiles of Susa have been useful. There also are reliefs showing tributary people, and many Persian seals are carved with battle scenes and representations of soldiers. Also in Greek vase painting, the Persian Wars and Persian soldiers have been common themes.[3] The inscription on the cliff faces at Behistun ordered by King Darius, c. 520 BCE provides a narrative, but only for one to two years. Also, it was ordered by Darius to support his claim to be king and written primarily to justify his own actions rather than as a historical record.[4] If we want to get a clearer picture or see an overall pattern in Persian history, we must turn to literary sources.

As early as the sixth century BCE, the Greeks were developing prose writing and taking an interest in historical writing. As a result, we must look at Greek literary sources in order to better understand the history of the Persian Empire.[5] It is somewhat ironic that the details about the great victories as well as the defeats of the Persian Empire come down to us from the Greeks, the empire's greatest enemy, when it is usually the conquerors who write their own glorious history.[6] There is little doubt that most of our information on the Achaemenid Empire and the Persian Wars comes from Herodotus; however, many questions have been raised concerning his credibility, veracity and objectivity. Anyone doing research on the Achaemenid Empire and the Persian Wars must have an understanding of the strengths and weaknesses of Herodotus. As I began my research, I was overwhelmed by the number of books that have been published on Herodotus. In addition, I don't read Greek, German or French, so I am limited to works in English or translated into English. With these limitations in mind I have consulted some experts on Herodotus and will explore his strengths, weaknesses, reliability and applicability to research on the Battle of Marathon.

Herodotus opens his book by identifying his goal. He says, "I hope to do two things: to preserve the memory of the past by putting on record the astonishing achievements both of our own and of the Asiatic peoples; secondly, and more particularly, to show how the two races came into conflict."[7] Michael Flower believes that Herodotus may have written because he believed the Greeks, who fought in the Persian Wars, like Tom Brokaw's "greatest generation" who fought in World War II, had done something as great as or even greater than the Achaeans who had won the Trojan War, and he wanted to make sure that they, too, were remembered. He goes on to point out that Herodotus does not claim that the Persians were weak and cowardly or that their leaders were despicable and led an evil empire.[8] Another historian says that Herodotus was influenced by "fifth century rationalism and the epic tradition." He believes that the epic tradition won out, and thus Herodotus did not write history as we have come to expect it to be written. As a result, he did not get into technical details about the Persian Wars, but rather wrote about the "great and wonderful actions of the Greeks and barbarians," as in the epic tradition of Homer.[9]

While we have no exact date, it appears Herodotus was born between 490 and 480 BCE and thus was probably not born when the Battle of Marathon took place and probably had no recollection of the Persian invasion of Greece in 480.[10] He was born in Halicarnassus in Caria (southwest Asia Minor bordering on Ionia), which made him a Persian citizen. His parents were noble and he was well educated, which allowed him to associate with aristocrats when he traveled, and that meant he would have had access to important information. To gather information, Herodotus traveled to Egypt, Gaza, Tyre, and down the Euphrates to Babylon. He also may have visited parts of Asia Minor, Greek colonies on the Black Sea and perhaps even Scythia.[11] Cawkwell accepts that Herodotus traveled to Sardis and Gaza and perhaps to Babylon but not does not feel he ever got beyond Babylon into Asia.[12] Detlev Fehling is skeptical that Herodotus ever traveled anywhere, and he has received support for his view from O. Kimball Armayor and Stephanie West. This extreme position will be examined later when the "Liar School of Herodotus" is discussed.[13]

Next, one must discuss the sources Herodotus used while writing *The Histories*. The problem is that Herodotus tells us that he used many oral sources, but he does not identify them nor does he include a bibliography of written sources. As a result we are left with drawing inferences and making educated guesses about his sources. As mentioned above, there were no Persian archives for Herodotus to consult, and even if there were, he did not speak or read the language. So he was limited to oral traditions passed on to him by Greek speakers whom he met on his travels.[14]

In his book *The History of Persia*, J.M. Cook considers possible sources from which Herodotus may have gained the detailed information he gives on the Persian Empire. Cook suggests that Herodotus gained information concerning the Persian war councils from Artemesia, despot of Halicarnassus. Herodotus tells the story of how Artemesia rammed another Persian trireme at Salamis which resulted in Xerxes making his famous statement, "My men have become women and my women men."[15] At the same time, we pick up the rumors that she rammed the ship in order to escape pursuit. These rumors were spread by her opposition, which included Herodotus' parents.[16] Another probable source for what occurred during the war councils was Demaratos, the exiled king of Sparta, who would have been in a position to relate details of Xerxes' military affairs.[17] J. Wells suggests that there is a more important source that had even more access to the Persian court. He believes that source was Zopyrus, the great-grandson of Megabyzus, who was one of the seven nobles who helped Darius take the throne. The father of Zopyrus was Megabyzus, the grandson of the above Megabyzus, who was one of Xerxes' six generals, and Zopyrus' grandfather was governor of Babylon about which Herodotus included great detail. Zopyrus deserted Persia in c. 441–440 and died within the year; however, it is possible that Herodotus met Zopyrus and spent several months with him in Athens before Herodotus sailed west to Thurii.[18] Cook also notes that Herodotus spent time on Samos and may have gotten information from those who had known Syloson, who had befriended Darius before he became king, and Darius restored Syloson to rule in Samos.[19] Demokedes of Kroton, a captured Greek doctor, treated Darius successfully and was rewarded by being allowed to live at court. Later he was sent on a Persian reconnaissance mission to the west from which he escaped to Italy. He then returned to Kroton, and Herodotus may have had contact with him. Others believe that Herodotus may have gained military information from the descendants of Artabazos, one of Xerxes' generals, who later was the governor of Hellespontine Phrygia.[20] Information concerning Otanes, another of the seven who helped Darius gain the throne, may have come to Herodotus during his time on Samos, as it was Otanes who had reinstated Syloson as the ruler of the island.[21] During his travels, Herodotus spent perhaps four years in Athens, became friends with Sophocles and probably got to know Pericles.[22] Thus, he had an extended time period in which to talk with the participants in the Persian Wars who were still alive. Lazenby believes that he would have been able to meet with those who fought at Marathon as well as those who fought at Plataea and beyond. Just as with the Persians, however, he does not identify particular sources.[23]

While we can speculate about his sources, we must also consider the credibility and veracity of his account. Macan and How and Wells agree that Herodotus is the earliest extant historical source for the Persian Wars, with only the painting of Marathon in the *Stoa Poikile* being able to be shown as drawn from contemporary sources.[24] Cook believes that Herodotus contains a great wealth of information, some of which is exaggerated and other that borders on mythical, but on the whole feels "there seems to be a firm substratum of genuine historical knowledge which was obtained from Persian and Median sources."[25] Lazenby reinforces Cook's view by claiming that we are fortunate to have such a good source as Herodotus. He points out that Herodotus was "nearly contemporary with the Persian invasions, able to talk to people who participated, checked stories to some extent and was a man of wide knowledge and broad sympathies, sound common sense and considerable humor."[26] Before bestowing sainthood on Herodotus, however, we certainly must recognize that his information varies in quality.

Hammond, even though he considers Herodotus an honest historian, believes we must use Herodotus with three different levels of confidence. He says we should have little doubt if he saw or experienced something, but that we must deal carefully if Herodotus is describing an event based on interviews with participants of long-past events or battles. Finally, he says we must use extreme caution when Herodotus describes long-past events from which no living participants remained.[27] Others believe that while there is not much evidence with which to check Herodotus, that which does exist has a tendency to support him, and his most accurate books from a historical standpoint are his last three books.[28] It is also pointed out that

Herodotus himself does not give equal credence to all of his material. He claims that he must record what others say even if he is not convinced of its truthfulness, and others point out that he attempted to check stories for accuracy. Jacoby, the great German expert on Herodotus, sees Herodotus as an honest historian, who is perhaps naïve and who failed to understand some issues and even may have been the victim of unscrupulous informants.[29] Still there is no doubt that Herodotus must be criticized for his acceptance or exaggeration of numbers involved in Xerxes' invasion of Greece, although this is not a problem unique to Herodotus, as others give huge numbers for the Persian armies fighting against Alexander the Great.[30]

One may be honest, use reliable information, but still be a biased person who selectively uses or ignores material to support his biased viewpoint. Was Herodotus biased when writing his histories? We might ask the question, can any historian be completely objective? All of us have personal and cultural biases, but it is the job of historians to overcome them as best they can. They are taught a method of research in which they should consistently check that "their descriptions, interpretations, and explanations are well supported by the data concerning their subjects that is available to them." In addition, the work of historians is subject to peer review that will help identify and condemn bias when it is found.[31] But Herodotus was not a trained historian. In fact, he was in the process of creating the discipline of history. So his conception of historical truth is not likely to be the same as ours. And yet, when we examine Herodotus, it seems that his score would be quite high if he was evaluated on the degree to which his work is free of bias. The consensus of modern historians seems to be that Herodotus was not a mouthpiece for Athens as some have maintained, was not biased in favor of the Alcmaeonidae, and was not an apologist for the Oracle of Delphi.[32] To be sure, Herodotus described the "freedom-loving" Greeks defeating the Persians led by an autocratic king. But at the same time he treated the Persians with respect. He described how a Persian male's worth is determined by his valor in battle and how Persian boys were taught three things: "to ride the horse, to shoot the bow, and to speak the truth."[33] In describing the Battle of Plataea, Herodotus says, "the Persians were not inferior in courage or strength, but they did not have hoplites arms."[34] Scott in his commentary concludes the following about Herodotus' view of democracy: "The impression from the histories as a whole is that he was neither pro nor anti, but disliked oppression and approved of fair government of whatever complexion, even, perhaps, that of a tyrant."[35]

To this point, most historians seem to accept Herodotus as an honest historian, who, through his travels and collection of oral sources, provides us with a vast amount of generally reliable information about the Achaemenid Empire and the Persian Wars. To be sure, the quality of information varies, and he must be approached with caution, as with most historical sources; however, there is another group of critics known as the "Liar School of Herodotus" who treat him with much less respect. In the late 19th century, authors A.H. Sayce and H. Penofsky came to the conclusion that Herodotus created sources to fit his needs.[36] That view was pretty much ignored until 1989 when Detlev Fehling published his book, *Herodotus and His Sources*. He claims that the apologists for Herodotus "tend to think that all they have to do to prove a point is to indicate a certain possibility." He agrees that Herodotus had written sources but concludes that when Herodotus referred to local sources, they "were in fact his own inventions."[37] Regarding his travels, Fehling believes that nearly all his statements based on autopsy are "pure fiction," and we must consider "the extreme possibility that he never left his native Greece." Fehling concludes, "It may justly be concluded that Herodotus had only the roughest framework of genuine historical information and filled that out ... by his own creative powers."[38]

O. Kimball Armayor has reached conclusions which support Fehling's viewpoint. In examining Herodotus' evidence on his trip to the Black Sea, Armayor concludes, "we cannot go on treating his stories as serious evidence of the fifth century Black Sea." He also states that "Herodotus' great catalogs of the Orient" are totally incorrect and includes three examples to prove his point.[39] He points out that Herodotus' measurements of the Black Sea, Hellespont and the Propontus are "badly wrong." He rejects the possibility that Herodotus saw the six-finger-thick, 600-Amphoreis Brazen Vessel of Exampaios or the wooly-haired Colchians and concludes,

> We cannot go on indefinitely trying to account for what he found in them on the basis of a simpleminded and confused autopsy. It is difficult to understand how one of such wide and varied Greek genius might have grown confused enough to set down in full earnest these impressions of the Pontus if he really went to see for himself. Either he did go and remained content to tell his readers what they wanted and expected to hear in the first place even though it was not true, or he did not go.[40]

Finally, in his book *Herodotus' Autopsy of the Fayoum: Lake Moeris and the Labyrinth*, Armayor totally rejects Herodotus' veracity. In his book, he states that Lake Moeris and the labyrinth that Herodotus describes in book 2.148–150 did not even exist when Herodotus lived. He quotes the work of Miss Caton-Thompson and Miss Gardner in 1929 as evidence of Herodotus' "lies."[41] Based on their geological and archaeological work, they concluded, "Herodotus could never have found a great, high-level lake in the fifth century Fayoum because all evidence of geology and archaeology makes that lake retreat into insignificance long before history began." Based on their article and Gardiner's work on the name "Moeris," Armayor concludes that people have been wrong in saying Moeris referred to a lake when in reality it referred to a town or perhaps a canal. He then argues that the Ionians misinterpreted Egyptian myths, terms and traditions and spoke of Lake Moeris as if it had existed, which Herodotus accepted as fact. Thus he concludes, "We have tried to insist that Lake Moeris belonged to fifth-century Egypt when it almost certainly belonged to sixth-century Ionia."[42] Concerning Herodotus' Labyrinth in the Fayoum he concludes, "Where can we find such a Labyrinth? Not in the real world of fifth-century Egypt, and certainly not in the real world of AD 20th century Egypt. Whatever else Herodotus' Labyrinth may have been, it was never real."[43]

Stephanie West supports Armayor's view concerning the accuracy of Herodotus using epigraphic evidence. She says he does not refer to a great many inscriptions, but those to which he does refer he gets wrong. She goes on to state, "I do not believe, nor would it be *a priori* probable, that his handling of inscriptions is somehow atypical of his methods in general."[44] Armayor's work on the labyrinth and Lake Moeris seems based upon solid archaeological and geological evidence, and West in her review of his book believes that his work "should not be neglected by anyone with a serious interest in Herodotus.[45]

However, upon further investigation, it appears that Armayor's research was not sufficient. In his review of Armayor's book, J.A.S. Evans points out that the research of 1929 has been discredited by the latest geological survey. In 1968, Southern Methodist University, the Polish Academy of Science, and the Geological Survey of Egypt discovered evidence that a lake of 2,200 square kilometers did exist in the time of Herodotus in the area in which Herodotus claimed to have seen Lake Moeris. Evans concludes, "In fact, it is hard to find much to recommend in this book. It fails to prove his point and is not a reliable guide to recent research in the Fayoum area."[46]

At first reading, the arguments of Fehling, Armayor and West seem impressive and convincing; however, upon further reading of reviews of their work one comes to see why most historians do not accept their conclusions. In his book *The Liar School of Herodotus,* W. Kendrick Pritchett claims that Fehling has insufficient knowledge "of the nature of the Greek world, of the area on its edge, especially, and the extent of its interaction with them."[47] He uses his encyclopedic knowledge of geography, topography and archaeology to undercut Fehling's evidence. He accuses Fehling of lacking archaeological knowledge and of having a limited view of what the Greeks might have believed. Pritchett goes on to list 39 claims that Fehling says Herodotus made with no evidence or sources to back them up. He then proceeds to show where Fehling is incorrect by quoting primary sources, ancient secondary sources, 18th- and 19th-century travelers, and topographical information. For example, in book 2.104 Herodotus says the Cholcians are really Egyptians because they are "black skinned and woolly haired," practiced circumcision and produce linen by the same distinctive method. Concerning this statement, Fehling says, "To describe the average Egyptian in these terms is peculiar to say the least; and for Herodotus' Cholcians the description could not be more wide of the mark.... I have also shown ... that the similarity and common Negroid appearance attributed to the Cholcians and the Egyptians in 2.104.2 is unfounded. We may well wonder how such a claim ever came to be made."[48] Pritchett responds by saying,

> We collected 12 sources of testimonia, including Pindar, Hippocrates, Diodorus, two authors of a periplous, Ammianus, and Christian writers, as well as modern literature, on the color of the Cholcians (although different words for color are used and differently interpreted) and their alleged Ethiopian or Egyptian origin, the distinction or Herodotus being immaterial, as Snowden has stated (*The Blacks in Antiquity* Cambridge, Mass. 1970 p. 121). The problem of race on the African continent bulks large in modern literature. We note that in the *UNESCO General History of Africa 2* (Berkeley 1981), the editor of the series, G. Mokhtar, Professor in the Arab Republic in Egypt, devotes the entire first chapter to reviewing the anthropological evidence about Egyptian race, concluding that "the ancient Egyptians are unquestionably among the black races." On page 59, J. Vercoutter endorses this position, "Ancient Egypt was peopled, from its Neolithic infancy to the end of the native dynasties, by black Africans." On pages 36–37, Mokhtar endorses all of Herodotus' statements about what he takes to be the Negroid character of the Egyptians, maintaining also that Herodotus was correct in the 2.104 passage concerning the Cholcians.[49]

Pritchett then takes a look at the evidence Stephanie West used to support her conclusions. In 46 pages Pritchett examines 20 different examples that West used to support her conclusion that Herodotus mishandles, misinterprets epigrams and found it "hard to accept that he could have seen what he says he saw."[50] As an example Pritchett explains that in book 3.84–88, Herodotus tells us that Darius became king because his horse whinnied first and lightning appeared in the sky. He goes on to say, Darius "set up a stone and had a relief carved on it in which was depicted a man on horseback with an inscription which said, 'Darius, son of Hystaspes acquired possession of the kingship of the Persians by the merit of his horse ... and of his groom Oibares.'" Concerning this story West comments,

> We are given no indication of the location of this monument. Nor is Herodotus' interpretation credible: if Darius had circumvented the arrangements whereby the choice of ruler was to be left to heaven, he would not have broadcast his skullduggery; but his whole account of the conspiracy which brought Darius to power bristles with so many blatant improbabilities that this conclusion will surprise no one. It looks as if the story of Darius' ruse (together, no doubt, with much of the immediately preceding narrative) represents a Greek fantasy.[51]

Regarding the accuracy of Herodotus' story, Pritchett turns to J.M. Cook for support concerning its accuracy. In his book, *The Persian Empire*, Cook states,

> Here we at last have a counter check on Herodotus. In his Behistun inscription Darius gives his account of the sequence of events before coming on to the rebellions he had to crush after his accession. The central claim is the same in both: Cambyses had had his brother killed and it was a pretender that the seven conspired to assassinate.[52]

Cook then goes on to explain that no Greek "writer ever showed the slightest acquaintance with it." He also says that Herodotus did not know of the Behistun inscription, and yet he had "precise information ... about the deliberations of the seven before and after the coup. It is clear that somehow he had heard an account of the events that had originally been transmitted orally from one of the seven."[53] For further support of Herodotus, he includes quotes from A.T. Young in the *Cambridge Ancient History* (1988 edition) and A.D. Lawrence in his *Commentary on Herodotus*. Concerning the story about Darius' horse whinnying, Pritchett points out that the trick used by Oibares to accomplish the trick was also covered by Justin and also Ctesias, certainly not one of Herodotus' admirers. Pritchett concludes his examination of this one example used by West by saying that without investigating Persian history or religion, a 20th century rationalist has charged Herodotus with "skullduggery," "blatant improbabilities," and creating a "Greek fantasy," although she does not tell us what is Greek about hippomancy or sun worship.[54] Finally Pritchett concludes his examination of the "Liar School of Herodotus" by stating,

> To stigmatize Herodotus as a liar and his "apologists" as credulous is to throw away at the outset the key to the interpretation of what he writes, to falsify history to our own anachronisms, and to treat as negligible what may be the most valuable thing in the narrative before us—the disclosure of the world age in which he lived. Herodotus was an observer of customs untrammeled by the desire to fit all that he had seen into a theory; a reporter of what he had seen even if he did not understand, and what he had heard, if it seemed for any reason worth reporting, without his necessarily believing it.[55]

In his review of Fehling's book, Hugh Bowden agrees with Pritchett's point that Armayor is "narrowly read." Bowden concludes his review by saying, "Fehling is blessed with a great imagination but a poor grasp of the facts."[56] Lazenby sums up his reaction to Fehling by stating,

> In effect, we are being asked to accept that the first historian was also the first historical novelist, inventing sources, even conflicting ones, before anyone had really tried to use real ones. Nor does the view make nearly enough allowance for the almost infinite possibilities of misunderstanding and misremembering that can arise when one talks to people of different languages and cultures, either directly or even worse through interpreters, probably without even taking notes, let alone tape recording what is said.[57]

Robert Fowler, in his article "Herodotus and His Contemporaries," asked why Herodotus would express skepticism about some sources if he was not serious about doing history. "Thucydides ... knew Herodotus was serious about doing history; he knew that his were the best available methods of discovering truth about the past. So far from faking his sources, Herodotus found new ways to deal with them."[58] Reacting to Fehling, Oswyn Murray in his article, "Herodotus and Oral History," said, "To postulate deliberate and wholesale deception rather than faulty execution, requires an answer to the question, who invented the model which Herodotus is thought to have abused? It implies a proto–Herodotus before Herodotus."[59]

Since these preliminary chapters are leading up to the Battle of Marathon, it is important to look at Herodotus as a military historian. The generally accepted view of historians is that Herodotus had little knowledge of warfare or strategy and tactics because he had no military experience and was unable to talk to top officers of the Persians and Greeks.[60] Adcock says that Herodotus had many good traits, but being a military person was not one of them. He thinks Herodotus was writing in an epic style which does justice to the great characters and events but "contributes little to our understanding of the art of war."[61] In his commentary on book 6, Scott explains the lack of detail concerning the Battle of Marathon as originating in oral traditions that did not value remembering past events in great detail. Also, by the time Herodotus could interview participants who were still living, 40 years had passed and details were forgotten, misremembered and even changed as they were passed down.[62] Hignett believes that Herodotus has been heavily criticized and that his ignorance of military affairs has been exaggerated. He obviously does not bother with describing Greek tactics but does talk of Persian strategy and tactics. He believes that Herodotus can be trusted when he describes actions by armies but not to be trusted as to why the action was taken. Also he feels Herodotus must be severely censured for accepting the ridiculous numbers that he describes during Xerxes' invasion of Greece.[63] Lazenby says that Herodotus' coverage of military affairs at times appears "superficial or even naïve." He also says that some believe that he was not able to judge professional soldiers because of his own inexperience; however, he thinks that perhaps the Greek strategy and tactics at that time were not very professional either, and Herodotus is simply describing events. He goes on to state that the Greeks did not have military schools or seek to study past campaigns. Also, there is little indication that the Greek leaders had any great experience. So maybe Herodotus was as well qualified as any of his contemporaries in military affairs.[64]

Arthur Ferrill argues that Herodotus has been misjudged as a military historian. He agrees with Lazenby that the Greek generals were not professional and states that they were instead politicians. He adds that the "hoplite phalanx demanded no more than a superficial appreciation of strategy and tactics." He says that it was the Greek generals who were ignorant of strategy and tactics rather than Herodotus.[65] Responding to the criticism of the ridiculous numbers concerning the Persian force used by Herodotus, he states that Herodotus used the numbers because they were traditional and "because they suited the grandeur of his theme." He feels that Herodotus understood the main point, which was that the Persians outnumbered the Greeks and that this influenced their strategy and tactics. Herodotus understood why Thermopylae was chosen and realized that the Persian numbers could overwhelm the Greeks on an open plain; however, he also understood that the Greeks had the advantage in hand-to-hand combat because of their armor and weapons. He believes that the epic tradition dominated Herodotus, so that he did not make any effort to go into depth about strategy and tactics, or to give detailed descriptions of the battles. Rather, he talks more about the great actions of individuals. Ferrill believes that Herodotus could have produced a more classical military history if he had chosen, as demonstrated by his discussion of the strategy before the Battle of Salamis, which Ferrill calls "impeccable."[66]

What conclusions can be reached concerning Herodotus after this long discussion? It appears that the conclusions that Lazenby and Hignett reach on the dependability and usefulness of Herodotus are most convincing. Lazenby says that perhaps we should not even be concerned with his credibility, since if his information is not true, "we might as well stop studying the Persian Wars." He then goes on to say, "The more one studies Herodotus, the more one concludes that there is little that he says about the two Persian invasions which can be proved to be wrong, and one is continually struck by the realization that there is a lot more acute observation and analysis in what he says than at first one thinks."[67] Hignett concludes that Herodotus "provides the only sure basis for a modern reconstruction of the Persian War, as no reliance can be placed on the other ancient accounts where they differ from Herodotus." But he goes on to say one must be aware of Herodotus' weaknesses and eliminate the fictions, gossip and legends; however, one must "make sure to the best of his ability that any statement or report in Herodotus really is untenable before he rejects it."[68]

While there is little doubt that Herodotus is the main source on the Persian Wars, other ancient sources also must be investigated as they could possibly complement Herodotus or supplement his account. Aeschylus, who fought at Marathon, and probably at Salamis, was both a witness and participant, who also left a written account. His play, *The Persians*, was presented first in 473–472, so it was seen by many participants in the battles, which meant he could not have changed the historical account without alienating his audience. Macan states that he considers him an "authentic source of real knowledge."[69] But the problem is that the play was not written as history or even a historical poem, but rather as a drama that includes historical characters. For the purpose of studying the Battle of Marathon, little is to be gained from Aeschylus other than as an eyewitness to the size of the Persian fleet during Xerxes' invasion. Pindar, who was also a contemporary of the Persian Wars, has left little that helps us with our study. Perhaps if we had his entire corpus of works he could have been a valuable source.[70]

Ctesias was a Greek physician who was born in Cnidus. He was captured by the Persian army and spent seven years at the Persian court where he served as physician for Artaxerxes II, his wife, his children and his mother from 404 to 397 BCE.[71] He wrote *Persica*, which was divided into 23 books and covered the history of Persia from Cyrus through Xerxes. At first glance he would seem to be the perfect source to complement, to supplement, and perhaps even provide an opportunity to check some of Herodotus' facts; however, upon closer examination we discover differently. While his works have been lost, Photius, a Byzantine scholar and patriarch of Constantinople in the ninth century AD wrote an epitome of Ctesias' last 17 books. Photius begins his epitome with an overview, and we immediately see we have a problem. Photius begins with an overview of Ctesias in which he states,

> On practically every matter he [Ctesias] presents a history opposed to that of Herodotus. In many places he convicts Herodotus of being a liar, and he calls him a *logopoios*. While Ctesias

lived later than Herodotus, he says that he was "an eyewitness of most of the things he recounts or else heard them from the Persians themselves. That which it was impossible for him to witness he claims to have heard from those who had."[72]

Ctesias incorrectly says that Datis was killed at Marathon and that Xerxes' invasion was caused because the Greeks refused to return the corpse of Datis. He places the Battle of Salamis after the Battle of Plataea and totally omits the Battle of Artemisium. Drews says Ctesias is good if one is interested in the sexual activities of Persian kings but that he ignores Persia's role in the Peloponnesian War and is basically useless regarding political or military history, as his sources seem to have been other physicians, cooks, translators and other low-level functionaries who gossiped during their leisure time.[73]

Xenophon (c. 430–c. 354) wrote long after Herodotus and did not write concerning the Persian Wars. J.B. Bury believes Xenophon is well known because so many of his writings have survived and not because he is deserving of his reputation.[74] While he does not write about the Persian Wars, Head and Sekunda consider him a valuable source for information on the Persian military. While Xenophon's *Cyropedia* is essentially historical fiction, they believe much valid information can be gleaned from it.[75]

Ephorus of Cyme (c. 405–c. 370 BCE) appears to be an excellent complementary source to Herodotus. He lived within 50 years of him, he was a "historian by profession" and he wrote about the Persian Wars as part of his Universal History, which was divided into 30 books. While his work did not survive, we do know a lot about it as it appears that Diodorus Siculus followed it closely. Macan, however, states that "Ephorus probably did as much as any one man ever did to corrupt history in the name of history."[76] It appears that Ephorus took Herodotus' *Histories* and attempted to make it more explicit, rational and understandable while also adding to his account and contradicting him at times. When he contradicts Herodotus, at no time does he identify a primary source to support his case. Hignett adds that Ephorus' additions to the story of the Persian Wars "are at best products of constructive inference and at worst they are pure fiction." He includes as an example the "absurd fiction that Leonidas led a surprise attack on the Persian camp and penetrated to the royal tent, but Xerxes was already gone."[77]

Diodorus Siculus was born c. 90 BCE on Sicily and died c. 30 BCE. He spent 30 years writing his "Library," which was divided into 40 books, 15 of which have survived.[78] He used Herodotus, Ephorus, Polybius, Thucydides, Xenophon and Theopompus among others as his sources; however, Bury has little respect for Diodorus and sees his main value as being that he included portions from the works of other writers whose works have been lost, such as the works of Ephorus.[79] He is also criticized for questionable autopsy, lack of military experience, fictional speeches and patriotic bias.[80] While his volume on the Battle of Marathon has been lost, some of his books which have survived, especially books 11 through 14, are helpful in regard to naval affairs in spite of the criticism of his work.

Cornelius Nepos was born in northern Italy c. 99 and died c. 24 BCE. He was a friend of Cicero and was perhaps the first biographer to compare Romans with foreigners.[81] Only two lives have survived from his biographies of Romans and Greeks; however, one was on Miltiades, in which many believe we have Ephorus' account of the Battle of Marathon preserved.[82] Many believe that Nepos' story of Marathon "has a coherence and plausibility, which has led many modern writers to him for its truth." However, How says that while at first sight Nepos' story appears superior to Herodotus' account, he goes on to conclude, "yet a closer examination shows that there is more truth in the doubts and inconsistencies of the historian than in the neat solutions of Cornelius Nepos."[83] Macan is even stronger in his conclusion regarding Cornelius Nepos. He states, "There is hardly a single item to be found in Cornelius, which can be treated as authoritative."[84] Peter Krentz, however, says, "Nepos has his champions, from George Grote in the nineteenth century to Johan Henrik Schreiner in the twenty-first."[85] S. Casson feels that "Marathon, perhaps the most important battle in Antiquity, is the least accurately described." He goes on to describe at least three points in Nepos that can be used to supplement Herodotus. He lists them as follows: "(1) The story that the Greek position was in *radicibus montiu*, (2) the *'novaars'* by which something approximating to barbed wire supplied the Greek lack of cavalry, (3) the use of their favorable position to prevent enfilade."[86]

Macan says that going from Cornelius Nepos to Plutarch (c. AD 46–c. AD 120) is like going from brass to gold.[87] His biographies are far superior to those of Nepos, and his lives of Themistocles and Aristides provide almost a complete picture of the Persian Wars, although he does not include a life of Miltiades which is a great loss. He became an Athenian citizen, traveled throughout Greece and was familiar with the battlefields and traditions. He was dependent on literary sources and preserved some fragments of information, and he was able to supplement Herodotus with some details; but when he contradicts Herodotus he is usually wrong.[88] In addition to his *Parallel Lives*, he wrote an odd piece called *The Malice of Herodotus*. There has been some disagreement over his authorship, but now it appears to be a settled question.[89] His goal in the book was to "rescue the good name of his ancestors, and of the Corinthians, and of all those others traduced in Herodotus."[90] His object was to destroy Herodotus, but too often he simply quotes Herodotus and denies what he says but gives no evidence to support his view. He has some success, but only when using Herodotus' materials.[91] In his introduction, his translator points out many errors in *The Malice of Herodotus* and says of his work, "It often seems coarse and hurried; valid criticisms of Herodotus are not pursued effectively, and other criticisms are made invalid by misrepresentations as much as by misunderstandings." He concludes by saying, "It will surely sharpen and increase our appreciation of Herodotus."[92]

2

The Persian Military

To understand the Battle of Marathon, it is necessary to investigate the Persian military system. The problem is that we have few sources from Persia on this topic, so we must look at Greek sources such as Herodotus and Xenophon for much of our information.

The Persian Army

The Persian king was in command of the military and was expected to personally lead the army in major campaigns. In an empire as large as Persia, to deal with every local problem, every revolt and every expeditionary force would require the king to spend all of his time on military affairs and take him away from governing his empire for long periods of time. Therefore he would give the provincial satraps military authority to deal with the local issues; however, for larger problems such as the Ionian Revolt or the campaigns in Thrace he would appoint generals to carry out the mission. These generals were usually of Persian nobility and often members of the Achaemenid family such as Mardonius who was Darius' nephew and son-in-law.[1]

The Persian army used a decimal system of organization. Herodotus tells us that the commanders appointed *myriarchs* (*baivarabam* in Persian), who commanded 10,000 troops and *chiliarchs* (*hazarapatis*), who commanded 1,000 troops. They in turn appointed *hekatonarchs* (*satapatis*), who commanded 100 troops and *dekarchs* (*dathabatis*), who commanded 10 troops. Xenophon in his *Cyropedia* also talks of an officer who commanded five troops (*pascadathapatis*) and another who commanded 50 troops. The *pascadathapatis* seems to have been a deputy to the commander of 10. The *dekarchs* (*dathabatis*) normally carried a short spear and stood in front of his troops who lined up behind him, while the deputy would have lined up at the rear of the troops. He goes on to say that there "were other officers in communicating orders to the various units and national contingents." The Immortals were the best-known *baivarabam* in the Persian army. They were handpicked from the best recruits in the army and served as the king's personal division. They were called the Immortals because they were always kept at full strength. If a man was killed, wounded or ill he was immediately replaced.[2]

Hignett feels that "on paper the organization of the Persian army was superior to the Greek," and Lazenby states that "one potential military advantage the Persians enjoyed in comparison with the Greeks was the unity of command."[3] After describing the organizational structure of the Persian military, Sekunda goes on to say, "The perfect symmetry of the system ... was not always maintained, and the parade status of units frequently fell below establishment." He gives examples of documents such as in Aswan where a *satapatis* had fallen from its usual hundred men to 50 to 60 men, and in Judea where a *satapatis* had fallen to 30 to 40 men based on ration records.[4]

Education and Training of Persian Boys

Like Spartan boys, Persian boys spent their first five years with women, after which they began their training for the army. Herodotus tells us that "from the age of five to the age 20 they teach their sons just three things: to ride horses, to shoot the bow, and to speak the truth."[5] The Persian term *arta* is associated with learning to speak the truth. It is usually translated as "truth justice," but it means "above all conforming with the established order in heaven and on earth." As a result of their training, young Persians saw it as their most important duty to obey the king unconditionally and most importantly to serve in the army.[6]

The boys were divided into companies of 50, each led by a son of the king or a satrap and were conditioned by running races and riding. They were taught to endure harsh weather and cross difficult streams as well as to take care of their horses and flocks and find wild fruits and nuts. They ate bread, barley cake, cardamom, and roasted or boiled meat.[7] Xenophon emphasizes the physical training and hunting aspects of the education, but he also describes the intellectual aspects of their training in which they learned from "wise men" about the history of Persia and its great men.[8] There is some confusion as to the length of service men spent in the army. Strabo tells us that military service lasted from age 20 until age 24, at which time they were demobilized but could be called up until the age of 50. Xenophon on the other hand says that they entered military service at age 17 for 10 years, after which they could be mobilized for an additional 25 years.[9]

The training that the Persian boys received was arduous and inclusive, but it appears that it was only open to the Persian nobility. Xenophon states that it is open to those "who live off the work of others" but that those "who need to work for their living" are excluded. It may also have been open to the sons of nobles who married into the local nobility in the provinces.[10] We do not know if Persian infantry received the same type of training as the cavalry, as they were not as wealthy as the cavalry troops.[11] It is questionable as to whether or not the Persian officers received any special training for their positions since at least most of the highest officers received their commands because of their family connections or their social position.[12]

Since Persians were the core of the army, military virtues and sons were all important. Herodotus states, "A man's worth is demonstrated first of all by his valor in battle, but next to that by fathering many sons, and the king sends gifts throughout the whole year to the man who in that year can show off the most sons. They believe that there is strength in numbers."[13]

A Professional Army?

What exactly was the Persian army? Was it a professional standing army like the U.S. Army? Was it a feudal army, was it a mercenary army or was it a multinational horde of untrained peasants? Dr. Farrokh claims that Cyrus had no actual army in the professional sense. It was only after Media and Persia were united that the professional Median *spada* became the basis for the imperial Achaemenid army. He says the Achaemenids continued the Assyrian practice of giving land to their elite soldiers in return for service.[14] Xenophon states that there are about "120,000 Persians," and Sekunda thinks that the number may be either the number of Persian nobility or the total of the national army.[15] Cawkwell asks if a true national army was ever available to the king, and he concludes that it was not. He quotes Darius in his Behistun Inscription as saying, "The Persian and Median army, which goes with me, this was a small force." Isocrates talks about "the army which goes around with the King," but Xenophon makes clear that it was only the 10,000 Immortals.[16] The king would have to draw on troops from the provinces if he wanted to mount a large campaign, but that did not mean that the king was limited in his military resources.

There were four different types of troops available to the king in the provinces. The satraps had troops of their own that they maintained as bodyguard units that were available to the king. An example of this can be seen in Oroites, satrap of Phrygia, Lydia, and Ionia under Darius. He had 1,000 Persians as his bodyguard unit. We do not know how they were maintained, so they could be similar to the second group, which were military colonists. As mentioned above, the Achaemenids gave land to elite soldiers in return for service. The king could call them up as needed. It appears that the Persians may have continued Babylonian practices after they conquered them. The military land in Babylonia was organized into *hatrus*, which was like a collective fief and was granted to a group of soldiers. They were divided into three different types called bow lands, horse lands and chariot lands which were used to support the troops.[17]

Darius granted the satraps a great deal of power and autonomy. They lived in royal style, had large agricultural estates, passed laws and collected taxes. To keep them under the king's control, they were assigned Persian secretaries who reported back to the king. In addition, garrisons of imperial troops were established in the satrapies.[18] An example is Memphis, which had a state arsenal and fort that contained about 16,000 troops based on their grain quota.[19] The king paid those who performed garrison duty, so were they loyal to him? At one point the satrap of Sardis with a bodyguard of 1,000 Persians appeared to be overstepping his authority. Darius sent messages which included an order to the bodyguard troops to no longer obey the satrap and to kill him. The troops killed him without hesitancy.[20] Mercenary troops could also be hired for specific campaigns. Xenophon describes being attacked by hoplites from Assyria and Hykanian cavalry.[21]

Finally, the king could order provisional levies. While we are uncertain how the local levies raised troops, it does not mean that they were totally untrained peasants. Certainly their enthusiasm for war and their training were less than the Persians; however, most of the troops that were raised by the king had much more experience and military training than the usual picture of untrained peasants fresh from their villages. Head points out that the Persians "were willing to take over the indigenous military organizations of their subject provinces." As an example of the type of forces that the Persians may have conscripted, he describes the Egyptian soldiers, who were not simply from peasants but "hereditary warriors from the traditional warrior castes."[22] Thus, the common perception of Persian armies consisting of hordes of untrained and undisciplined troops does not ring true. In fact, the "impression one gets of a motley array should be erased from the mind and not allowed to color one's picture of the great armies we hear of throughout Achaemenid history."[23] We must be careful not to underestimate the power of the forces that the king of Persia had available to him. It is important to remember that in about 30 years, the Persians had conquered an empire that stretched from the Strymon River in the Balkans to the Indus River in India and from the shores of the Black Sea to Aswan in Egypt.[24]

Glazed brick friezes found in Susa show soldiers from Immortal regiments wearing the traditional long Persian robe. Herodotus tells us that the Persians adopted the Median dress, and it appears that the change probably took place during the reign of Darius when the Persian robe was discarded for the tunic and trousers and cloak of the Medes.[25] Two styles of soft caps were used by Persian soldiers. One had a high domed crown with a single lappet hanging down at the rear. Herodotus called the second style the *ticara*, which was a felt hat with three lappets, two on the sides and one in the rear. The two side lappets could be tied under the chin or over the mouth.[26] The Persian soldiers wore leather shoes. There is little indication of Persians wearing body armor, although Herodotus does mention some troops wearing "breastplates of iron fashioned to look like fish scales" and some wearing "breastplates of linen."[27] But it appears that body armor was not in general use in the fifth century BCE.

Did the Persian soldiers wear a uniform? Sekunda says that "a number of literary passages do point to the fact that the Greek authorities recognized that the Achaemenid army was clothed and equipped in identical style." He feels the centralized nature of the Achaemenid Empire led it to develop uniforms much earlier than the Greeks, who did not utilize uniforms until the end of the fourth century. Head, on the other hand, says that there is "little hint of uniformity" and uses the Issos Mosaic and the Darius Vase to support his viewpoint.[28]

The Persian Cavalry

The Persian army was an infantry army when Cyrus met the Lydian army in battle. The Lydians had a large and well-trained cavalry and were on the verge of defeating Cyrus until he committed camels from his baggage train to the battle. The Lydian cavalry had never faced camels, and their horses were frightened by the size and smell of the camels and that effectively eliminated the Lydian cavalry from the battle. Cyrus could not depend on the tactic working in future battles, so it became imperative for him to develop a cavalry arm for his army. He called upon the Medes to provide cavalry troops as they were fine horsemen; however, Cyrus was unsure of their loyalty so he also created a Persian cavalry force.[29] Using wealth and land from his conquests, Cyrus distributed horses and money to support the creation of a cavalry force. He looked to his nobles to create this force and stated that "henceforth they should ride everywhere, and that it should be considered a disgrace for a Persian nobleman to be seen on foot."[30] Once established, the importance of the cavalry can be seen in the dominant position that learning to ride and shoot the bow played in the education of Persian boys.[31]

The Persians became successful horse breeders, and by the time of the Battle of Marathon, large numbers of horses were available to the cavalry. Herodotus tells us that the satrap of Babylonia had a "private herd of 800 stallions and 16,000 mares" for breeding purposes. Strabo tells us that the Persian kings had 50,000 mares in the fertile pastures in Media and that the Satrap of Armenia sent 20,000 foals to the Persian king each year. Coppodocia provided 1,500 horses to Persia each year, and Cilicia included 360 white horses in its yearly tribute.[32] It is estimated that the horses were about 14 hands tall, weighing about 1,000 pounds, and the reliefs at the palace in Persepolis show 10 different breeds.[33]

Cavalry caused difficult logistical and transportation problems. A 1,000-pound horse would require about "6.8 pounds of digestible nutrients" each day. This could be met with 5 pounds of barley and 6.5 pounds of dried grass or with 5 pounds of barley and 5.75 pounds of bran. Horses also required .5 to .6 gallons of water for each 100 pounds of weight of the horse. An additional problem was that the food and water requirements changed depending upon the temperature as well as the amount of exercise the horse got. On a land campaign one might expect the food requirements to be met by allowing the horses to graze freely in local pastures and the water requirement to be met from local wells, streams and rivers. However, on further investigation one finds that suddenly changing the type of food, water and grass that the horses received could lead to the horses developing flatulent colic, which can incapacitate a horse for weeks or cause foundering, in which the horse develops hoof problems which prevent their use.[34]

Since logistics was one of the strengths of the Persian army, they would carry fodder and water for their horses; however, transporting their horses along with their food, water and tack was a difficult task when the campaign was by sea. They solved the transportation problem by building special horse transports which carried the horses, riders and their food, water and tack. After being fed fodder onboard ship for an extended time, it would have been dangerous to suddenly switch to pasturage, so the Persians hobbled their horses rather than letting them graze in new pastures and brought fodder and water to their horses. This would also free up soldiers who would have had to guard the horses if they had grazed freely.[35]

Using Marathon as an example and assuming the Persians had 1,000 cavalry, Shrimpton explains how the process might have occurred. He says that 1,000 horses would need about 10 tons of hay, a few tons of grain and about 8,000 gallons of water each day. He says that the Persians could have brought in fodder each day by ship from Euboea. He adds that horses should drink before eating, so they would have to bring in water from local water sources.[36]

Over time, Median dress was also adopted by the Persian cavalry because of its suitability for riding. It included trousers, a long-sleeved tunic and a sleeved cloak that reached down to the knees and was worn on the shoulders, leaving their arms free.[37] Herodotus states that "some of the horsemen wore helmets forged from bronze and iron," but probably the majority wore felt caps like the infantry.[38] Fifteen thousand nobles known as kinsmen or *Huvaka* were at the top of the social system in Persia. From this group, an elite regiment of cavalrymen was created, some of whom were dressed in "in gold tunics and silver embroidered trousers."[39]

Men in the cavalry were expected to provide their own equipment. While the Persian palace reliefs do not include cavalry, Cook summarized the equipment required of a cavalryman's fief in southern Mesopotamia in 422 BCE: "Besides money (a mina of silver), and food, the requirement read something like, horse in harness, saddle cloth, iron cuirass, helmet with felt neck guard, shield, 130 arrows, an iron shield attachment, and an iron club and two javelins—there is no mention of additional armor for the horse, such as some late Achaemenid heavy cavalry seem to have had."[40] It appears that over time the Persians developed more heavy cavalry; however, at the time of the Battle of Marathon the Persians utilized a more light and agile cavalry force, so the iron cuirass, helmet and shield were not part of their equipment.[41]

The Persian cavalry man was essentially a mounted infantry man. He sat on a saddle cloth, and since he had no stirrups, he could be easily unseated from his horse, although this view has been challenged by Sidnell. Evans describes his horse as "a mobile platform from which he could launch his weapons."[42] The light, agile Persian cavalry in the early fifth century was used mainly to harass the enemy forces and to attempt to cause confusion in their ranks. They tried to interfere with lines of communication, cut off food and water supplies and charge the enemy; however, they did not actually come into contact with them. Rather, they shot their arrows and threw their javelins and then withdrew. They also had the ability to accurately fire their arrows as they rode away. If there was sufficient space, they could encircle the enemy and continuously harass them with arrows and javelins.[43] Rawlinson states,

> The light Calvary was celebrated for the quickness and dexterity of its maneuvers. It had the loose organization of modern Bashi-Bazouks or Cossacks; it hung in clouds on the enemy—assailed, retreated, rallied, re-advanced—fled, and even in-flight was formidable, since each rider was trained to discharge arrows backwards, with a surer aim against the pursuing foe.[44]

Sidnell describes the cavalry as swarming around the enemy with little formation, bombarding the enemy with arrows and javelins while relying on their horses' speed and maneuverability to avoid close combat until the odds were in their favor.[45] The goal of the tactic was to induce the enemy to flee or to disrupt their formation by "inflicting casualties on the front ranks and forcing the rear ranks to stumble over the fallen as they advance, or step around them, thus interfering with their rank-mates." At some point the cavalry then withdrew to avoid arrows from their own archers and joined the infantry in pouring more arrows into the ranks of their enemy. From their new position the cavalry would be in position to sweep down on enemy troops should they break formation and to ride down individual soldiers as they ran, or if by chance their own infantry should instead break they could cover its retreat.[46] In 496 during the Cypriot revolt, the Persians learned that coming into direct contact with hoplites in close formation with cavalry was ineffective.[47] Evans states, "An axiom of warfare is that horses will not charge into a solid line that they can neither get through nor jump over." At the same time, cavalry could be very effective in dispatching individual hoplites if the hoplites broke ranks or if they were caught unsupported on open ground.[48]

While most people have emphasized the importance of the cavalry to the Persian army, Christopher Tuplin in two articles published in 2010 has raised questions concerning that viewpoint. He believes that the importance of the cavalry in the Persian army has been exaggerated, pointing out that in the 444 military episodes that he examined from Greek and Latin texts, he found only 76 that involved the cavalry. He also claims that iconography seems to indicate that the cavalry's main weapon was the spear and that he found little or no evidence of the cavalry firing arrows as they harassed the enemy troops. Rather, he emphasized the role of the cavalry outside the bounds of a formal battle. He said the cavalry was used to scout and survey the enemy and terrain, attack enemy supply lines, run down enemies in flight and/or to defend their soldiers if they were in retreat or fleeing. He adds that the cavalry could participate in the battle by harassing the enemy's flanks if they were not protected by cavalry.[49]

He goes on to say that there is little evidence to show that the "Greeks found Persian cavalry inherently exotic or awesome" or that the Greeks thought the Persians used their cavalry in a superior manner. He adds that Datis and Artaphernes did not believe that it was necessary "to deploy a substantial cavalry force to defeat a hoplite force." Finally he says that it "remains purely conjecture that early Persian successes against Asiatic Greeks were predicated to any degree on the ability of Persian cavalry to sweep aside infantry."[50]

The Persian Navy

Since Persia was a landlocked area, Cyrus carried out his conquests with his army not needing a naval force; however, his son Cambyses, prior to his invasion of Egypt in 525 BCE realized that he needed a navy in order to offset the Egyptian fleet as well as to carry supplies for his army.[51] Herodotus tells us that the Persians described Cambyses as being "a better man than his father since he had everything that his father had given him, and in addition had acquired control of Egypt and the sea."[52] While it is true that Cambyses created the Persian navy, it was the conquests of Phoenicia and Ionia by Cyrus that made it possible.[53] It is generally accepted that Cambyses created the Persian navy and that it played an important role in Persian successes; however, there is disagreement on how the navy was organized.

One viewpoint is that there was no regular Persian navy, but rather a navy that was created when it was needed by calling up the navies of its subject areas such as Phoenicia, Egypt and Ionia. When Cambyses created the Persian navy, it was totally dependent upon the Phoenicians for its ships, but later other areas also provided ships.[54] By calling up naval ships only when needed, the Persians were assured a navy was available "without the expense and trouble of maintaining a regular Persian navy."[55] At the Battle of Lade, Herodotus describes the Persian naval forces as follows: "The Phoenicians were the most ardent for battle, and serving with them were the recently subjugated Cyprians, as well is the Cilicians and the Egyptians."[56] In describing Xerxes' navy during his invasion of Greece, Herodotus lists over 11 specific areas providing ships, ranging from the 300 ships provided by the Phoenicians with the Syrians to 25 ships provided by Halicarnassus.[57] Regarding the Persian navy, Rawlinson states,

> Though the Persians were not themselves a nautical people, they were quite aware of the great importance of a navy, and spared no pains to provide themselves with an efficient one. The conquests of Phoenicia, Cyprus, Egypt, and the Greek islands were undertaken, it is probable, mainly with this object; and these parts of the empire were always valued chiefly as possessing skilled seaman, vessels, and dockyards, from which the great King could draw an almost inexhaustible supply of warships and transports.[58]

In 1983, H.T. Wallinga took issue with the above viewpoint and claimed that the Persian navy was truly a national navy that did not depend upon subject areas to provide ships. Rather, he believes that Persia provided the ships and its subject areas simply provided the crews. For support he quotes Diodorus who stated that Xerxes' navy "numbered more than 1,200, 320 of which were Greek: the crews were furnished by the Greeks, the ships supplied by the King." Wallinga claims that Diodorus' information came from Ephoros, a naval historian, who came from Kyme which was an important Persian naval base.[59] In his book *Ships and Sea-Power before the Great Persian War,* Wallinga states that Herodotus' description of Xerxes' navy does not controvert Diodorus and explains how some areas might have had their own ships to contribute.[60] Wallinga goes on to explain that it is difficult to accept that an imperial power "would have given to its subjects a major role in its defense as well as providing them with the military means to revolt." Finally, he claims that Miletus in 500 and Cyprus and 498 "did not have warships of their own."[61]

Wallinga's unconventional viewpoint on the Persian navy seems to be gaining some acceptance. Lionel Scott in his historical commentary on Herodotus' book 6 would seem to lean toward Wallinga's viewpoint. He says that it appears that the Persian navy was at bases when not in use. He suggests bases existed at Aleion Pedion in Cilicia, Cyme and on Samos, with possible bases at Abdera and Myus, although he seems to think that Abdera and Myus were probably just convenient anchorages. He also suggests that some ships may have been kept in local ports, but "we might envisage oars and sails being kept under secure conditions, to be released only on a Persian say-so."[62] While J.S. Morrison, Anthony Graham Keen and F.J.A.M. Meijer criticize many aspects of Wallinga's views on triremes in their reviews of his book, they all seem to be more open to his views on the creation of the Persian navy, so perhaps Wallinga's viewpoint on the Persian navy is becoming more acceptable than the traditional view.[63]

According to Herodotus, the Persian navy included triremes, triaconters, pentecounters, light boats and horse transports.[64] Horse transports were made specifically for that purpose and were "large, clumsy vessels." Lighter craft for the transport of corn were also utilized, although triremes were also modified to carry troops, horses and supplies. They were even used to build bridges.[65] While there is no consensus on when the trireme was invented or by whom, it appears certain that the trireme was the backbone of the Persian navy at the time of the Battle of Marathon, while Athens had few, if any, triremes until after Themistocles' naval bill in 483 BCE.[66]

The Persian triremes were built using Phoenician designs, which differed from the Greek trireme. The Greeks added a third level of rowers by adding an outrigger, whereas the Persians accomplished the third level by adding to the ships' height The trireme was 110 to 120 feet in length, 15 feet in width, had three banks of rowers and had a mast with a square sail. The rudder was made up of two bladed oars, one on each side of the stern united by a crossbar. The trireme was equipped with a bronze ram similar to the style used in the seventh and sixth centuries which was long and tapered to a single point.[67]

The triremes carried 170 rowers arranged in three files—the upper file (*thranites*) numbered 62, the middle file (*zygian*) numbered 54, and the lower file (*thalamios*) also numbered 54. In addition they carried 14 marines, some spare rowers and oars.[68] Herodotus says that in 480 BCE the Persian triremes carried 200 men per ship and 30 Medes, Persians or Saki serving as marines.[69] Does that mean Phoenician triremes were larger than Greek triremes? Wallinga does not feel that there is sufficient evidence to reach such a conclusion, but rather that it is a misinterpretation of the number of rowers and crew on pentecounters.[70] Cook, on the other hand, proposes that the Persians had a continuous deck on their triremes as opposed to the Greeks, who had partial decks, and this allowed the Persian triremes to carry more marines.[71] The crews were drawn from all over the empire, but the marines were elite troops drawn only from Persians, Medes and Saki.[72] Persian triremes were not as heavy as the Greek triremes and were more fragile; however, they made up for it by being the better sailing ships.[73]

Size of the Persian Navy

How large was the Persian navy? Again, without Persian archives and with few available Persian sources, one has to depend upon Greek sources to come up with an estimated size. Perhaps the best way to get an estimate of the size of the Persian navy is to examine it when all elements of it were pulled together for the invasion of Greece in 480 BCE Aeschylus, our only contemporary source, in his play *The Persians* states, "Xerxes led 1,000 ships; their number. Well I know; 200 more and 7, that swept the seas with speediest sail: that was their full amount."[74] H. J. Rose in his commentary on Aeschylus states that "no one now accepts Xerxes' strength as anything like 1,207 keel; as with all events at Salamis, the exaggeration is perhaps around 100 percent."[75] According to Herodotus, "the total number of triremes came to 1,207," and he gives a detailed list of where all of the ships came from as follows: Cilicians—100, Pimphylians—30, Lycians—50, Dorians—30, Ionians—100, Islanders—17, Aeolians—60, Pontic Region—100, Phoencians—300, Egyptians—200, and Cyprians—150.[76] While Aeschylus and Herodotus are generally in agreement on the number of triremes, historians have been arguing about the numbers for at least the last 150 years.

Writing in 1848, George Grote, in his multivolume *History of Greece,* sees Herodotus' number of 1,207 triremes as acceptable because he got the number from Aeschylus, an eyewitness at Salamis; however, he rejects Herodotus' 3,000 smaller ships and 1.7 million infantry.[77] Writing at the turn of the 20th century, R.W. Macan, in his commentary on Herodotus, feels that Herodotus' number of 1,207 triremes is a reasonable number considering the fact that 600 triremes had been at the Battle of Lade, on the Scythian campaign and at the Battle of Marathon.[78] How and Wells in their commentary on Herodotus in 1908 also find "the traditional number of the King's navy (1,000 or 1,207) far more credible than that of the army."[79] The German historian H. Welzhofer accepts Herodotus' figure of 1,207 ships but claims that only about 400 were warships, while E. Meyer claims the fleet only had 600 to 800 ships.[80] J. B. Bury suggests that the fleet must be reduced to "perhaps 800."[81] J. A. R. Munro also proposes 800 as a reasonable number for Xerxes' fleet.[82] Hans Delbruck, one of the earliest military historians, rejects Herodotus' number of 1,207 ships and claims that the Persians "certainly did not have more than 200 to 300."[83] In his article "The Fleet of Xerxes," W. W. Tarn states that "we are not justified in jettisoning all Herodotus' numbers and taking the guesswork unless and until we have made every effort to extract sense from them." He goes on to examine the four divisions of the fleet that Herodotus lists and reaches the conclusion that it makes no sense given the numbers of 1,200 triremes. Rather, he claims that there were five divisions of ships of 120 each for a total of 600 ships.[84] "A fleet of 600 triremes would, I suppose, be quite unmanageable in fact; but five separate fleets of 120 each would not." He goes on to claim that "no other power in antiquity ever collected a fleet of 600 warships. Octavian may have controlled 500 partly borrowed from Anthony and organized as two distinct leagues in different seas."[85] In 1948, A.T. Olmstead, in his *History of the*

Persian Empire, accepts Herodotus' figure of 1,200 triremes; while J. M. Cook in his *The Persian Empire,* published in 1983, thinks there may be some exaggeration in Herodotus, but he concludes, "The Persian fleet cannot have been much less than 1,000."[86]

In the 1960s two major works appeared on the Greek and Persian Wars. C. Hignett of Oxford University addressed the problem of the number of ships in Xerxes' fleet in his book *Xerxes' Invasion of Greece.* He believes that if one accepts Herodotus' statement that the Persian fleet was only slightly larger than the Greek fleet at the Battle of Salamis, then the 1,207 number "must be an invention." He feels that the Persian fleet could not have been much larger than 600 and wonders if the 1,207 number was an attempt "to credit Xerxes with a fleet larger than that which Agamemnon led against Troy."[87] Burn, writing about the same time in his book *Persia and the Greeks,* suggests that the 1,207 number may have been based on "Greek intelligence reports.... Never-the-less the figures are certainly far too high." He does not believe that Herodotus adequately explains why only about 600 Persian ships were at Salamis after starting with 1,207 ships. He does not, however, suggest a more accurate number.[88]

In 2004 George Cawkwell in his book *The Greek Wars: The Failure of Persia,* states that "Herodotus' total of 1,207 triremes and 3,000 lesser crafts is not worthy of discussion." He also rejects the number of 600 triremes, which "has attained some sort of respectability." His basic argument is that there is a "contrast between the large numbers in the Persian fleet prior to the Greek invasion and the smaller fleets after the Greek invasion. He says that after the Greek invasion the typical Persian fleet was about 300 or less, with only Arian listing a fleet of 400 in the year 334 BCE He concludes, "Even if Arian's figure of 400 is correct and 334 is an exception, the point is clear that, in the fourth century, Persian fleets were regularly no more than 300." He then asks how it was different in the fifth century. He examined naval actions after 480 and says, "It may be affirmed that the Persian navies of the fifth century were never much in excess of 300 ships."[89] He concludes, "The figure of 300, however, appears so constantly and in such varied circumstances that it would seem that 300 was what different kings regarded as suitable. After all, fleets like armies need to be kept supplied.... For proper understanding of Persian power one must emancipate oneself from the navy list as well as the army list of Herodotus."[90]

H.T. Wallinga, a maritime historian from the University of Utrecht, has written several books in which he reaches a radically different conclusion from Cawkwell and others who challenge Herodotus' number of 1,207 ships. Wallinga says his rule "has been to accept Herodotus' (Aeschylus') factual information until a contradiction is overwhelming." He begins his argument by pointing out the large number of ancient writers that have put the size of the Persian fleet at from 1,000 to 1,200 or more ships.[91] He then explains that Cambyses created the Persian navy, because as he planned his invasion of Egypt, he realized that Egypt with its allies had a fleet of about 300 ships. Wallinga says that explains why the Persian fleet was created with about 300 ships and how 300 became a key number in the Persian navy. This initial fleet of the Persians depended upon the Phoenicians to supply rowers. Darius later added an Aegean fleet of 300 that depended upon Ionian rowers. In 500–499 BCE the eastern fleet of the Persian navy was enlarged to 600 ships after 300 ships in the Aegean fleet had been seized by the Ionians during their revolt. They were also adding to the 300 Persian ships that they seized by building additional triremes. According to

Herodotus, when the Persians discovered that the Ionian fleet had 353 ships, "the Persian generals ... became frightened that they would be unable to prevail over it, and thus fail to become masters of the sea." This statement in Herodotus has been used to challenge Herodotus' figure of 600 ships, as why would the generals be frightened of 353 ships if they had 600? Wallinga rejects this viewpoint by claiming the Persians had 600 ships but they were short of crews, so they could not fully man the entire 600 ships.[92]

Just as the army figures presented by Herodotus are rejected because of their unrealistic, size, so too is the number of Persians ships questioned because of the huge number of men required to man the 1,200 triremes. If we take 170 rowers times 1,200 ships, it gives us the huge number of 204,000 rowers required to row the Persian fleet. Perhaps there were sufficient rowers available in the Persian Empire, but to "mobilize them all would have paralyzed whole sections of the economy, especially the trade of the Phoenicians and other seaboard peoples."[93] These figures would certainly seem to indicate that Herodotus' number of ships is wrong and that the Persian navy must have been much smaller; however, Wallinga points out that the problem is with the number of rowers needed, not the number of ships. He explains that triremes that were adapted to transport horses and or troops could have been rowed by as few as 60 men. Obviously fighting ships would need more rowers, but even they could have crews of different sizes depending upon the tactics to be employed. He concludes, "In practice, the degree of manning will have depended on a whole number of factors: the availability of oarsmen in the first place; financial means; the attended or expected character of the operations; and perhaps others."[94] If all or most of Xerxes' fleet were moved by skeleton crews of about 60, the number of rowers needed would be about 75,000. It is still a very large number but less than the 102,000 to 120,000 rowers needed to fully man the 600 ships that many historians consider reasonable. Even taking the lowest number suggested of 300 triremes, the total of 56,100 rowers required is not that much lower than the 72,000 to 75,000 needed to move the 1,200 Persian ships using Wallinga's approach. His explanation would also answer the concern that many historians raise about the large difference that existed between the size of the Persian fleet when it started and the number of Persian ships present at the battles of Artemesium and Salamis. The rowers were consolidated upon fewer ships to bring the total rowers up to the required 170 for a fully manned fighting ship. That would explain why the Persian fleet was not much larger than the Greek fleet at the Battle of Salamis.[95]

Peter Green in his book, *The Great Persian Wars*, feels that the total of 1,207 ships advanced by Aeschylus and Herodotus "is by no means impossible as a general estimate of total available resources; but, all our evidence suggests it was far too large for the actual fleets, which fought at Artemisium and Salamis.[96] Green goes on to ask how Herodotus gained his information. He concludes that Xerxes himself provided the information to the Greeks by releasing the Greek spies captured at Sardis in an effort to intimidate the Greeks and to influence poleis that had not yet decided whether to capitulate or fight. He even suggests that the spies were given "muster-rolls, naval lists and other handouts from the quartermaster general's staff."[97]

The purpose of the above discussion was not to support or criticize Herodotus' and Aeschylus' number of 1,207 triremes in Xerxes' naval force in 480 BCE but rather to reach a fair estimate of the potential size of the entire Persian fleet. On this point Cawkwell argues that in the fifth century it is doubtful if the Persian Empire could raise a fleet of more than 300 ships; however a large number of historians appear ready to agree to the proposition that it was a possibility that the vast Persian Empire could raise a fleet of 1,200 triremes. But before we can conclude that the Persian navy may have had 1,200 triremes, we must consider whether the Persian Empire could pay for such a vast fleet. Also, could the empire muster the seamen required to man such a large fleet? First, let us address the financial consideration. Wallinga estimates the costs that Persia would incur in creating a navy and then projects the costs out for 20 years, about the life of the trireme. He includes the following items:

1. Cost of building a trireme and maintaining it.
2. Infrastructural needs such as slipways and ship sheds.
3. Defense of the naval bases.
4. Permanent patrols like the Delian League used.
5. Large-scale operations by the fleet.

To calculate the costs, he used figures similar to those incurred by the Athenian fleet and reached a figure of 7,890 talents for 20 years, or about 400 talents per year.[98] While Wallinga admits these cost estimates are very rough, they at least give an indication of the huge costs of a navy. Also, the navy was enlarged, which would add considerably to the costs. This probably accounts for Darius' monetizing part of the tribute system in order to pay for the navy, as he had doubled the size of the navy with the addition of the Aegean fleet.[99] While 400 or more talents per year was a very large number, Persia also had a huge income from its empire. Darius changed the tax code and had his officials determine the yield of agricultural lands in each region and taxed them at 20 percent of normal yield.[100] Darius divided his empire into 20 provincial satrapies and assigned each a tribute that they would pay. Herodotus listed each satrap and its tribute and came up with a total of 8,700 talents income for the king.[101] Pierre Briant writing in 2002 says that some historians claim the figures given by Herodotus are not credible just as his army totals lack credibility; however, he states, "Despite several conversion and arithmetic errors, it is apparent that the numerical information he gives must be considered reliable." He goes on to say, "The precision suggests quite strongly that he had access—through unknown (and doubtless indirect) channels—to official documents such as, for example, (written or oral) from the archives of Sardis and elsewhere."[102] He then explains that areas such as the Arabs and Ethiopia, which were exempt from tribute, still made gifts and that the king of Ethiopia provided two quarts of unrefined gold, 200 ebony logs, five Ethiopian boys and 20 elephant tusks every two years. Every year the Arabs sent 1,000 talents of incense. The king also received taxes on merchandise, cultivation of the soil, cattle, poll taxes and a tax on mines.[103] Based upon the above figures the Persian Empire certainly was capable of paying for a fleet of 1,200 triremes even if the estimated costs were doubled to 800 talents or more per year.

Another issue that must be addressed is whether the Persian Empire could come up with the necessary rowers that a fleet of 1,200 triremes required. Each trireme required 170 rowers, so 1,200 triremes required 204,000 rowers. If you add the 30 to 40 marines per trireme, that adds an additional 36,000 individuals, which brings the total to nearly 250,000 men for the navy alone, a huge number for that time in history. As discussed above, Wallinga deals partially with this problem by suggesting that the Persians did not fully man each trireme. Rather 60 rowers would move the fleet, and then when it came time for battle, they would concentrate their crews on fewer triremes that were fully manned. If they did that for 1,200 ships it would reduce the rowers required to 72,000 rowers, a more reasonable number, although still very large. Wallinga goes on to suggest that all sea fighting did not necessarily involve the maneuver of *diekplous*, which required full crews in order to sail through or around the enemy fleet and attack their more vulnerable sides and sterns and attempt to ram them. Lazenby points out that *diekplous* were seldom used. There were also different tactical possibilities which would allow different manning levels of the triremes and thus allow more ships in the battle since they did not all require full crews. There are also cases of the Greeks undermanning their triremes.[104]

But even if Wallinga, Casson and others are correct, could the Persians have maintained a fleet of 1,200 triremes? The Delian League's fleet of 450 triremes would require 76,500 rowers using the figure of 170 rowers per trireme unless, of course, if the Athenians also undermanned their triremes. Athens maintained the fleet with money from the members of the Delian League, who gave money in place of ships and crews. A.W. Gomme has estimated the population of Athens at about 316,000 total population in 431 BCE and Athens was able to maintain, and man, the ships for the Delian League.[105] To be sure, perhaps Athens was able to draw rowers from other areas, but there is little evidence to demonstrate this fact. Estimates of the population of the Persian Empire range from 17 million to 35 million under the Achaemenids.[106] The empire reached its peak under Darius, so one might suggest that the Persian Empire of 30 million or even 10 million, taking a ridiculously low number, was able to maintain a fleet of 1200 triremes if Athens, a city of 315,000 or even 400,000, could maintain a fleet of 450 triremes.

Persian Weapons and Armor

Herodotus describes the weapons used by Persian soldiers as follows: "They were armed with short spears, longbows, and arrows made of reeds. From their belt they fastened daggers, which hung down along the right thigh."[107] In his commentary on Herodotus, Macan states that Herodotus' description of a Persian soldier accurately meets the "appearance of the soldiers on the frieze of the Apadana of Xerxes in Susa."[108] The spear of the Persian was about 2 m (6.56 feet), was made of tough cornel wood and had a wide sharp blade with a long socket. The spear carried by the last five rows may have been longer, perhaps 3.5 m (11.48 feet); however, one must be careful in estimating the length from artistic images, as often the artists filled in the available space rather than showing the actual size of the weapon.[109] The sword that the Persian soldiers carried was called the *akenakes*; it was made from one piece of metal and was designed for thrusting rather than cutting. It appears that there was no standard size for the sword. Rawlinson describes the sword carried by the common soldier as being about 15 to 16 inches long and calls it little more than a dagger.[110] In his book on the Persian army, Head includes line drawings to scale of recovered *akenakes* that range from 40 cm (16 inches) to 80 cm (31 inches) in length.[111] Manouchehr Khorasani includes examples of excavated *akenakes* from the Museum of Tehran that measure from 41 cm (16.1 inches) to 65 cm (23 inches). He includes a gold *akenakes* from the museum that has been dated to about 500 BCE and which obviously belonged to a noble Persian officer as it was made of gold.[112] From this information, perhaps we can speculate that at about the time of the Battle of Marathon, the Persian swords were 41 cm or shorter, as it is doubtful that a common soldier would have had a sword longer than their officer's sword. Concerning the longer *akenakes* that were included by Head and Khorasani, they were perhaps from a later date, or perhaps they belonged to officers in the elite guard units such as the Immortals.

The bow was the most important weapon for the Persian army. The Persian tactics included using infantry archers to cause confusion by firing volleys of arrows while the cavalry harassed the enemy's flanks by throwing javelins and shooting arrows both while attacking and riding away to avoid direct contact with the enemy.[113] As the bow was developed in the Near East, it became clear that simple bows lacked power and broke too easily. Therefore, over time, a compound bow was developed in which two layers of the same material were used, but it was found that more powerful bows that did not break easily could be created by combining wood, sinew and bone, which when glued together became known as a composite bow.[114] When drawn, the horn acted to resist compression while the sinew stretched, only to pull back into shape when the bowstring was released. They were expensive and it took up to a year to produce a good bow and 10 years to produce a superb bow.[115] Experiments have demonstrated that composite bows are more powerful and twice as strong as simple bows. Also, they can be smaller and still retain their power. Zutterman concludes, "They therefore have more strength, far more range and their small size results in more mobility.[116]

The Persian army used a variety of bow types. The three most commonly identified are the Yrzi composite recurved bow, the Elamite bow with duck-headed ears and the Scythian bow. They range in size from 90 cm (35.4 inches) to 120 cm (47.2 inches). The infantry used the longer bows while the cavalry used the shorter bows. The Persian soldiers carried their bows over their shoulders or in bow cases at their side. Khorasani suggests nobles and officers had bow cases, but Head includes several illustrations showing common soldiers also carrying bow cases. The soldiers carried their quivers by attaching them to their belt. It has been suggested that Persian soldiers carried 62 to 75 arrows with them, and more were stored on carts from which they could be supplied by pages or could go to get more themselves.[117] By using the smaller bows, Zutterman claims that Persian cavalrymen "could turn their upper bodies all the way to the rear of the horse and shoot, giving the cavalry an extra advantage while retreating." Thus the Persian cavalry was a threat both when they rode at the enemy and when they rode away from the enemy to avoid direct contact.

Since the bow was the primary weapon of the Persian army, its effective range was very important. Delbruck claims the effective range of the Persian bowl was 100 to 150 paces.[118] Wallace MacLeod in his article, "The Range of the Ancient Bow," states, "This review of the evidence suggests that bow men were quite accurate up to 50 to 60 m; that their effective range extended to at least 160–175 m, but not as far as 350–450 m; and that 500 m was an exceptional flight shot." He claims there are records that can serve as an external check on composite bows like those used by the Persians, and he concludes that opponents could come under fire from Persian arrows perhaps at 250 m.[119]

Hammond claims that McLeod's estimate of 200 to 300 m for a bow's effective range is an exaggeration and sets 150 m as a reasonable compromise between the many estimates put forth. He goes on to state that McLeod based his conclusions on incendiary arrow distances and that incendiary arrows did not need penetrating power, which negates McLeod's figure.[120] McLeod responded that "the tinder binding—bulky enough to keep a spark through the trajectory ... would interfere with the smooth flow of air past the shaft and curtail the range. It follows that, if a fire arrow from the Areopagus could reach the Acropolis 155 m away, a war arrow from the same bow would carry even further. As additional evidence, McLeod points out that the Byzantine measurement called the "bow shot" would fall between 290 and 335 m.[121] Peter Krentz in his book, *The Battle of Marathon,* leans toward the view of McLeod stating that the effective range for archers using the Persian bow was 175 to 190 yards (160–173 m), with exceptional archers reaching 250 yards (228 m). To support his conclusion he uses Herodotus' statement that the Persians shot fire arrows from the Areopagus hill to the Acropolis at a range "of about 500 feet with a vertical rise of about 100 feet."[122]

The Persian officer in charge of 10 men (*dathabatis*) stood in the front of his men to protect them. He carried a spear and a large rectangular shield called a *spara* which was about 1.5 m (4.92 feet) tall and about .60 to .80 m (1.96–2.62 feet) wide. The shield was made of raw leather that had been soaked in water and hard reeds that were threaded through "specially cut holes in closely set vertical lines." As the leather dried it contracted, resulting in a shield that was hard, highly resilient and at the same time light in weight. Often a pointed stake was attached to the shield so that the person bearing it could stick it into the ground to form a wall with other shields to protect the archers and to free up his hands to use his spear.[123] The last person in the line was the assistant *dathabatis* who was responsible for keeping the archers in their proper order and position. While the shield was light and strong, it was not designed for hand-to-hand combat as it was too large and unwieldy.

Herodotus describes the soldiers in the Persian army as wearing "breastplates of iron fashioned to look like fish scales." Wozniak points out that there have been archaeological finds of "scales, armor plates and whole fragments of scale armor" and says that the quality of the armor was very impressive as the very small scales were carefully arranged, which resulted in armor that was "extremely elastic."[124] Head says that while Herodotus mentions the scale armor, only one example of it has been found in Greek vase painting, while all the other images show Persian soldiers either wearing quilted linen cuirasses, leather cuirasses or no armor at all. He also explains that Herodotus says later in his work that the Persians lost because their equipment did not match that of the hoplites.[125] From the evidence of vase paintings, he suggests that few soldiers in the Persian army had scale armor but that others had other types of armor, though he does think the soldiers in the elite guard units very well may have had scale armor. He does admit that perhaps the scale armor was under the Persian tunics and thus not visible, but he does not seem to think that very likely.[126] A problem in discussing Persian armament and weapons is that a typical Persian army was made up of a great variety of different soldiers. It seems likely that the Persians, Medes and Saka might indeed have had better armor and weapons as they were the best troops of the empire and they were the core of the army; however, they were often only a small part of the army. For example, at Marathon, many historians estimate that there were only several thousand Persian soldiers, and we are uncertain from where the rest of the troops were recruited. Perhaps Herodotus was right in describing a Persian soldier's armor, but because the vast majority of troops were not Persian, he was also right in saying a reason for the Persian defeat was that their equipment did not match up with the Greek equipment.

A Persian Campaign

When the Persian army went campaigning they were cautious and methodical in their approach. They carefully planned their logistics, and a supply of corn that would last for several months was carried by the baggage train. In addition a fleet with additional supplies accompanied the army if possible. Because of the large size of their armies and the accompanying baggage train, rapid marches were not possible. Night movements were seldom used, and the Persians sometimes fortified their camps. Once entering enemy territory, they sent out cavalry scouts to search for the enemy. When they made camp they tried to allow seven to eight miles between them and their enemy in order to avoid surprises. Whenever possible they camped on an open plain with a water source available.[127] As with most armies, the Persians preferred to pick their battlefield, and it would be an open plain if possible. Their tactical approach was built around archers and cavalry. The infantry massed its archers in ranks of 10 behind shield walls made of *sparas* and the cavalry was massed in front or on the flanks of the infantry.[128] As the infantry archers sent arrows in volleys into the enemy ranks, the cavalry harassed the enemy's flanks. They would charge the enemy flanks, release their arrows and javelins and then retire before making contact with the infantry. As they retired they were skilled enough to continue to fire arrows at the enemy. They then charged again and repeated the tactics as often as needed. The goal was to disrupt the enemy's lines, cause confusion and demoralize the enemy. When that was accomplished, the infantry closed with the disorganized enemy and used their *akenakes* to end the battle.[129]

Jim Lacey, professor of strategy, war and policy at the Marine War College, gives an excellent summary of the tactics of the Persian army in military terms. He writes,

> The Persian Army ... relied on the coordinated action of its combined arms, centered on massed archery, to inflict sufficient losses to shatter an enemy's cohesion.... As the archers pinned down the enemy force and thinned its ranks, the cavalry would start moving off in a series of flanking or encircling movements. As long as the enemy remained unbroken, the cavalry would keep away.... While unbroken infantry could hold off cavalry indefinitely, once an infantry formation began wavering, it was useless. A thousand pounds of charging flesh with a screaming rider wielding a spear or sword was a terrifying sight. Under such an attack, a decimated line that was already stepping back always broke. At this point ... the infantry started forward. Armed with their *akenakes* (short swords) and short spears they delivered the coup de grace.[130]

3

The Greek Military

When describing the ancient Greek military, the words that come to mind immediately are *hoplite* and *phalanx*. *Hoplite* refers to the heavy infantrymen who were equipped with a common panoply. Many people, such as F.D. Adcock, claim that "hoplites are troops who take their name from their shields," which was the *hoplon*.[1] J. F. Lazenby and David Whitehead challenged that view in an article in 1996. They claim that "hoplites took their name from their arms and armor as a whole, their hoopla.... Accordingly hoplite was nothing more than a heavily-armed infantry man."[2] They state that there is little actual ancient evidence to support the traditional viewpoint and examine the ancient passages used to support the view that *hoplon* meant shield and conclude that they do not support the traditional definition.[3] Van Wees writing in 2004 supports the view of Lazenby and Whitehead, while Schwartz writing in 2009 raises doubts concerning their definition.[4] While there is disagreement on whether the hoplite drew his name from a shield, there is no disagreement that the hoplite was defined by a shield and spear. The phalanx is defined as "a body of infantry drawn up in close order in several ranks which are also close together."[5] Although there may be disagreement on the details of how the phalanx operated, Adcock's definition seems acceptable. While Peter Connolly believes that it is "impossible to trace the early development of the phalanx," it seems to be generally accepted that it had developed in Corinth by c. 650 BCE.[6] John Salman states that "no evidence can demonstrate formally that phalanx tactics were used before c. 650 BCE but that there are some pointers in that direction." He believes that phalanx tactics probably existed before 650 BCE but that vase painters lacked the skills to depict it. He argues that it is reasonable to assume that earlier painters had made "less successful attempts at depicting the same subject.[7]

In the past 60 years a great deal of information has emerged concerning the hoplite's panoply from archaeology, analysis of vase paintings, analysis of fragments from lyric poets and comments from later Greek historians; however, there is not agreement on how it should be interpreted. H. Lorimer believes the changes in the round shield "swung on a *talamon*" was a technological breakthrough that led to phalanx tactics and that it occurred c. 700 BCE.[8] Cartledge agrees with Lorimer that "the invention of the *porpax* and the *antilabe* tells us that concern for protection in the front was outweighing the need for maneuverability and for protection on the flank and rear—in other words the changing tactics in the direction of organized, hand-to-hand fighting was already in place."[9] After examining the archaeological evidence concerning Greek armor and weapons, A. M. Snodgrass looked at the chronology of the development of the hoplite panoply and phalanx tactics. In his article "The Hoplite Reform and History," he concludes that many of the elements of the panoply existed earlier than 700 BCE but not before 750 BCE Contrary to Lorimer's conclusion, Snodgrass believes that the evidence shows that "adoption of the hoplite panoply was a long, drawn out piecemeal process which did not entail any radical change in tactics."[10] Victor Davis Hanson in his article, "Hoplite Technology in Phalanx Battle," believes that Snodgrass' gradual adoption is the more influential hypothesis, but emphasizes the fact that both schools of thought "postulate that new tactics, either around 700 or 650 BCE followed the adoption of new equipment."[11]

Greek Armor and Weapons

While sources on the early development of hoplites and phalanx tactics are very limited, we are lucky to have available large numbers of body armor, helmets and also remains of weapons and shields found in archaeological excavations at sites like Delphi and especially at Olympia. Fortunately it was a religious custom to dedicate some weapons to sacred sites after hoplite battles. Also after 650 BCE many vase paintings exist that illustrate hoplite warfare.[12]

All the hoplites in a phalanx did not have the same panoply or even a complete panoply; however, one cannot imagine a hoplite without a shield for defense and a spear to attack. Also, these are two elements of the hoplite panoply that do not change over the 300 years of the hoplite era. With this in mind we will proceed to examine the shield and spear first and then look at the other elements of a hoplite's panoply.

The Hoplite Shield

In his book *Arms and Armor of the Greeks,* Snodgrass describes the shield as follows:

> It was much larger than the round shield of the preceding era: the regular diameter is about 3 feet and one exceptional example was found to be nearly 4 feet across. The shape is gently convex, except that the rim is usually flat. The basic material was wood, reinforced with bronze. The whole shield sometimes had a bronze facing, and the rim was invariably faced with bronze, usually with a cable declaration. On the inner side was a bronze strip sometimes short but more often running right across the shield and bowed out in the middle to form a loop through which the left forearm was passed, up to just below the elbow. This armband or *porpax* as the Greeks called it was a new invention and peculiar to this kind of shield. At the edge of the shield was a handle—the *antilabe*—a leather thong which was gripped by the left hand.[13]

The hoplite or Argive shield first made its appearance c. 700 BCE While it may have evolved from the round one-handled grip shield used earlier, it had few similarities other than being round. Its grip configuration was completely changed, as an arm band (*porpax*) was placed at the center of the shield, and a leather thong or rope handgrip (*antilabe*) was added near the rim. The *antilabe* was formed by running a leather thong or rope around the inside of the shield which originally may have also been used as a "cable truss to add additional support to the inner face of the dome."[14] The hoplite's left forearm was put through the *porpax*, and then the leather *antilabe* was grasped by his hand. In addition the shield had a bronze reinforced rim and was much more concave than previous shields. The core was usually made from laths fastened to the rim and often of several thin layers that were crossed and glued together, similar to plywood, which increased its strength and resiliency. A lathe was then used to form the shallow dome shape, which meant the center was thinner than the outer edge. This core of the shield was covered early on in ox hide or bronze but later mostly in bronze. The covering helped prevent the wood from splintering and spread the force of the blow over a greater area. The bronze covering was unusually thin, probably less than 1 mm, and while the bronze added little extra protection, it was easily polished to look impressive, and some even think they could use the sun's reflection to blind their enemy. The construction of the shield included a rim or lip that extended about 4.5 cm (1.77 inches) all around the shield. Even if the entire shield was not covered in bronze, the rim was covered so as to prevent blows from penetrating the wood and separating the wooden laths. Finally the inside of the shield was padded with leather; however, it was thin and added little extra protection. It might have been used to make it more comfortable to carry the weight of the shield on the hoplite's shoulder. The rim or lip allowed the hoplite to rest the shield on his shoulder to take some of the weight off of his left arm. When discussing the concavity of the shield and the importance of being able to rest it upon the shoulder, Hansen suggests that "this concavity, so radical in conception rather than the more heralded armgrips and handgrips, was the real revolution in armament: it allowed a disproportionately large piece of equipment to be carried by even a small man (of some 150 pounds)."[15] Matthew believes that the hoplite shield "must have been custom made to suit the individual" as the *antilabe* would have to be a certain length in order for the shield to be balanced and able to have part of its weight carried by the hoplite's shoulder. If the *antilabe* was too short or too long, the entire weight of the shield would be borne by the arm itself. He adds that some artistic representations show the *antilabe* as consisting of being a handle attached to the outer edge. This he says reinforces his view that the shield would have to be custom made as the handle would have to be placed carefully for the individual using the shield.[16] The wood core of the shield formed a shallow bowl that was about 10 cm (3.9 inches) deep, although vase paintings show shields with an even deeper bowl. The laths determined the distance between the *propax* and the *antilabe,* which accounts for the different sizes of shields that have been found, although only the *antilabe* could be attached at different points.[17] The convex shape of the shield provided a "greater thickness of wood to be penetrated by weapons impacting at oblique angles." Berundias claims that the shallow dome of the *aspis* could be a structural problem as force on the flattened surface could cause the rim to be forced outward and cause the dome to pop "inside out." To prevent this, the *aspis* had a thickened rim which resisted the force trying to push the rim outwards, and it was reinforced by a bronze sheath whose tensile strength resisted stretching.[18]

    One of the drawbacks of the hoplite shield was its size and weight. Listings of the shields dedicated at Olympia show an average diameter of between 80 cm (31.4 inches) and 100 cm (39.4 inches), with one specimen actually measuring 120 cm (47.2 inches).[19] There appears to be general agreement that shields weighed between 6.2 kg (13.7 pounds) to 8 kg (17.6 pounds); however, Krentz, in his book *The Battle of Marathon,* suggests that while in late archaic times "hoplites could have carried shields in the 15 pound range, most probably carried a lighter one, under 11 or even 10 pounds."[20] Since the hoplite shield was heavy, the advantage of the two-handed grip is obvious. It allowed the hoplite to support the weight of the shield on both the elbow and wrist, and because of its concavity also upon the shoulder. When the shield was resting on the shoulder, it meant that the shield was carried at a slant with its lower edge extending out, which "greatly enlarged its zone of protection.[21] While the two-handed shield brought with it advantages, it also created problems. Carrying the shield at a slant also made it more difficult for spears and arrows to penetrate the shield; however, on the negative side the slant could cause the spear or arrow to glance off of the shield into the hoplite's face. Also, if the shield was kicked at its lower edge, it could cause the shield to be pushed into his throat region.[22]

The previous one-handled shield allowed the soldier to switch hands to rest his arm and also to protect each side; however, the hoplite with the two-handed shield could not switch hands. In addition, the large, heavy, awkward shield was held by his weaker left arm. He had to hold it waist high with "his elbow bent and forearm straight and parallel to the ground, the hand clenched to the grip. If the hoplite bent down or slipped, it would scrape the ground, "which could certainly occur, as the average hoplite at that time was about 5'6."[23] It was also impossible for the hoplite to bring the shield over to protect his right side. Flank attacks were always a concern for the extreme right file as they had no protection for the right side, nor could the shield offer any protection for his back, as the two-handled shield did not have a carrying strap like the one-handled shield, which had allowed the hoplite to sling the shield on his back to protect him as he ran from the enemy in defeat. Finally, the size and weight of the shield made it exceedingly difficult to maintain it in an extended position, and as a hoplite became tired he lost his concentration and instinctively lowered his shield.[24]

Effectiveness of the Shield as a Defensive Weapon

In order to provide the maximum surface area to protect the hoplite, the thickness of the shield had to be reduced in order to reach a weight that was possible for a five-foot-six-inch, 150-pound hoplite to handle. As a result the shield seldom was more than an inch to an inch and a half thick. By the fifth century, shields were often covered fully in bronze, but this covering added little to its protective ability; however, it was generally adequate to withstand spear and sword thrusts at close quarters since it was difficult for the hoplite to get much power behind his thrusts with the spear or sword. While the shield was mostly adequate, it often cracked or fell apart in the front ranks as the two sides made the initial impact.[25] Snodgrass states that shields could be pierced by the offensive weapons available at the time, and Sekunda feels that shields were generally reliable against thrusting spears and swords but not as effective against arrows and javelins.[26] Vase paintings also show many shields being pierced or damaged.[27]

Blyth states that it would take between 20 to 40 joules of kinetic energy per cubic centimeter of wood displaced to perforate the 20-mm-thick hoplite shield that is held at the Vatican. He goes on to say, "The tests show that the 9 mm gaboon ply [shield] was very nearly thick enough to provide a satisfactory defense against hand spears, and a good birch ply shield of, say, 12 mm, with a thin layer of bronze might require up to 60 J for a perforation of 15 mm diameter, and that would provide enough protection against both spears and javelins."²⁸ He then turns his attention to the shield's effectiveness against arrows and makes the following statement:

> However, such a shield would require only 15 J for perforation by a 7 mm arrow, provided that the arrow did not break as it penetrated. Reckoning that the arrow would require about 7 J more, in order to do damage on the other side, and that it would lose about 5 J in traveling the first 80 m, we should expect the infantry arrows launched with an energy of 25 to 35 J to represent a danger to shields at close range, but the cavalry arrows launched with 20 to 25 J to be harmless unless they came in at a sufficiently wide angle to miss the shield.²⁹

While the shield may have been more susceptible to being perforated by arrows, this was not a major concern since the shield had been developed for phalanx tactics and the shield appears to have performed admirably. Also, the bow was little used by Greek armies during archaic times.

The Hoplite Spear

You cannot have a hoplite without a shield for defense or a hoplite without a spear for offense. These two items of the hoplite panoply are essential and had the least alteration during the 300 years of hoplite dominance.³⁰ In fourth-century Athens, when the government supplied weapons, they gave the ephebes a shield and spear upon completion of their training.³¹ Concerning the importance of the spear, Cartledge states, "The spear was to offense what the shield was to defense: Aeschylus represented the Persian Wars as a victory of the Dorian spear over the Asiatic bow, and Tyrtaios could refer to the Spartan army simply as Spearman."³²

Ash wood was used for spear shafts in the heroic age, but cornel wood was used through the classical age. Later pinewood and wild olive as well as oak may have been used, but none were as good as the ash wood.³³ Sekunda claims that only ash could be used to provide shafts strong enough and light enough to handle and that while ash trees were found in the mountains of Greece, many cities imported their supplies.³⁴ Schwartz points out that cornell cherry and ash were both dense and fairly elastic without being overly flexible. He also points out that remains found inside a butt-spike were pinewood and goes on to say it is no surprise that we have records of spear shafts breaking since pine is not a hard wood and is "prone to splitting" and would break under the pressure that would occur during a battle, especially during the charge.³⁵

The spearhead on the hoplite spear was usually made of iron, which was harder than bronze and not that much heavier, although some bronze spearheads were reintroduced in the sixth and fifth centuries. The spearheads were socketed and the shafts were secured with pitch and rivets. The spearheads were between 20 cm (8 inches) and 30 cm (1 foot) long, although some longer spearheads were found which were thought to be ceremonial as they were up to 1 m long and highly decorated. There was no set standard, but the usual spearhead was a leaf-shaped blade with a strong central rib for support and a diameter of about 16 to 19 mm. The average spearhead weighed about 153 g (5.4 ounces).³⁶

At the opposite end from the spearhead, the hoplite spear had a butt-spike (*sauroter*) made of bronze. It was usually a solid cast bronze four-sided spike, which ranged in length from 20 cm (8 inches) to 50 cm (20 inches) and weighed on average about 329 g (11.6 ounces) and served as a counterweight to the spearhead.[37] The *sauroter* being about 2.1 times as heavy as the spearhead not only served as a counterweight but shifted the point of balance for the hoplite spear toward the rear of the spear, which allowed the hoplite to hold the spear closer to the rear, thus extending the reach of the spear. The point of balance for the spear was about 89 cm from the rear point of the *sauroter*.[38]

The butt-spike apparently served multiple functions. Its small diameter allowed it to be stuck into even hard ground when the spear was not in use. In addition, it stopped rot and wear in the wood and prevented splintering. Since many spear shafts broke in the first impact, the butt-spike provided an excellent second weapon by allowing the hoplite to reverse the shaft and use the butt-spike as a new short spear, unless the shaft was too shattered to be of use. Of course, even if the spearhead was not broken off, the butt-spike could be of great value during combat if the hoplite found himself too far into the enemy phalanx with enemy hoplites behind him. A backward jab with the butt-spike could be very effective. Finally the butt-spike was useful for the rear ranks that carried their spears upright. If they came upon enemy hoplites that were wounded or had simply fallen to the ground, they could kill the enemy hoplites with a powerful downward stroke with the butt-spike that could penetrate the cuirass of the enemy without having "to reverse the spear or bend over with the short sword."[39] Paul Bardunias suggests that the *sauroter* was also important because it allowed the hoplites in the rear ranks to plant their spears in the ground and use them as an aid in pushing forward during *othismos*.[40] Blyth calls the butt-spike the "only armor piercing device." Armor found at sanctuaries has shown square holes which many think were made by the butt-spike, but Hansen suggests that the holes may have been made by spikes used to display the armor.[41]

Sekunda acknowledges the claims that the butt-spike served as a secondary weapon but says that there is little evidence to support this view.[42] Christopher Matthew, an experimental archaeologist, is even stronger in his rejection of the possible use of the *sauroter* (butt-spike) as a secondary weapon. He claims that there is "no" literary evidence, nor "are there any representations of a hoplite engaging an opponent with the rear end of a broken spear in vase illustrations, relief carvings or statuary." He then claims that in a test he conducted, the *sauroter* was unable to "penetrate a flat target bronze plate 1 mm thick" and thus would be useless as a weapon. Regarding the square holes found in some armor at Olympia, he states that the holes were 5 to 8 mm in size, while a *sauroter* would leave a hole "at least 9 × 9 mm in size" if it was to cause serious injury. He agrees with Hansen that the holes were the result of damage caused by chisels while setting up the armor as a trophy.[43]

It has been estimated that the diameter of the spear shaft, irrespective of the wood used, was about 25 mm (.98 inches), but the shaft would have to have been tapered in order to fit into the socket of the spearhead and the butt-spike, which was about 19 mm in diameter. The shaft could not be 19 mm along its entire length, as spears with such a diameter would show "a considerable 'droop' toward the front end of the weapon." In addition a shaft of 19 mm would be more easily broken. Replacement spear shafts created in the field were probably not fully tapered, as creating a long taper required professional expertise. In the field the entire shaft produced would be about 25 mm, with only a small section at each end reshaped to 19 mm to fit into the sockets of the spearhead and the butt-spike.[44] While no hoplite spears complete with shaft have been found, we have many spearheads and butt-spikes to examine. Most estimates place the length of the hoplite spear between 7 and 8 feet based upon vase paintings; however, Sekunda claims that "on vase paintings the hoplite spear is normally short for artistic convenience, but occasionally shown at its true length of up to 9 feet."[45] Based upon the density and weight of cornell cherry wood and oak wood and using the spearheads and butt-spikes that have been found by archaeologists, estimates for the weight of the typical hoplite spear range from 1.388 kg (2.95 pounds) to 21.95 kg (4.29 pounds).[46]

There were two ways that the hoplite could grip his spear—the overhand grip (high position) and the underhand grip (low position). Vase paintings usually show the hoplite using the overhand grip in order to use a downward thrust, which produced the most power; however, the opposing hoplite's shield and armor greatly reduced the target area of the spear to the face and neck. The underhand grip or low position of the spear on the other hand allowed the hoplite to strike under the shield at the unprotected groin and thighs of his opponent. The problem with the underhand grip is it only produces about 14 percent of the impact energy of the overhand grip. Thus the shield and armor could not be penetrated by an underhand thrust.[47] Matthew, writing in 2012, claims that previous scholars have neglected to examine a third way a hoplite could hold the spear which he calls the "underarm" technique in which the spear is held tucked beneath the armpit. He says that scholars may have considered the underarm position as an elevated version of the underhand grip or low position; however, he claims that under closer examination the underhand grip/low position and the underarm position are quite different. In both the overhand grip and the underhand grip, the hoplite's forearm is perpendicular to the spear shaft, while in the underarm position the hoplite's forearm is not perpendicular to the spear shaft but rather can be placed above, beneath or alongside the shaft running parallel to the long axis of the spear. He then adds that the pitch of the spear is changed "through the vertical movement of the entire forearm, pivoting at the elbow, using the muscles of the upper arm rather than relying on the flex of the wrist. Finally he states that the spear "can also be elevated by rotating the shoulder and raising the entire arm above the head while keeping the grip in position." At this point the "spear moves out from the armpit and is held away from the body." He calls this position a "reverse" position which he considers the fourth combat position.[48]

Blyth states that the hoplite spear was designed to "cut flesh and perhaps leather rather than to pierce bronze or wood." Based upon their experiments, Gabriel and Metz conclude that "the spear was not a terribly effective weapon unless it struck the face under the chin or in the space between the neck collar and chest armor."[49] Schwartz agrees that "a spear wielded with one hand only lacks penetration power.... Consequently it is unlikely that sufficient power could be generated with a one hand thrust to penetrate bronze armor (or shields)." He goes on to say that penetration may have taken place if sufficient momentum had been gained during the first impact of the front ranks. Certainly, the forearms and upper legs were vulnerable, but they seldom received killing wounds.[50] The spear shaft was long and thin with a diameter ranging from 16 mm (.62 inches) to 19 mm (.74 inches), which made it susceptible to breaking during the initial impact. We also hear of the spear being broken by a sword blow, and Herodotus (9.62.2) tells of Persians who "seized the Hellene's spears and broke them." The spear could also become stuck in an enemy's body, and a "sideways wrench on the handgrip with a force of the order of 358N (80 foot-pounds) would break the shaft just behind the socket."[51] Matthew says that statements concerning Persians breaking hoplite spears are simply incorrect. He bases this view on field tests using spears of 25 mm and 19 mm in diameter and found that individuals were incapable of breaking spears of either diameter. He concludes that the Persians only "managed to break or hack through the Greek spears using a weapon wielded in the right hand.[52] When the phalanx attacked, the middle ranks held their spears upright, which provided some protection against missiles and also kept their butt-spikes clear of the ranks behind them. The first two ranks lowered their spears as they attacked, which meant that the immediate ranks behind them faced their butt-spikes and accidents could occur.[53]

Body Armor

While the spear and shield of the hoplite remained virtually unchanged over time, body armor went through many changes. Eero Jarva in his book *Archaiologia on Archaic Greek Body Armour*[54] identifies five types of body armor as follows:

Type I—the well-known bronze bell cuirass is identified by "an outward-jutting bottom edge" which allowed the hoplite to squat or sit and also deflected a downward thrust of his opponent's spear. The negative is that the extended lower lip also guided an underhand thrust with a spear into the groin area. The cuirass also had a collar that would help deflect upward spear thrusts. The bronze plates used in making the bell cuirass range from .5 mm (.015 inches) to 3 mm (.125 inches).[55] The bell cuirass seems to have provided good protection from the hoplite spear. It would take 137 foot-pounds of energy to penetrate 2 mm of armor, and an overhand thrust with a spear only generated 70.8 foot-pounds.[56] Jarva dates the bell cuirass back to the eighth century and believes it remained in use through the sixth century, possibly as late as 540 BCE.[57]

Type II—the only difference between the bell cuirass and type II cuirass was the absence of the jutting-out lower edge. Evidence is only found in vase paintings, and it appears to have been very rare.

Type III—also called the muscle cuirass. It first becomes seen in vase painting, c. 480 BCE and is an improvement over types I and II. It is unique in its "very naturalistic, though perhaps somewhat heroically exaggerated, moldings of upper body musculature. A major change is the addition of a belly guard, and it also had leather or metal-reinforced leather *ptereygia* to protect the groin and upper legs.[58]

While all the bronze plate cuirasses provided excellent protection, they also had many negative traits. A big drawback was the weight of the cuirass which interfered with mobility. Jarva gives estimates for the bronze cuirass as ranging from 3.36 kg (7.4 pounds) to 3.85 kg (8.48 pounds), but goes on to state that a 2 mm cuirass with *pterygia* could reach as high as 10 kg (22 pounds), while Krentz gives estimates ranging from 7.7 pounds to 12.1 pounds.[59] In addition to weight, the tight-fitting cuirass allowed little ventilation. In the summer when most of the campaigns took place, the temperatures were very high, with average temperatures ranging from 23.8°C (83.3°F) in the shade to as high as a maximum of 42.6°C (108°F) in the Peloponnesus. The bronze of the cuirass acted as a solar collector which made the surface hot to touch. Hoplites wore felt or linen under their armor to help with the heat and roughness of the bronze armor. Very quickly the undergarments became soaked with sweat, having few outlets from which to evaporate. As a result, heat prostration and dehydration were major problems for the hoplites. Conversely the armor caused a problem in the spring as cold weather and thunderstorms made the hoplite extremely uncomfortable and even led to hypothermia as the bronze would effectively siphon away body heat.[60]

As a result of the weight, cost, and negative features of the bronze cuirass, composite cuirasses were developed.[61] Snodgrass comments that it appears that it was decided in the mid-sixth century that change was required as the body armor was too heavy and unwieldy.[62] Jarva identifies the shoulder piece corselet as type IV and calls it "the most common Greek breastplate during the archaic period, along side of the Bell cuirass. There are no surviving corselets of this type since they were made with materials that have long since disappeared. They are first found represented on vase painting around 560 BCE It appears that many were made from one piece of leather, usually ox hide because of its thickness and toughness. They had *pteryges* that were often covered with bronze scales to protect the upper legs and groin area. In addition to leather, Jarva also identifies a type IV made of many layers of linen. While they appear on vase paintings, "the structure of the linen corselet is not described in extant written sources."[63]

Connelly suggests that the linen corselet was made by gluing together many different layers of linen to form a stiff shirt that was about .5 cm thick. The corselet reached to the hips, and *pteryges* were formed by cutting slits in the linen; they were reinforced by gluing similar strips to the inside of the *pteryges* to cover the open spaces between them. He explains that he made a sample linen corselet which he found comfortable once he got used to it and felt he could move easily with it.[64] Krentz describes one made by a member of the Hoplite Association, which contained a dozen or so layers and that weighed eight pounds.[65] In addition to the weight advantage, the composite corselet was less affected by the cold and heat and allowed better air circulation than the bronze cuirass. Also, leather and linen were softer and more comfortable than bronze and allowed greater mobility, though it is also pointed out that the corselet still hindered arm movement and made it difficult for the hoplite to reach across his chest with his shield in order to protect his right side.

In his conclusion, Jarva states that bronze, despite its cost and negative qualities, still had appeal because of its "shining, golden appearance." He quotes Onasander, who said "the advancing companies appear more dangerous by gleam of weapons, and terrible sight brings fear and confusion to the hearts of the enemy." He also points out that leather corselets were relatively cheap but that "a fine linen corselet could easily raise the price of a panoply to the annual wage of a skilled workman." He finally points out that leather corselets appeared much more often in artistic works toward the end of the archaic period.[66]

The helmet used by hoplites evolved from two prototypes—the Kagle and the primitive Corinthian. Connelly traces the development of the Kagle, which disappeared in the seventh century, and the Illyrian which was a derivation of the Kagle type and continued to be used until the fifth century; however, he states that the Corinthian and its various versions was by far the most popular helmet in Greece. Jarva estimates that over 350 examples of helmets have been found, and 250, or 71.4 percent, are Corinthian.[67] Snodgrass states that the first

Corinthian helmet appears on vase paintings c. 700 BCE and was widely used until the early fifth century, when suddenly it seldom appears in paintings. He describes it as follows:

> The helmet is a remarkable one: in a single sheet of metal it covers almost the whole head from the collarbone upwards. The cheek pieces, instead of hanging, merely sweep forwards continuing the lower rim of the helmet, and a leave only a small, roughly T-shaped aperture for the eyes, nose and mouth.[68]

The helmet had padding that was made of leather, felt or sponge to prevent chafing, to protect the head from the hot surface temperature from the sun in the summer, and also to add some cushioning to absorb blows to the helmet. Finally, the helmet had a crest of horsehair, often brightly dyed, usually attached to the helmet but sometimes attached to a short stem on top of the helmet. It seems that the crest was designed to make the hoplite appear taller and more threatening, but it could also help absorb blows to the top of the helmet; however, it made the helmet more unstable and unwieldy. Cartledge believes that the horsehair crests also "satisfied demands that were at least psychological or aesthetic."[69]

The Corinthian helmet went through many refinements and had reached a very advanced form by the late sixth century. The later Corinthian helmet's rims were longer and lower in shape and had notches in the sides so that the helmet set more squarely on the neck and shoulders. The cheek guards and nose guards "jutted forward at a raking angle," and the cheek guards were elongated so that they protected the neck and throat. In addition, the forehead part of the helmet and the nose guard were made thicker while the rest of the helmet was kept thin for lightness. Jarva gives figures of 6 mm (2.3 inches) to 8 mm (3.1 inches) for the nose guard. Finally, the later helmets all have some sort of opening for the ears in an attempt to improve hearing for the hoplite.[70]

Snodgrass points out that the trend in helmets, as in other parts of the panoply, was toward lightness. Jarva estimates helmets weighed between 1.2 and 1.5 kg (2.6–3.3 pounds), Hansen estimates the average weight at 2.27 kg (5 pounds), and Schwartz lists 1.6 kg (3.5 pounds) with extremes between 1.1 kg (2.42 pounds) and 1.9 kg (4.1 pounds) and quotes Franz at about 2 kg (4.4 pounds); however, Krentz claims late Corinthian helmets had been reduced in thickness and width and with padding weighed 2.6 pounds (1.1 kg), but he also believes many hoplites wore "Attic" helmets which weighed even less.[71] Schwartz compares the weight of the Corinthian helmet to modern World War I helmets which averaged 1.08 kg (2.3 pounds) and concludes, "The Corinthian helmet was heavy by almost any definition of the word."[72]

In 1970 P. H. Blyth applied engineering science and mathematics to the study of how effective Greek armor would be against hand weapons and bows and arrows. He looked at the differences between annealed bronze used in early Corinthian helmets and the high-tin-content bronze that was cold worked for late Corinthian helmets, and also at the different hardness scores between the two. The improved hardness of cold-worked bronze helmets allowed lighter helmets to be produced while at the same time maintaining a high level of protection. He also examined the amount of energy produced by hand weapons and bows and arrows and how much kinetic energy was required to perforate the bronze plate armor.[73]

When Blyth examined armor found at Olympia, he found the following: about 150 helmets show only dents, with no scarring by metal (some, however, have pieces missing because of corrosion).

1. Forty to Fifty have small indentations which could be due to stones.
2. Three have possibly been perforated in battle.
3. Seventeen show cuts or stamps which could have been made in battle. Of these, all but five are due to slashing blows, but none is convincing evidence of a fatal blow.
4. Nine show perforation by square or circular indentures, with the helmet removed—in many cases near the edge and at the rear, as if for hanging the helmet up. The holes may have been made by a nail, or by the butt-spikes of a spear. These holes have a diameter of between .5 and .8 cm.
5. Six at least (and possibly all of the doubtful greaves) have been thrust through with a blade while empty, often outward.[74]

Blyth concludes that Greek armorers were highly skilled as they used high-tin-content bronze and were able to create complex shapes while working the metal. He adds that this view is supported by the "small amount of serious battle damage in surviving helmets."[75] He says that "a Greek hoplite could quite happily rely upon his bronze helmet to keep out both Persian and Scythian arrows and on his breast plate and greaves if he wore them."[76] The helmet also provided excellent protection against blows from a sword or other weapons to the head. Gabriel and Metz include some interesting facts from modern studies on blows to the head. They state,

> Modern studies of skull fractures conducted by the American military demonstrate that it takes a minimum of 90 foot-pounds delivered over one square inch to fracture the human skull with a blow delivered to the front of the head. If the blow was delivered to the temporal/parietal region, 45 foot-pounds will produce a fracture. A blow to the zygomatic region, the bony arch on either side of the face and around the eye, requires only 18 foot-pounds force to produce a fracture.... In fact, studies show that a force of between 56 and 79 foot-pounds to the skull produces unconsciousness, although forces of 17 to 36 foot-pounds have been routinely sustained without even dazing the victim. Even without a helmet the human skull can withstand tremendous impact without dazing or rendering its owner unconscious. It requires 585 foot-pounds of energy impacting upon a helmet to render the soldier unconscious. The most the human arm could generate in our experiments was 101 foot-pounds. In their experiment, the 101 foot-pounds was produced by a mace. Other weapons that the Greeks might have faced included the sword (77.5 foot-pounds), the javelin (67.1 foot-pounds), the arrow (47.4 foot-pounds), the overhand spear thrust (70.8 foot-pounds), the underhand spear thrust (13.5 foot-pounds) and the sling (16 foot-pounds).[77]

Hanson describes the late Corinthian helmet, which was still in use at the beginning of the fifth century, as follows: "Its sleek cheek and neck guard, the eerie cutouts for the eyes and the impressive ridge at the top of the face gave unmatched protection and lent a sense of terror to the warrior." But he also feels that the helmet must have been a most unpleasant piece of equipment to wear, and it greatly hindered the sight and hearing of the hoplite.[78] He believes that the sight and hearing was so bad for the hoplite that the simple "formation and tactics of phalanx warfare ... grew, at least in part, out of the lack of direct communication between soldiers and their commanders; dueling, skirmishing, and hit-and-run attacks were out of the question with such headgear." He also believes that the isolation hoplites felt as a result of their helmet could feed the fear and panic that at times spread through a phalanx. Individual hoplites had little concept of how the overall battle was going and could react to the fear and panic of a few hoplites around him which could lead him to run even though in other areas his forces were being victorious.[79] J. P. Franz challenges the idea that the helmet limited vision and caused a problem for the hoplite. He states, "The large eye apertures shaped after the form of the eye, provide very good side view."[80] Schwartz, who translated the German statement of Franz, disagrees with his conclusion and describes his own experiment with a model of the Corinthian helmet. He made a replica of a typical Corinthian helmet using measurements taken from helmets in the Archaeological Museum at Olympia. He found that when not wearing a helmet the range of vision was 1.5 m to each side at 1 m distance and 1 m to each side at .5 m distance. When wearing the helmet the person could see clearly 1 m at a distance of 1 m, but outside that distance things were blurry, while at .5 m distance nothing could be seen outside of .5 m. While he felt he could not be completely accurate, he did feel confident in stating that the Corinthian helmet definitely obscured the vision of a hoplite.[81]

Another problem with the helmet was that it was not custom made for the individual, so often the fit was poor. As a result of blows to the helmet, it could move up, down or sideways, greatly affecting the vision of the hoplite. In addition, the tight-fitting bronze helmet generated a great deal of heat around the eyes, mouth and nose and made breathing difficult because the air in the helmet would become stuffy, hot, and humid, and the dust on summer battlefields would add to the breathing problems.[82]

The Corinthian helmet had padding of felt, sponge or leather which helped to absorb blows to the helmet; however, the helmet lacked a suspension system used in modern military helmets to prevent physical contact between the area of impact and the skull. While helmets were seldom perforated and padding helped, severe blows to the helmet could cause serious head trauma, resulting in severe contusions, concussions and being knocked unconscious.[83]

While the Corinthian helmet certainly provided unmatched protection, Schwartz asks "whether the protective advantages of the helmet's design outweighed the considerable drawbacks" of the helmet. In considering the question, he goes on to say that the helmet was heavy and its small eye openings definitely restricted the vision of the hoplite. Another problem is that often the helmets did not fit perfectly, and the crest and crest holder made it top-heavy so that it would shift on the hoplite's head during the battle which could affect the hoplite's sight even more. The helmet also affected the hoplite's hearing as the archaic helmets did not have ear openings. In addition, the long hair and beards of the hoplites as well as the padding in the helmet caused more muffling of sound. It is possible that basically all the hoplite heard was his own breathing, which was loud and labored as the helmets were not ventilated and most of the fighting occurred in the hot summer months which made breathing even more difficult.[84]

The answer to Schwartz's question appears to be that the drawbacks of the helmets were not offset by the protective traits of helmet, as the Corinthian helmet suddenly disappears during the fifth century and is replaced by the Attic helmet and eventually by a pointed cap (*pilos*).[85] The so-called Attic helmet had hinged cheek guards, an opening for the ears to improve hearing, no nose guard, and much larger openings for the eyes to improve vision. No surviving Greek Attic helmets have been found, although examples from Italy do exist.[86]

Greaves

While the hoplite shield protected much of his body, it did not cover his lower legs. Snodgrass points out that greaves were found in Mycenaean times but that the modern greave appears in vase painting only around 675 BCE Jarva identifies five different types of greaves, but they were all similar and hammered out of thin bronze sheets. Over time they grew longer and eventually covered the entire knee.[87] The greaves were lined with either felt or leather and were pulled open and snapped on around the calf muscles and were held in place by the elasticity of the bronze. Both Schwartz and Hansen comment on the fact that movement would cause chafing and slipping, which could require the hoplite to rebend them for more comfort.[88] The greaves range from .5 mm to 2 mm in thickness, their weight being between 1.2 kilograms (2.6 pounds) and 2.2 kg (4.8 pounds). The greaves were very important as the bone is "directly beneath the skin and the area is very sensitive: a wound here was likely to be incapacitating or cause a hoplite to collapse in pain."[89] Even though thin, the greaves seem to have offered good protection against hand weapons and missiles of all kinds. Their resistance was probably more the result of their round surfaces than of their thickness. When he examined armor, Jarva found "that damage is rarer on greaves than on helmets."[90]

Other Body Armor

In addition to greaves, examples have been found of upper and lower arm guards, thigh guards, ankle guards and foot guards. Jarva identifies three types of upper arm guards worn on the right arm that was not protected by the hoplite's shield but concludes that due to the small number of originals discovered, their use was very limited. The evidence for lower arm guards being used in archaic Greece is even more limited. Most evidence for thigh guards is found in iconography, and Jarva and Lorimer disagree on its validity.[91] E. Collins in excavations at Olympia found 50 original ankle guards, but little evidence is found in archaic Greek art. Jarva concludes that "their use was quite limited in relation to greaves." Concerning foot guards, Jarva states, "This form of protection enjoyed little popularity, judging from the fact that only three such pieces have been found at Olympia and there is little evidence of them in iconography."[92] Irrespective of their popularity, it appears that all arm and leg guards except for greaves disappeared from use by the end of the sixth century.[93]

Swords

All hoplites carried a sword as their backup weapon. Anderson says it was definitely secondary as he explains that "there is no classical Greek word for swordsman, and the Greek speaks of plunder, captives, and lands won by the spear, where we might say by the sword."[94] The hoplite's sword evolved from the 75 cm (29.5 inches) straight, double-edged sword used by the Mycenaeans. By the fifth century the sword had evolved to a straight, two-edged sword with a variable length rarely exceeding 60 cm (23 inches). The sword blade grew broader from the hilt for about two-thirds of its length where it tapered to a point. There is uncertainty about the weight of the sword, but Jarva estimates that it was between 1.5 kg (3.3 pounds) and 2 kg (4.4 pounds). It had a leaf-shaped blade and a cylindrical pommel for balance and could be used for thrusting or slashing. The hoplite carried it in a sheath hung over his shoulder under his left arm so that he could quickly draw it if his spear was broken or lost.[95]

During the fifth century, a single-edged slashing sword called a *kopis* became more common. The back of the sword was nearly straight, but the cutting edge was curved and the maximum width was near the tip. It varied in length between 50 cm (19 inches) and 70 cm (27 inches). It was a terrifying weapon as it was capable of beheading an opponent or easily removing a limb.[96] Even though it was an intimidating weapon, it still definitely remained a secondary weapon. In order to have sufficient power behind the slash, the hoplite would have to raise his arm back and over his head, and this would expose his right side and armpit to counter-blows by his opponent. Also, a slashing weapon is not as effective at piercing armor as the force is spread over a greater area rather than being centered at the point of a weapon such as an arrow or a spear. As a result the *kopis* achieved less fatal results than thrusting weapons.[97] Finally, Schwartz points out that the *kopis* would be difficult to swing during a closely packed hoplite battle, making it even more difficult to get much power behind the sword. He speculates that "possibly it was primarily intended for great slashing blows in the pursuit or otherwise on the retreat: in this situation, when their ranks were broken and there was room to swing it, the *kopis* would be both devastatingly effective and owing to its terrifying appearance and effect, also a decided psychological asset that might win a pursued hoplite crucial seconds."[98]

The Hoplite Panoply

The standard panoply for the hoplite included the shield, spear, helmet, breastplate, greaves, a sword and in some cases thigh- and arm-guards; although the latter two were not generally used.[99] Based upon his investigation of armor at Olympia, Jarva concludes, "Summarizing the above discussion about the definition of the panoply, it may be said that in practice it was not a fixed thing but a variable concept, which at a minimum included a helmet, shield, spear and perhaps also a dagger or sword, and could naturally include at maximum the full selection of the items discussed."[100] While there is little disagreement that the above describes what a fully equipped hoplite carried, there is not agreement as to how many hoplites were fully equipped.

Hans van Wees states that a Greek needed only a spear and a shield to be termed a hoplite and feels that most wore less than the full panoply. He admits that iconography shows most hoplites wearing the full panoply, but he points to the armor found at Olympia to support his view. From hundreds of pieces of armor, he extrapolates that one in three hoplites wore greaves and one in 10 wore a bronze cuirass.[101] Assuming that the armor at Olympia is somewhat representative of the amount actually worn by hoplites, Jarva suggests that the greaves and bronze cuirass were worn by the hoplites in the front ranks, while the middle ranks might be occupied by hoplites equipped with the minimum, such as the spear and the shield.[102] Schwartz is not willing to accept the assumptions of Jarva and van Wees that the armor dedicated at Olympia is somewhat representative of the amount worn by hoplites. He states, "We have no way of knowing what was dedicated or why, and we cannot be certain that everything was dedicated. Sometimes only the best items were selected for dedication, and quite possibly at other times the victors kept what they liked."[103]

The weight of the hoplite's panoply would obviously affect how he fought and how long he could fight before becoming exhausted. Here again there is wide disparity on the issue. In examining the weight of the panoply, Jarva found estimates ranging from 12 kg (26.4 pounds) to 40 kg (88 pounds) at the extreme but concludes that the typical well-armored hoplite carried less than 30 kg (66 pounds).[104] There seems to be general agreement that the panoply of the hoplite became lighter in weight toward the end of the archaic period, but there is still a wide disparity as Jarva and Schwartz estimate the typical hoplite carrying between 25 and 30 kg, while Krentz believes that the weight ranged from 12 to 20.4 kg.[105]

During the archaic period the hoplites were farmers who fought to defend their land. One author describes the hoplites as "an untrained amateur fighting a decisive battle during a break in the agricultural schedule."[106] Aristotle in his *Politics* tells us it was not Spartan training and discipline that made them so successful but rather the fact that they had training while the other poleis had none. Xenophon also draws the conclusion that Spartan training led to superiority when the other poleis had none.[107]

Why was there no training for hoplites? Perhaps it was partially because the farmer/hoplites felt it would take too much time away from their agriculture work, but also because the ideology of the time "favored a form of extreme amateurism, hostile to any form of specialized military training."[108] In addition, hoplite warfare required "utmost courage, excellent physical condition and endurance, but little specialized training or skill with weapons."[109] In Xenophon's *Cyropedia* he says men took naturally to weapons. He quotes one character as saying, "Let me tell you, when I was a little boy I would grab the sword, as soon as I saw one, and I knew instinctively, without having learned from any, how to hold it." Van Wees suggests that boys learned to handle weapons informally within the family and also learned from the hunt; however, he also says, "if such limited and informal train was deemed adequate for hoplites, the general level of competence must have been quite low."[110] Hanson agrees that handling spears and swords in massed combat required little skill as there is little chance of missing the enemy massed in front of you; therefore little training was required.[111]

Later on in the fifth century one could learn fighting skills from private instructors (*hoplomachoi*), but acceptance of private instructors was limited. In Plato's *Laches,* a distinguished general attacks such instructors "as cowards and incompetents, and their art as worthless." His main objection is that there is simply not much to be learned about handling weapons, and he adds, "anyone claiming to be a trained fighter will be regarded as a boaster."[112] Much later in the 330s BCE, Athenians of "pure stock and free status" were enrolled as ephebes at age 18. After taking an oath "not to dishonor his arms, not desert his post, to extend the territory of his homeland and to defend its laws and religious cults," he began his military training which lasted for two years. During his training he was paid, and at the end of the training, he was presented with a spear and shield by Athens.[113]

There seems to be a dearth of sources regarding the military command structure of the Greeks, but most historians seem to agree that it was simple and remained "at a rudimentary level—not only by modern, but also by Macedonian, Hellenistic and Roman standards."[114] No officer class existed in Athens during archaic times, and generals (*stratagos*) and their brigadiers (*tariarchs*) were elected; they were often ambitious politicians who had no specialized military training. Once they were elected it appears that the generals received no training for the job, and their duties were basically to collect and deploy the troops. Perhaps also the general chose the time and place of battle, if it had not already been chosen by his opponent. In addition, generals had few of the powers or privileges of modern military officers. Salutes were not required, officers' armor and equipment were not different, rations and living conditions were not different, and hoplites offered suggestions and addressed generals in terms not acceptable in a modern army. Finally, generals could be accused in court for actions taken during their time in office.[115]

Perhaps the generals' most important function was to "boost morale and kindle passions for the fight" by giving a speech and motivating by example.[116] The general usually placed himself in the right wing of the phalanx, which was the most dangerous position. It certainly motivated his men to see him fighting in the forefront where the most killing took place. Hanson suggests that the general's death could cause panic, but Schwartz feels that his death might "rouse the front ranks to fight all the more fiercely."[117]

The Hoplite

Prior to the hoplite revolution, fighting was dominated by the noble class; however, with the development of the hoplite phalanx, more fighting men were needed, so the duty and privilege of fighting as a hoplite was extended to the independent small farmers of the polis. Thus, the typical hoplite was a small farmer who owned between 10 and 15 acres, which was worth between 2,000 and 3,000 drachmas, and was able to supply himself with the hoplite panoply, which was quite expensive. Estimates for the cost of the hoplite panoply run from 25 to 30 drachmas (about one month's wages) for the minimum panoply of a shield and spear, to 75 to 100 drachmas (about three months' wages) for a full bronze panoply.[118] While the panoply was expensive, less affluent farmers could possibly afford a panoply by purchasing spears and shields of less quality, by purchasing equipment from booty that was put on the open market or by utilizing equipment passed down from generation to generation, even if it did not fit perfectly.[119] Regardless of the exact cost of the hoplite panoply, it was still expensive and beyond the ability of many Greeks to pay, with the result that the hoplite phalanx was always much smaller than the number of citizens in the polis.[120] The Greeks saw their service as hoplites as fulfilling their obligations as citizens to their polis and its gods.[121] In addition they were fighting for their land and their families. To the farmers his land was everything, and he was not willing to allow its defense to be handed over to others. Greece is 80 percent mountains, and there is not much good land for farming. As a result, disagreements between poleis over borderlands were frequent, and even disagreements over pasture rights could escalate into warfare. Also, war was seen as a natural way by which individuals could prove their courage, bravery and valor.[122] Tyrtaios states,

> It is a noble thing for a brave man to fall fighting among the foremost, doing battle for his father land.... So let us fight for our land and let us die for our children without sparing ourselves. Young men, fight shoulder to shoulder in do not begin shameful flight or be afraid. Make your heart great and brave. Do not restrain yourselves in fighting the enemy or flee and abandon those from whom age has stolen agility.... This is suitable for the young man while

he has the bloom of youth. He is a thing of admiration to men and desirable to women as long as he lives and he is fair when he falls as well. So let each stand his ground firmly with his feet well set apart and bite his lip.[123]

Greek farmers were willing to fight and die for their land and families; however, they did not feel any responsibility to fight if their own lands or lives were not threatened. This is seen by the little aid that Athens gained against Persia at the Battle of Marathon.[124] While farmers fought as hoplites, they were first and foremost farmers. They were part-time amateur soldiers who were willing to take only small amounts of time from their agricultural duties. As pointed out earlier in the chapter, they were unwilling to take time to train, and they expected campaigns to be short and to be held when their agricultural duties were limited. Campaigns were often taken before harvest season when farmers were relatively free and enemy crops were vulnerable.[125]

Describing what makes a good hoplite, Tyrtaios states, "For no man ever proves himself a good man in war, unless he can endure to face the blood and slaughter, go close against the enemy and fight with his hands."[126] The small independent farmer was well prepared to play this role. Working in his field for long hours gave him strength and endurance; dealing with crop failures, droughts and storms prepared him to face adversity; and butchering his pigs, sheep and cows prepared him to face the blood and gore of the battlefield.[127]

Since Greece is 80 percent mountains, it raises the question as to why the Greeks did not defend the mountain passes, which would require fewer troops and allow the farmers to concentrate on their agricultural duties. Everett Wheeler calls it the "geographic paradox of the phalanx: mountainous Greece developed a heavy infantry formation as a national tactical characteristic despite the relative scarcity of level, unbroken terrain suitable for it."[128] Perhaps the mountain passes could have been held and prevented invasions, but a totally different military system would have been needed. The troops would have required specialized training in mountain warfare and weapons such as the bow, sling and javelin. They would have had to have permanent bases, be paid by the state and have a logistical system to keep them supplied. In addition, an officer class would be required to supervise them. In fact a professional army would need to be created and maintained by the state.[129] This would have been totally contrary to the Greeks' belief in amateurism. Also the farmer was willing to buy his own panoply, but he was not willing to pay taxes to support a professional army. The farmers felt that it was important to fight in person and not turn over control to others who might squander his resources. Finally, could such a system ensure that campaigns would be short, decided in one battle, and be relatively nonlethal when it was developed under the ritualized agonal warfare of the hoplite system?[130]

Other Troops

Thucydides (4.94) tells us that "light troops regularly armed there were none in the army, nor had there ever been any at Athens." It appears that cavalry and light armed troops became marginal in the seventh century as the hoplite phalanx developed.[131] Hansen claims that "like bowmen on the other end of the social scales horsemen were often ridiculed and pilloried in Greek literature as either the pretentious or the timid, who chose not to serve with the mass." He goes on to say that "until the Peloponnesian War, landed infantrymen developed a system that deliberately made missiles and mounted warriors incidental to success in battle. The system reflected contemporary social, economic and political aspects of agrarianism."[132] Another view is that light armed soldiers played an active role throughout the archaic period. Hans van Wees believes that light armed troops, cavalry, and hoplites were all intertwined on the battlefield until the classical hoplite phalanx emerged in the fifth century. Peter Krentz thinks that the "exclusive hoplite phalanx did not exist before Marathon" and believes it is probable that the "archaic Greek phalanx included a variety of fighters so that it was closer to what we read in Homer than to what Thucydides describes."[133]

The Phalanx

The traditional definition of the phalanx might be that it was a battle formation of massive hoplites drawn up in close order with interlocked shields usually made up of eight ranks of hoplites, although the depth could vary from 4 to 50 ranks depending upon the date and battle one examines. It would advance in an orderly manner to make contact with opponents in hand-to-hand combat.[134] The width of the phalanx would vary according to the total number of men available to fight divided by the ranks. For example, 9,000 hoplites drawn up in ranks of eight would have 1,125 files and a battle front of 1,125 yards, or about .66 miles.

Whatever the depth of the phalanx, only the first two ranks came into direct contact with the enemy, given the length of the hoplites' spear. One might ask the question, why eight ranks deep if only the first two ranks were able to use their weapons against their foe? It would seem to be more logical to have a wider and shallower phalanx as it would bring more weapons into contact with the enemy. Also, a wider, shallower phalanx would give a greater chance of enveloping the enemy. The reason for the deeper phalanx appears to be that it's very difficult to move a wide, shallow line of hoplites into battle without the line losing cohesion and not arriving in a well-ordered manner. A narrower, deeper phalanx would encounter fewer obstacles in the terrain and the rear ranks would help keep the front ranks in better order.[135]

The Greek phalanx was divided into three different parts—the right wing, the center, and the left wing. The right wing was considered the most important location and the most dangerous part of the phalanx, and the bravest and best troops were placed in that location along with the general who was in command. The left wing was considered the second most important part as they faced the enemy's right wing. Herodotus (6.111) tells us that it was the custom of Athens that the *polemarchon* always commanded the right wing.

While it is obvious that the bravest and best fighters were placed in the first two ranks which make contact with the enemy, the question arises as to how the rest of the ranks were organized. What about those soldiers who were less dependable? It may seem logical to place such soldiers in the rear ranks; however, Delbruck points out that putting "unreliable men, slaves, in the rearmost ranks" would be a mistake as they might break ranks and run at the slightest provocation and cause panic that could lead to defeat. Therefore, it would seem best to put a second group of reliable men, after the front ranks were filled, in the rearmost ranks and the least reliable in the middle ranks, where they would be pulled forward by the bravest and best and pushed forward and prevented from taking flight by the rearmost ranks.[136]

The hoplite's shield was his most important defensive weapon; however, the two-handled shield also created problems. Since he held it with his left arm and his left hand gripped near its rim, it provided excellent protection for his left side, but it also left his right side unprotected; however, this problem could be solved by lining up close to the hoplite on his right so that his neighbor's shield would provide protection for his unprotected right side. According to Thucydides, this led to a quirk in all hoplite armies. He says that all armies were similar in that when they went into action they got forced to move right as each hoplite did his best "to shelter his unarmed side with the shield of the man next to him on the right, thinking that the closer the shields are locked together the better will he be protected."[137]

The next question that needs to be addressed is the amount of space that existed between the files in the phalanx. Asklepiodotos identifies three different intervals between the files. He tells us that their marching order involved 4 cubits (6 feet) between the files, but in their attack order (*synnaspismos*), the interval was 2 cubits (3 feet), and when they were in their defensive order (*pyknosis*) it was reduced to 1 cubit (1.5 feet).[138]

The traditional view of the hoplite phalanx is that the hoplites marched in close order with intervals of three feet between the files. The phalanxes fought until one phalanx created gaps in the opposing phalanx that led to victory. The key to victory was to maintain cohesiveness and not allow penetration of the phalanx by the enemy hoplites. The traditional view of close-order fighting had been challenged as early as 1942,[139] but challenges increased starting in the 1980s. Those who challenge the traditional viewpoint suggest that the archaic phalanx evolved from Homeric times in which similar weapons and armor were utilized and in which some close-order fighting took place as well as individual encounters. They then claim, based upon iconography, that the archaic phalanx included not only hoplites but also archers and light infantry who fought within the phalanx, utilizing the hoplites for protection. They state that the archaic phalanx advanced in close order to avoid losing cohesiveness, but as they neared the enemy the phalanx switched to the loose order of six feet between files, which allowed space and fluidity so that individual hoplites could engage enemy hoplites in individual combat. They reject the view that the hoplite panoply prevented hoplites from freely moving across the battlefield and engaging individuals in combat. They believe that the two-handled hoplite shield actually helped the hoplite to fight as an individual, as he could handle more weight and also grip the shield tighter and at an angle so that blows glanced off of it. The lack of protection for his left side was overcome by taking a sideways-on stance so that the shield covered his full body, thus overcoming the argument that close-order fighting was necessary in order to gain protection from one's neighbor's shield. While the sideways-on stance offered full-body protection for the hoplite's front, he still needed protection from possible attacks from the side, as his Corinthian helmet greatly limited his sight and hearing. Krentz believes that staying within a spear's thrust, or six feet, would offer such protection. The above viewpoint sees the archaic phalanx as slowly evolving from Homeric origins which included light-armed fighters as well as hoplites, to the classical phalanx in which only hoplites fought in close-order formation. Those who hold it also believe that the phalanx did not reach that evolutionary level in which only hoplites were in the phalanx until after the Persian Wars.[140]

The case for the new view of hoplite phalanx fighting is perhaps best summed up by Hans van Wees in his 2004 book, *Greek Warfare: Myths and Realities*. Using fragments of Tyrtaios' poems and iconography he attempts to demonstrate that the hoplite phalanx evolved very slowly and that it was organized in loose order, with hoplites fighting individually in a way similar to Homeric times until after the Persian Wars. Adam Schwartz in his 2009 book titled *Reinstating the Hoplite: Arms and Armour and Phalanx Fighting in Archaic and Classical Greece*, challenges van Wees' conclusions. Concerning van Wees' use of the poems of Tyrtaios, Schwartz concludes that Tyrtaios does not support a more fluid and open form of fighting. He says that not only did he not find Tyrtaios supporting the open form of fighting but instead support for a compact phalanx. Tyrtaios calls on the Spartans "to stand completely fast and die sooner than yield a step." He claims that in open combat it would be pointless to urge hoplites to die before giving a step as in open hand-to-hand combat it would be wise to withdraw if one was being pressed, since no one was dependent on that individual other than himself. They could then recover and reenter the battle and still play a role in it.[141]

Paul Bardunias, writing in 2011, approaches the hoplite battle from the perspective of an expert in group behavior and attempts to reconcile some of the differences between the "heretical" and "orthodox" viewpoints. He claims that that van Wees' inclusion of archers, horsemen and others acting along with hoplites could have occurred within a close self-ordered phalanx. He says that the *aspis* "acted as a literal meters-stick. Men did not need to make any judgment on their frontage other than lining up shield rim to shield rim in human crowds." He sees it as possible that individuals could move to the front line to throw a missile and then retire from combat once the two groups of hoplites advanced upon each other. As the two groups advanced on each other, they would become denser as men piled up, and when they came shield to shield, the literal *othismos* could result.[142]

Bardunias goes on to claim that *othismos* has been misunderstood, because the physics of *othismos* has not been correctly stated. He explains that when the rear ranks push forward, the front ranks would not be able to "hold their shields away from their bodies and bodies and shields became pressed to torsos." Once the ranks became compressed, they reached "critical density," which is defined as "at least eight people pressed together with less than 1.5 m of spacing per person. By simply leaning against the man in front like a line of dominoes, 30–70 percent of body mass can be conveyed forward." The amount of force generated by a file of eight hoplites could produce enough force to "kill a man by asphyxia." He goes on to explain that since they were simply leaning forward they could maintain such force for a long time.[143]

This would seem to support the views of Frasier and the "heretical" view that *othismos* was not as traditionalists claim; however, Bardunias goes on to explain that the unique concave construction of the *aspis* allowed the hoplite to survive by "protecting his torso from compression." Crowds pushing forward can produce 1,000 pounds of force and have been known to "bend metal retaining structures." But the large diameter of the shield and concave shape "protected the diaphragm and allowed the hoplite to draw breath." In describing a hoplite battle, Bardunias says that the phalanxes charged at each other, but did not charge into each other at a run due to the natural fear of running into a massive number of enemy spears. He explains that spear fighting would take place for a time, but spears would be broken and close contact ensued if neither side gave way. Swords would be used and the rear ranks would press the two phalanxes together, and the hoplites would use their shields to cover their chest and protect their diaphragms. He claims that "images of hoplites show a variety of strikes that could be used with their upraised right arm over the shields." During the push, maximum pressure can be maintained only if there is resistance. If one side stepped back, "their foes would have to pack in tight again before maximum force can be transferred." When one side could no longer maintain their pushing, the rear ranks would break and flee, and the victorious phalanx would "target the backs of their routed foes."[144]

Regarding the "orthodox" and "heretical" viewpoints concerning *othismos*, Christopher Matthew states that "what neither side appears to have considered is the possibility that hoplite warfare was much more dynamic and variable than the predictable engagements that either of these two theories would suggest." He claims that it was physically impossible to get closer than 2 m to a hoplite phalanx in close order because of the extended spears. Rather, he says most battles were "conducted at spear length" because they could not break through the opponent's spears. While Matthew sees most hoplite battles fitting closer to the "heretical" theory, he does agree that some phalanxes did collide "shield against shield" with *othismos* resulting, but adds that it could only occur if two loose-order phalanxes charged each other. He also claims that in many cases if neither side was victorious in the "push phase," both sides would step back and weapons combat would reoccur.[145]

Much of the support for the new view of phalanx organization and fighting comes from iconography. The problem with iconography is that interpretations vary. Cartledge bemoans the scarcity of evidence available for archaic Greece and says that "visual artists, despite their interest in the warrior as a subject had no professional concern to represent the equipment or exertions with photographic fidelity, even when they possessed the requisite technical skill."[146] After a long discussion of archaic iconographic items, Schwartz concludes, "The differences between van Wees' interpretation and mine show that very different approaches are possible, and that an attempt towards interpretation is bedeviled by the ambiguity inherent in early iconography."[147] Even Krentz who supports van Wees' view of the archaic phalanx states that "representations in art are notoriously difficult to interpret"; however, he goes on to point out that very few vase paintings from the archaic period show phalanx formations in close order. He refers to the Beazley Archive Pottery Database in Oxford and points out that of 1,761 vases, only 17, or 1 percent, show "warriors in group," while there are hundreds showing hoplites in groups of 3 or more men standing still, advancing, or running but not showing tight formations.[148]

Schwartz counters that the technical difficulty of representing a phalanx in action is the reason there are so few representations of phalanx fighting in archaic iconography. He states, "This is something that is forbiddingly difficult to do with any degree of accuracy, and especially so given the lack of understanding of true depth and perspective." He goes on to say, "Not so, however, with single combat. Two single combatants can be portrayed in a number of ways that emphasize the toughness of the combat and which underlined the physical, individual aspect of it."[149] Based upon his examination of archaic iconography and literary sources, Schwartz concludes,

There is nothing substantial, then, in either iconography or datable archaic literature to support the notion that hoplites fighting from c. 750 wasn't in any respect more fluid or fought between more mobile warriors than those described in later sources.... As for the iconographical and literary evidence, there can be little doubt that there is in fact ample evidence of phalanx tactics. The presence of an additional spear for the hoplites and of light armed troops is not in itself incompatible with phalanx tactics, and therefore not sufficient evidence to dismantle the prevalent notion of a hoplite phalanx, supported by other, more mobile troop types. If there are elements that point to open battle order in iconography and literature and the Homeric battles, there are even more similarities to hoplite phalanx fighting.[150]

At this point we have eminent scholars who have all examined the same literary, archaeological, and iconographic sources but have reached very different conclusions. Perhaps by looking at the individual farmer-hoplite fighter we can get a better understanding of how the phalanx operated. Greek farmers were willing to serve as hoplites, provide their own panoply, and die if need be to protect their land and their family; however, they were not willing to pay property taxes to support a professional army, army garrisons, or an officer class. They were not willing to take time from their real work, which was agricultural work, to train for war. They were willing to fight and die in order to control the military and keep campaigns short so as not to interfere with their agricultural duties. Hansen calls them "polemen" whose muscle rather than technique was the key. The hoplite was a professional farmer but an amateur soldier. Would he have been interested or willing to take on individuals in battle when he had no special skills? He could assume his opponent was also an amateur, but what if he had more skill? What about the fear the hoplite feels as he is about to go into battle. Ancient battle accounts emphasize courage, bravery, and heroism and don't mention much about fear and cowardice.[151] But were ancient soldiers any different than soldiers today? Modern postwar studies, after World War II, found that "more than 90 percent of the respondents acknowledged pre-battle fear ranging from violent beating of the heart to the occasional losing control of the bowels or bladder."[152] The studies involved highly trained and disciplined soldiers, some of whom were career professionals. There can be little doubt that the amateur Greek hoplites felt this fear, as even the professional Spartans exhibited symptoms of fear and there were even five or six instances where Greek phalanxes broke and ran before contact was ever made.[153]

Hoplite warfare involved hand-to-hand combat between opposing forces. In his book *Battle Studies: Ancient and Modern Battle,* Col. Du Picq states that "man taxes his ingenuity to be able to kill without the risk of being killed. His bravery is born of his strength and it is not absolute. Before a stranger he flees without shame. The instinct of self-preservation is so powerful that he does not feel disgraced in obeying it."[154] Fear is contagious, but there is no doubt that individuals feel a duty to fight for their cause; however, if they see others flee, "the social pressure is lifted and the average soldier will respond as if he had been given a release from duty, for he knows that his personal failure is made inconspicuous by the general dissolution."[155] S. L. A. Marshall, the official historian of the European theater of operations during World War II, wrote, "Man is a gregarious animal. He wants company. In his hour of greatest danger his herd instinct drives him toward his fellows. It is a source of comfort to him to be close to another man."[156] The hoplite phalanx met this need by its close-order method of fighting and by organizing it around the tribal structure so that individuals were surrounded by neighbors, family members, and relatives, which gave the hoplite a sense of security but also made him less likely to break and run when those closest to him would see his cowardice.[157] It would be natural for "panic and fear" to spread from the front ranks to the rear ranks, as the front ranks were the first to come into contact with the enemy phalanx. The hoplite phalanx dealt with this problem by having the bravest and best hoplites in the front ranks, and they placed the second best and bravest group of hoplites in the rear ranks so that if panic did develop, the rear ranks would prevent the middle ranks from breaking and running. Hoplite battle is dirty, bloody and noisy. His helmet interferes with his sight and he can hear little. But in a close formation, he doesn't have to look for the enemy nor for his fellow hoplites. He can feel his neighbors, and as a mass they collide with the enemy. It's not him against one other hoplite; it's the whole mass versus the enemy mass, and that fact helped the hoplite deal with his fear. For this reason, perhaps, the traditional view of hoplites fighting in close order is the more accurate view.

Light Armed Troops

While light armed troops were mentioned above, let us look at the subject in more depth. Both Krentz and van Wees firmly believe that the archaic phalanx included various other fighters such as archers, slingers and javelin throwers up until the Persian Wars.[158] After examining archaic iconography, van Wees states,

> The number of archers in archaic art is minute compared to the number of hoplites—and much smaller than in geometric art—but it does not follow that the archaic phalanx included only a handful of them. Their rarity was not a reflection of their small numbers in archaic armies, but of their lower prestige. As close combat came to be ever more highly valued, and as light-armed became dependent on hoplites for protection, their status fell and artists began to represent them less often.[159]

He also quotes a fragment from Tyrtaios which states, "You light-armed, squatting under shield here and there, must throw great rocks and hurl smooth javelins while you stand close by the heavy-armed."[160] Hanson agrees with van Wees that the poor in Athens, who were unable to purchase the hoplite panoply, "never achieved military parity with their social betters," but he feels they were still able to make a military contribution by serving as light-armed soldiers.[161]

There is little doubt but that the light-armed troops were part of the archaic Greek military, but most historians do not see them being included in the hoplite phalanx as suggested by van Wees and Krentz. Delbruck claims that the bow was traditionally respected in Athens but goes on to say,

> But since the time the phalanx was formed of spear carriers, the bow was pushed into the background, since the two arms, even if not mutually exclusive, can be combined only with great difficulty. One can picture the archers, sling men and javelin throwers in front of, beside, and behind the phalanx. Whenever they were deployed forward of the front line, they must have disappeared before the clash of the two phalanxes, and therefore would necessarily have withdrawn around the flanks. If they attempted to push back through the phalanx itself, the resulting disorder and delay would cause much more damage than the advantage from the losses that they might have inflicted on the enemy.[162]

Pritchett describes one battle in which 5,000 skirmishers on each side fought while the hoplites watched; however, he adds that the "skirmish had no perceptible effect on the outcome of the battle."[163]

Agonal Warfare

Traditional historians have viewed warfare between hoplite phalanxes as using an *agonal* model. They describe it as similar to a contest or competition or a "bloody sport," rather than as an attempt to annihilate the enemy. Disputes between poleis were to be determined "by open pitched battle, devoid of trickery or maneuver and decided by the head-on-clash of rival phalanxes." There was a tacit understanding between Greek poleis that you did not ambush or otherwise try to surprise a hoplite force.[164] Greek warfare became much ritualized, with limited aims which were often to determine status and prestige for the victor rather than total conquest and destruction of the enemy. Hoplite battles have been described as "battle by mutual consent"; neither side interfered in its opponent's deployment, and they even kept their lines equal so that neither side would be outflanked.[165]

Over time Greek warfare became ritualized. Once it was decided to go to war, heralds or ambassadors were sent to announce the war to the opponent. One side offered battle and usually it was accepted, as to decline battle would be seen as cowardly and a loss of honor. Neither side would enter battle without sacrifices to the gods. Before they went into battle, sacrifices were made to determine the will of the gods. Negative signs could lead to one side withdrawing, without a loss of honor, as the gods were against the battle; however, usually they simply made more sacrifices until they got the result that they desired.[166] Just before the armies began their advance into battle, another sacrifice was made, only this time it was to appease the gods rather than to determine their will. Once the battle was over, the victors erected a trophy to the gods, and the defeated side sent heralds requesting a truce to collect their wounded and dead. These two actions showed that both sides accepted the outcome of the battle and recognized the victor. It would be considered an offense against the gods if the victor did not allow the defeated hoplites to recover their dead and wounded; however, the victor would strip the bodies of armor and weapons and any valuables before allowing the dead and wounded to be recovered. The victor usually dedicated 10 percent of the booty to the gods at a shrine such as Delphi or Olympia.[167]

A Hoplite Battle

Hoplite battles usually took place after the hoplites had enjoyed their midday meal, when they were relaxed, well fed and ready to fight. Certainly wine was a normal part of the hoplites' rations, so there is little doubt that they had wine before battle, and some feel they may have taken more than their customary amount in order to help control their fear and steady their nerves as they faced the enemy phalanx and perhaps their own death.[168] Following the ritual, a sacrifice was made to determine the will of the gods, after which the general addressed his soldiers to encourage them concerning the coming battle. Some say he "harangued" the troops, reminding them of their duty and challenging them to win for their honor, their family, and their state.[169] Many feel the general provided the most motivation by placing himself in the most dangerous position in the phalanx, the right wing. Following a second sacrifice which was made to propitiate the gods, the trumpets sounded and the phalanx began to advance. As they advanced they often sang the paean which helped them to maintain their order as they advanced. During the advance, hoplites carried their spears on their right shoulder, and on command the front two ranks lowered them and used the underhand grip. The hoplites began their advance at a walk and began to gain speed in order to have momentum as they neared the opposing phalanx. It was the general's duty to make the decisive decision as to when they should go to double time or run in order to have maximum momentum when the phalanxes collided. It was a crucial decision: if they started too early to go to double time, the hoplites would be exhausted when making contact, but if they started too late the opposing phalanx had the advantage of more momentum. Usually at about the point at which the phalanxes were 200 yards apart, the order to go to double time was given.[170]

As the hoplites advanced they did not remotely resemble the well-disciplined, well-ordered army that we envision when we think of the Roman army. They were amateur soldiers, and they quickly became disordered as they advanced; they "resembled more the rush of an armed mob than the march of disciplined troops in careful formation."[171] As they advanced, noise on the battlefield grew louder as shields, breastplates and spears rubbed together, and as soldiers were singing and shouting encouragement to each other until finally they let out the collective war cry of *elelu* or *alala* as they began the final charge.[172]

The key to success was to keep the hoplites moving forward despite the fear, noise, confusion, and dust of the battlefield. According to S. L.A. Marshall, an army is simply a collection of individuals working together; but it is also a crowd, and if it loses its momentum it can "revert to crowd form" and give in to the panic that often occurs in a crowd.[173] If the phalanx continued forward and broke into a double-time run when 200 yards separated the phalanxes, they would come into contact within 40 seconds to several minutes depending upon the speed of their approach.[174] As they advanced, they held their spears on the right shoulder, but they lowered them to an underhand thrusting position when the order to go to double time or to run was given. Some historians believe that they switched their grip to an overhand thrusting position in order to be able to strike over their opponent's shield; however, others claim that they kept them at the underhand position hoping to be able to thrust under their opponent's shield at his groin or at his legs above his greaves.[175]

When the phalanxes collided, there was a great noise as shields struck shields, and spears shattered from the impact and even shields cracked and split. If the hoplite's spear did not shatter, he switched to the overhand grip, as it was the only way that he could get sufficient force into his thrust from a standing position against his armored opponent. He tried to thrust over the shield of his enemy at his face, neck or shoulders. If his spear shattered but still had some length, he reversed it and used the butt-spike to jab at his opponent. If his spear was too shattered to use, he switched to his sword to use against his opponent. His goal was to strike a blow to disable his opponent and thus create a gap in the enemy phalanx.[176] Some scholars claim that the phalanxes did not collide at full speed when they charged. According to van Wees, the hoplite did not run the final 200 yards to gain momentum for his spear thrusts, but rather to "relieve his pent-up emotions, to minimize his exposure to missiles and with any luck to frighten the enemy." Instead of colliding, the hoplites must have slowed down at the very end and come to a stop before making contact. At that point they engaged in hand-to-hand combat.[177] Others claim that two phalanxes running at each other "could not smash together in a horrendous crash, as few in the first two ranks, officers and the best fighters, would have survived."[178]

Othismos

If one of the phalanxes did not crumble after the initial collision, whether they collided at speed or if they held back before the collision, they soon entered the *othismos,* or "push of shields," which is also called by some the "mass shove." During the *othismos* the goal was to push against the enemy phalanx in order to force them back, disrupt their organization, and break into their ranks, at which point the enemy phalanx generally broke and ran. Up to the *othismos* only the front two ranks in the phalanx came into contact with the enemy and they did all the fighting; however, during the *othismos* the rear ranks assumed a critical role in the battle.[179] It was recognized in archaic Greece that if two phalanxes of equal numbers met, it was the phalanx with the most ranks that was usually successful, as it was able create the greatest momentum through the use of the superior weight or mass of its ranks. This was accomplished by having the hoplites in the rear ranks press "with the center of a shield against the back of the man to his front, and he probably steadied his balance at times with his upright spear shaft as he leaned forward."[180] At some point during the *othismos*, one phalanx or elements of it would begin to be pushed back. Even if only parts of the phalanx were pushed back, the cohesion of the phalanx would be broken and the shift in momentum would be felt by the individual hoplites. Fear that had been kept under control by the cohesiveness of the phalanx and the closeness of his fellow hoplites would suddenly come to the fore, which led to panic as the hoplites saw their phalanx beginning to dissolve. The hoplite was ingrained with the belief that he must stand fast for the good of all, but once he sees that others are not standing fast, the average soldier will respond as if he had been given a release from duty and he will consider his personal survival as paramount and feel free to flee the battlefield.[181]

If the phalanx was broken, there were two possible actions which could be taken by the defeated hoplites. They could attempt to retreat and establish a rear guard to allow others to escape; however, this seldom occurred as the hoplites were amateur soldiers with little training, and such an action would require discipline and well-trained troops.[182] Another possibility was that small groups of hoplites could stick together and offer enough of a threat that pursuing hoplites would choose easier targets. This probably was most likely to happen if individuals controlled their panic; however, in most cases what occurred was that the panicked hoplites simply dropped their shields and weapons and ran for their lives as the tired, victorious hoplites, weighted down by their armor and weapons, would have trouble catching them and would not pursue them for a long period of time.[183] If cavalry was present, the fleeing hoplites were in much greater danger; however, cavalry was seldom used during archaic battles except in Thessaly.[184]

As early as 1942 the concept of the *othismos* as a push of shields or a mass shove was rejected by A.D. Fraser, and since then many scholars have joined in challenging the traditional view of the *othismos*. Fraser claimed that the idea that the rear ranks placed their shields on those in front of them and pushed them was not conceivable as the "front-liners are subjected to a degree of squeezing that is distressing to contemplate" and their weapons would be useless.[185] Rather he said the rear ranks were passive in the battle as the frontline troops sought out individual warriors to engage in combat; thus the rear ranks served as reserves and relieved the frontline troops when they were wounded, killed or exhausted.[186] While the view that the rear ranks served as a reserve has been rejected by later scholars, many still agree that the rear ranks did not physically push the front ranks forward with their shields. Rather the rear ranks are seen as being important as they prevented the front ranks from giving way and attempting to flee, which would be impossible because of the press of the rear ranks.[187] While the rear ranks were passive during the initial fighting, if gaps were developed in the front line from casualties, those in the rear ranks could step forward to fill the gap. The rear ranks did not provide the physical pressure envisioned by the traditional view, but rather asserted psychological pressure on the enemy phalanx. Van Wees states, "The deeper the enemy's formation, the larger the number of soldiers ready to take the place of casualties, and the slimmer one's chances of breaking through. The prospect of having to fight one's way through not just 8 but 16, 25, or 50 ranks was deeply demoralizing."[188] Another criticism of the traditional view is that the hoplites could not have continued the mass shove for more than a short time before exhaustion set in, and yet many battles often went on for a long time.[189]

They also believe that when the archaic poets wrote of "shields striking against shields" and that shoving occurred, they were referring to individuals using their shields as an offensive weapon and not as a mass shoving contest.[190] Finally, the nontraditionalists contend that ancient evidence cannot support the idea that *othismos* consisted of the rear ranks packing down behind those in front and literally pushing the enemy into defeat.[191] Others contend that even if *othismos* was used, it was used figuratively rather than literally. They use examples such as "Miltiades pushed away the Apsintheans by walling off the Chersonese peninsula," and news reports such as "the push toward Baghdad" to illustrate the figurative use of the word *push*.[192] Krentz claims that the word *othismos* is seldom used and that "unlike the noun *othismos*, the verb *otheo* (push) and its compounds occur frequently in classical historians." He also points out that *otheo* is used to describe actions in naval battles where there was obviously no "mass shove."[193] In contrast, Schwartz states, "the examples of *othismos* meaning bodily push are too many and too unambiguous to be safely ignored or explained away, as 29.7 percent of the 41 battles that he examined contained "*explicit references* to *othismos*." The 12 battles that contained "explicit references" include Plataea 479, Mykale 479, Pylos 425, Solygeia 425, Delion 424, Mantineia 418, Syracuse 415, Miletos 412, Koroneia 394, Corinth 392, Leuktra 371, and Kynoskephalai 364.[194]

The different schools of thought about phalanx fighting are usually called the "orthodox" and the "heretics."[195] The traditionalists list 17 references to *othismos* in classical historians, while the heretics say *othismos* is seldom used and what evidence exists "cannot support the view that the *othismos* consisted of the ranks packing down behind those in front and literally pushing the enemy into defeat."[196] With such differing viewpoints on phalanx warfare, it might seem that there is little hope of coming to some agreement or synthesis. Even Krentz has admitted that he has not convinced anyone of his viewpoint. And yet, perhaps the two viewpoints do not have to be mutually exclusive. Writing in *The Cambridge History of Greek and Roman Warfare,* Wheeler says, "If defining hoplite battle as a shoving match is too extreme, denying *othismos* likewise goes too far."[197] Even Cawkwell, who agrees with the "heretics" on many points, agrees that *othismos* occurs; although he claims it occurs "late in the battle when the other side shows signs of exhaustion."[198] Schwartz writing in 2009 dedicates 17 pages to examining the various views of *othismos* and concludes,

> *Othismos,* then, may well have been a more or less conscious group effort, but not necessarily directed by [a] commanding officer or indeed by any principle other than the instinctive urge to advance: in other words, *othismos* [w]as probably every bit as chaotic as the hand-to-hand melee, executed [in] bursts of varying lengths with varying degrees of success, and with different numbers of file members participating in the various sectors of the battlefield. Consequently, it is not a question of only either *othismos* or "normal" fighting: rather, hoplite battles comprise[d] both. One does not in any way exclude the other provided that they are regarded as perfectly compossible elements [in] the constant and chaotic flux of battle.[199]

Jim Lacey, writing in 2011, is somewhat harsh on the heretic school when he says, "Heretics are substituting their imaginations for an overwhelming body of literature and archaeological evidence that supports the traditional view"; however, he also says that "the purpose of the phalanx push—the *othismos*—was to break open the opposing phalanx, and one can suppose that such an act could easily lead to individual fighting as one or both phalanxes began to lose cohesion."[200] Wheeler believes that either defining hoplite warfare as a shoving match or denying it totally is too extreme but says the goal was to tear a gap in the opponent's line which could produce a general collapse as the phalanx was fragile.[201] Keeping the above in mind, a possible conclusion might be that while there is no doubt that the *othismos* took place, the *othismos* did not determine the outcome of all hoplite battles. Schwartz points out that of 41 battles, 29.27 percent contain explicit references to *othismos*;[202] however, the outcome of many hoplite battles was determined before the *othismos* became necessary.

Battle Casualties

After examining 17 battles between 472 BCE and 371 BCE Krentz found a pattern on casualties in hoplite battles. He found that the defeated phalanx suffered losses of 10 to 20 percent (14 percent average) with 3 to 10 percent (5 percent average) being killed in the victorious phalanx.[203] Gabriel and Metz analyzed 14 battles from 2250 BCE to 45 BCE and found that the defeated side lost about 37.7 percent killed in action while the victors averaged about 5.5 percent. In addition they claim that the defeated army also experienced 35.4 percent wounds serious enough to be abandoned on the field of battle.[204] While Krentz and Gabriel and Metz basically agree on the casualties victorious phalanxes experienced, they disagree on the casualties experienced by the defeated phalanx; however, there are problems in applying either set of figures on casualties to the archaic period. In Krentz's case his figures are based upon battles from 472 BCE to 371 BCE when the classical phalanx was dominant and the troops received much more training than in archaic times. Also by this time, the hoplites were using a much lighter version of the panoply. Can we extrapolate from his figures and have confidence that the figures apply to the battles between archaic phalanxes? Similar concerns also apply to Gabriel and Metz's figures. They only include one battle before Hellenistic times and are much more dependent on Alexander the Great's battles and Roman battles, when casualty rates were much higher. Whatever figures are used for casualties in the archaic period, it appears that there were probably more wounded than killed in hoplite battles.[205]

Gabriel and Metz believe that in hoplite battles, wounds were more common than deathblows, except when the defeated were being pursued: however, they also believe that large numbers of wounded ended up dying from their wounds. Using Frohlich's analysis of the *Iliad*, they point out that of the 147 wounds in Homer's *Iliad*, 114 ended in death, for a death rate of 77.7 percent.[206] Can we apply this figure with confidence to archaic hoplite battles? It would appear that the answer is no, since the fighting in the *Iliad* revolved around the siege of Troy, and many of the head wounds would have resulted from missiles and rocks being dropped on Greek soldiers from the walls of Troy; however, this would not happen in a hoplite battle. In addition, while the Homeric soldiers were heavily armored, they did not fight in a close-order formation which gave much greater protection to the individual hoplites in the archaic phalanx. Hanson suggests that because of the heavy panoply of the hoplites and lack of light-armed troops to pursue the defeated hoplites, casualties would be much lower in archaic battles than in the battles during the fifth and fourth centuries. In addition he claims archaic hoplite battles were at a slower pace than the battles after Marathon. He concludes, "In general, velocity, the centuries old twin of lethality, seems to have been absent from the Greek battlefields before Marathon. Lumbering rather than sprinting hoplites may explain why in the first two centuries of the polis there were fewer casualties that even in the relatively nonlethal battles of the fifth and fourth centuries."[207]

The wounded hoplites could be divided into two categories. The first category was those with minor wounds such as flesh wounds, contusions, or simple fractures.[208] These wounded hoplites were generally treated with success and were able to return home and fight another day. The second category was those with serious wounds. They were generally penetration wounds from the spear, slashing wounds from the sword, head injuries, brain injuries, collapsed lungs, and compound fractures.[209] It is estimated that 80 percent of the seriously wounded would die on the day of the battle and 30 to 35 percent of the survivors would die after they returned home. About 50 percent of those who survived the battle probably had permanent disabilities.[210] Many of the wounded died as a result of infections which were caused by cloth carried into the wound by the spear or sword or from dirt that got into the wound when the hoplite fell to the ground wounded. Estimates are that 6 percent would get tetanus infections, of which 80 percent would die; 5 percent would get gangrenous infections, of which 80 to 100 percent would die within a week; and 1.7 percent would get septicemia infections from arterial or venous wounds, of which 83 to 100 percent would die in 6 to 10 days. Ultimately about 25 percent would die of their wounds from infections.[211]

While hoplite warfare was bloody, killed many, and left many disabled, its goal "was to limit rather than glorify war, and thereby save rather than destroy lives." All the rituals associated with hoplite battles were "designed to reinforce the idea that further killing was not merely senseless but unnecessary as well."[212] The 5 percent casualties suffered by the victorious polis were certainly easily absorbed, but even for the defeated polis, "the outcome of hoplite pitched battle left the property and culture of the defeated intact, robbed only of some 15 percent of their male citizens, many of whom were already past the prime of their life."[213]

The help that the wounded could get from Greek physicians was limited. Medicine developed within each culture, and there was little that was gained from other cultures. During the archaic period, Greek medical practices were not as well developed as many of the earlier civilizations in the Middle East.[214] The early Greeks believed, as did many others, that illness was caused by "sin, broken taboo, and the anger of the gods" and attempted to deal with it by "placating the gods through rituals and sacrifice." Battle wounds, however, did require a more practical approach. There are many examples of doctors treating wounds in the *Iliad,* which includes "doctors utilizing songs, spells, and incantations." But there are also examples of empirical medical techniques such as cutting out arrowheads, washing out wounds, and applying roots and bandages."[215] Hansen points out that the Greeks effectively bound torn tissue to stop blood loss and used linen and cotton bandages over open wounds." They also "used wool or lint plugs, or even plasters of gum and wheat were used as sponges to soak up blood and cleanse the wound." He concludes, however, that "treatment of simple service wounds or uncomplicated fractures marked the limit of the expertise" wounded hoplites could expect.[216]

Aftermath of the Battle

Once the losing phalanx broke, the pursuit of the hoplite was relatively short-lived, and the victors quickly returned to deal with their dead and wounded.[217] The victorious general set up a trophy as proof of their victory. The trophy usually consisted of armor and weapons from the enemy attached to a tree or stakes, often at the point where the enemy phalanx first broke.[218] Usually victorious generals viewed the dead, a custom that went on for several millennia, "to examine closely the remains of those who had killed many of his men and were for the first and last time to be approached with impunity."[219] The victorious hoplites then stripped the enemy bodies of their armor, weapons and any valuables they might find such as finger rings.[220]

The booty was usually put together; however, the general had probably promised to dedicate some of the spoils to a particular god or shrine, often up to 10 percent of the total. The rest of the booty could be divided among the troops, given to "booty sellers" who auctioned it off to raise money for the state, given to the hoplites to replace damaged or destroyed weapons and equipment, or simply sold on the open market.[221] The spoils that were dedicated could go to temples in the polis and/or to Panhellenic sanctuaries. Usually the dedicated armor and weapons were taken from the best of the captured spoils, and it was often called "the top of the heap" or the "pick of the crop." The donated weapons and equipment brought glory to the Panhellenic shrines, but it also increased "the admiration and fear that other Greeks felt for the favored dedicators."[222] The armor and weapons that were dedicated to temples in the polis added to the pride and confidence of the people and the hoplites. It appears that "the dedication of the spoils could be the climax of triumphant thanksgiving celebrations" and would also help to "unite the state in triumph."[223]

Once the pursuit of the fleeing hoplites ended and the victor's trophy had been erected, the defeated polis admitted their defeat by formally sending heralds to the victorious polis asking for a truce to collect their dead. The truce was generally granted, as the respect shown to the dead was probably the result of "divine ordinance and sanction."[224] After the truce had been granted, the defeated hoplites carried out the gruesome task of identifying the bodies of friends, neighbors, brothers, and other kin, and it was a difficult task. In addition to the emotional pain they must have felt, there were other practical problems that they faced. The bodies were returned nude, stripped of any characteristic armor, weapons, or clothes that might have helped identify a body. The bodies may also have received disfiguring wounds to the neck and head. The campaign season was during the summer, when temperatures were routinely between 32°C and 37°C (90°F–100°F), which combined with the sun could hasten decomposition, and the resulting gases could turn the corpses into "grotesque caricatures of human beings." In addition wild animals and birds may have been at the bodies, and the bodies were probably covered in dirt and blood, which had to be washed off before they could be identified. Finally, the corpses may have received further abuse from being mutilated or trampled as they fell under the victorious phalanx when it drove through the defeated phalanx. In spite of all the difficulties, Vaughn sums it up by saying, "Perhaps the relatively small losses (in modern terms) in battles, the accuracy of muster lists, and the presence of family and close friends in the ranks usually allowed for a rough 'process of elimination,' which left only a few hoplite dead positively unidentified."[225]

The Greeks expected their generals to preside over the identification of the dead and their burial and to show proper reverence for the dead in order to show those that survived that they would receive similar care in the future if they should die in battle.[226] Even in naval battles the generals were expected to retrieve what they could of their dead. This was not a duty that a general should take lightly. After a naval battle in 406, the Athenian generals did not immediately retrieve their dead and a storm came up which caused them to fail in their duty. Despite the storm the generals were held accountable and six were executed.[227]

After the identification of the dead, the corpses were usually buried in a mass grave at the site of the battle. The names of those killed in battle were listed in a public place in the polis for all to see.[228] The Athenians cremated their dead and usually brought "the ashes, bone, and teeth home for burial; starting probably in the 460s they held the annual funeral ceremony described by Thucydides."[229]

Fate of Defeated Hoplites

There was no concept of prisoners of war having certain protections in ancient Greece. Rather it was clear to the Greeks that those who were defeated and captured were at the mercy of their captors, and they faced three possibilities—massacre, enslavement, or detention for ransom.[230] While the agonal model of warfare implies that the defeated hoplites would be treated less harshly than was typical in ancient times, it is difficult to know if this was true during the archaic period as no written sources of hoplite battles are available. It is clear, however, that if captured hoplites were ransomed, it was done to make a profit off the prisoners and not for humanitarian reasons.[231]

Pierre Ducrey analyzed 120 battles in ancient Greece and found that 24 ended with massacres, 28 ended with enslavement, and 68 ended with captivity, being exchanged or enrolled in the victor's army.[232] Pritchett believes that ransoming of individuals was usually an individual matter and that it occurred infrequently. He also says that there were some cases when captives were sent home to the victorious polis to work for the state as in the case of 20,000 prisoners taken at Eurymedon (467 BCE being used by Athens in the Laurium silver mines.[233]

The problem with the above data is that virtually all of it comes from the classical period and later, with much of it coming from the Peloponnesian War when we know that the agonal model of warfare broke down; however, it would seem that the choices of a massacre, enslavement, and ransom were also the options available in the archaic period. Did the agonal model mitigate the harsher options? It would seem doubtful, as it would seem natural that the hoplites that had seen their kinsmen and friends being killed in the heat of battle could easily give in to their lust for enemy blood and massacre the defeated enemy. Also enslavements were done for economic gain, and it is doubtful that the farmer-hoplite was not as interested in economic gain as the hoplites in classical Greece.

4

The Rise of Persia

In 612 BCE Nineveh, the capital city of the Assyrian Empire, was sacked marking the end of their empire. The Assyrians had controlled Mesopotamia (Iraq), much of modern-day Iran, Syria and Palestine for most of the past six centuries. The empire was defeated by a coalition of the Medes, a growing power northern Iran, and a renewed Babylonian Empire. The Median Empire controlled Iran, parts of Afghanistan, northeastern Iraq and part of Anatolia. The Neo-Babylonian Empire controlled southern Iraq and much of northwestern Iraq as well as Syria and Palestine. The defeat of the Assyrian Empire allowed Egypt to regain its independence, and the new kingdom of Lydia emerged in western Anatolia.[1]

The Persians were part of the Median Empire; however, they had their own ruling family—the Achaemenians. While they were a subordinate people, they were still considered important, evidenced by the fact that Astyages, the king of Media had his daughter marry Cambyses, the Achaemenian king of Ansha, the home of the Persians. It is assumed that the Persians were considered important because they had supplied first-rate infantry to complement the outstanding Median cavalry of the Median army. From this marriage, Cyrus, the founder of the Persian Empire, was born.[2]

We have little historical information about Cyrus's birth and childhood. Herodotus tells the story that King Astyages had a dream that was interpreted to mean that his "daughter's offspring would be king in his stead."[3] As a result when his daughter gave birth, Astyages ordered Harpagus, his most loyal steward, to kill the baby. After agreeing, Harpagus found that he could not kill the child and instead ordered a cowherd to take the child and expose him in the mountains so that he would die. The cowherd's wife, who had given birth to a stillborn son, convinced her husband to expose her dead child and for them to raise Cyrus as their own child. Three days later the cowherd showed Harpagus' men the body the stillborn baby as proof that he'd carried out his instructions.[4]

When he was 10 years old, Cyrus was chosen to play the role of a king in a game, and he had another boy flogged when the boy refused to obey him. The boy, who was flogged, was the son of a prominent noble who complained to Astyages, and he ordered his cowherd to appear before him with his son. After seeing the boy, Astyages felt that the boy looked familiar and forced the cowherd to tell the true story. King Astyages then confronted Harpagus, who defended himself by saying he had been deceived by the cowherd. Feeling betrayed by Harpagus, King Astyages asked him to send his son to meet Cyrus and then invited Harpagus to have dinner with him. The king then had the son of Harpagus killed and had his servants cook some of the son's flesh, which he served to Harpagus for dinner. When

Harpagus found out what the king had done, he said, "Everything the king did was pleasing." With that reply he took leftover meat, and he went home to bury his son.[5]

When King Astyages discovered that Cyrus was alive, he called upon his magi (priests) for advice as to how he should proceed. They told him, "If the boy has survived and becomes king by chance, take courage and be of good cheer! Because he will not rebel a second time." The king was relieved and sent Cyrus to be raised by his parents.[6]

What do we know about Cyrus' life after he learned who he really was? Herodotus simply says "Cyrus grew into manhood and was the most stalwart of his peers as well as the most popular."[7] Xenophon, however, in his *Cyropaedia,* gives us more information as to what his education may have included. In the Persian system of education he would have been sent to school to learn justice and righteousness. Emphasis was placed on developing gratitude, as the "ungrateful man is the most likely to forget his duty to the gods to his parents to his father land and his friends." They were also instructed in temperance and self-restraint and "taught to shoot the bow and fling the javelin." Participating in hunting was considered "the best possible training for the needs of war," as students learned how to endure heat and cold and to march and run at top speed.[8]

In 560 BCE Cyrus ascended to the throne of Ashann but still recognized King Astyages as his overlord. In 550 Cyrus rebelled against his overlord and grandfather King Astyages. What led to his rebellion is uncertain; however, Herodotus tells a story in which Astyages "began to treat the Medes harshly." So Harpagus worked with important nobles to end Astyages' reign in order to get revenge on Astyages for killing his son. He then made an alliance with Cyrus.[9] When King Astyages discovered that Cyrus had convinced the Persians to take action against him, Astyages sent a messenger ordering Cyrus to appear before him. Cyrus told the messenger to inform Astyages "that he would be in the king's presence sooner than the king would wish." Astyages called out his army and appointed Harpagus as general. When the battle took place, it turned into a rout for the Persians, as Harpagus and his followers joined with Cyrus and many other Medes fled the battlefield. As a result, Cyrus gained control of the Median Empire, but probably because of the role of Harpagus and his followers in defeating Astyages, Cyrus treated the Medes more as partners than as subjects.[10]

After the fall of the Assyrian Empire, the kingdoms of Lydia and Media fought for five years with neither kingdom able to establish dominance. In 585 BCE at the River of Halys, the two armies met, but no battle took place because of a solar eclipse. A truce was arranged with the Halys River becoming their common border, and the truce was reinforced with the marriage of the daughter of the Lydian king to the son of the Median king. In 560 BCE King Croesus of Lydia expanded westward into Ionia and added the Greek cities to his empire.[11] With his western and eastern borders settled, a period of peace followed, and Lydia became very wealthy; however, with the defeat of the Median Empire by Cyrus, the status quo changed.

King Croesus now became concerned about his eastern border. Perhaps he saw a chance to expand east as a result of the defeat of the Medes, or perhaps he feared the rising power of Persia and thought to take preemptory action before Persia became too strong. Herodotus tells us that Croesus wanted vengeance because Cyrus had overthrown his brother-in-law King Astyages. While we are unsure of the reason, it appears Croesus contemplated a war with Persia; however, before making a final decision Croesus consulted the oracle at Delphi after donating 1,000 pounds of gold bars and statuary and all of his wife's necklaces to the oracle.[12] When Croesus asked if he should make war on the Persians, the oracle responded that "if Croesus were to wage war against the Persians, he would destroy a great empire." In addition the oracle "advised him to find the most powerful Hellenes and make them friends and supporters." As a result, Croesus sent ambassadors to Sparta and instructed them to say, "Lacedaemonians, the gods' oracle told me to acquire the Hellene as friend and supporter. You, I have learned, are the leaders of Hellas, and so I invite you to comply with the oracle; and I am eager to become your friend and military ally without treachery or guile.... Because he had chosen them as friends in preference to all other Hellenes the Spartans welcomed the alliance with Croesus."[13]

Previously, Croesus had used diplomacy to gain promises of support for Lydia against Cyrus from Babylonia and Egypt; however, instead of waiting for his allies to join him, Croesus believed that immediate action was required. Based on the fact that he had an excellent army, which included heavy Greek infantry from the Ionian Greek cities as well as outstanding Median cavalry, and confidence in the oracle at Delphi's response, he moved against Persia with only his own forces.[14] Croesus took his army across the Halys River which was the border with Media and took the city of Pteria. Cyrus quickly responded to Croesus' invasion and marched toward Pteria, gathering more troops along the way until his army was larger than the army of Croesus. The armies met near Pteria, and the battle "was fierce, with many falling on both sides. It finally ended when night fell, with neither side gaining the victory."[15]

Believing that he had not won victory only because his army was outnumbered, King Croesus decided to withdraw to Sardis and call upon his allies and wait for the spring campaign season to continue the war. When he arrived at Sardis, he sent heralds to Babylonia, Egypt and Sparta and asked them to assemble at Sardis in four months. He then disbanded his infantry, allowing them to return to their homes, and told them to reassemble in the spring for the final campaign against Persia. Then, he believed that with his allies he would complete the defeat of Cyrus.

Even though winter was approaching, Cyrus, instead of returning to Persia as expected, decided to follow Croesus in an attempt to win the war before Croesus could be reinforced by his allies. When Cyrus' army arrived in Sardis unexpectedly, Croesus was in a weakened state as he had disbanded his infantry; however, instead of staying behind the walls of Sardis and waiting for help from his allies, he again offered battle, confident that his elite cavalry could carry the day.[16]

Cyrus recognized that his cavalry was no match for that of the Lydians, so, at the suggestion of Harpagus, he ordered the camels from his supply train to be placed in front of his infantry. The horses of the Lydian cavalry were so spooked by the smell and sight of the camels that the cavalry had to dismount and fight as infantry. As a result, Cyrus won an overwhelming victory, but Croesus and the survivors from the battle reached the safety of the walls of Sardis. Cyrus had no choice but to lay siege to the city.[17]

It appeared that the walls of Sardis were impregnable and that Croesus would be able to hold out until the spring when his allies arrived with reinforcements; however, one part of the wall of Sardis was weakly guarded because it was protected by a steep cliff at its base. On one occasion a Persian soldier observed a Lydian soldier who climbed down the cliff to retrieve a fallen helmet. The soldier observed how it had been done, and the Persians, following his lead, climbed the cliff and penetrated the wall at that weak point and the city was taken.[18]

The fate of King Croesus after the fall of Sardis is uncertain. Bacchylides (520 BCE–450 BCE), in a poem that predates Herodotus' account by at least 30 years, claims that Croesus had a wooden pyre built and when the Persians took Sardis he and his family mounted the pyre and he ordered his servants to light the pyre, but Zeus intervened with a "black-cloaking cloud and doused the yellow flame," and Apollo bore Croesus and his family away to a place "far north beyond the north wind to live with a mythical people devoted to Apollo."[19] Herodotus, however, says that King Croesus was captured by the Persians and Cyrus had Croesus placed upon a pyre and ordered it lit. After hearing Croesus call out the name of Solon, Cyrus ordered the fire extinguished, but the Persians were unable to do so. At that point Croesus cried out to Apollo and a "cloud suddenly converged out of the clear, calm sky and a storm burst out, and rain poured down in floods extinguishing the fire." Cyrus then freed Croesus and accepted his advice to not sack Sardis, as Croesus advised, "Sire, it is not my city, or my wealth any longer.... It is rather your property that you are plundering and looting."[20] Because of that advice, King Cyrus decided to keep Croesus as one of his advisers.

J.A.S. Evans writes that the *Nabonidus Chronicle* from Babylonia seems to contradict Bacchylides and Herodotus when it "states that Cyrus annihilated the King of Lu-, and if Lu- means Lydia, as seems most likely, this would be *prima facie* evidence for Croesus' death"; however, he goes on to point out that "the verb used for annihilate can mean "destroy as a military power" as well as "to kill." Evans then quotes Richard Frye, an Iranian scholar, who says, "One should perhaps trust the Greek historian, unless he is proved wrong."[21] Ctesias tells how Croesus was captured after taking sanctuary in a temple of Apollo. He was "bound in fetters three times, but each time he was freed by an invisible force." He was then taken to the palace and "tied up more securely. But, with thunder and lightning, he was again freed." At that point Cyrus released him and gave him the city of Barene near Ecbatana, along with 5,000 cavalry and 10,000 light-armed soldiers.[22]

What conclusions can be drawn from the above sources? Evans claims that "Bacchylides is more plausible than Herodotus and that Croesus immolated himself when Sardis fell."[23] If, however, Croesus had been captured, it seems logical that Cyrus would not have wanted to alienate the Lydians by executing their king as evidenced by his decision to let Astyages live and to also allow Nibonidus to live. Evans even points out that "it was Cyrus's policy to appear merciful; long before Julius Caesar, he had discovered the political uses of clemency."[24]

After the fall of Sardis, the Ionian Greek cities became worried about how Cyrus would interpret their rejection of his request for support in his war with Lydia. After his victory over King Croesus, they sent envoys to Cyrus asking to be allowed to be "subject to him on the same terms on which they had formerly been subject to Croesus."[25] Cyrus rejected their offer, so the Ionian cities sent messengers to Sparta requesting help. The Spartans refused to send military help but did sent envoys to Cyrus to "declare to Cyrus in the name of the Lacedaemonians that he must not inflict reckless damage on any city in Hellenic territory, since the Lacedaemonians would not tolerate it." Cyrus responded to the envoys, stating, "I have never yet feared any man who have a place in the center of the city set aside for being together, swearing false oaths, and cheating one another, and if I live long enough, Lacedaemonians will have troubles of their own about which to converse, rather than those of the Ionians."[26] The first diplomatic contact between the Greek mainland and the Persian Empire did not bode well for future relations between mainland Greece and Persia.

Cyrus turned control of Sardis over to a Persian governor and assigned a Lydian, Paktyes, to manage its wealth as he turned his army toward the territory in the east, not considering the Ionian issue important enough for his personal concern. After Cyrus had left with his army, Paktyes led a revolt and used the gold to buy a mercenary army. When Cyrus heard about the revolt of Paktyes, he threatened to enslave the entire city; however, Croesus convinced Cyrus not to punish the entire city because of the actions of Paktyes. Rather, he suggested that Cyrus should take away all the weapons and military equipment from the people in Sardis and encourage them to become merchants and shopkeepers so that there would be no revolutions in the future. Cyrus accepted Croesus' advice and ordered Mazares, a Mede, to take part of the army and put down the revolt and implement the changes suggested by Croesus. When Mazares and his army approached Sardis, Paktyes fled to Cyme, and his army disintegrated.[27]

Shortly after putting down the revolt in Sardis, Mazares suddenly died and was replaced by Harpagus, who had helped Cyrus defeat Astyages. Harpagus then took his army and marched on the Ionian cities to bring them under Persian control. Rather than uniting together and offering battle against Harpagus, the Ionian cities "shut themselves up within their walls," as they felt confident that they could resist a siege since they could be supplied by sea, as Harpagus did not have a navy at his disposal. But the Ionians had underestimated Harpagus. Instead of trying to starve the cities into submission, Harpagus had his army build great earth mounds against the walls of the cities which allowed the Persians to breach them. In several cities, the population chose to abandon their cities and escape using their navies, hoping to found colonies elsewhere. The remaining Ionians "fought courageously for their country. But they suffered defeat and conquest and then stayed in their cities, submitting to Persian rule." With the defeat of the Ionian cities, many of the Ionian islands also submitted to the Persians.[28] Concerning the resistance of the Ionian cities, Lacey comments, "Given his Greek audience, Herodotus could not say plainly that the Ionians cravenly surrendered on the approach of the Persian army." But he goes on to say that all the cities fell in one campaigning season, so it appears that there were few if any prolonged sieges.[29]

From their actions against the Ionian Greeks, Lacey believes that the Persians drew several conclusions about fighting Greeks. After their defeat of the Ionians, the Persians believed that even in a crisis the Ionian Greek cities were not able to overcome their "petty rivalries" and differences of opinions in order to present a united front against the Persians. They saw that a combination using military force along with diplomacy and bribery was successful in ending the Ionian Revolt. Incorrectly they concluded that the same approach would work if they had to fight the mainland Greeks.[30]

Between the fall of Sardis in 546 and Cyrus' attack on Babylon in 539, Herodotus is silent about Cyrus' actions. We know that Cyrus moved east with his army and that he sent part of his army back to Sardis under Mazares and Harpagus to deal with the revolt of Paktyes as well as to bring the Ionian Greek cities under Persian control. Historians speculate that perhaps there was unrest and possibly revolts in the east that required Cyrus' attention, or perhaps he felt that it was more important to add new territory to his empire in the East. It is known that the territories of Parthia, Drangiana, Aria, Chorasmia, Bactria, Sogchana, Gandhara, parts of Scythia, Sattagydia, Arachosia and Maka, which had not been under the control of the Median Empire, were part of the Persian Empire when Darius became king. Cambyses put his effort into conquering Egypt, so we can assume that Cyrus brought the above areas into the Persian Empire between 546 BCE and 539 BCE.[31]

After Cyrus had completed his conquests in the East, he turned his attention to the Neo-Babylonian Empire. Babylon was the wealthiest city in Mesopotamia and also perhaps the best-protected city in the ancient world. Herodotus says that the city was protected by a "deep, wide moat full of water" and a wall "76 feet in width, 304 feet in height." In addition, within the outer wall "there is another wall ... which is not much weaker but is narrower than the outer one. In the center of one of the city's two districts, they have built the Royal Palace, fortified and surrounded by a huge impregnable wall."[32] While Herodotus has probably exaggerated the height and width of the wall, it is obvious that Babylon would be difficult to take.

In 539 the Neo-Babylonian Empire was ruled by Nobonidus, an elderly general who had overthrown the sons of King Nebuchadnezzar. Nobonidus alienated the priests of Babylon by his religious policies. He had spent a great deal of time and money restoring a temple to Sin, the moon god, because his mother had been a priestess at the temple. In addition he placed Sin, a relatively minor god, above Marduk, who had previously been the supreme god in Babylon. In addition, Nobonidus spent much time away from Babylon, restoring the temple and later campaigning in Arabia, with the result that he was not present for Marduk's New Year festival. This not only offended the priests but also the people of Babylon as they "felt that the King's participation was the surest guarantee of good harvests and continued prosperity." Finally, the merchant class was tired of the high taxes imposed to pay for his campaign into Arabia.[33]

It seems that Cyrus might have begun operations against the Neo-Babylonian Empire as early as 541 BCE Lacey believes that Cyrus ordered probing attacks along the Babylonian border looking for weaknesses and also testing the Babylonian army. With Nibonidus campaigning in Arabia, there was little interest in the frontier on the part of the government in Babylon, and this caused the inhabitants to question Babylonian support. In addition, Cyrus sent agents to contact the various peoples like the Jews after they had been conquered and settled in Babylonia. His actions must have experienced some success as Cyrus is mentioned in the Old Testament 23 times, often in glowing terms.[34]

In 539 BCE Cyrus launched his attack on the Neo-Babylonian Empire. The frontier areas, feeling a lack of support from Babylon, appeared unwilling to put up strong resistance. In fact, a provincial governor, Gobyras, went over to Cyrus' side along with all his forces. As a result Cyrus won a major victory over Nabonidus and his army near the city of Opis. At that point, Cyrus split his army, giving Gobyras command of one portion of the army with orders to move on Babylon, while Cyrus with his portion of the army pursued Nabonidus and the defeated Babylonian army. Nabonidus retreated to the walled city of Sippar, but the city closed its gates and refused him entry. He then retreated toward Babylon. When Cyrus arrived with his army at Sippar, the city opened its gate and greeted him as a liberating hero.[35]

While Cyrus and his army were pursuing Nabonidus' forces, Gobyras and his army reached Babylon and entered the city without a fight. When Nabonidus finally arrived at Babylon, he found that the city was in enemy hands, and he was taken captive by Gobyras.[36] Herodotus, however, tells a different story. He claims that Nabonidus reached Babylon safely and that Babylon was well prepared for an attack from Cyrus. The city had plenty of water available from the Euphrates River, which ran through the city, and had gathered enough food to withstand a siege of many years. When Cyrus was unable to breach the walls, he "diverted the river through a channel ... and made the river fordable. When the river level fell where it entered the city, Cyrus' troops were able to enter the city and surprise the Babylonians. The city quickly fell and Cyrus had added the territory of the Neo-Babylonian Empire to the Persian Empire.[37]

We have another version of the fall of Babylon from Berossus, a Babylonian scholar who, using Babylonian sources in the third century, wrote a history of Babylon called *Babyloniaca*. While we do not have his total text, we have some fragments. He wrote, "Nabonneidus learnt of Cyrus's coming attack and ordered his army to assemble and meet him, but he lost the battle and had to flee with a few followers to Borsipp." After taking Babylon, Cyrus had the walls of the outer city razed, because they presented too strong a defense for the city.[38] Another version comes from the Cyrus Cylinder. It was discovered in Babylon in the area of Marduk, the chief Babylonian god, and tells us that Nobonidus:

> 8. repeatedly did that which was bad for the city. Daily he destroyed all with an unending yoke.
> 9. In response to their lament the Enil of the gods drew very angry....
> 11. He [Marduk] searched through all the countries, he examined....
> 12. he sought a just ruler to suit his heart, he took him by the hand: Cyrus, king of Anshan....
> 15. He ordered him to go to Babylon....
> 17. Without battle and fighting he let him enter his city of Babylon. He saved Babylon from its oppression. Nabonidus, the king who did not honor him, he handed over to him.[39]

While Herodotus' story is engaging, the consensus seems to be that the religious policies of Nabonidus and his extended absences campaigning in Arabia cost him the support of the important priests as well as the people, so Cyrus was able to take the city without a battle. As with Croesus we are uncertain as to the fate of Nabonidus. Berossus claims that "Cyrus received him graciously, exiled him from Babylonia, but gave him Carmania instead. Nabonidus spent the rest of his life in that country and died there."[40] Herodotus is silent on the fate of Nabonidus, but some chroniclers claimed that the Babylonian monarch was sent into exile while others recorded that Cyrus had him executed."[41]

With the defeat of the Neo-Babylonian Empire, Cyrus controlled three of the four empires that came into existence with the fall of the Assyrian Empire as well as the additional eastern territory conquered by Cyrus between 546 at 539, which extended all the way to India. From Cyrus' victory over the Babylonians in 539 to 530, Herodotus is once again silent on Cyrus' actions. In 530 he tells that Cyrus proposed marriage to Tomyris, queen of the Massagetai. Realizing that Cyrus wanted her kingdom rather than herself, Queen Tomyris rejected his proposal. In response, he raised his army and marched on her kingdom, which was located east of the Caspian Sea near the Aral Sea. She offered him and his army free entry into her kingdom to do battle or offered to enter Persia to do battle. Following Croesus' advice not to let any foreign army into Persia, Cyrus entered the territory of the Massagetai and defeated part of her army by using deceit, which resulted in Cyrus capturing the son of Tomyris.

Queen Tomyris offered to allow Cyrus and his army to leave her territory if he released her son. When Cyrus refused to release her son, she vowed vengeance. Tomyris attacked with the rest of her army, and a great battle ensued. Herodotus describes the battle as "the most violent of all battles ever fought by barbarians.... For a long time they fought fiercely and neither side was willing to flee. But at last the Massagetai prevailed. A large part of the Persian army perished in this battle, and in particular, Cyrus himself met his end."[42]

Ctesias agrees that Cyrus was killed in battle, but he claims that it occurred while Cyrus was campaigning against the Derbica, who may have lived near the Oxus River. According to Ctesias, the Persians were ambushed by the Deberca who used elephants, which put the Persian "cavalry to flight; Cyrus himself fell from his horse, and an Indian man ... drove a javelin below the hip joint into the upper part of his thigh, and this caused his death."[43] Xenophon on the other hand claims that Cyrus died at home surrounded by his family. He says, "Cyrus was an old man, he returned to Persia for the seventh time in his reign ... he called for his children ... he summoned his friends and Persian governors. When they were all present, he began to speak.... At the end of this speech, he gave his right hand to everybody, covered himself, and so died."[44]

Upon his death, Cyrus was succeeded by his son Cambyses.[45] It is unclear why Cyrus had not moved against the kingdom of Egypt during his reign; however, Cambyses made the decision to invade Egypt. According to Herodotus, Cambyses "became extremely enraged with Egypt." He was "enraged" because Amasis, the Pharaoh, deceived him by sending a woman impersonating his daughter when Cambyses proposed marrying Amasis' daughter. When he discovered the subterfuge, Cambyses decided to invade Egypt.[46] Ctesias agrees with Herodotus concerning the subterfuge of Amasis but claims that Cambyses loved the impersonator and went to war not because he was deceived, but rather because Amasis had killed the impersonator's father.[47]

While the story about Cambyses' proposal to Amasis to marry his daughter may be true, it seems unlikely that Cambyses would truly go to war over just that incident. Rather, it seems more likely that Cambyses wanted to show that he too could add to the Persian Empire, and with his eastern border pretty well set, Egypt would be the logical next target, as it was the only great kingdom left unconquered from the old Assyrian Empire.[48]

As with the invasion of Lydia and Babylonia, the Persians received help from within the enemy army. Phanes, an important mercenary from Halicarnassus, had a dispute with Amasis and fled to Persia to sell his services and information to Cambyses. Amasis sent his most reliable eunuch in pursuit, and he intercepted Phanes; however, Phanes escaped by getting his guards drunk, and he finally reached Cambyses as he was completing his plans for the invasion of Egypt. Phanes shared "precise information concerning Egypt" and also advised Cambyses "to send a petition to the king of the Arabians asking him to provide a safe passage for his army through his country."[49]

Previously Amasis had felt secure in Egypt as it was protected by the Sinai desert, and the fact that Persia lacked a navy to attack from the sea; however, with Cyrus' conquest of Babylonia, Phoenicia had voluntarily surrendered to Persia, thus giving Persia access to its navy.[50] Recognizing the threat that the Persian navy represented, Amasis attempted to create alliances with islands in the eastern Mediterranean in order to strengthen his navy. While he thought he had achieved his goal, his "allies" instead sent their fleets to assist Persia.[51]

As the Persian army neared the desert, the Arabian king "ordered camel skins to be filled with water and loaded onto his camels which he had sent to the desert region where they waited for the army of Cambyses."[52] Amasis died before Cambyses and his army reached Egypt, but his son, Psammenitos, who succeeded him, led out his army to await the Persian army at the Pelusian mouth of the Nile River. Before the armies engaged, the Greek and Carian mercenaries in the Egyptian army brought the sons of Phanes out in front of the armies and killed them and drank their blood to punish Phanes for his betrayal of them. At that point the armies engaged in battle in which the fighting became so fierce that a large number of men fell on both sides, but finally the Egyptians were routed. Psammenitos and the remnants of his army fled to the city of Memphis to take shelter behind its walls. Cambyses sent a ship along with Persian heralds to "invite Egyptians to enter into an agreement." The Egyptians attacked the ship and killed all the crew members and the heralds. The Persians laid siege to the city until the Egyptians finally surrendered. After seeing the defeat and surrender of Egypt, Libya, its neighbor, surrendered without a battle, as well is the cities of Cyrene and Barke.[53]

Nine days after the fall of Memphis, Cambyses brought the son of Psammenitos and 2,000 other sons of Egyptian nobles and had them executed as punishment for the attack on the Persian ship carrying the heralds. Based upon the response of Psammenitos to the executions, Cambyses allowed him to live. Herodotus refers to the Persian custom to honor those captured and to often return them as administrators of the conquered areas; however, Psammenitos got involved in a plot and was later executed.[54]

Cambyses then began to consolidate his rule over Egypt by mounting expeditions against the Ammonians and the Siva Oasis on the southwest border Egypt and Nubia in the south. Herodotus tells us that the army sent to the Siva Oasis was lost in a sandstorm and never reached the Ammonians nor returned to Egypt. He also tells us that Cambyses set off "against the Ethiopians without ordering any provisions for food, or giving any rational consideration to the fact that he was about to lead his army to the edges of the earth." He goes on to say that in spite of food shortages Cambyses refused to turn back until some of his troops turned to cannibalism. At that point he returned to Egypt, but he had lost most of his army.

Herodotus blames Cambyses' actions and setbacks on him being somewhat insane. Herodotus then proceeds to give various instances to prove Cambyses' descent into insanity. Herodotus says that Cambyses ordered the governors of Memphis killed when he thought they lied about why the Egyptians were celebrating the epiphany of the god Apis, as he thought they were celebrating his defeat. He then ordered the sacred calf, Apis, brought before him, and he stabbed Apis with a knife which led to the death of the calf, which was considered sacred by the Egyptians. Cambyses also sent Prexaspes to Persia to kill his brother, Smerdis, because Cambyses had a dream of Smerdis sitting on the royal throne. Herodotus also tells us that Cambyses married two of his sisters and killed one of his sister-wives because of a remark she made that angered him. Adding to his bizarre behavior, Herodotus tells us that Cambyses "went into the sanctuary of the Kabeiroi, where no one other than the priest is allowed to enter according to the laws of God and men. Here he subjected all the statues to a long session of mockery and then burned them." Herodotus concludes, "I am convinced by all the evidence that Cambyses was seriously deranged."[55]

While Herodotus claims to have reached his conclusion about Cambyses based upon evidence, most modern historians take exception to his view of Cambyses. Amelie Kuhrt states that "trying to present a balanced assessment of the reign of Cambyses is a difficult task, because of the nature of the evidence at our disposal. It is dominated by Herodotus' extremely biased account of the Persian conquest of Egypt, which has created an influential image of Cambyses as an ever more crazed despot."[56] Yet Kuhrt also believes that Herodotus' "stories includes many perfectly credible elements," and points out that he "is the only surviving writer to provide what seems to be a fairly reliable account of the progress of the Persian conquest of Egypt"; however, she also points out that later writers and archaeological evidence point to the success of the campaigns that Cambyses mounted to secure the borders of Egypt, and yet Herodotus calls them failures.[57] Kuhrt points out that archaeological work in 1988, 1991 and 2005 shows that the Persians were successful in both of the campaigns to the southwest border and over the southern border of Egypt.[58] Strabo states that "when Cambyses conquered Egypt, he advanced with the Egyptians as far as Meroe," which was located far beyond the Egyptian border in Nubia.[59] Diodorus Siculus adds that certain trees called Persae were introduced into Egypt from Ethiopia "when Cambyses conquered those nations."[60]

Lacey takes issue with Herodotus when he says that Cambyses moved against Nubia with inadequate preparation. He states, "Given the meticulous preparations Cambyses had made for the invasion of Egypt, it seems odd that he would conduct a second major invasion without any preparation."[61] He believes that perhaps Cambyses sent out a reconnaissance force toward the Siwa Oasis which may have been lost. He also advances the thought that Cambyses was successful in taking much of Nubia, but heavy fighting and perhaps logistical problems caused him to settle for his gains and return to Egypt. Finally he thinks Cambyses may have received news of unrest or popular revolts back in Persia.[62]

While there are no Egyptian records of a narrative nature concerning the invasion of Cambyses, there are some documents that challenge Herodotus' story about Cambyses' sacrilege against the Apis bull. In his autobiography, Udjahorresne, a naval commander, scholar and priest at the time of Cambyses' invasion, tells how Cambyses expelled foreigners living in the Temple of Neith, the chief deity of the city, and "commanded them to purify the Temple of Neith and to restore it to all its people." He goes on to say that Cambyses "betook himself to the Temple of Neith. He touched the ground before her great majesty as every king had done."[63] An Egyptian hieroglyphics stella from 524 BCE describes how the Apis bull was embalmed and placed "in the necropolis, which had been prepared by Cambyses. Offerings of clothing, gold ornaments and semi-precious stones were made" in accordance with the words of his Majesty...."[64] An inscription on a granite sarcophagus translated in 2000 CE states, "Cambyses—may he live forever! He has made a fine monument for his father Apis—Osiris with a great granite sarcophagus, dedicated by the king of upper and lower Egypt ... Cambyses—may he live forever."[65] While the Egyptian sources are limited, those available certainly do not support Herodotus' story about Cambyses' sacrilege against the Apis bull and Osiris, and they also raise questions concerning the reliability of other comments made by Herodotus concerning Cambyses' actions in Egypt.

While Cambyses was in Egypt, one of the magi (priests) he had left in charge of his household learned that Smerdis, the brother of Cambyses, had been killed but that it was being kept secret and that most people thought he was still alive. This magus had a brother that resembled Smerdis and his name was also Smerdis. He took his brother, Smerdis, passed him off as the real Smerdis, and declared that Cambyses was no longer king but that Smerdis was the true king. When Cambyses was informed of the revolt and was assured by Prexaspes that he had indeed killed his brother Smerdis, he wanted to quickly lead his army back to Persia and against the false ruler. As Cambyses mounted his horse he accidentally stabbed himself in his thigh when his sword's scabbard fell off. As his wound became infected, Cambyses called the most notable Persians to him and confessed that he had had his brother Smerdis killed and demanded that they not allow the Medians to regain control of the empire. After his wound became gangrenous, Cambyses died after ruling for seven years and five months.[66]

According to Herodotus, the magus, who was impersonating Smerdis, the brother of Cambyses and son of Cyrus, ruled for seven months, during which "he performed many generous deeds to benefit his subjects," but he then goes on to tell how Smerdis' true identity was discovered. He claims that Otanes, an eminent Persian noble, began to suspect that the "Magus was not Smerdis, son of Cyrus, and who he really was." He asked his daughter, who was one of Smerdis' wives, to find out if Smerdis had ears, as Smerdis the magus had had his ears cut off by Cyrus because of some "grave offense." When his daughter discovered Smerdis had no ears, she informed her father, who now knew that Smerdis was an impersonator.[67] Once Otanes' suspicions were confirmed, he informed Aspathines and Gobyras, two leading Persian nobles, who believed him, as they had also developed suspicions about Smerdis. They each agreed to bring "the man he trusted most into their group." The three individuals that they brought in were Intaphrenes, Megabysos and Hydarnes which brought the group up to six. When Darius, son of Hytaspes, arrived in Susa, the group decided to include him as the seventh member.[68]

When the group of seven nobles discussed their next action, Darius called for an immediate attack on Smerdis. Otanes suggested waiting for more support, but Darius' speech won over the other nobles. Meanwhile the two magi attempted to win over Prexaspes and planned to have him publicly recognize Smerdis as the true son of Cyrus. When Prexaspes publicly appeared before the Persians called together by Smerdis, instead of supporting Smerdis' claim, he announced that he had "been forced by Cambyses to kill the true Smerdis, son of Cyrus, and revealed that the magi were now reigning." He then called upon the Persians to overthrow the magi, and at that point Prexaspes "hurled himself headfirst down from the tower. Thus Prexaspes ended his life as he had lived it: an admirable man."[69]

After hearing of the actions of Prexaspes, the seven nobles again discussed their plan, and once more Darius' arguments won out over the arguments of Otanes, who called for delay. Once the decision had been made, the seven conspirators went to the palace, and the guards admitted them because of their high rank. In the courtyard, however, they met resistance from the eunuchs, but they pushed through them and entered the palace. In the palace they came upon the two magi and their supporters; and in the ensuing fight two of the seven were wounded, but Darius and Gobyras cornered Smerdis in a bedroom and killed him. After killing the two magi, the victors cut off their heads and carried them out to the courtyard and explained what the magi had done. The people joined with Darius and the other nobles and hunted down the supporters of the magi, whom they killed.[70]

Five days after their victory, the seven nobles met together to discuss the future of the Persian government. They discussed three different methods of ruling—"rule by majority," "rule by an oligarchy" and "rule by monarchy." Darius' arguments for rule by monarchy won over all the other nobles except for Otanes, who withdrew his name from being considered for the position of king, and the other six nobles decided that the king would be chosen by chance from among them. It was decided that at sunrise the next day the six nobles would ride outside the city and the rider whose horse "made the first sound would have the kingship." Darius had a "clever groom" who took steps to make sure that Darius' stallion made the first sound. Darius' horse made the first sound, and thus Darius became king of the Persian Empire.[71]

As pointed out earlier, we have few Persian sources concerning the Achaemenid period, so we usually have little with which to evaluate the accuracy of Herodotus' stories; however, regarding the rise of Darius, we have the Behistun inscription with which to check Herodotus' account. The Behistun inscription is "generally thought to be the earliest old Persian inscription," and it is "the longest and the only one to discuss specific political events: it provides crucial and almost contemporary information on Cambyses, the revolt of Bardiya and Darius' accession."[72] The Behistun inscription seems to validate much of Herodotus' account as the inscription describes how Darius overthrew the magus who claimed to be the son of Cyrus. In addition, five of the six conspirators who joined with Darius to overthrow the false Smerdis in Herodotus' account are also named in the Behistun inscription; however, the Behistun inscription also raises problems.[73] For example Herodotus claims that the conspirators killed Smerdis in the palace at Susa, while in the Behistun inscription, Darius states that at "a fortress by the name of Sikayahuvati, a district by the name Nisaya, in Media, that is where I killed him."[74] In addition, we must be aware that the Behistun inscription was not an attempt at historical writing, but rather it was the result of an attempt by Darius to "legitimate his newly won power. Darius, quite naturally dedicated the Behistun inscription to the exultation of his own accomplishments."[75]

Another issue that arises from both Herodotus and the Behistun inscription is whether Smerdis was in fact an imposter or the real son of Cyrus. In referring to the story of Smerdis as being an imposter, Cook states, "The story smells and few scholars now seem prepared to believe that it really was a pretender that the seven killed."[76] Briant also asks, "Was Gaumata really the usurper called 'Magus' by Darius, or was he just an invention of Darius, because he was anxious to conceal that it was really he who had overthrown Bardiya, the true son of Cyrus?"[77] Both of the above historians raise the question of how the assassination of Bardiya could have been kept secret for four or five years. Even Herodotus points out that the nobles who were with Cambyses when he died "were profoundly skeptical that the Magi were in control of the government; they assumed that Cambyses said what he did about the death of Smerdis to discredit his brother and turn all Persia against him."[78] Briant goes on to develop a hypothesis in which he explains why and how Darius carried off the "deception" about Smerdis and answers the accusations against Smerdis raised in the Behistun inscription.[79] But Briant also states, "It must be remembered that nothing has been established with certainty at the present time, given the available evidence."[80]

Lacey weighs in on the discussion by agreeing that the argument that the real Smerdis had not been killed has much going for it, as it tells us why many people believed that Smerdis was not a pretender and how the murder of Cambyses' brother could have been kept secret from the Persian nobility and people. But he also points out that the above versions have problems. He points out that there is no actual evidence to support the case. Also he thinks that if it had been the real Smerdis that had been deposed, the enemies of Darius would have spread the story and Herodotus would have heard it. He goes on to say that it would have been the perfect story to show the deceitfulness of Darius which his audience would have loved. Lacey then concludes, "Therefore, with no evidence to the contrary available, it would be unwise not to accept the essence of what the existing sources present us."[81]

With the death of Smerdis, whether by Darius or earlier on the orders of Cambyses, there was no legitimate male heir to the Persian throne. When Darius emerges from the seven conspirators to be recognized as king, he implies that he is the rightful king because of his ancestry. The Behistun inscription states,

> I am Darius, the great King, King of Kings, King of Persia, King of peoples/countries, son of Vishtaspa, grandson of Arshama, an Achaemenid. Darius the king proclaims: My father is Vishtaspa; Vishtaspa's father is Arshama; Arshama's father is Ariaramna; Ariaramna's father is Cispish; Cispish's father is Hakhaimanish. Darius the king proclaims: For this reason we are called Achaemenids. From long ago we are royal. Darius the king proclaims: eight of our family were kings before; I am the ninth; nine kings are we in succession. Darius the king proclaims: By the favor of Auramazda Darius the king proclaims: The kingdom which had been taken away from our family, I re-established, I put it back in its place.[82]

Briant points out that there are no ancient sources which demonstrate that Darius had a genealogical claim to the throne. But he also states, "making Darius into a usurper, as has been customary, does not make much sense either," as none of the other six conspirators could claim better dynastic credentials. Briant concludes by saying that Darius did not become king because of his ancestry; rather, "as a result the power that he arrogated to himself, he established the dynastic rights of his ancestors."[83]

Other than describing the marriage of Darius to "imminent Persian women," Herodotus is silent as to the immediate events that took place after Darius became king.[84] However, from the Behistun inscription we find that Darius faced widespread revolts and uprisings as he became king. The Behistun inscription states, "Darius the king proclaims: this (is) what has been done by me in Babylon. Darius the king proclaims: this (is) what I have done by the favor of Auramazda, in one and the same year, after I became king. I have fought 19 battles. By the favour of Auramazda, I defeated them and took nine kings prisoner."[85] After putting down the initial revolts in 522 BCE Darius moved northeast to secure his northern border against the Scythians, who been increasing their raids while he had been preoccupied with putting down revolts. Using a unique maneuver of launching "an amphibious assault" on the rear of the Scythian army, Darius won a great victory. As a result, he added the Saka to his empire which gave him access to the cavalry of the Saka, which was among the finest in the world. With his northeast border more secure, he turned to deal with Oroites, the satrap of Lydia and Ionia, who had refused to send troops during Darius' campaigns. Rather than sending troops, Darius simply sent a letter to the Satrap's "1,000 elite Persian troops" who served as his bodyguard. Darius instructed them to kill the satrap, and the Persian troops, who were loyal to the king, carried out the order with no hesitation. Meanwhile, Darius continued to campaign in the East and added territory in the Indus Valley to his empire.[86]

With his northern, eastern and southern boundaries relatively settled, Darius turned to the west and Europe as an area in which to expand. He called for troops, ships and engineers who were to build a bridge across the Thracian Bosporus. After crossing over the bridge into Thrace he ordered the bridge to be dismantled and for the ships to sail to the Danube and wait for his army. After defeating the various tribes in Thrace he reached the Danube River. Again a bridge of boats was built, and Darius and his army crossed over the Danube into Scythia. He left the Ionian tyrants who were traveling with him behind to guard the bridge and told them to leave if he had not returned within 60 days.[87]

The Scythians had called upon neighboring kings for help against the Persians but many refused, so the Scythians decided not to meet the Persians in open battle but rather to retreat, destroying all potential supplies for the Persians and fight a war of attrition. While the Persian army was pursuing the Scythian army, some Scythian cavalry got behind the Persians and tried to convince the Ionians guarding the bridge over the Danube to break up the bridge and go home so as to strand Darius and his army in Scythia. They told the Ionians that this would leave Darius stranded, and as a result the Ionians would have their freedom. Miltiades, the tyrant of Chersonese and an Athenian, argued in support of the Scythian proposal. Histiaeus, the tyrant of Miletus, argued that they should maintain the bridge because if Darius should be defeated, they would be removed from power because they only held power because of the support of King Darius. The majority of the tyrants agreed with Histiaeus, and they agreed to remove some of the ships in the bridge to impress the Scythians but to leave enough ships so that they could quickly reassemble the bridge should Darius and his army appear. When Darius appeared, the bridge was reassembled, and Darius and his army were saved. Darius then returned to Sardis, but he left behind Megabazos with an army of 80,000 with orders to subjugate any cities in the area of the Hellespont who did not submit to Persia. After Megabazos achieved that goal he moved further south in Thrace conquering the tribes that he met. He then he sent envoys to King Amyntas, of Macedon, who agreed to submit "earth and water" to the king of Persia.[88]

After Darius returned to Sardis he decided to reward Koes of Mytilene for the advice he gave him concerning the Danube bridge and Histiaeus for the support that he had shown to Darius when the Scythians had tried to convince the Ionians to break up the bridge and strand him and his army in Scythia. Darius offered them "each a gift of their choosing" and Koes responded by asking to be made tyrant of Mytilene while Histiaeus asked for Myrcinus in southern Thrace so he could build a city. Darius granted both of their requests and they left Sardis.[89]

When Megabazos returned to Sardis after completing his campaign in the Hellespont and southern Thrace, he expressed concern that Darius had allowed "a dangerously clever Greek" permission to build a city at Myrcinus because it would allow Histiaeus access to timber to build ships and oars, silver mines and "multitudes of both Hellenes and barbarians."

Megabazos was concerned that Histiaeus could possibly cause problems for Darius in the future, and to avoid war within his own empire he said Darius should "send for him and stop him, but treat him gently and when you have him in your grasp see to it that he never returns to the territory of the Hellenes."[90] Appreciating Megabazos' "keen foresight," Darius sent a message to Histiaeus saying that he had need of him and asked Histiaeus to come to Sardis so that he could inform him "of important projects which I am planning." When Histiaeus arrived at Sardis, Darius made the following offer, "Leave Miletus and your newly founded city in Thrace. Follow me to Susa and share in everything I have. Be my table companion and my counselor."[91]

While Herodotus implies that Darius was unaware of the strategic and economic value of Myrcinus and that Darius appreciated Megabazos' warning, many historians take issue with this interpretation. Blamire questions the validity of Herodotus' source and claims that "it is impossible to accept Herodotus' implication that Darius was totally ignorant of its (Myrcinus) strategic and economic assets.[92] Harris points out that Myrcinus sitting on the Strymon River was well situated as it controlled the major land route down the Thracian coast. In addition it was at the intersection with the trade routes from central Europe and also was the "hub" for the roads from the gold and silver mines in Thracia.[93] Questions also arise concerning how Histiaeus and Koes made their decision about their reward. Based upon evidence as to how Darius bestowed governorships and financial gifts in the past, it is obvious that Darius would not grant the rewards to Histiaeus and Koes unless it was in his political interest to do so.[94]

There can be little doubt but that Megabazos had great hostility toward Histiaeus; however, there is not agreement among historians concerning the role he played in Histiaeus' recall from Myrcinus. Harris suggests that Megabazos' denunciation of Histiaeus may have led Darius to remove both of them from the area in order to avoid the constant conflicts that too often occurred between the Greeks and Persians at Darius' court.[95] Blamire rejects the traditional view that Megabazos caused the recall of Histiaeus. He claims Darius felt that he had to "cancel his grant and take Histiaeus with him. Another governor for Myrcinus would readily be available if required but there was no other Greek upon whom Darius could equally depend for his Foreign Ministry."[96] Georges sees other motives for Darius recalling Histiaeus. He says that Darius, a usurper, was looking for new men. He claims that Darius, in order to ensure his own control, had put down the many revolts that faced him. Once the revolts had been put down, he had to work out a system of personal alliances within the Persian nobility and among the provincial areas that he controlled. Among the Ionian Greeks he did it by creating tyrants in Ionian cities and rewarding them for their loyalty. He points out that Darius gave Histiaeus multiple titles as well as "direct access to his person." Histiaeus was not an adviser in name only; rather, his place in the imperial household was only slightly below the king's groom and the king's cupbearer. By taking him to Susa, Darius had made Histiaeus one of the most influential Greeks in the empire.[97]

With the end of the campaign in Scythia and Thrace, it is perhaps a good time to evaluate Darius' military achievements by 510 BCE By this time Darius had put down all who had revolted when he became king. He had also secured his northeastern border, expanded east to a secure border at the Indus River, and the southern border was also settled. While his campaign against the Scythians beyond the Danube River was unsuccessful, he had created a secure border between Scythia and Thrace at the Danube River, and he had added the rest of Thrace to his empire. Finally, the king of Macedonia had submitted to Darius by submitting "earth and water." Thrace was a major addition to the empire as it had an abundance of important minerals, including silver mines, and large amounts of timber for building ships and making oars.[98]

With the end of his major campaigns, Darius turned to governing his vast empire. Billows believes that Darius' deeds probably were enough to earn the title of Darius the Great; however, he believes that Darius' greatest achievement was his reorganization of the empire which "set it upon a businesslike footing" and "enabled the Empire to function smoothly and last for another 150 or more years."[99]

Herodotus tells us that Darius "established 20 satrapies, which is what we call provinces in Persia, and after he had designated the provinces and the governors in charge of them, he assigned to each nation the tribute it would pay to him."[100] While no date is given, Herodotus goes on to list the 20 satrapies along with the tribute each owed. When you add the tributes each owed, the total came to 14,560 talents of silver.[101] This number has little meaning to us today, and it is difficult to compare ancient money to money today; however, Billows has attempted to help us understand what a large amount it was. He does this by comparing Persia's income to that of Athens at its height of power. He states,

> It isn't really possible to express ancient sums of money usefully in modern terms, but a comparison may help. The Athenians at the height of their power in the mid fifth century received an annual tribute from their allies of not quite 400 talents. From this they were able to build and maintain the most powerful fleet in the ancient world, to conduct mostly successful warfare against the Persians and (at times) the Spartans, to build some of the most expensive and widely admired buildings in the ancient world (most famously the Parthenon), and to create a reserve fund that by 432 BCE amounted to 10,000 talents. The annual tribute received by the Persian kings was more than 30 times that received by the Athenians that enabled them to do all these things. Stupendous is hardly a sufficient term to describe the size of this tribute income.[102]

In addition to the above income, tribute was not assessed upon some areas, but they still gave gifts. The Ethiopians and residents around Nysa contributed two quarts of unrefined gold, 200 logs of ebony, five Ethiopian boys and 20 large elephant tusks every year. The Colchians sent 100 boys and 100 girls every four years. Finally the Arabians gave 1,000 talents of frankincense each year.[103]

The satraps in the Persian Empire had a great deal of power. They had money, Persian troops, controlled a great deal of land and were often a far distance from the capital. They were also allowed to take their whole family with them, and the office was often passed from father to son. There was certainly potential for the creation of "satrapal principalities" as evidenced by the actions of Oroites that were covered above. However, the satrap was totally dependent upon the king for his power, and the king alone could dismiss him; it seems that the satraps "were watched over by a Corps of Royal spies, reporting any rebelliousness or dereliction to the king." Regarding the power of the satrap over his Persian troops, it is clear that he had to gain permission from the king before undertaking campaigns. It is also very clear that the Persian troops took their orders from the king, no matter how far the satrap's territory was from the king or the amount of time that the troops had been attached to the satrap, as evidenced by Oroites' Persian troops' willingness to kill him upon a letter from the king ordering them to do so.[104]

In summary, when the mainland Greeks came into conflict with the Persian Empire in c. 500 BCE the Greeks faced an empire that controlled the largest landmass of any empire up to that date, an empire that was well governed, an empire that had a large and effective army and navy and an empire that had huge financial resources.

5

The Ionian Revolt

Herodotus and the Ionian Revolt

Herodotus is our only surviving literary source for the Ionian Revolt, and as is pointed out in Chapter 1, many questions have been raised concerning his credibility, veracity and objectivity.[1] G.B. Gray and M. Cary, writing in the 1926 edition of *The Cambridge Ancient History*, point out that "we possess the account of Herodotus, and the Ionian Revolt marks the very point at which he begins to attempt a continuous narrative. Unfortunately this chapter of his story reveals Herodotus almost at his worst."[2] Herodotus enjoyed little support from ancient critics because of "his alleged mendacity and gullibility and his lack of scientific spirit of historiography when compared with Thucydides."[3] Lateiner sums up the unsatisfactory aspects of Herodotus' account as follows:

> Herodotus' account of the Ionian Rebellion is unsatisfactory in the following respects: his narrative of facts is skimpy and fragmented; his attribution of trivial motives to the Ionians, especially to individuals, seems to have been biased by hostile sources, hostile especially to Histiaeus and Aristagoras; the absolute chronology of the revolt is the despair of commentators and historians; even the relative chronology poses problems; the biographical elements are full of the romantic, the fabulous, and the melodramatic; Herodotus' own condemnatory stance toward the Ionians as a group and towards the revolt as a hopeless gesture colors the entire narrative; and Herodotus' notorious, if exaggerated, weakness in strategic questions, military and political, makes the modern historians task all the more difficult.[4]

Cawkwell, writing in 2005, also criticizes Herodotus as he states, "The view adopted in this book amounts to substantial rejection of Herodotus, and I can do no more than state what I believe to have been the truth." He goes on to give three major criticisms of Herodotus' account. He says that Herodotus is "too personal," simply dismissed the Ionian Revolt as hopeless and never understood "the nature and operation of the Persian Empire."[5] Cawkwell also believes that Herodotus' bias was influenced by the Athenian isolationists and that the Alcmaeonidae greatly influenced him to the detriment of Ionia.[6]

Murray, writing in the 1988 edition of *The Cambridge Ancient History,* takes a different approach. He says that there is no evidence, either literary or material, that gives us any idea that there was a better source available than Herodotus, nor is there a basis upon which to construct one. Since Herodotus' version is based upon oral sources, Murray says that we must evaluate it based on the "characteristics of oral tradition and for their reliability as history, not with methods appropriate to a documentary tradition." He goes on to claim that Herodotus based his history of Ionia upon a priestly tradition and thus is not as reliable as his history of mainland Greece which was based upon more rational sources. He further denies that Herodotus was biased against the Ionians. Rather, he claims "the oral traditions of a defeated people behave quite differently from those of a victorious one" and goes on to say that Herodotus was simply "accepting the verdict of that society upon itself."[7]

W. G. Forest addresses the charge that Herodotus is naïve or "too personal" and that he ignores economic, social and political causes for the Ionian Revolt. He points out that Herodotus lacked the "language of sophisticated analysis" which modern historians use. He also points out that Herodotus felt he had to include information that he was told even if he did not believe it or even if it appeared absurd. He then states that Herodotus was a brilliant storyteller and chose to write a descriptive history as opposed to analytical history. Finally he reminds us that most of Herodotus' information came from oral sources and oral tradition, which "tends to recall the startling, the colorful, the scandalous and the heroic," and that Herodotus was "writing of, if not in, a time when individuals did matter more than historians now think they matter or mattered at any time."[8] Addressing the same question that Herodotus is too simple and focuses too much upon individuals instead of the bigger question of why the Ionians revolted, Peter Krentz claims that "Herodotus supplies plenty of threads for weaving a larger, more complex tapestry."[9]

The noted scholar of Persia, A. T. Olmstead, points out that Herodotus was a Persian subject who was able to travel throughout the empire, and because of the "Persian peace" he was able to utilize Persian official sources both oral and written. He claims that Herodotus was pro–Greek but not "violently anti–Persian" and that he "presents honestly the facts to the best of his ability, and if he has not always detected partisan distortions, his facts generally permit us to correct the interpretation."[10] Waters agrees with Olmstead concerning "partisan distortions," as he reminds us that Herodotus was dependent upon "oral sources of a fair degree of unreliability, which had already acquired a certain cast, or prejudice."[11]

J. Neville also agrees with Olmstead that Herodotus was honest in his approach to his writing and that he did not deliberately exclude evidence in an attempt to put the Ionian Revolt in a bad light. He claims Herodotus was impartial as he described both countries and individuals. He did not describe Greeks as good or Persians as bad as some have claimed. Rather Herodotus included good, bad and indifferent material on all nations, and he is no different in his approach to the Ionians. Neville believes that we should be more aware of the problems faced as he tried to gather information for his work. Finally, he believes that Herodotus did an excellent job in organizing his material and thinks that his coverage of the Ionian Revolt is inadequate only if we try to compare it with modern historical writings.[12]

Evans points out that while Hecataeus opposed the revolt, he was still chosen as an envoy to Artaphernes, which showed that Hecataeus "was not compromised with the Persians." He goes on to suggest that Hecataeus "may have been responsible, at least in part, for Herodotus' bias against ... the Ionian revolt."[13]

H. T. Wallinga contends that we should not be surprised by the negative view of the Ionian Revolt held by the sources consulted by Herodotus. He points out that when Herodotus was writing *The Histories,* the Ionians were free only because of the failure of the Persian attempt to conquer Greece. He goes on to state, "Insofar as the Ionians had contributed anything in 480, it had been with few exceptions-on the Persian side. No wonder therefore that Herodotus disapproved of the Ionians, considered their resistance to Cyrus futile, scorned the motives of their revolt, disparaged their achievements and felt contempt for their leaders; no wonder either that they viewed the revolt in the first place as the cause of their disaster."[14]

There is little doubt that Herodotus visited Samos, and because of his own aristocratic background, he had access to the aristocratic families on Samos. Certainly one of the major criticisms of Herodotus is his apologia for the part played by Samos in the Ionian Revolt, as the "treacherous bargain made by the Samians with Aiakes to desert is excused, the blame being laid on the overwhelming might of the king's armies and the refusal of the Ionian crews to train, which made resistance hopeless and gave the Samians some sort of justification for deserting."[15]

Lateiner asks the question whether Herodotus was duped by his Samians informants. He goes on to say, "It is true to say that he thrusts the bare fact of their treachery between two attempts to excuse it and the account as a whole superficially whitewashes the Samians." Lateiner then proceeds to examine six more items relating to Samian sources and suggests "that Herodotus here too kept his wits about him in reporting events, although his determined explicit judgment of the entire rebellion as a mistake colors this instance as well as the rest of the section that comprises books V–VI."[16] J. Neville reinforces Lateiner's view when he says, "Unless further evidence turns up to prove, beyond reasonable doubt, that Herodotus was malignantly denigrating the Ionians in their national patriotic bid for freedom from a harsh and despotic overlord, I would suggest that the more sober, less partisan view of Herodotus is infinitely preferable."[17] Concerning Herodotus' prejudice, Chapman adds, "Such prejudice, if it merely expresses the author's considered opinion, is fair comment even if it is wrong. It is only damaging if it is a sign of deliberate distortion of facts to suit a preconceived verdict."[18]

Since there are so many different viewpoints concerning Herodotus and his value as a source for the Ionian Revolt, is it possible to reach any consensus about him? First, all agree, even his strongest critics like Lang and Cawkwell, that Herodotus is our only surviving literary source. Without Herodotus it is impossible to write a history of the Ionian Revolt.[19] Secondly, many historians would also agree with Olmsted's view that Herodotus "presents honestly the facts to the best of his ability, and if he has not always detected partisan distortions his facts generally permit us to correct the interpretation." Finally Chapman believes that Herodotus is right on most of the major points concerning the Ionian Revolt. He says that the we can be sure of the following items. The Ionian cities were unhappy with the tyrants Persia installed and revolted and deposed them. The revolt broke out after the failure of the Naxian expedition, and Aristagoras was its early leader. Athens and Eretria sent aid and participated in the attack on Sardis, but they both withdrew after the battle at Ephesus; however, Byzantium, Caria, Caunus and most of Cyprus joined the revolt. The Persians retook Cyprus and in spite of a naval defeat at Cyprus took the offensive and began to retake Ionian cities. Aristagoras left Miletus, and Histiaeus attempted to return to Miletus but failed. The Ionians were defeated in the sea battle at Lade because the Samians deserted the in the midst of the battle, after which Miletus was taken by the Persians. At that point the revolt was over except for mopping-up operations by the Persians. Histiaeus was captured and killed by Artaphernes. The Ionian Revolt had lasted for six years. He then goes on to state, "It is the detail within the general framework which has been criticized."[20]

This chapter's description of the Ionian Revolt will be based upon the general facts presented by Herodotus and at the same time explore the different views and interpretations concerning the details of the Ionian Revolt.

The Naxos Campaign

In c. 500 BCE wealthy aristocrats who had been exiled from the island of Naxos arrived in Miletus seeking help from their "guest-friend" Histiaeus, the tyrant of Miletus; however, when they arrived they discovered that Histiaeus was at Susa serving as an adviser to the Persian king.[21] As a result they approached Aristagoras, who was the cousin and son-in-law of Histiaeus, and who had been left in charge of Miletus when Histiaeus went to Susa in c. 514/13 BCE.[22] They asked Aristagoras if he would supply them with forces to return them to power in Naxos. Using the pretext of honoring the guest-friendship that they had with Histiaeus, Aristagoras proposed to help them while in reality he hoped to gain control over Naxos by helping them to return. While he offered to help them, he also claimed that he had inadequate resources to succeed against Naxos which had 8,000 hoplites and many warships; however, he offered to go to Artaphernes, the satrap at Sardis and the brother of King Darius, to seek his help. The Naxians were pleased and told Aristagoras to "promise gifts and expenses for Artaphernes' army which they themselves would pay."[23]

When Aristagoras approached Artaphernes, he told him that while Naxos was "not a very large island, it was fair and fertile and close to Ionia. Moreover, it contained abundant wealth and slaves." He told Artaphernes that he had "a large sum of money ready for him in addition to the expenses of the army" and that in conquering Naxos, Artaphernes could gain control of the islands of Paros, Andros and the Cyclades islands which would serve as a good base from which to attack the "large and prosperous" island of Euboea, and he told Artaphernes that 100 ships would be able to carry out the entire mission. Artaphernes replied that he would supply 200 ships instead of the 100 ships and seek the approval of King Darius. When King Darius approved the plan, Artaphernes equipped 200 triremes and appointed Megabates, a first cousin to Darius, to be his military commander.[24]

The fleet picked up Aristagoras and his Ionian army at Miletus and sailed toward the Hellespont in order to mislead the Naxians concerning its mission. At the island of Chios the fleet halted in order to gain the north wind to sail down and surprise Naxos. At this point an incident took place that greatly impacted the outcome of the mission. While making rounds of the ships, Megabates found an unguarded ship and ordered the captain, Skylax of Myndos, to be punished by being tied up with his head sticking out of an oar hole in the ship. Aristagoras was informed that his guest-friend, Skylax, was being mistreated and appealed to Megabates to release him. When Megabates refused, Aristagoras released Skylax on his own and pointed out to Megabates that he, Aristagoras, was in overall command of the mission. According to Herodotus, Megabates was so infuriated by Aristagoras' actions that he sent some men by boat to warn the Naxians of the upcoming assault by the fleet.[25]

Being forewarned, the Naxians "brought everything from their fields to within the city walls and prepared for a siege by stockpiling food, water and wine and by reinforcing their wall." When Aristagoras and the fleet arrived, they discovered the Naxians behind their walls, so they laid siege to the city. After four months with little success, the supplies were getting low and the costs were running much higher than had been expected, with the result that Aristagoras had to spend much of his own money. Recognizing that the siege was failing, it was abandoned, and the Persian fleet returned to the mainland.[26]

From reading Herodotus it appears that Artaphernes was enthusiastic about Aristagoras' proposal and offered to double the number ships he would provide to 200 so as to ensure the success of the plan. Wallinga has asked whether the original request of 100 triremes would have been adequate to accomplish the goal. He points out that Naxos probably had a few triremes, many merchant ships and perhaps 80 to 90 pentekonters and small galleys, not all of which would be available on short notice. Based upon the above numbers, Wallinga claims 100 triremes would have been more than sufficient even if 80 triremes had to be used as troop carriers in order to have sufficient forces to face Naxos' 8,000 hoplites. Why then did Artaphernes raise the total from 100 to 200 ships?

Wallinga raises the possibility that either Artaphernes had more grandiose plans for the fleet after Naxos fell or he feared interference from other Greeks, perhaps from the mainland. He claims that either is a possibility, but then he suggests that perhaps Artaphernes was concerned about bringing together 100 Ionian ships in which the crews could seize the ships and use them against Artaphernes. A solution to that particular problem was for Artaphernes to double the number of ships and "make crews as mixed a lot as possible so that the community of interests was minimal" and the Persian commanders would have more control. The crews of the Naxian expedition included Carians, Lesbians, and Aiolians from Kyme and Ionians.[27] Lateiner suggests a simpler reason for the change in the number of ships. He states that Darius had decided to reduce the Ionians' "independent policymaking" and Darius' decision to "double the Ionian expeditionary force against Naxos and add his gift of a Persian commander and Persian troops was meant to indicate who was in control."[28]

Herodotus' statement that Megabates warned the Naxians of the coming invasion has been challenged by many historians. Arthur Keaveney writing in 1988 stated that ancient historians are in rare agreement that Megabates did not warn the Naxians. He then presented a list of suspects who may have warned the Naxians, and his list follows:

1. Megabates, like Herodotus says.
2. Aristagoras, the person most suspected by those claiming Megabates was innocent.
3. An anonymous Greek seaman.
4. A Naxian who changed his mind.
5. Nobody warned the Naxians. Secrets are hard to keep, and Naxos heard enough to be suspicious and to be prepared.[29]

Keaveney claims there is no evidence to support choices 3 and 4, so he eliminates them. He rejects choice 5 on the "grounds that it is misconceived." Perhaps Aristagoras did it "in the heat of the moment," but Keaveney rejects that idea because Aristagoras had no motive, since "he had successfully asserted his authority, freed Skylax and for good measure reminded Megabates to his face as to who was in charge," so he rejects choice 2. Thus, he concludes, 1 is the only choice that is left.[30]

After pointing out that scholars were universally opposed to Herodotus' view of Megabates, Keaveney, by the process of elimination, reached the same conclusion as Herodotus.

How does he support his case? He first explains that it is clear that in any disagreement between Megabates and Aristagoras, King Darius would certainly support the Persian rather than the Greek. Thus Keaveney claims that Megabates would have little to fear if he did betray the expedition. He goes on to say that Megabates certainly must have disliked being placed under the command of Aristagoras, but he accepted his situation until Aristagoras overruled him in the case of Skylax and publicly embarrassed him. He then planned revenge, as any Persian noble would, and took steps to ruin the expedition and destroy the career of Aristagoras.[31]

Harris rejects Herodotus' version that Megabates betrayed the Naxian expedition. He explained that its failure would be a disaster for Aristagoras but that Megabates would also have been affected by the failure of the plan. He goes on to argue that it is difficult to believe that a high-ranking Persian noble and close relative of the king would commit "such an act of treason from childishly vindictive motives." In addition Harris claims that it is not necessary that anyone even betrayed the expedition. He points out that Naxos was a well-fortified island with 8,000 hoplites available for its defense. He agrees that the fleet took an unusual route in an effort to surprise Naxos; however, he also explains that a successful surprise attack required much more cooperation, timing and discipline, which the problems between Aristagoras and Megabates made impossible. He adds that it would have been difficult to keep the goal of such a large-scale operation secret during the long period of preparations.[32]

Evans thinks that it was not necessary that there had to be a person who betrayed the Naxian expedition. He says it would not have been difficult for Naxos to learn about the goal of the expedition without any help from a member of the expedition. He thinks that the charge against Megabates was simply the result of rumors spread among the sailors looking for someone to blame for the failure of the operation. While he does not think Megabates was guilty, he believes it shows how unpopular Megabates was and as a result Aristagoras emerged as a national hero.[33]

Georges also doubts that Megabates would subvert the Naxian expedition which was important to his king and also to his personal advancement. He feels that it was probably a Greek who betrayed the expedition "for profit, private friendship, or fear and envy of Miletus' power." He goes on to point out that the failure of the expedition also appears to have impacted Megabates' future career as he held no other known command."[34]

Lang takes a different approach in rejecting Herodotus' view of Megabates. She starts by accepting Grundy's view that Aristagoras used the request of the Naxian exile as an opportunity to mobilize the Ionian fleet to be used in a revolt. Once the fleet was mobilized, Aristagoras planned to dispose of the Persian commanders and raise the "standard of revolt." When Artaphernes doubled the size of the fleet, the Ionians were no longer dominant, so they had to go along with preparing for the Naxian expedition; however, Aristagoras had no intention of helping Persia add Naxos to its empire, so Naxos was warned and the expedition failed.[35]

At this point, can we draw any conclusions concerning the guilt or innocence of Megabates? After recognizing that most scholars reject Herodotus' view concerning Megabates, Keaveney proceeds to defend Herodotus' view along with Forrest, while others accuse anonymous Greeks, the Naxian exiles or Aristagoras. Some argue that no one betrayed the expedition because it was impossible to keep the goal of the expedition secret. Perhaps this is a case where there is no "proven" answer but each person must decide among the conflicting viewpoints. And yet it seems that one can take motive into account, for, as Grundy points out, "why should motive be disregarded in the court of history when it is regarded as an essential factor in the court of law?"[36] It would seem that Megabates had the least motive to betray the expedition.

Outbreak of the Revolt

When Aristagoras returned to Miletus after the failure of the Naxos campaign he feared for his future. His personal finances were in trouble because of the money that he had spent on the campaign, and he had failed to provide Artaphernes with the territory he had promised. In addition he feared that Artaphernes would listen to Megabates and remove him from his position at Miletus. Thus he began planning the revolt in order to maintain his position of power at Miletus. Coincidentally, during the time he was planning a revolt a slave-messenger arrived from Histiaeus in Susa telling Aristagoras to revolt. Histiaeus wanted a revolt because "he resented being detained at Susa and he felt he would never be allowed to return to Miletus again." While he wanted to inform Aristagoras, he feared that a message would be intercepted, so he had the head of his most trusted slave shaved and wrote the message on his head. After the slave had grown his hair back he was sent to Aristagoras who was told to shave his head.

With the support of Histiaeus, Aristagoras consulted other Ionians and all of them agreed with his plan to revolt except for Hecataeus, the famous geographer-historian of Asia Minor. Hecataeus reminded them of the great power of Persia and recited "a list of all the peoples under his rule." Hecataeus failed to convince Aristagoras and the others of his viewpoint, so he next suggested that they should first gain control of the sea and that then they should seize the treasure that Croesus had dedicated to Apollo at Didyma near Miletus, which would give them money to finance the revolt; however, again Aristagoras and his supporters rejected Hecataeus' advice and proceeded with the plan to revolt without seizing the treasure at Didyma.[37]

The fleet from the Naxos campaign was still docked at Myous near Miletus, so it was decided to send Iatrogoras to Myous where he successfully won over the sailors of the fleet and arrested many of the Greek commanders. Next, to win over the people, Aristagoras "claimed he was letting go of his tyranny, and he established *isonomy* [equality under the law]." With the fleet under his control Aristagoras then expelled the tyrants from other cities in Ionia and turned the tyrants that were arrested at Myous over to their own cities in order to gain support of those cities. Thus the Ionian Revolt began.[38]

Herodotus is criticized for being too simplistic in his motives for the revolt and giving too much importance to individuals as causing the revolt. But as Forrest has pointed out, Herodotus lacked the language skills and analytic tools of modern historians, and he also points out that Herodotus used oral sources and oral tradition which placed greater emphasis upon individuals, and he was writing at a time when individual actions were considered more important in influencing outcomes. So, should we be surprised about his concentration on individuals? That being said, we still must examine more factors in order to understand why the Ionian Revolt took place. Even accepting the explanation of why Aristagoras decided to revolt, we still must answer the question of why the other Ionians joined him in rising up against the mighty Persian Empire, and that question can only be answered by examining a broader array of causes.

Gray and Cary, who wrote in the 1926 edition of *The Cambridge Ancient History*, explained that Ionia was experiencing an economic crisis, but they also suggest that there is little evidence that Persia intended to hurt Ionian trade or that Persia ever gave preferential treatment to Phoenicia, the greatest rival in Greek trade. Yet they point out that the Persian conquest of Egypt ruined Ionian trade with Naucratis, the Greek city in Egypt, while the Carthaginian destruction of Sybaris in Italy undercut Milesian trade in the western Mediterranean. Finally, Persian action in Thrace prevented Miletus from exploiting the material resources, such as silver, to pay for grain imports that they needed from Thrace.[39]

Murray writing in the 1988 edition of *The Cambridge Ancient History* agrees that the expansion of Persia into the west was disastrous for the Greek trading cities of Ionia. Those cities had dominated the trade of the Aegean Sea as well as the Black Sea. As a result the Ionian cities had trading interests from Egypt in the south to Sicily in the western Mediterranean. He claims that the Persian conquests and military operations greatly disrupted the trade of the Ionian cities and the Mediterranean economy. He points out that Naucratis in Egypt was the greatest hub for Greek trade and its source for corn, but after Persia conquered Egypt in 525 BCE there is a period of about 25 years in which Greek pottery does not appear in the archaeological record at Naucatis. He states that the Scythian expedition of Darius interfered with Greek trade in corn and slaves and that Persian action in the Propontus and Thrace also interfered with Greek trade for "timber, hides, silver and again slaves." Finally he claims that the Persian conquests of Lydia and Egypt removed markets for luxury goods that were manufactured and/or supplied by the major Ionian cities. Also Egypt had employed many Greek mercenaries, and Persia's conquest removed this opportunity for employment and income for the Ionian economy. He concludes by saying that the Ionian cities had seen their trading prospects and economies deteriorate after the Persian conquest of Egypt. He believes the Ionian Revolt was "both the consequence and consummation of the process."[40]

Harris in his study of "Ionia under Persia" states that compared to conditions under Babylon and Assyria, life in the Persian Empire was an improvement. He then proceeds to examine the financial burdens imposed by a satrapy system in which the locals had to pay for all the administrative structures, court system, internal security forces and the satrap's own court, which in some cases were quite extravagant; however he does point out that expenses varied according to the satrap. They also had to pay the Imperial levy, which while it was high it does not appear to have been unreasonable. But in addition they had to pay for imperial garrisons of troops and cavalry. Finally special taxes were imposed to pay for the king and his army if they passed through the province, or they had to pay for a member of the royal household or private individual honored by the king. He concludes that direct tribute assessments were reasonable; however, taking into account the total taxes, fees and assessments, the Ionians faced a heavy financial burden.[41]

In the sixth century BCE, Ionia had about 250,000 free inhabitants, but it could not supply its population with sufficient food except through trade and the importation of food from colonies and the surrounding area. As a result the Ionian economy was "uniquely vulnerable to the shocks of political importance in many quarters of the Mediterranean world where her trade connections existed." Harris basically agrees with Murray as he lists the destruction of Sybaris, the Persian conquest of Egypt, the Persian control of Thrace, and the Persian conquest of Byzantium as being among the factors impacting the Ionian economy. He also, however, points out that the good system of roads, methods of communication and the peace and order maintained by the Persian Empire were very beneficial to Ionian commerce. In addition he says that large numbers of Ionians found work within the Persian administration and fleet.[42] But Harris believes that the negative impact of economic problems outweighed the positive benefits of Persian rule and Darius became a convenient target to blame for the difficulties the Ionians experienced, whether or not the Persian Empire was responsible. He concludes, "Thus, for reasons well-founded or ill-founded, rational or irrational, there can be no doubt that an accumulation of economic grievances significantly influenced the outbreak of the revolt."[43]

Georges writing in 2000 rejects the economic arguments of Murray and Harris. He claims that in late archaic Greece there was a major increase in trade and manufacture in the trading area of the Pontus, Egypt and the Greek cities in Ionia. He claims that Persia's action in Thrace did not cut off the supply of silver to Ionia but rather increased it, as Ionia first coined silver after the Persians had taken control of Thrace. He believes Darius' naval policy and administrative reforms actually helped maintain the "Ionians' profitable role" as he introduced a genuine Persian coinage and opened a second mint in Ionia. He believes that the coined wealth did not leave Ionia but remained in the islands of the Aegean Sea and the areas in Asia Minor controlled by the Greeks and Carians. He further claims that Persia replaced the Lydian and Egyptian markets for luxury goods and gave the Ionians new trading opportunities by "integrating them into their empire as a naval arm in their advance into Europe and the Aegean archipelago."[44]

Krentz, writing in 2010 agrees that those who claim the Ionian economy was damaged by Persian expansion are incorrect, as they and not only contradict "Herodotus who says that Miletus was at its economic peak," but their claims do not "fit the external evidence of increased monumental building, increased private dedications, and increased silver coinage." While he believes that the Greeks of Asia prospered under the Persians, he also says that they had economic grievances. Their first grievance was that the king had confiscated vast amounts of land in Ionia and given large estates to Persians willing to move to Ionia to help defend it. Their second grievance was the Imperial tribute which, although not intolerable, was still required, required being the key word. Their final grievance was the required military service, which could involve thousands of men and great expense.[45]

Cawkwell agrees with Krentz that the Ionian economy was not in decline prior to the Ionian Revolt and agrees that Herodotus is probably correct when he describes Miletus as being at its peak of prosperity. He also agrees that the king's grants of Ionian land to Persian nobles may have been the cause of bitter resentment. He states, "It is unlikely that the revolt was inspired by Persian taxation, rather than by Persian domination as a whole of which the collection of tribute was only one aspect."[46]

When the Ionian tyrants were discussing the proposal to break up the bridge over the Danube in order to strand Darius and his army in Scythia, Histiaeus argued in favor of maintaining the bridge, and he stated that "it was because of Darius that each of them now governed his city as tyrant, and if the power of Darius were destroyed, he himself would not be able to keep ruling Miletus, nor would anyone else be able to rule his own city either. For, he said, all of their cities would prefer democracy to tyranny.[47] J.B. Bury refers to the "widespread hatred of the despotic constitution which smoldered in the cities and the despotic constitutions that were part of the Persian system."[48] Gray and Cary point out that the tyrannies established by Persia had outlived their "usefulness and had come to be resented as a burden and a humiliation."[49] Blamire agrees, claiming that the principal grievance of the Ionians "was Persia's retention of the outmoded system of tyranny."[50] Harris agrees that the Persians "using puppet-tyrants" from their own citizenry as instruments of imperial authority "rankled" the Ionians the most; however, he also points out that from the Persian perspective it may have been seen as "a concession to local sentiment in the Greek states" as Persia used local leaders in other areas such as Cilicia and Judah.[51]

The development of tyranny in Ionia had initially been "an outgrowth of social change and internal unrest," just as it had developed in the rest of the Greek world, and it was part of the movement toward "more popular forms of government." However, King Darius was a great administrator, and his reorganization of the imperial system that had emerged from the reins of Cyrus and Cambyses was dramatic. He set up the satrapy system to govern his empire, codified the laws, made economic changes, established and standardized the imperial levy and established military levies.[52] As a result of Darius' reorganization, Samos, Chios and Miletus lost the special privileges that they had previously enjoyed. In addition his reorganization impacted the tyrants of the cities and how they were chosen. Previously the Ionian tyrants probably "represented an indigenous political phenomenon"; however, after his reorganization, tyrants were appointed by the king.[53] After the reorganization, tyrants were generally chosen from groups or individuals who had "some claim to legitimacy, who earned the confidence of the king ... and came from the wealthy oligarchical segments of the populations." Prior to the reign of King Darius, the Ionian Greek cities had been allowed a great deal of local autonomy. Some claim that it is only after the reorganization of Darius that "systematic interference in the local autonomy of the Greek cities began." The newly appointed tyrants of Darius were well aware that they served at the will of the king and that it was their job to control the local politics of their cities.[54]

As with most Greek cities, internal politics in Ionian cities often consisted of conflicts between "warring factions of the rich and the poor, called the *Ploutis* (wealth) and *Cheiromcha* (labor)," which caused great discord within the cities.[55] Histiaeus and his party were set up in Miletus with the support of Persia in order to "stabilize the political life of the city." At this point the "new tyrants" appointed by Darius seem to have taken on an "anti-Hellenic character as vassalage to the great king." Rather than helping Persia achieve its goal, the Persian approach of appointing and supporting tyrants seems to be a major failure in their Ionian policy. Harris states,

> The oligarchical groups had not only failed to hold Ionia firm for Persia, but had actually reversed the position and provoked revolt, when popular feeling against tyrants became so strong that the collapse of the whole system of puppet tyrants appeared imminent. The tyrants were thus used as scapegoats by their own oligarchical supporters, who joined in ejecting them from office when the revolt broke out, with Aristagoras and his "friends" at Miletus leading the way by turning "democratic."[56]

He concludes by stating that Aristagoras shrewdly took advantage of the situation in Ionia in 500 BCE Aristagoras realized that the hatred of the tyrants appointed by Persia was so great that he stepped down as tyrant and established *isonomia* in Miletus to win over the people, and his actions were very successful.[57]

Cawkwell states that the Ionians were not revolting against Persian rule as much as against the tyrants that Persia had installed. He recognizes the view that the Ionian cities wanted to be allowed to move toward more democratic rule as had occurred in many cities such as Athens; however, he finds the support for this viewpoint weak. He claims that the "tyrants were opposed not because they were tyrants but because they were instruments of Persian power."[58]

Evans suggests that the Ionian Revolt was a nationalistic movement that was caused by a desire of the subject Greek cities for more unity. He goes on to claim that the growing unity was a result of the Persians bringing a united Ionian fleet together for the Scythian and Naxian campaigns.[59] Graf agrees that the "general consensus" is that the Ionian Revolt was a national movement, although he includes opposition to "puppet-tyrannies" as an underlying cause.[60] Evans goes on to claim that "the immediate cause of the revolt seems to have been massive discontent among the sailors who returned from the Naxian expedition." Aristagoras, who emerged from his confrontation with Megabates as a national hero, saw his opportunity and took advantage of the "unique opportunity" of the fleet being at Myous to make his move to be leader of the revolt.[61]

Sparta and Athens

After Aristagoras had given up his tyranny at Miletus and ejected the tyrants from other Ionian cities, he had the cities appoint generals who probably also served as chief magistrates of the cities. Aristagoras then turned to finding additional allies.[62] Fortunately for Aristagoras and the Ionians, the revolt began in the winter at the end of the campaign season, as this gave them time to organize an attempt to find more allies before they would have to face the Persian forces the following year. In fact, they had even more time as the Persians lacked sufficient resources in West Asia to cope with a large-scale revolt. The nearest garrison of Persian troops was in Sardis, and it was probably not large enough to put down the revolt without additional resources. In order to raise sufficient numbers, the Persians would have to raise levies, which took so much time that the Persians were unable to undertake any massive campaign until the campaign season of 497.[63]

Arriving at Sparta, with a "bronze tablet on which a map of the entire world was engraved, including all rivers and every sea," Aristagoras appealed to King Cleomenes, saying that the Spartans as "leaders of Hellas" should help the Ionians free themselves from the slavery imposed upon them by Persia. Aristagoras reminded the Spartans that the Ionians were "of the same blood" as them and told them that Sparta could easily defeat the Persians as the Persians were not valiant and "fight with bows and short spears and wear trousers and turbans on their heads" while the Spartans "have attained the highest degree of excellence in war." Using his bronze map, Aristagoras pointed to the lands near Ionia and described their fertile land, mineral resources and wealth, concluding with the statement that Sparta would emerge from the war with wealth that would rival that of Zeus.

After considering the proposal of Aristagoras for three days, Cleomenes asked how far it was from the sea of the Ionians to the Persian king. Aristagoras made the mistake of telling Cleomenes that it "was a journey of three months on land," at which point Cleomenes told Aristagoras to leave Sparta, as they would never agree to travel such a long distance from Sparta. Later Aristagoras, carrying an olive branch, approached Cleomenes at his home as a suppliant and asked him to reconsider his decision in front of Cleomenes' nine-year-old daughter, Gorgo. Aristagoras at first offered Cleomenes 10 talents to change his mind and ultimately raised his offer to 50 talents as Cleomenes continued to refuse to change his decision. At that point Cleomenes' daughter "blurted out, father your guest-friend is going to corrupt you unless you leave and stay away from him." Taking his daughter's advice, Cleomenes left the room, and Aristagoras departed from Sparta.[64]

While Herodotus simply lists the distances involved in Ionia as the reason that Cleomenes would be unable to get approval to help the Ionians, Lateiner gives three additional reasons besides "the perennial danger of helot revolt." First he points out that previous marine expeditions by Sparta against Samos and Athens had been unsuccessful and that the lines of communication would be impossible for the Spartans to maintain. Secondly he claims that Sparta's longtime rival Argos was hostile and would be a threat to Sparta if its army was in Ionia. Thirdly, Aegina and Corinth, who had the most ships in the Peloponnesian League, each had strong reasons for not helping Ionia. Without their fleet Sparta could do nothing.[65] Jakob A.O. Larsen adds that the Peloponnesian League had recently "adopted the principle that Sparta could not demand military cooperation of its allies without first securing the approval of the assembly of the league." He goes on to suggest that the assembly of the league would have probably rejected such a proposal with the opposition being led by "Corinth and probably Aegina." Larsen concludes by saying "the domestic conditions in Greece were such as to make Spartan intervention in the Ionian revolt impossible."[66]

Cawkwell argues that in addition to promising territory and wealth, Aristagoras also would have pointed out that it was in the self interest of the Greeks on the mainland to support the Ionians. He believes that by 500 BCE based on the fact that the Persians had absorbed West Asia, taken the offshore islands, and occupied much of Thrace and made an alliance with Macedonia, it must have been obvious to all the Greeks that the Persians were moving to control the Aegean area. He thinks Aristagoras might have appealed to Sparta and Athens in the following terms: "We are in revolt, and need help. It is plain that you will fight in defense of your liberty, either with us in Ionia or without us in Greece itself. You cannot avoid the fight."[67]

Aristagoras next traveled to Athens and appealed for aid at the assembly. While he took the same approach as he had taken in Sparta, he added to his appeal that "Miletus was originally an Athenian colony, and therefore, since the Athenians were a great power, it was only fair and reasonable for them to offer protection to the Milesians." Herodotus claims that "there was nothing he failed to promise them, since he was now in dire need and at last he managed to win them over," and they offered 20 ships to support the Ionians. At that point Herodotus added some editorial comments, saying "it would seem to be easier to deceive and impose upon a whole throng of people than to do so to just one individual since he had failed with Cleomenes of Lacedaemon, who was alone, but then succeeded with

30,000 Athenians." He completes his comments by claiming, "These ships turned out to be the beginning of evils for both Hellenes and barbarians."[68]

While 20 ships from Athens seems like a rather anemic response from Athens, that conclusion would only be true after the silver strikes in Attica that allowed Athens to build its great fleet in the 480s. In 499 BCE the 20 ships Athens committed accounted for nearly half of their fleet of 50 ships. At this time Athens had "neither the equipment nor the capital to venture more."[69] In the summer of 489 BCE the Athenians arrived at Miletus along with five triremes from Eretria on the island of Euboea. Eretria sent five ships to repay Miletus for its support of her in a war with Chalcis in the seventh century.

Aristagoras arranged an expedition against Artaphernes' capital at Sardis and placed it under the leadership of his brother, Charopinos. Using Ephesian guides, the joint force of Ionians, Athenians and Eretrians caught Sardis unprepared and captured most of the city, except for the Acropolis, without resistance. The Acropolis was defended by Artaphernes with a large force of Persians. As the Greeks began to plunder the city, a soldier set fire to a house and the fire got out of control and burned much of the city, which included the sanctuary of the local goddess, Kybele, the mother of the gods and goddesses of the Phrygians and Lydians. Later the Persians would use this incident to justify the destruction of Greek temples and sanctuaries when the Ionians had been defeated. When the Ionian force saw Persian reinforcements arriving, they withdrew back to Ephesus where the Persian troops caught up with them. A battle was fought and the Greeks were defeated with heavy casualties. After the battle, the Athenians returned to Athens, and no further aid was sent to Ionia despite many appeals by Aristagoras.[70]

When King Darius was informed of the burning of Sardis by the Ionians, he expressed little concern about the Ionians because he knew they could not escape retribution for their revolt; however, he asked for information about the Athenians. After he had been told, he took a bow and shot an arrow into the sky and said, "Zeus, let it be granted to me to punish the Athenians." Then he appointed one of his servants to remind him three times at every dinner to "Remember the Athenians."[71]

Why did the Athenians leave after the battle at Ephesus and not return? Lateiner suggests that "Athenian self interest as well her fears concerning Aegina" controlled Athenian policy. He thinks that Athens saw the possibility that cooperation with the Ionians could serve as a counterweight to Spartan influence, but after arriving in Ionia and meeting the Persians in battle, they "realized that they were unprepared to take on Darius's military."[72] Grundy suggests that perhaps war broke out with Aegina and that affected Athens' decision, but he also states that the date of the outbreak of the war with Aegina is uncertain. He further suggests that the burning of Sardis alienated the Lydians, which meant that the Lydians would not rise up against Persia and this caused the Athenians to rethink their position. In addition, the battle at Ephesus may have changed their opinion concerning the revolt and given them an "overly pessimistic view of the prospects of the revolt." Finally he states that "another possible cause may have been a change in the preponderance of political parties at Athens during that year."[73]

A major question concerning the Battle of Sardis is how the Persians were caught so unprepared that the Greeks were able to take the city without resistance. In his treatise *The Malice of Herodotus,* Plutarch claims that the attack on Sardis took place in order to raise the siege of Miletus by the Persians and that this account was recorded by Lysanius of Mallos in his *History of Eretria*.[74] While few historians give much credence to this work by Plutarch, Grundy, while recognizing "the bitter animus of the treatise," believes that his statement about the siege of Miletus "is so manifestly in accord with the situation at that time that it is impossible to reject it as untrue." He believes that with an entire winter to prepare, it is inconceivable that Artaphernes would have "allowed months to elapse without taking measures to crush the rising before it became formidable." He states that Artaphernes was an experienced administrator with 10 years of governing the Ionians, so it appears obvious that he would have attacked the center of the revolt which was Miletus.[75]

Grundy also believes that the bold plan to attack Sardis completely upset Artaphernes' plans. Not only did he have to raise his siege of Miletus, but he also had to hurry back with his army to Sardis, as it was to be his base of operations to put down the Ionian Revolt. He states the attack on Sardis was a brilliant idea and gives Aristagoras the credit for coming up with it and claims the plan demonstrated Aristagoras' high ability if not genius."[76] Gray and Cary agree that Plutarch's story answers the question of why the Persians were caught unprepared. They claim that from the Persian point of view the best idea was to make a swift attack on the rebels' headquarters, and they believe "Artaphernes lacked neither the men nor the energy to carry out the stroke." They close their argument by saying, "the Greeks, we conclude, were first put into check by the Persians, but they relieved the pressure by offering check to the Persians in turn, and as Artaphernes had thrown his pieces too far forward, they caught him at a disadvantage."[77]

Georges offers an alternative explanation of why little action was taken for so many months after the Ionians took the fleet and deposed the tyrants. He claims that the Ionians took no action because they hoped to work out an agreement with Artaphernes mutually beneficial to both. He says that the Ionians had successfully taken over the fleet and driven out the tyrants. At that point he claims that their goal was to return to the autonomy they had enjoyed before Darius' reorganization plan and perhaps achieve an adjustment in the imperial levies. He concludes saying that the Ionians certainly could not have expected the Persians to allow them to be totally independent. Georges also claims that the Persians wanted to avoid war with the Ionians. The Persians would have to depend upon the Phoenician navy, which might not necessarily be cooperative based on their past history. Also it would mean that their navy would be split into two parts and fighting each other just when Darius was planning a major campaign in the west by sea. But this changed when Athens and Eretria arrived in Ionia to provide support. Now instead of being a local dispute, it became a war against foreign invaders and forced both the Ionians and Persians to give up hope for a peaceful resolution.[78]

Herodotus states that the Battle of Ephesus was a severe defeat for the Ionians; however, many historians question the accuracy of that statement. Harris, who claimed that the Sardis expedition was simply a raiding force designed to buy time for the Ionians, feels that the expedition was a great success as it gave the cities a period of time, perhaps up to a year, in which they could build and consolidate their positions as the burning of Sardis convinced the Persians of the need to bring up more levies of troops which was a time-consuming project. He goes on to state that the "defeat at Ephesus was merely a minor brush of the returning force with the enemy." Harris also asks whether the revolt would have spread so rapidly if the Ionians had suffered a severe defeat.[79] Lang agrees with Harris' viewpoint, and she questions the "importance of the defeat at Ephesus, if indeed it was a defeat and not a regrouping."[80] Grundy also questions the severity of the defeat at Ephesus, claiming, "There are several very serious reasons, however, for believing that the result of the battle has been greatly exaggerated."[81] The Ionian attack on Sardis, whatever the severity of the defeat which followed at Ephesus, was a great success, as it provided "the psychological spark that kindled the wide expansion of the revolt."[82] While the chronology is difficult if not impossible to reconstruct accurately, the revolt spread rapidly to Byzantium and the Hellespont, to Caria, and Cyprus.[83]

It appears at this point that Darius called Histiaeus to him and told him how Aristagoras had broken his allegiance to Persia and wondered whether this could have happened without Histiaeus knowing about it. Histiaeus assured Darius of his loyalty and defended himself, saying, "For it is probably because of my absence that the Ionians are now doing what they have for a long time yearned to do. If I had been there in Ionia, not a single city would have made such a move." He then asked Darius to send him to Ionia and he would "restore everything to its former order and deliver into your hands the governor of Miletus." Herodotus claims that Histiaeus "successfully misled the king," and Darius gave him permission to go to Ionia but ordered him to return to Susa when he had accomplished his task.[84]

Herodotus' account concerning Darius and Histiaeus causes problems for modern historians. First of all the chronology of their meeting and his return to Ionia is uncertain. Macan sets his return to Ionia in the summer of 496, Chapman sets his return at the end of 498 and Gray and Cary set his return in 497.[85] While the exact date of Histiaeus' return may not be overly important, his intentions and to whom he was loyal do matter. Chapman saw Histiaeus as a co-conspirator with Aristagoras and says, "It is not credible that Darius should suspect the truth and then let him go." He goes on to state that Histiaeus' actions are "better explained if his aim was to settle affairs by negotiation and restore Ionia to subject status, than if he was the brains behind, and potential leader of, the revolt."[86] Harris believes that since Histiaeus had been in Susa for many years, a journey of three months from Ionia, it is doubtful that he could have played any important role in the outbreak of the Ionian Revolt. But he says it is obvious that Histiaeus planned to help settle the revolt in the hope that he could return and again become a power in Miletus and Ionia.[87]

Blamire is more explicit on Histiaeus' motives and goals. He believes that Histiaeus' nostalgia for Ionia influenced him and that he wanted to settle the revolt in order to "obtain a position of personal supremacy" in Ionia by combining Greek cities in Ionia and the Aegean into "a political unit subject to Persia with the creation of himself as its satrap."[88] Gray and Cary agree that Darius accepted Histiaeus' offer to pacify the rebels, but they point out that the revolt began to turn in Persia's favor before Histiaeus could accomplish his goal.[89]

Manville takes a very different view of Histiaeus and Aristagoras. He believes that there was a power struggle between Aristagoras and Histiaeus for control of Miletus as evidenced by Aristagoras not seeking Histiaeus' help with the Naxian campaign but instead going directly to Artaphernes. The failed Naxian expedition had hurt the prestige of Histiaeus in both Susa and Miletus. Aristagoras had put Histiaeus into a difficult position as Darius still could hold Histiaeus responsible for Aristagoras' actions. If Aristagoras had succeeded at Naxos he might have become the tyrant of Miletus; however, he had failed and it now was incumbent on Histiaeus to be sure that he was not damaged by his deputy's mistakes. Histiaeus hoped that if he could suppress Aristagoras and the revolt, he would be allowed to return to Miletus as its leader.[90]

The first major action taken by Persia was against the island of Cyprus because it was "the key to all of naval operations in the Mediterranean." The island was predominately Greek, but there were also Phoenician interests centered in the city of Amathus. Gorgos was the king of the principal city of Salamis, but he refused to join the Ionian Revolt. Onesilos, the younger brother of Gorgos, overthrew his brother and led Salamis into joining the Ionian Revolt. All the other cities joined the revolt except for Amathus, which Onesilos attacked and put under siege probably in the summer of 497.[91]

Both the Ionian Greeks and the Persians were aware of the importance of Cyprus as it was in a position to dominate "the only practicable military line of communication between Asia Minor and the Euphrates Valley ... with the shore of the Levant." Grundy states that Cyprus was "of inestimable value either to a power attacking Asia Minor from the East, or to one defending it from the West" and would have put the Ionian Greeks in a position to "threaten at its weakest point the Persian line of communication with the Western satrapies." In addition for the Greeks, Cyprus would have been an ideal "base for trade with the wealthy East and would have placed the Greek trader in possession of a sea route of his own instead of the one that faced fierce Phoenician competition or having to use a land route through Asia Minor" which was slower, more expensive and which passed through many different peoples.[92] Because of the above reasons, the Persians mounted their first major campaign against Cyprus, and the joint Ionian Council immediately sent a fleet to Cyprus when Onesilos asked for help.[93]

It appears that the Ionian fleet arrived about the same time as the Phoenicians fleet crossed over from Cilicia and landed the Persian army. The Phoenician fleet then sailed around the Keys of Cyprus toward Salamis. The Cyprians offered the Ionians the choice of fighting on the sea or on the land, and the Ionians chose to fight on the sea and let the Cyprians fight the Persian army.[94] The Cyprians placed their best troops led by Onesilos opposite the Persians led by their general Artybios. In a hard-fought battle Onesilos killed Artybios, but Stesenor, the tyrant of the city of Khourion, deserted with his forces and was followed by the war chariots from Salamis. At this point the Persians gained the upper hand, and the battle turned into a rout, with Onesilos and Aristokypos, the king of Soli, being killed.[95]

According to Herodotus the sea battle took place at the same time as the land battle; however, in the sea battle the Ionians won a great victory and Herodotus says that the ships from Samos especially distinguished themselves. Cary and Gray claim that since "nothing further is heard of the Phoenician fleet for three years, its defeat was probably complete enough to cripple it."[96] When the Ionian fleet heard of the death of Onesilos and the defeat of the Cyprian army, the fleet returned to Ionia.[97]

On Cyprus the Persian army laid siege to the cities that had revolted except for Salamis, which Gorgos, the previous king and Onesilos' brother, had turned over to the Persians. Murray says that the Persian army was very professional and had developed a very successful approach to laying siege to walled cities. The Persian army did not depend upon catapults or other forms of artillery. Rather their engineers utilized siege mounds to access the cities. They probably used "impressed local labor" and prisoners to build the mounds. As they worked they were protected by Persian archers. Using the results of excavations at Paphus on Cyprus, Murray gives details of the Persian techniques. He explains that the Persians faced a city with a large ditch with a well-built stone-faced wall of mud brick behind it. Against this they raised a siege mound that was slowly extended over the ditch and against the wall. The excavated mound revealed a large amount of statues and stones from a local sanctuary as well as a concentration of three-winged arrows used by the Persian army and crude four-sided javelins and stones ranging in size from 2.7 to 21.8 kg that were used by the defenders. The Persians placed archers in siege towers to keep defenders off the wall. There were also signs that the defenders attempted undercut the siege mound by digging four different mines under it, but obviously they failed.[98]

In 496 BCE Persia had sufficient troops at Sardis to create three armies under three different generals, married to daughters of King Darius. Daurises took his army to the Hellespont where he retook the cities of Dardanos, Abydos, Perkote, Lampsacus and Paisos, after which he was directed to take his army to deal with the revolt in Caria. Hymaees took his army to the Propontus where he captured Kios. When Daurises took his army to Caria, Hymaees marched to the Hellespont where he was very successful in capturing Ilium (Troy) and the Gergithians; however, he then fell ill and died in the vicinity of Ilium. The third general, Otanes, along with Artaphernes, led an army against Ionia where they captured Klazomena and Cyme in Aeolis.[99]

According to Herodotus it is after the above victories by the Persian armies that "Aristagoras revealed how weak-spirited he really was" as he realized that the revolt was not going to succeed and he began to plan his escape. He called together his supporters in Miletus and suggested that they would "all be better off if they had some place of refuge in case they were forced to leave Miletus." He offered to lead them to set up a colony in Sardinia or to lead them to Myrcinus in Thrace. He ultimately decided upon Myrcinus, and after turning Miletus over to Pytagoas, an important citizen, he led his supporters to Myrcinus. While in Myrcinus, Aristagoras became involved in a war in the local area and was killed while laying siege to a Thracian city.[100]

When Daurises arrived in Caria with his army, he found a very different situation from the Hellespont campaign. The Carians had been expecting an attack, so they were prepared to fight. Also the Carians were more used to battle and had large numbers of professional soldiers who had fought in other lands among their troops.[101] The Carians gathered their forces at the White Pillars at the Marsayas River where they had a discussion among themselves as to whether they should cross the river and fight with the river at their backs so there would be no escape which would motivate the soldiers to stand and fight, or whether they should allow the Persians to cross the river and have the river at their backs. The Carians wisely decided to allow the Persians to cross the river, but the Persians were still victorious after a hard-fought battle because of their superior numbers. The Persians lost 2,000 men while the Carians lost 10,000 men.[102] The Carians who survived fled to Labaunda where they were trapped in a sanctuary of Zeus Statios. The Carians were considering surrendering when reinforcements from Miletus and its allies arrived. The reinforced Carians attacked the Persians, but once again they were defeated, this time even worse than the first time, with the Milesians taking the worst casualties. With victory within their grasp, the Persian army during a night march to attack the Carians' cities "stumbled" into an ambush set up by the Carians, and the Persian army was annihilated and all their generals, including Daurises, were killed.[103]

How did the Carians manage to come up with sufficient forces to defeat the Persians after they had just experienced two devastating losses to the Persians? In Herodotus' account the three battles occur one after another with seemingly little time between them. Grundy suggests that perhaps the Persians had also suffered losses in the first two battles and thus had to wait for more reinforcements to arrive before making their final advance. Such a delay would allow the Carians to rally and come up with sufficient forces to set the ambush that destroyed the Persian army.[104] Looking at Herodotus' statement in 5.121 that "afterword the Carians recovered from their disaster and renewed the struggle," Harris thinks that it is plausible to interpret the statement as allowing a period of time, perhaps substantial, between the second defeat of the Carians and the third battle in which they were victorious. He then suggests that after the second victory the Persians felt no reason to give the Carians any reasonable terms for surrender. He believes that winter intervened between the battles, giving the Carians time to draw together additional forces to make a final stand in defense of their cities. He also thinks that the Persians probably believed that their two victories had eliminated any large-scale resistance and that they had entered "the mopping up phase" of the campaign. Thus they were caught totally by surprise in the night ambush and their army was annihilated.[105]

At this point Herodotus describes Histiaeus arriving in Sardis. During a discussion about the Ionian Revolt Artaphernes concluded the discussion by saying, "Well, then, let me tell you how and why it happened, Histiaeus: you stitched up the shoe and Aristagoras put it on." Histiaeus, fearing what action Artaphernes might take against him, fled during the night to Chios. When he arrived in Chios, the Chians arrested him and confined him, believing him to be an agent of King Darius; however Histiaeus managed to convince the Chians that he really favored the revolt and they released him. Histiaeus then sent letters to individual Persians in Sardis with whom he had discussed a possible revolt against Artaphernes; however, Artaphernes intercepted the letters and executed the conspirators. Histiaeus then asked the Chians to restore him to Miletus, but the Milesians rejected him because they were happy to be rid of Aristagoras and "they had no desire whatsoever to accept another tyrant into their land."[106]

After being rejected, Histiaeus attempted to take Miletus by force in a night attack, but he failed and was wounded in the attempt. He returned to Chios and asked for ships to command, but the Chians refused to grant them. Histiaeus then made his way to Lesbos and convinced them to give him eight ships which he took to Byzantium where he seized ships "sailing out of the Pontus, except for those whose crews asserted that they were willing to follow the commands of Histiaeus."[107] There is a great deal of controversy concerning Herodotus' account of Aristagoras and Histiaeus, so the views of modern historians on these individuals will be covered in a later section in this chapter.

After the disastrous defeat of the Persian in Caria, Herodotus suddenly becomes quiet about any further role for the Carians in the revolt. In fact he has little to say about any other actions by either the Ionians or the Persians until the final assault on Miletus and the Battle of Lade. Regarding Caria, Grundy suggests that after the Persian defeat in Caria, Artaphernes turned to diplomacy in an effort to detach the Carians from the revolt. He hypothesizes that Artaphernes nullified their role in the revolt by "offering her a share of the spoils of the enemy." He supports his hypothesis by pointing to the "non-participation of Carians in the years following the Persian defeat, and the unexpected grant to a Carian city" after the fall of Miletus.[108] Cary and Gray acknowledge that the campaign seasons of 496 and 495 are blank in Herodotus and attempt to explain the lack of action by saying, "the defeat of their fleet at Cyprus and of their army in Caria compelled the Persians to mark time; the disunion of the Greeks prevented them from making a counter-attack."[109]

In 494 the Persians combined their armies into one and advanced against Miletus, which was seen as the most important target area. In addition they brought together their navy made up of Phoenician, Cyprian, Cilician and Egyptian ships which also advanced on Miletus. While the Persians were gathering their forces, the Ionian cities sent their representatives to the Panionian near Mycale to plan their response.[110] Only eight of the league cities attended the meeting, and while we know that Klazomena fell to the Persians under Otanes, Colophon, Ephesus, and Lebedos were also absent. Perhaps these three cities had also been captured, or perhaps they had made their own peace with Persia by that time.[111] The Ionian Council decided not to attempt to meet the Persian army on land but rather to have Miletus defend its own walls; however, the decision was made to meet the Persians at sea where the Ionian fleet had experienced success in the past by assembling "a naval force that would include every one of their ships without exception." The ships were ordered to meet at a small island near Miletus called Lade.[112]

The Ionians were able to assemble a naval force of 353 triremes which included 80 ships from Miletus, 12 ships from Priene, 3 ships from Myous, 17 ships from Teos, 100 ships from Chios, 8 ships from Erythrai, 3 ships from Phoceae, 70 ships from Lesbos and 60 ships from Samos. Lateiner points out that the Ionians were the dominant naval force at that time and that its 353 triremes were greater than the 320 ships the Greeks massed at Artemisium and just short of the 380 Greek ships at the battle Salamis.[113] Harris does not think that the figure of 353 triremes is exaggerated as he points out that the Ionians seized 200 ships after the Naxos campaign and that for them to construct 153 additional ships by 494 does not seem unreasonable.[114]

Herodotus claims that the Persian fleet had 600 ships, but this number is not so easily accepted. Grundy has no trouble accepting 600 ships, calling it a "naval levy"; however, Harris accepts Hignett's view that 600 is a "stereotypical figure ... for any large fleet" since it appears so often, as in the Scythian campaign, the Battle of Lade and the Marathon campaign. Harris then goes on to point out that "the behavior of the Persians at Lade strongly suggests that they had no great numerical superiority over the Greeks."[115]

Concerning the Ionian strategy at Miletus, Lateiner states that it was unreasonable from the Greek point of view to think that they could defeat the massive resources of the Persian army. Even if they were successful in a battle on land, the Persians could simply call up what appeared to be unlimited levies of troops until the Ionians were defeated or ran out of troops; however, an Ionian victory at sea was "no idle dream," and such a victory would have enormous benefits.[116] Harris describes these benefits:

> A decisive victory over the Persian fleet would have had several important and perhaps decisive results. The Ionians would have been assured control of the Aegean for some time to come, which would have left the island states invulnerable to Persian attack and would have

secured the mainland states from blockade by sea. Furthermore, a Greek victory would have prevented the reestablishment of Persian power on the European side of the waterway to the Euxine and its vital grain trade. Thus failure to wrest control of the sea from the Greeks might very well have permanently wrecked the Persian process of bringing the revolt to an end. The battle of Lade is therefore properly viewed as one of the most decisive battles in all of Greek history.[117]

After the Ionian ships had gathered at Lade, they met and chose Dionysius of Phocaea as their commander, even though he brought only three ships with him. Perhaps that is one reason he was chosen to lead them in addition to the fact that he was an excellent seamen. If the admiral of one of the four major sea powers was chosen, it may have created jealousy and disunity. For seven days Dionysius trained the Ionian ships and crews in column formation and also trained the rowers to execute the *diekplous*, a maneuver in which ships rowed through the line of enemy ships and then turned back to ram them. The training was hard and the sun was hot, and Herodotus tells us that after seven days the crews of the ships rebelled and refused further training and "pitched their tents on the island and remained in their shade, refusing to board their ships or practice their maneuvers."[118]

Meanwhile, when the Persian fleet arrived off Miletus and "the Persian generals learned how large the Ionian fleet was, they became frightened that they would be unable to prevail over it" and they hesitated to go into battle. Instead they called together the tyrants that had been deposed by the Ionians and asked them to contact their former subjects and tell them that if they would detach themselves from the Ionian fleet "no harm will come to them, nor will their sacred or private property be set on fire; ... But if they refuse to follow this advice and still preferred to engage us in battle despite our offer, ... We shall lead them into captivity as slaves, and we shall turn their sons into eunuchs and drag their virgin daughters away."[119] When the deposed tyrants made contact with the contingents from their cities, they were met with refusal from all those they contacted.

After the Ionians turned against Dionysius, Aiakes, the deposed tyrant of Samos, again asked the Samians to break their alliance with the Ionians. This time the Samian contingent was more open to Aiakes' proposal as they "had observed the Ionians' extreme lack of discipline," and they felt that as a result the Ionians would be unable to defeat the Persian fleet; and even if they did manage to win, "they knew that they would certainly have to face another one five times as large."[120] Lateiner points out that there were probably additional reasons for Samos agreeing to defect to the enemy. Samos had been the major sea power before the conquest of Ionia by the Persians, and Miletus was given preferential treatment by Cyrus. Also the population of Samos had been greatly reduced by a Persian massacre when Syloson had been reinstalled as tyrant in 515 BCE Finally, Samos had been a bitter rival of Miletus for the past 200 years. The Persian successes in its counterattacks on the mainland and the defeat of the Cyprians had caused Samos to lose enthusiasm for the revolt. They probably wondered why they should aid Miletus, Chios and Lesbos when none of them had come to the aid off Samos when they had pleaded for help in 515 BCE The Samians may have also thought that Persia would grant Samos the "most favored status" that Miletus had used so effectively to multiply its wealth. Finally, they may have thought that with the defeat and punishment of Miletus, Chios and Lesbos, Samos would once again become the leading naval power in Ionia.[121]

In his study *Medism: Greek Collaboration with Achaemenid Persia*, Graf states, "The contentious Greek states were frequently found to have remained divided and many of them viewed compromise with the foreign invaders an attractive means to achieve supremacy over their rivals."[122] After the revolt was crushed, Samos was the only island that was not sacked and burned, and their temples and sanctuaries were also spared. In addition, Samos became the headquarters for the Persian fleet with all the economic advantages it brought with it. From the above discussion is Samos' decision a surprise?

The Ionians needed to take action as soon as possible since their base at Lade "was cramped, unhealthy and hard to supply." All their food and water had to be brought to the island by boat. The Persians on the other hand dominated all the territory outside the walls of Miletus and had easy access to water and food.[123] Yet it was the Persians who attacked first, feeling comfortable that their appeals to the Samians had reached fertile soil; however, the Ionians were not caught unprepared.[124]

The Ionians sailed out and, just as they had practiced under Dionysius, prepared to execute the *diekplous* in order to route the Persian fleet; however, just as the forces closed for battle, the Samian fleet of 60 ships, their total fleet except for 11 that stayed to fight, raised their sails and abandoned their colleagues, sailing to Samos. This caused the Lesbian fleet of 70 ships to also raise their sails and leave the battle, followed by the majority of the other ships. The Chian fleet of 100 ships "did not think it right to act as cowards," so they stayed to fight, performed the *diekplous* and took many of the Persian ships, but at the cost of most of their own ships. The few that survived sailed to Chios. The 11 Samians ships that stayed fought honorably to their death and were later rewarded with a pillar erected in Samos by their government that listed their names and proclaimed that they "had proved themselves to be brave and valiant men."[125]

When Dionysius of Phocaea recognized that the battle was lost, he seized three of the Persian ships and sailed to Phoenicia where he captured many merchant ships and "amassed a large sum of money," after which he sailed to Sicily where he became a pirate, but he only attacked Carthaginian and Tyrrhenian ships, never attacking Hellenic ships. Some of the survivors of the defeated Chian ships reached Mycale and set off on foot to return to Chios. When they entered Ephesian territory, a women's ritual honoring Demeter was taking place outside the city walls of Ephesus. Claiming that they were unaware of the Chians' identity, the Ephesian army attacked and killed the Chians as they thought that the Chians were pursuing the women performing the ritual.[126] Harris points out that Ephesus had not been a strong supporter of the revolt, and he believes the Ephesians wiped out the Chian survivors in all probability in an effort "to restore themselves in favor with the Persians."[127]

After their victory at Lade the Persians laid siege to Miletus by land, and sea and in the sixth year of the Ionian Revolt, Miletus fell to the Persians. Herodotus claims the fall of Miletus confirmed the oracle from Delphi. The oracle had stated,

> The time will come, Milisians, divisors of evil deeds, and When many will feast on you: a splendid gift for them; Your wives will wash the feet of many long-haired men, And others will assume the care of my own temple at Didyma.[128]

As promised in their appeal to the tyrants before the Battle of Lade, the Persians treated Miletus in an uncharacteristically harsh manner. Gillis believes that they were treated so harshly not only because Miletus had been the center of the revolt but also because Miletus had been given special privileges starting with King Cyrus. Therefore, he thinks the Persians considered that Miletus' role in the revolt was "especially heinous and demanded special punishment."[129] The majority of the men of Miletus were killed and the women and children were enslaved. The sanctuary at Didyma was plundered and burned, and the "Milesians who had been captured alive were taken to Susa where the king resettled them in the city of Ampe on the Persian Gulf." The territory around Miletus was kept by the Persians; however, the Hill country was granted to the Carian city of Pedasa probably on the basis of an agreement made to end the revolt in Caria.[130]

Aristagoras and Histiaeus

Since Aristagoras and Histiaeus played such an important role in the account of the Ionian Revolt by Herodotus and due to the fact that their motives and actions are open to various interpretations, it becomes necessary to devote a section to these two individuals.

Grundy claims that Aristagoras made plans to revolt against Persia before the Naxos campaign and possibly long before the campaign, but he agrees with Herodotus that the Naxian campaign was the "immediate efficient cause of the revolt." In fact he claims that Aristagoras jumped at the opportunity to help the Naxian exiles as that would bring together the Ionian fleet which Aristagoras could use as the backbone of his revolt. Grundy asks why Aristagoras didn't start the revolt before the Naxos campaign. He explains that even though the fleet was Ionian, it contained a large detachment of Persians which had to leave the fleet before it could be seized. In addition, he points out that by beginning the revolt at the end of the campaign season, it gave Aristagoras and the rebels time to gain allies in preparation for facing the Persians. He then goes on to address the "tale of a man with the tattooed head." He states that there is no reason to "suspect the truth of it" and claims it probably proves that Histiaeus had been in the preplanning for the revolt before he "made his involuntary journey to Susa." In addition Grundy points out that Histiaeus' position at Susa had shown Aristagoras that "the Persian authorities had no intention whatever of allowing even the most faithful and most favored Greek tyrant to acquire a position of real power on the coast." Therefore the only reason Aristagoras would take on the plight of the Naxian exiles was to use it as an excuse to gather the Ionian fleet together.[131]

Lang agrees with Grundy that Aristagoras had plans for revolt prior to the Naxos campaign. She points out there was little chance that Aristagoras could achieve power over Naxos, saying that even if Persia gained control of Naxos, it is doubtful that Darius would have considered allowing the tyrant of Miletus to also control the Cyclades. She agrees that Histiaeus was involved in planning the revolt long before 499 BCE and believes Histiaeus chose Myrcinus because of its wealth which could be used to support a revolt in the future and also would serve as an excellent base from which to attack "Persian installations in the North." She suggests that Histiaeus "left the leadership of the revolt" with Aristagoras and that Histiaeus would be able to aid the revolt while "in the Persian bosom" and that being in Susa he would know when the best time was to attack. She also agrees with Grundy that the message from Histiaeus to Aristagoras was telling him that it was a good time to revolt.[132]

After examining Grundy's arguments, Blamire concluded that Grundy's claim was not supported by the evidence. Harris is in agreement with Blamire, claiming that "Grundy's radical revision of the story creates more difficulties than it solves." He states that to accept Grundy's theory requires one to reject the picture that Herodotus gives us regarding Aristagoras and then would require us to reinterpret evidence every time Aristagoras enters the picture. He also claims "there is not a shred of evidence that a full-blown conspiracy of revolt existed before ... the Naxian expedition." But he adds that if there was such a conspiracy, it seems "impossible that the Greek tyrants that commanded the naval contingents could have been kept in ignorance for the best part of two years." He concludes that there is no reason to reject Herodotus' version "that at the inception of the Naxos campaign, Aristagoras was playing his own game."[133]

While Grundy and Lang accepted Histiaeus' message to Aristagoras using the tattooed slave as historical, many historians do not. Chapman states that "we can hardly take the details of the story seriously and many historians have regarded the account as agreeable fiction; even if we do believe that some sort of message was sent, the timing was too good to be true." He then examines the possibility that Histiaeus and Aristagoras were in contact and that he encouraged Aristagoras in general terms to revolt; however, Chapman considers it "doubtful" and claims "the absence of any plausible motives" for Histiaeus to revolt against Darius.[134] Blamire says that the story of the tattooed slave is "legend," but claiming it is a legend does not deny the possibility that Histiaeus and Aristagoras were in communication; however, he states that for the idea that Histiaeus and Aristagoras were secretly communicating with each other, "it will have to be shown that the circumstances of the time were such as to render any alternative hypothesis untenable," and no one accepting that Histiaeus was responsible for the revolt has been "successful in showing this."[135] Georges suggests that Artaphernes forced Aristagoras to revolt and that Aristagoras needed to convince others that he had Histiaeus' approval. He points out that the "tattooed slave" was a well-known folklore figure and that Aristagoras might have arranged to have the messenger from Histiaeus tattooed so that he could produce the slave as proof that Histiaeus supported him as he worked to win approval of his plans in Milesia.[136] Manville thinks that a message on a slave's head is simply "too romantic" to be even considered true. He considers however that a more orthodox message is possible, except the arrival of the message just as Aristagoras is considering revolting is too contrived to be true. And yet he states that the failure of the Naxos expedition might have caused Histiaeus and Aristagoras to consider a revolt at the same time. However, his interpretation of a possible message is very different. He believes that Histiaeus still considered himself answerable to Darius, for what occurred in Miletus was still of concern to Darius, and Aristagoras' failure at Naxos caused him to worry as to how Darius might react. So he decided that he needed to take action to be sure that Aristagoras' mistakes did not reflect poorly on him. He felt that if he was successful in resolving the problems at Miletus, Darius might reward him by letting him return to power in Miletus.[137]

How are we to see Aristagoras? Herodotus describes Aristagoras as an individual out for himself, who uses the Naxian exiles in an attempt to increase his power and prestige and who starts the Ionian Revolt in order to extricate himself from the difficult position he found himself in after the failure of the Naxos expedition. Herodotus has Aristagoras plan the Sardis expedition but tells us that Aristagoras does not lead it, rather staying in Miletus, implying that he was not a courageous leader. In addition, when the Persians begin their counterattack and Cyprus falls, Aristagoras "revealed how weak spirited he really was" and began to think about saving himself.[138]

Many historians have criticized Herodotus for the way he describes Aristagoras and Histiaeus, claiming he was biased and purposely made them look bad. Grundy paints a very different picture of Aristagoras. He says that the early measures that Aristagoras took during the revolt "showed high ability, if not genius" and states that "the period during which the revolt was formidable" was when Aristagoras played the leading role in it. He defends Aristagoras' move to Myrcinus by saying that Aristagoras was suggesting that a place of retreat should be established should one be required. He explains that Aristagoras took his proposal to his fellow conspirators and had them vote on it. Only after the majority supported his action did Aristagoras and his supporters leave Miletus after he had put a prominent citizen in charge there. He concludes, Aristagoras "went out to secure a refuge for his fellow citizens and died in so doing. He never returned because he could not return."[139]

Evans sees Aristagoras as having mixed motives. Self-interest was obviously in the forefront of his decision making, but he also sees Aristagoras as idealistic. He describes him as "a man who could champion the unfortunate Myndian captain, Scylax, against a cousin of the great King, was quite capable of championing Greece against Persia with ideals as high as any Miltiades or Themistocles could muster." He goes on to point out that "successful rebels become heroes; unsuccessful ones are less fortunate."[140]

Lang believes that Herodotus is unfair in placing the blame for the Ionian Revolt on Aristagoras' personal quarrel with Artaphernes. She claims that while Herodotus belittles the success of the Sardis expedition planned by Aristagoras, in fact it must have been a "tremendous success" because it put the Persians on the defensive and encouraged others to join the revolt. She also claims Aristagoras is not given credit for his strategic thinking and that his leaving Miletus, rather than demonstrating a weak spirit, was an attempt to plan for the future should a refuge be needed. She also sees it as a move to create a diversion and force the Persians to spread their troops.[141]

Manville sees Aristagoras in a struggle with Histiaeus for control of Miletus. Aristagoras was Histiaeus' deputy in Miletus, but he had been in control probably for 14 years when the Ionian Revolt broke out. Manville believes Aristagoras went to Artaphernes for support of his Naxian expedition, "forsaking Histiaeus." But while he goes on to say that we do not have to believe that Aristagoras was a "treacherous and ungrateful deputy," we also have no evidence to show that he was not. When the Naxian expedition failed, Aristagoras feared not only Artaphernes' response but also Histiaeus'. He says that Aristagoras was a more radical leader than Histiaeus might have expected. Aristagoras' rapid organization of the revolt ensured that it would be long and bitter. Regarding Aristagoras staying at Miletus during the attack on Sardis, he suggests that Aristagoras might have feared Histiaeus' return and that civil war over control of Miletus could break out. Finally, when Aristagoras left for Myrcinus he believes that Aristagoras was seeking power, not refuge, and that desire for power led to his death in Thrace.[142]

Georges makes an interesting comparison of Aristagoras to Cleisthenes. He believes that Aristagoras faced threats to his power, since he drew his authority from Histiaeus, from both the oligarchic right and "advocates of free politics" within Miletus. He learned from Cleisthenes, who had put himself at "the head of the forces for change" when his political power was threatened. Thus Aristagoras had championed the cause of *isonomia* and probably converted his tyranny to see the new regime into being."[143] Cawkwell, writing in 2005, gives the strongest endorsement of Aristagoras. He states,

> The truth can no longer be avoided. I believe that de Sanctis was right when he pronounced Aristagoras one of the heroes of Greek liberty. Herodotus' account of him is so plainly unsatisfactory that one inevitably suspects that his denigration of Aristagoras was a result of prejudice, apologia, and misunderstanding. He makes Aristagoras a coward choosing escape to Thrace when his ill-conceived self seeking plans miscarried. I see him as a man of political vision, who when the mainland Greeks failed him took the sensible decision to move the Ionians to a colony on the Strymon.[144]

About the time that Aristagoras was leaving Miletus, Histiaeus was arriving in Ionia on a mission from Darius to end the revolt. In the court at Susa, Histiaeus faced much criticism even though he learned the Persian language. Many disliked him because of "his excessive influence with the king," and among them were powerful men like Megabazos, the general who had opposed Histiaeus receiving Myrcinus; Harpagus, a general who might have been a descendent of Harpagus who had helped Cyrus expand his power by betraying the Medes; and Artaphernes, Darius' half brother; however, Darius retained faith in Histiaeus and sent him to Ionia to bring an end to the revolt.[145]

Histiaeus went to Sardis in an attempt to gain support for his mission from Artaphernes. Some argue that he should have gone directly to Miletus if his goal was to negotiate. They ask why he stopped at Sardis and suggest he had other motives than negotiating; however, the royal road leads to Sardis, and any actions that he would take would require the support of the local satrap. It is also pointed out that Artaphernes wanted revenge for the burning of Sardis and would make "the perfect sponsor for Histiaeus' return to Miletus"; however, his timing was not good. By the time he arrived, Aristagoras had left Miletus, the Cyprian revolt had been quelled and the revolt seemed to be on the downturn. Thus Artaphernes, who had no love for Histiaeus or any Greek at Persian court, "would have no further dealings with cunning Greeks." Instead he accused Histiaeus of being complicit in the revolt, and Histiaeus quickly made plans to leave Sardis for fear of Artaphernes' possible actions against him.[146] Chapman adds that the breakdown between Histiaeus and Artaphernes occurred over the best means to end the revolt. Histiaeus favored diplomacy as it would make him look good to the king, while the Persian successes in Cyprus and Asia Minor "may have encouraged Artaphernes to press for a final and crushing victory."[147]

Georges suggests that Artaphernes did not have the total trust of Darius. He explains that Darius sent generals and administrators close to him to serve Artaphernes. He then goes on to state that Histiaeus must have convinced important Persians in Sardis that he had the support of Darius when he spoke with them about a possible revolt against Artaphernes. Georges points out that Darius had waited until after the Ionian Revolt had failed before he raised new forces for the occupation of Thrace. Then Darius took steps against Artaphernes by bringing in new generals and appointed new advisers to Artaphernes before he removed Artaphernes himself.[148] Blamire points out that Darius had little trust in his satraps, and he believes that Darius' decision to allow Histiaeus to leave Susa was part of a plot against Artaphernes. He adds that Artaphernes' efforts to expand his territory created many enemies for him among his fellow Persians.

After fleeing from Sardis, Histiaeus went to Chios where he was arrested as an agent of the Persian king. Histiaeus managed to convince the Chians that he was not a Persian agent and rather was in favor of the revolt and that he had encouraged Aristagoras to revolt in the first place.[149] While in Chios, Histiaeus sent letters to the Persians in Sardis, with whom he had discussed revolting against Artaphernes. But the messenger carrying letters, probably expecting a major payday, took them instead to Artaphernes. Artaphernes sent them on to the Persians but had the messenger return their replies to him. When he had the replies, he ordered the Persians arrested and executed.[150]

Realizing that his plot against Artaphernes had failed, Histiaeus asked the Chians to return him to Miletus; however, the Milesians refused him entrance to their city because they were "rid of Aristagoras and did not want another tyrant" in their land.[151] Blamire claims that he was not rejected because they did not want another tyrant but rather because of his reputation—"that of an ex-tyrant and an agent of Darius."[152] After being rejected entry, Histiaeus returned at night with troops and attempted to gain entry to the city by force. He was once again prevented, and this time he was wounded in the attempt.

After failing to gain entry to Miletus the second time, Histiaeus returned to Chios and asked to be put in command of some ships. The Chians refused his request, and Histiaeus crossed over to Mytilene on Lesbos and convinced them to give him the command of eight triremes. Herodotus tells us that he took the ships to Byzantium where he "seized ships that were sailing out of the Pontus, except for those whose crews asserted they were willing to follow Histiaeus."[153] While not using the specific term, Herodotus certainly implies that Histiaeus has simply become a pirate.

Grundy asked the question, if Histiaeus had become a pirate, why did the Ionians allow him to act in such a manner? He points out that Lesbos is but a two-day sail from Byzantium and that they certainly had sufficient ships to stop his piracy. As a result Grundy suggests that Histiaeus was "acting in the interest of those cities that had persevered in the revolt against those other Greek cities that had made or sought to make terms with the Persians."[154] Lang agrees that Histiaeus was not involved in piracy but rather thinks Histiaeus was working to support Ionian interest in the north as the revolt was failing in the south but could possibly be expanded in the north.[155] Blamire rejects as nonsense a view that Histiaeus was trying to starve the Ionians into submission with his blockade of the Bosporus straits. Rather, he believes Histiaeus was trying to drive up the price of grain which would allow him to make a great profit when he released supplies that he had captured.[156] Harris points out that the Persians had retaken the cities on the Asiatic side of the Hellespont but that the Greek cities on the European side were still free; however, controlling the cities on the Asiatic side meant that the Persians could harass shipping passing through the Bosporus straits. Therefore, he says that Histiaeus was not trying to blockade Ionian trade through the Bosporus nor was he trying to establish a power base in the north Aegean. Rather he suggests Histiaeus received a commission to take his fleet to Byzantium to "guard the grain routes from enemy harassment."[157]

When Histiaeus was informed about the result of the Battle of Lade, he left his affairs with a deputy and took his fleet and troops from Lesbos and sailed to Chios. When he was denied entrance to the island by a garrison, he attacked the garrison and took it. After taking Chios, Histiaeus attacked and laid siege to the island of Thasos "with a large force of Ionians and Aeolians"; however, when he heard the Phoenician fleet was sailing north from Miletus he returned to Lesbos with his entire army. What were Histiaeus' motives and goals for his actions? In two verses Herodotus describes Histiaeus' actions but gives us no indication of his motives or goals.[158] Blamire believes that Histiaeus' position near Byzantium was safe as long as the revolt continued, as neither side had the resources or time to deal with him; however, with the Battle of Lade that situation changed. He suggests that Histiaeus attacked Chios and Thasos in an effort to create a "sphere of influence" for himself. Thasos was his most important objective, as it was close to the gold mines of Thrace and also was the place that had the "remotest chance of resisting the tide of Persian conquests." Blamire also describes "a more ambitious program" for Histiaeus put forth by German scholars. They suggest that Histiaeus wanted to create an independent *Inselreich* (island state/empire). They also claim that Histiaeus remained a loyal subject of Darius so that an *Inselreich* under Histiaeus would remain subject to Persia. While it is an intriguing theory, Blamire claims "it lacks even a shred of supporting evidence."[159]

Grundy thinks that the results of the Battle of Lade drove Histiaeus to desperation but that he had a plan to save himself and his supporters. He believes his thoughts returned to Thrace and Myrcinus where he could establish a "rallying-point for the irreconcilables among the insurgents. He sought to resume in a modified form a design he had been forced to lay aside nearly 20 years before." But if that was his plan, why did he attack Chios? There are two interpretations of Histiaeus' actions. Herodotus makes Histiaeus hostile toward the Chians and wanted to "emphasize the despicable behavior of the various sections of the insurgents to one another when their fortunes had become desperate." Another view is that Histiaeus expected to be peacefully accepted at Chios and only attacked the garrison which would not admit him. That view points out that it is "remarkable there is no mention of any bloodshed save in the case of the attack on the garrison." Grundy points out that with the Persian victory at Lade the inhabitants of Ionia could expect a "terrible retribution" from the Persians, so there must have been thousands of Ionians seeking escape or refuge on the Ionian coast. Chios, which was off the coast of Ionia, was a natural place for the refugees to flock. By taking Chios, Histiaeus would find a large number of people willing to follow him if it meant possible escape from the Persians.

Once he had gathered more supporters and troops, he attacked Thasos. Why did he attack Thasos? He attacked Thasos because it fit into his plan, as Thasos had "considerable possessions on the lower Strymon" near Myrcinus; however, it was doubtful that Thasos would welcome a new power in the area which had brought them so much wealth in the gold mines in the region. Thus with the additional troops that he had gathered at Chios, Histiaeus attacked Thasos and laid siege to the city. Timing was very important as he had freedom of action only as long as the Phoenician fleet was still occupied in the south; however, before Thasos was taken, the Phoenician fleet began to move north and the Lesbians in his force demanded the return to Lesbos either to defend the island or to evacuate its inhabitants. When Histiaeus arrived at Lesbos they discovered the food supply of the island was exhausted, probably because of the many refugees fleeing from the Persians.[160]

In order to get food for his army and the inhabitants of Lesbos, Histiaeus and his army crossed over to the mainland at Atarneus to gather the grain from the plain of the Caicus River; however, as they were gathering the grain they were attacked by a Persian army under Harpagus, which happened to be in the area. A long battle ensued until the Persian cavalry made the final charge that decided the battle. Most of the Greek forces were destroyed and Histiaeus was taken alive. Herodotus states that Histiaeus "succumbed to such a cowardly desire to live" that he fled the battlefield. When a Persian soldier caught him and was about to kill him, Histiaeus called out in Persian "that he was Histiaeus of Miletus." Herodotus tells us that Darius probably would have forgiven Histiaeus "for his offense and that he would have suffered no harm"; however, Artaphernes and Harpagus also were concerned that Darius might forgive him. As a result they took Histiaeus and "hanged him from a stake" to make sure he could not appeal to the king, and they then cut off his head, embalmed it and brought it to the king.[161] Harris suggests that Artaphernes was quick to kill Histiaeus because the satrap might have been obliged to explain why he had wrecked a hopeful and royally approved diplomatic initiative on the basis of a personal grudge.[162] When Darius learned of the fate of Histiaeus, he reprimanded Artaphernes and Harpagus for not bringing Histiaeus before him alive. He ordered them "to wash the head, wrap it up tightly and to bury it."[163]

What conclusions can be reached concerning Histiaeus? Blamire blames Herodotus partially for the difficulty in judging Histiaeus. He says that it is the job of historians to ask questions about his sources and to decide if his informants "had any obvious motive for lying or distorting the truth." He goes on to state that "Histiaeus' personal enemies did have such motives, but the question is simply not one that Herodotus always troubles to ask."[164] Grundy says that Histiaeus had a plan but that too often "he miscalculated the means necessary to affect his design within the limited time within which it could possibly be successful. His cleverness was greater than his ability. He possessed the finesse of the schemer but lacked the practical reason of a man of action."[165] Manville points to his shifting loyalties to describe Histiaeus. He claims that Histiaeus often appears loyal to Darius, but at other times it seems that he is loyal to Ionia. He says Histiaeus' changing loyalties lead to different interpretations concerning Histiaeus by various historians. Manville claims that ultimately Histiaeus was loyal to no one but himself.[166]

After their victory at Lade, the Persian fleet was ordered to restore Aiakes as tyrant of Samos because of his work before the Battle of Lade. In addition the Persians were ordered not to burn the temples and sanctuaries on Samos because most of their ships had deserted at Lade. After reinstalling Aiakes on Samos, the Ionian fleet returned to Miletus for the winter.[167] The following year the Persian fleet moved north and took the islands of Chios, Lesbos and Tenedos with little resistance. When they took an island, they would "net" the people, which meant that the troops would join hands walking across the island so that no people could escape them. When the Persian army took mainland cities they also captured the people, but they could not "net" the areas. The Persians then carried out the threats that they had made before the Battle of Lade by castrating the most handsome boys, carrying off the most beautiful virgins to the king, killing the men and turning the women and children into slaves as well as burning the cities and their temples and sanctuaries. The fleet then sailed to the Hellespont retaking all the cities on the European side and Chersonese. It was at this time that Miltiades, the hero at Marathon, fled from the Chersonese back to Athens.[168]

After subduing the Ionians, Artaphernes called for envoys from all the Ionian cities and informed them of some changes. First he made all the cities "sign compacts with one another so that they would submit their disputes to legal arbitration and refrain from pillaging and plundering one another," and Artaphernes informed them that he would enforce the procedure. Secondly he reformed the taxation system. He ordered a new survey of all the land and based tax assessments for the imperial tribute on the results of the new survey. Herodotus claims the system worked so well it was still in effect when he wrote *The Histories*.[169]

Georges believes that the economic settlement of Artaphernes was quite harsh as it attempted to raise the same revenue from Ionia as it did in the past even though the population had declined and territory had been lost. He believes that Artaphernes did little to improve conditions in Ionia but simply restored similar policies that had caused the Ionian Revolt in the first place. He says Artaphernes' policies made little sense if the Persians were going to continue to depend upon the Ionians to play an important role in their navy.[170] The following spring Mardonius, a son-in-law of Darius, arrived in Ionia in command of a new army and deposed all the tyrants in Ionia and established democratic governments.[171]

While the reforms of Mardonius appear to be a major change in the Persian approach to governing the Greek cities in the west, Austin sees problems with that viewpoint. He claims tyrants are found in Samos, Chios, Lampsacus and perhaps Cos. Rather than calling it a turning point in Persian governance, he sees it "as at least a façade of constitutional government."[172]

What can be concluded about the impact and importance of the Ionian Revolt? Murray sums up its impact on Ionia by claiming it brought an end to Ionia's period of prosperity. He says that the Ionian cities that had dominated the trade in the Mediterranean Sea and the Black Sea were no longer a dominant force, and their economy did not regain a dominant position for "over 500 years." He says that prior to the Ionian Revolution, Ionia had been the center of important intellectual developments "in Greek poetry, philosophy, science and history"; however, after the Ionian Revolt, the center for intellectual creativity shifted to mainland Greece and was not to be regained.[173]

Gray and Cary agree that the Ionians sacrificed their future but thinks that they also saved the European Greeks. Instead of causing the Persian invasion of Greece, they believe the revolt put off the Persian invasion for seven years and gave the Greeks an opportunity to learn from the mistakes of the Ionians. The Greeks on the mainland came to recognize the importance of controlling the sea and the need for unified action if they were to be able to resist the Persians.[174] Cawkwell writing in 2005 concurs with Cary and Gray but adds that without the revolt the European Greeks would have "been less prepared psychologically to resist." He also points out that without the Ionian Revolt, the invasion of Greece would have been led by Darius instead of Xerxes, and he believes the Persians may have succeeded under Darius' leadership.[175]

In his work *Ionia under Persia, 547–477*, Harris summarizes the impact Persia had upon Ionia and the impact of the Ionian Revolt as follows:

> Few chapters of Greek history are more tragic than the fate of the Ionian states after the coming of the Persians. These cities, which had become leaders in the development of Hellenic civilization, and had originated so much of what has become the enduring legacy of Greece to

the Western world, found their vital, exuberant development suddenly arrested when they came within the orbit of the greatest empire the ancient world had produced up to that time. Unwilling to submit to the shackles of Oriental despotism, many of the most enterprising and creative sons of Ionia had taken refuge in areas beyond the reach of the great King. Those who remained, conscious of the ebbing vitality of the civilization of the Ionian homeland had taken the desperate gamble on unaided revolt against the massive power of Persia. Although a failure, the revolt had not been without its glorious chapters, and it can credibly be argued that by their long and courageous resistance to re-subjugation the Ionians had saved the Greek world. They had shown their European kinsman the reality of the Persian threat and had demonstrated that Persia was far from invincible, but they also had shown the hopelessness of resistance to the barbarian without unity of purpose and unity of command. But the salvation of European Greece from the barbarian did not mean the restoration of Ionia to the leading role she once played in one world after. As unhappy subjects and tributaries to Athens in the Delian Confederacy, the Ionian states thereafter became and remained rigid pawns between Persia and Greece until the dawn of the Hellenistic age.[176]

6

Greece and Persia, 492–490

After Mardonius had retaken the European side of the Hellespont he moved into Thrace with his army, and a huge fleet moved through "advancing toward Eretria and Athens. Those two cities were the professed goals of the expedition, but what the Persians really intended was to subject as many Greek cities as they could."[1] Briant believes that there is little doubt but that Macedonian Thrace had taken advantage of the Ionian Revolt to undermine Persian control and sees Mardonius' mission as being to reestablish Persian authority in those areas.[2] Grundy agrees with Herodotus' view that the goal of Mardonius was European Greece and uses the large army and navy, perhaps with more than 600 ships, to support his viewpoint.[3] Gray and Cary writing in the 1926 edition of the *Cambridge Ancient History* and Murray in the 1988 edition claim that Mardonius' mission was limited to reconquering and stabilizing Persian control in Thrace and Macedonia.[4]

It appears that Mardonius faced minimal resistance as he moved against Thrace and Macedonia; however, at one point while in Macedonia his force was attacked by the Byrgoi, a Thracian tribe, and Mardonius was wounded. The attack accomplished little as "Mardonius did not leave these regions until he had made them Persian subjects." When the Persian fleet sailed around Mount Athos to join Mardonius' army in Macedonia, it was caught in a storm that was so strong "300 of their ships were destroyed with more than 20,000 men." Herodotus concludes his description of Mardonius' expedition by saying, "so after these disgraceful failures the expedition withdrew and headed for Asia."[5] Grundy agrees that the disaster at Mount Athos prevented the Persians from moving into Greece, as the fleet was not in condition for "further advances; possibly because the actual loss of supplies had been great; possibly because it was left too weak in numbers and equipment to face the inevitable fighting in Greek waters." Grundy does not see the mission as a "disgraceful failure," as "Macedonia and Thrace (the southern part of it) were re-conquered and remained passive in the hands of Persia for thirteen succeeding years." Regarding the impact that the disaster at Mount Athos had on Darius, Grundy claims it had no impact upon his desire to punish Athens and Eretria and to conquer Greece other than causing him to alter "his plan of action." Darius was convinced that the Greeks and the western part of his empire were always a threat to rise up in rebellion as they had the liberty of the cities in European Greece with which to compare their own "servitude in Asia."[6]

The disaster at Mount Athos had shown Darius that he had underestimated the difficulty of conquering Greece. He now decided that the "route through the islands of the Aegean" would be a faster and safer route for his troops to reach Greece.[7] The following year after Mardonius' expedition, Darius sent envoys to Thasos "ordering them to tear down their city wall and to bring their ships to Abdera in Thrace."[8] While Thasos had withstood the siege by Histiaeus and had been using their wealth to build warships and to strengthen their walls, they still submitted to Darius' demand with no resistance.

Darius then sent out heralds throughout the Aegean to "find out whether they intended to wage war with him or surrender to him" by having the heralds demand "earth and water." At the same time Darius sent heralds to "tribute-paying cities along the coast with orders to build warships and vessels to transport forces." According to Herodotus many cities from the mainland submitted "earth and water" along with "all the islands to whom heralds had come with the request," although the only island mentioned by name is Aegina. Later Herodotus claims that the "Athenians had cast these heralds, when they made their request, down into a pit and the Spartans had thrown theirs into a well, and the heralds were told to take their earth and water to the King from there!"[9]

The issue of the Persian heralds as described by Herodotus has drawn much discussion from modern historians. Grundy accepts Herodotus' version and sees sending heralds demanding "earth and water" as an attempt by Darius to "minimize the danger of the expedition by detaching as many of the states as possible from the defense before the attack was actually made."[10] Hignett considers the story of the heralds as "probably unhistorical."[11]

Raphael Sealey, in his article "The Pit and the Well: The Persian Heralds of 491 BCE," describes a work by K. J. Beloch, a German historian, in which Beloch claims that the Persian heralds sent in 491 are a duplication of those who had been sent in 481, and in reality the only authentic heralds were the ones sent in 481. Beloch also claims that no heralds were ever sent to Athens and claims the Athenians made up the story because they wanted to match the Spartans in demonstrating their strong reaction to the Persians. Sealey says that Beloch's viewpoint has been widely accepted, and he specifically mentions Hignett to illustrate his point; however, he then proceeds to explain why he rejects Beloch's view and rather accepts Herodotus' version that heralds were sent by Darius in 491. Sealey claims that Beloch based his hypothesis on the belief that Persia did not plan to conquer Greece but only planned to punish Athens and Eretria. Sealey rejects Beloch's premise and claims that Persian plans to conquer Greece were demonstrated as early as the Scythian campaign of Darius which was not designed to conquer the Scythians but rather to settle his northern border and to gain control of the coastal road in Thrace as a land route to Greece. He sees the Naxian campaign as an attempt to gain control of the Cyclades as bases for the fleet to stop for water and supplies.[12]

The Ionian Revolt interfered with Darius' plans until 492 when he sent Mardonius along with a fleet to reassert control over Thrace and Macedonia; however, the naval disaster at Mount Athos caused Darius to switch his thoughts to a sea route through the Cyclades. But before he could send a major force by sea he needed to gain the landing bases in Greece, and that was the purpose of the expedition against Eretria and Athens. After demonstrating that Darius intended to do more than just punish Athens and Eretria, Sealey turns his attention to the actions of Sparta and Athens. He claims that the heralds had been sent by Darius because Aegina's decision to give "earth and water" caused Sparta to take hostages from Aegina in order to prevent Persian encroachment into European Greek territory. He then examines the internal politics in Sparta and concludes "opinion within Sparta was becoming sharply divided on the question of policy toward Persia. So those favoring resistance tried to commit the city to their policy by carrying out an outrage against the Persian heralds." Concerning Athens, Sealey claims that Persian aggression was not the main concern of Athen's foreign policy. Rather Athens was preoccupied with the threat that Aegina represented. When Aegina gave "earth and water" the Athenians feared Persia would supply "armed help" to Aegina. In reaction he claims the Athenians were "again carried away by a wave of mass-emotion" and as a result they threw the Persian heralds into the pit.[13]

Graf examines the view of Beloch and adds that Beloch rejected heralds being sent to Athens as "it was the focus of the Persian attacks and objects of revenge," and thus Persia would not allow Athens to escape punishment by giving "earth and water." Herodotus points out that the Persian fleet attacked Naxos and Carystos and conscripted troops to join with them and took hostages from the other islands. Beloch claims such actions by the Persians were "clearly incongruous with the peaceful submission to the heralds' advance." Therefore Beloch concludes there had been no heralds. Graf explains that others have taken a more moderate position, claiming that heralds were sent "primarily to the Aegean Islands." Clearly if the Persians were to use the southern sea route they would need to assure themselves "of naval stations in the Cyclades." Concerning Beloch's use of the fact that Persia had taken troops and hostages from the islands, they answer Beloch by claiming that the islands promised to furnish "contingents to the Persian fleet" when they gave "earth and water." The hostages were simply a precautionary move by the Persians to ensure the loyalty of the contingents from the islands.[14]

Finally Graf concludes that "the heralds had been primarily sent to the Cyclades to prepare a safe passage through the Aegean for the Armada on its mission of revenge." He goes on to say that perhaps heralds were sent to some of the more "powerful and crucial mainland powers like Sparta." As a result many believe that the harsh treatment the heralds received at Sparta was "the only authentic element in the story." The actions of Athens however appear to be a "contrived tale, perhaps created in the post-war to rival and complement the episode at Sparta."[15]

Graf also presents two viewpoints concerning Aegina providing "earth and water." One view sees Athens and Aegina as both being in the Peloponnesian League and Sparta's taking hostages from Aegina as simply being an internal matter of the league. As a result this view sees the story about Aegina giving "earth and water" as "an Athenian slander, propagated afterwards to abate the island's distinguished record during the Persian wars." The counter viewpoint claims that as a result of the defeat of Aegina in the "unheralded war" in 493, "Aegina had no other recourse but to seek Persian aid." They go on to explain that after Marathon, Aegina again gained the upper hand in a struggle with Athens which allowed Aegina to break with Persia and join the Greeks in defending Greece in 480. Graf seems to lean toward the second viewpoint as he sees Aegina as an important base if Persia wanted to move into the Saronic Gulf, so it would seem obvious that Persia would send heralds to Aegina.[16]

Herodotus tells us that Darius was unhappy with the results of Mardonius' expedition, so he replaced Mardonius with Datis the Mede and Artaphernes, the nephew of Darius and the son of Artaphernes, the satrap at Sardis during the Ionian Revolt, and ordered them to go to Greece and to "enslave Athens and Eretria and to bring back the captives as slaves to his presence."[17] Rather than replacing Mardonius because of his failure in 492, it appears more likely that Darius replaced Mardonius because of the serious wound that he received during the attack by the Byrgoi in Thrace.[18]

Why did Darius appoint two generals to replace Mardonius? It appears that Datis was the commander of the expedition, so perhaps Artaphernes was sent along to "keep an eye on him"; or maybe one was to be in charge of the fleet and the other in charge of the army, or there may have been a plan to split their forces into separate groups at some time during the campaign. While it might not be a surprise that Artaphernes, the nephew of the king, was not given command of the expedition, it is unusual to see a Mede put in overall command. Who was Datis the Mede?[19]

It appears that Datis was not a young man, as he had sons who commanded troops during Xerxes' invasion in 480.[20] Burn says that if the Lindos Temple Chronicle is to be trusted, it appears that Datis was in command of the Persian fleet when it first entered the Aegean and that Datis was senior to Mardonius at that time.[21] Kuhrt in her *Corpus of Sources* includes an excerpt from Ctesias in which he claims that Datis returned from the Pontus "in command of the Persian fleet."[22] Lewis claims that Datis was a person of "very high personage" and uses information from the Persepolis Fortification Tablets to support his claim. The tablets state, Daiya (Datis) received a travel ration of 70 quarts of beer and wine when he carried "a sealed document to the King." Lewis points out that the king's sisters received 30 quarts of ration when they traveled and that he has only come across two individuals with a higher travel ration that Datis. Thus he must have been a very important individual. He states that it was always believed that Datis had experience during the Ionian Revolt, but the fortification tablet is the first clear evidence to support that belief.[23] Based upon his experience with the navy and his experience in dealing with the Greeks, it made Datis a good fit to replace Mardonius. Balcer claims that it was Datis who recommended that the Persians use the sea route through the Cyclades instead of the route that Mardonius had taken.[24]

Most historians seem to agree with Herodotus that the goal of the expedition under Datis and Artaphernes was to punish Athens and Eretria for their interference in the Ionian Revolt. Grundy sees the expedition against Athens and Eretria as the final step in ending the Ionian Revolt. The expedition was meant to demonstrate to the European Greeks that they must not interfere in the affairs of the Persian Empire and was also meant to show the Ionians that if they considered revolting in the future, they could not expect help from the European Greeks.[25] In addition the expedition would also deal with Naxos and bring the Cyclades under Persian control.[26]

Datis, Artaphernes and their army met up with the Persian fleet which included horse transports in Cilicia. Herodotus says the fleet included 600 ships but does not mention the number of troops, which is unusual.[27] After boarding their troops, the Persian fleet sailed into the Aegean Sea and sailed up toward Samos into the Icarian Sea and turned southwest to sail down to attack Naxos. Instead of resisting the Persians as they had with the Naxian expedition under Aristagoras in 499, the Naxians fled their city into the hills. After enslaving those Naxians they caught, the Persians burned the city and their sanctuaries and set sail for the other islands. Without waiting for the Persians, the Delians fled their island to Tenos, a nearby island. When Datis discovered where the Delians had fled, he sent heralds asking them to return to their island because "the King has instructed me not to harm the site on which two Gods were born, nor the rest of the island or its inhabitants." Datis then sacrificed

300 talents of frankincense upon the altar in Delos. After leaving Delos the Persian fleet sailed to other islands conscripting troops and taking hostages. When they reached Carystos, on the island of Euboea, the city refused to give hostages or to provide troops to attack Eretria and Athens. The Persians "besieged the city and ravaged the land" until the city submitted to the Persians.[28]

Murray suggests that the Greeks did not feel immediately threatened by the Persian fleet when it entered the Aegean, as they expected that Datis would follow Mardonius' route along the Thracian coast and would not reach Greece until late in the campaign season. Instead when the fleet emerged out of the Icarian Sea and sailed against Naxos, the Naxians were caught unprepared and fled to the hills, allowing the Persians to land unopposed. Murray credits Darius with developing the bold strategy of attacking by sea through the islands and credits the Phoenicians for doing the careful planning that such a sea expedition required.[29]

Concerning the story that Datis sacrificed "300 talents of frankincense," Krentz points out that those 300 talents would equal 7.5 tons or 38 camel loads of frankincense. So it would seem to be an exaggerated statement; however, Krentz goes on to state that he "is prepared to believe that Datis brought 300 talents of frankincense which could have been carried in one merchant ship." He points out that while 38 camel loads seems huge, Darius received 141 camel loads from Arabia alone each year. Is the number of 141 camel loads each year an unreasonable number? He does not think so, as we know that 7,000 to 10,000 camel loads of frankincense entered the Roman Empire each year during the first century CE.[30]

With the Cyclades under Persian control, the fleet sailed to Eretria. When the Eretrians learned of the Persian approach, they sent messengers to Athens asking for assistance. The Athenians offered to have 4,000 cleruchs in Chalcis, a city about 6.4 miles from Eretria, go to the aid of Eretria. The Eretrians were not united, and there were splits concerning the strategy that they should follow. There was no doubt that they should not march out to engage the Persian army; however, some believed that they should all flee to the hills while others, "expecting to win personal gains from the Persians," were prepared to betray the city. While some of the Eretrians may have fled to the hills, the decision was made to stay inside the city and defend their walls. When the cleruchs arrived from Chalcis, Aischines, son of Nothon, the leading man in Eretria, told them that the Eretrians were not united and told the cleruchs to "return to their own land so that they would not perish along with the Eretrians." Heeding his advice the cleruchs departed and crossed over to Oropus in Attica.[31]

The Persians, finding no opposition, landed their troops in three different locations and marched on Eretria. Since the Eretrians refused to come out to face the Persian army, the Persians assaulted the city for six days, during which many died on both sides. On the seventh day two prominent citizens "betrayed their city and surrendered it to the Persians." The Persians plundered the city and burned their sanctuaries in retribution for the sanctuaries burned in the attack on Sardis, and enslaved the people as ordered by Darius.[32]

When Eretria asked for help from Athens, the Athenians voted not to send any aid to Eretria from Athens, but Herodotus includes the story of the Athenians offering the cleruchs to help Eretria and modern historians have commented on it. To some historians it seems that the number of 4,000 cleruchs is too high; but Scott points out that Herodotus never states that the cleruchs were all Athenians, and many may not have been of hoplite status.

He claims that Athens "set up a self-governing but satellite community, over which she had sufficient authority to instruct them to help Eretria."[33] Historians also question Herodotus' account concerning why the cleruchs left Eretria. Grundy claims that Herodotus' defense of the cleruchs leaving Eretria "was intended by its creators to cloak the cowardice of these cleruchs."[34] Scott agrees that the story "suggests an ex-post-facto Athenian attempt in light of the victory at Marathon, to gloss over their embarrassment of having failed to offer Eretria even moral support, much less tangible help."[35] Gray and Cary agree with Scott. They point out that Athens certainly benefitted economically from the destruction of Miletus and Eretria, and Herodotus seems to be trying to prevent the thought that Athens had abandoned its allies for her own economic benefit.[36]

How did the cleruchs cross over the Eoboean channel to Oropus? Gray and Cary believe that the Athenian fleet probably had been sent to Oropus to keep communication with Eretria open and the fleet was used to ferry the cleruchs over to Oropus.[37] In Herodotus' account, the Cleruchs exit his story at Oropus; however, Scott suggests that most probably they returned to Chalcis when the Persians were defeated and thinks some of them may have fought at Marathon.[38]

Murray explains how difficult it was to land seaborne troops and cavalry in ancient times. The ships had to be rowed close to shore in an area that was sheltered, the water calm and no underwater obstacles present. So they had to have local intelligence concerning possible landing areas. When the ships were in shallow water, the troops disembarked into the water and waded ashore. The horse transports had "let-down flaps" to offload the horses, but they had to move quickly because the horses became restless as they became excited by the smell and sight of land. The greatest danger to the landing came if the defending force caught the troops and horses in the water, which made them very vulnerable to missile weapons. In order to confuse the Eretrians and to split their forces, the Persians planned to offload their forces at three different landing spots.[39] Herodotus identifies the landing areas as Timynai, Choerseai and Aigilia, but modern scholars have not agreed on their exact locations. While there is disagreement, all three landing areas are placed either west or east of Amarynthos within 6 to 11 km (3.7 to 6.8 miles) of Eretria. The landing areas were probably chosen because the land between the landing areas and Eretria was flat so that it was acceptable for the cavalry.[40]

Murray calls the Eretrians' decision to stay behind their walls sensible, as they had about 5,000 troops and the city was surrounded by a high stone wall.[41] Scott points out that "Eretria is one of the few cities where walls are positively attested for mainland Greece prior to the fifth century. Scott also believes the decision of the Eretrians to defend the walls made sense. He says that the size of the Athenian aid and the superior numbers of the Persians must have caused them to resist confronting the Persian force in battle. He also points out that Eretrians were "seafarers, not soldiers" and that they had little military experience since they had not fought a war in over 200 years. While some of the Eretrians fled to the mountainous interior of Euboea, others felt that good terms could be negotiated. Finally, the Eretrians were unsure of what Athens might do based on the limited help they were willing to give to Eretria.[42]

Based upon Greek experience, defense was always stronger than offense when one was defending a walled city; however, the Persians were not your typical enemy as they were very experienced and effective in the use of siege warfare.[43] Usually the Persians built a siege mound or dug tunnels under the walls of the city to help them collapse, but that was a time-consuming approach. Since they planned to also move against Athens, they probably took a more direct approach and used ladders to scale the walls and battering rams against the gates; however, for six days the Eretrians fought hard and held out, with many casualties occurring on both sides. On the seventh day Euphorbus and Philogros, both prominent citizens, betrayed Eretria to the Persians. It can be assumed that negotiations between the pro–Persian action and Datis had been going on during the battle, but little is known of the two men or what reward they received for their treachery.[44] The betrayal of Eretria seems to reinforce Graf's conclusion that "internal factionalism of the Greek world overshadowed any ideal of the polis as the object of the individual's loyalty. Personal rivalry was the norm of political life and the polis was essentially the arena for entertaining competition and obtaining success over rival aristocrats and factions."[45]

The Persians plundered Eretria and burned their sanctuaries and enslaved the people, but Herodotus does not give details so the severity of the Persian punishment is uncertain. Krentz claims that the Persians "deported 780 Eretrians including old men, women and children," as logistics prevented the Persians from removing the entire population since space on the ships was limited. Scott thinks the Persians took a few hundred Eretrians and points out that Eretria seemed to recover quickly, as she sent seven ships to defend Greece in 480 and 600 hoplites to the Battle of Plataea. While Eretria did not regain its "trading eminence, the city subsequently played as prominent a part in Greek affairs as any other polis."[46]

With the fall of Eretria, the Persians had several options as to how to carry out their attack on Athens. Since Athens had abandoned Chalcis, the Persians could cross into Boeotia, where Athens' enemy, Thebes, might join them and they could link up with Persian forces in Macedonia before attacking Athens with a stronger force. Or they could attack Athens immediately before Athens received any aid from Sparta. Finally, they could land "in the Argolid, where Argos would join them and the line of communication between Sparta and Athens would be cut." Datis decided that their best course of action was to attack Athens immediately, so after spending some days organizing their base at Eretria, the Persian fleet sailed down the European channel and landed at Marathon.[47]

Murray evaluates the success of the Persian expedition at this point in the campaign. He thinks that Darius' strategy against Greece had worked very well. His forces had taken Naxos, the Cyclades were added to his empire and Eretria had fallen. His forces had been increased as they had taken conscripts, his lines of supplies and communication were secure and he had sufficient supplies as Eretria had accumulated supplies in preparing for a Persian siege.[48]

7

The Battle

The Battle of Marathon According to Herodotus

When the Athenians learned that the Persians had landed at the plain of Marathon, the Athenian army immediately marched to Marathon to confront the Persian army. Prior to leaving Athens the generals sent Philippides, a long-distance runner, to Sparta to request their assistance. He arrived in Sparta "on the day after he had left" and spoke to the Spartans, saying, "Lacedaemonians, the Athenians beg you to rush to their defense and not look on passively as the most ancient city in Hellas falls into slavery imposed by barbarians. For in fact Eretria has already been enslaved, and thus Hellas has become weaker by one important city." The Spartans replied that they would send aid but that according to their law their army could not leave Sparta before the full moon.[1] Meanwhile the Athenian army had reached Marathon and had established their camp in "the precinct of Herakles." Soon after they had made camp the entire army of Plataea arrived at the Athenian camp to aid Athens as in the past Plataea had placed itself under the protection of Athens and Athens had supported them.[2]

When the 10 generals of the tribes of Athens met to discuss their course of action, they were evenly split and five favored confronting the Persians in battle while the other five opposed going to battle because their forces were too small. Callimachus, the Polemarchon, held the 11th and deciding vote, so Miltiades approached Callimachus and made the following appeal.

> It is now up to you, Callimachus, whether you will reduce Athens to slavery or ensure its freedom and thus leave to all posterity a memorial for yourself which will exceed even that of Harmodius and Arostogeiton [legendary tyrant slayers]. For from the time Athenians first came into existence up until the present, this is the greatest danger they have ever confronted. If they bow down before the Medes, it is clear from our past experience what they will suffer when handed over to Hippias; but if this city prevails it can become the first among all Greek cities. I shall explain to you how matters really stand and how the authority to decide this matter has come to rest with you. We 10 generals are evenly divided in our opinions, some urging that we join battle, others that we do not. If we fail to fight now I expect that intense factional strife will fall upon the Athenians and shake the resolve so violently that they will medize. But if we join battle before any rot can infect some of the Athenians, then, as long as the gods grant both sides equal treatment, we can prevail in this engagement. All this is now in your hands and depends on you. If you add your vote for my proposal, your ancestral land can be free and your city the first of Greek cities. But if you choose the side of those eager to prevent a battle, you will have the opposite of all the good things I have described.[3]

Callimachus was convinced by the arguments of Miltiades and voted to "join battle." After the vote was taken the generals who had favored going to battle turned their days of command to Miltiades; however, Miltiades did not order an attack until it was his day to command. Miltiades deployed the army with Callimachus in command of the key right wing as it was customary for the *polemarchon* to command it. The 10 tribes were then posted in their numerical order and the Plataeans were charged with holding the extreme left wing. In order to make sure that his battle line equaled the Persian battle line, Miltiades had to weaken his center, but he kept his wings "strong in number."[4]

After the required sacrifices were completed and proven favorable, the Athenian army "charged at a run toward the barbarians." The distance between the battle lines was eight stades, or about a mile.[5] As the Persians observed the Athenians attacking, they thought that the "Athenians were seized by some utterly self-destructive madness," as the Athenians were "few in number" and were attacking without cavalry or archers to support them. Herodotus claims that the Athenians were the first Greeks to charge at a run against their enemy and were also the first to "endure the sight of the Medes clothing and men wearing it" while the name Mede had previously struck "terror into Hellenes." The armies fought for "a long time" until the Persian center, made up of Medes and Sakai, their best troops, broke through the weakened Greek center and "chased them inland"; however, while the Persian center was being successful, the Athenians and Plataeans on the Greek wings routed the Persian wings, after which the Greek wings drew together and defeated the Persian center. The Greeks pursued the fleeing Persians until they reached the sea, where the Greeks attempted to seize the Persian ships and burn them; however, the Greeks had little success as only seven ships were seized, and during the attempt Callimachus was killed; Stesilaos, another general, was killed; as well as other famous Athenians.[6]

After escaping, the Persian fleet set sail and picked up the Eretrian captives from the island of Aigilia and sailed around Cape Sounion in an effort to reach Athens before its army could return. Later the Alcmaeonidae were blamed for a shield signal sent to the Persians after they had boarded their ships. While the Persians were sailing around Cape Sounion, the Athenian army was quickly marching back to Athens, and they arrived at the city before the Persian fleet and set up their camp in "another sanctuary of Herakles, the one in Kynosarges." When the Persian fleet arrived off of Phaleron, the Athenian harbor, and saw the Athenian army, they anchored their ships "for a while, and then sailed back to Asia."[7] Meanwhile a 2,000-man Spartan army reached Athens on the third day after the full moon. They were disappointed that they had missed the battle, but they asked "to see the Medes." After marching to Marathon, the Spartans "praised the Athenians for their achievement and went home."[8]

The magnitude of the Athenian victory becomes clear when Herodotus tells us that the Persians lost 6,400 men while the Greek dead were only 192. Herodotus then tells an amazing story of Epizelus, a courageous warrior who "was stricken with blindness, though he had not been struck or hit on any part of his body." Rather, he observed a "huge hoplite whose beard overshadowed his entire shield," and "this phantom passed by Epizelus and killed the man standing next to him." Finally, Herodotus tells us, "I do not believe that they [the Alcmaeonidae] could ever have displayed a shield to the Persians pursuant to an agreement that was motivated by any desire on their part to subject the Athenians to Hippias and the barbarians."[9]

Chapter 1 examined various viewpoints concerning Herodotus' reliability as a source for the Persian Wars and found Hignett's conclusion most convincing. He stated that "Herodotus provides the only sure basis for a modern reconstruction of the Persian wars, as no reliance can be placed on the other ancient accounts where they differ from Herodotus." But he goes on to say that one must be aware of Herodotus' weaknesses and eliminate the fictions, gossip and legends; however, one must "make sure to the best of his ability that any statement or report in Herodotus really is untenable before he rejects it."[10] Concerning only Herodotus' account of the Battle of Marathon, A. W. Gomme, in an article in 1952 stated, "Everyone knows that Herodotus' narrative of Marathon will not do."[11] The statement occurs often in literature concerning Herodotus and the Battle of Marathon, so it appears acceptable to most historians; however, how much of his narrative is acceptable and what to do about the problems identified with the narrative certainly varies among historians.

In his commentary on Herodotus, Macan in 1895 wrote, "There is now, strictly speaking, nothing older or more primary for the purpose of reconstructing the story of Marathon."[12] He then proceeds to his major problems with Herodotus' account. He charges Herodotus with exaggeration when he says that the Athenians were the first to charge the enemy in a run, the first to sustain the site of the Median dress and men, and that the name Medes was a terror to the Greeks. He accuses Herodotus of being guilty of using anachronisms when he discusses the role of the *polemarchon*, the relations between the *polemarchon* and the *strategoi* and the relation between Callimachus, Miltiades and the other *strategoi*. He points out that Herodotus specifically mentions the Persian cavalry is at Marathon but never mentions it as taking part in the battle, and he claims the existence of the shield signal referred to by Herodotus is questionable. He then proceeds to list key omissions in Herodotus' account of the battle: (1) the exact date, (2) numbers engaged, (3) names of commanders and their behavior on both sides, (4) topography of the battlefield, and (5) how or why the battle was fought at Marathon.[13]

J. B. Bury writing in 1896 is even harsher on Herodotus. He states, "Anyone who reads critically the Herodotean account must see that Herodotus had not the smallest idea why the battle was fought, and had a very inadequate notion of how it was fought. He has collected a number of details, some true, others absurd; which are without any inner connection."[14]

How and Wells in their 1912 commentary on Herodotus continued the negative assault on Herodotus' coverage of the Battle of Marathon. They state,

> Yet if Herodotus be our best authority, his account is in many points defective and in some positively misleading. Compared with his descriptions of Thermopylae and Artemisium, of Salamis and of Plataea, it is meager and lacking in detail though the tactics employed are more clearly indicated. This slightness of the narrative shows itself in the omission of numbers engaged on either side, an omission emphasized by the record of numbers of the Athenians in Persians slain. It shows itself also in the omission of all reference to the monuments on the field of battle, described by Pausanias, the tombs of the Athenians and of the Plataeans and slaves, the trophy of white marble, and the memorial of Miltiades. It is seen in the vagueness of the historian's topography which makes it unlikely that he ever visited the field of Marathon. Herodotus' knows indeed that Marathon looks on the sea but he says nothing of the mountains that look on Marathon, nothing of the watercourse dividing the little plain, or the marshes at either end. It is probable that Herodotus, like Thucydides and Theopompus deliberately rejected a good deal at patriotic fiction with which Athenian, and above all Phil-

iad, tradition had already overlaid the plain facts and so found himself unable to construct from his material a detailed history.[15]

After stating that Herodotus' narrative of Marathon will not do, Gomme went on to ask, if we do not accept Herodotus' account as written, can we add to his account or try to correct his errors, or should we simply admit that we know too little to write an account of Marathon? He rejects the idea that one could accept one part of Herodotus while rejecting other parts, because such an approach would lead to many different versions of the battle based upon what individuals accepted or rejected. He says that this would be unsatisfactory. He suggests using Herodotus' basic facts as correct since he probably got them from veterans of the battle, but not to accept reasons for taking an action, as his sources probably were unaware of the reasons behind decisions. As an example of his approach he says that we could accept the fact that there was a delay before the battle took place but that we might reject the reasons given by Herodotus. He goes on to say that we could accept the fact that Herodotus' omission of the Persian cavalry was correct as the veterans he talked to would have corrected him if he was wrong.[16]

Not all historians have seen Herodotus' narrative of the Battle of Marathon as inadequate. Hammond in his long article on the campaign and Battle of Marathon in 1968 states that he is basically in agreement with W. M. Leake, who in 1828 declared that Herodotus' work was basically correct and trustworthy although we should be willing to accept facts from later writers, as Herodotus may have omitted them as he did not think they were significant.[17] Hammond goes on to remind us that Herodotus was writing history and reciting in Athens to men who had participated in the Battle of Marathon, so the facts he presented must have been correct or he would have been corrected by the veterans present. He also points out that we need to remember that Herodotus was not writing a military history for scholars who wish to reconstruct the battle. Rather he was writing to preserve "great and marvelous deeds." As an example, Hammond says that if the Persian cavalry did not perform any marvelous deeds, Herodotus simply did not refer to that cavalry in his narrative. Also his audience was well aware of the details surrounding the battle, so he did not feel the need to include many details that we would like to know today.[18]

J.A.S. Evans writing in 1993 agrees that "Herodotus is inexact and even exasperating," but he points out that Herodotus is our earliest source and also our only consistent narrative; however, he also states that the oral sources that Herodotus used were tainted by interest groups that wanted to influence how the battle was viewed in the future. He goes on to claim that the Athenians used the Battle of Marathon to claim that they were the saviors of Greece and used Marathon and their actions at Salamis and Plataea to justify "Athenian imperialism." Evans claims that by the time Herodotus consulted oral sources, the role of Miltiades had been greatly enlarged, and the Miltiades myth and the myth that Athens' victory at Marathon had saved Greece may have misled Herodotus; however, he also thinks that Herodotus only bought into part of the myths, and for this reason his account is brief and leaves questions unanswered.[19]

Norman Doenges writing in 1998 agrees with Gomme's view of Herodotus but feels the problem is not with Herodotus but rather is caused by the "uneven quality" of the sources which were available to him when he wrote. He believes that when Herodotus had reliable information he wrote an accurate narrative and points to the voyage of the Persian campaign through the Cyclades and the attack on Eretria as examples; however, he believes his description of the events at Marathon are not reliable because he was not sufficiently critical of the popular accounts of the battle that he received in Athens. He thinks that Herodotus 6.111–114 is the only valuable section of his narrative, as his sources were probably veterans of the battle.[20]

Kurt Raaflaub, writing in 2010, believes that it is impossible to write a totally acceptable history of the Battle of Marathon using only Herodotus. As an example, Raaflaub uses narratives by Hammond and Evans, who both agree on the accuracy of Herodotus, but who have written very different versions of the battle using the same account. Raaflaub says that the problem is not that Herodotus is incorrect or misleading because his sources mislead him, but rather because his account of the campaign is simply too short and too elementary. Raaflaub believes that this is extraordinary since the Battle of Marathon had become so important in the "Athenian memory, identity and ideology" by the time Herodotus was writing. Why would Herodotus treat such an important battle in such brevity when his coverage of the Battle of Plataea demonstrates that he is capable of doing much better? Raaflaub concludes that it was a conscious choice on the part of Herodotus to describe Marathon as an Athenian victory but not to exaggerate its importance. Rather he planned to use Xerxes' invasion as the center of his history and to describe the role of the united Greek poleis in resisting Xerxes and saving Greek liberty.[21]

The 2,500-year anniversary of the Battle of Marathon was marked in 2010 CE Three new books on the Battle of Marathon were published in English in 2010–2011. They were *Marathon: How One Battle Changed Western Civilization* by Richard Billows, *The Battle of Marathon* by Peter Krentz and *The First Clash: The Miraculous Greek Victory at Marathon and Its Impact on Western Civilization* by Jim Lacey. All of these authors agree that Herodotus is our best extant literary source and generally accurate in its facts, and yet they write very different accounts of that battle. Peter Krentz in an article in 2011 has identified eight questions Herodotus' account raises with modern historians. A paraphrased list of his concerns follows:

1. Herodotus does not tell how many Greeks and Persians fought against each other.
2. Herodotus does not tell the location of the sanctuary of Herakles where the Greeks camped.
3. Herodotus' description of the command structure at Marathon appears to be an anachronism.
4. Herodotus does not clearly define the position of the battle lines.
5. Why did the Greeks not wait for the Spartans before attacking?
6. Herodotus describes horse transports but does not mention the Persian cavalry in the battle.
7. Herodotus says that the Greeks charged at a run for eight stades while most scholars consider that impossible.
8. Herodotus does not clearly explain why the Greeks won.[22]

Krentz then proceeds to answer how Billows, Lacey and he dealt with each of the identified concerns. Krentz's approach seems to be a logical and efficient way to cover the various views and positions on the Battle of Marathon. Thus this chapter will examine a similar list of issues raised by the study of the Battle of Marathon and summarize how various scholars have dealt with the issues identified.

Topography

General Frederick Maurice, in his article "The Campaign of Marathon," states that "ground and the conditions of time and space were then, as they are today, the dominating factors both in tactics and strategy."[23] Fred Allen Ray, in his book *Land Battles in Fifth Century BC Greece*, explains that "knowing the physical factors present in any past battle is critical to grasping what actually took place, with fighting techniques, types and numbers of troops and casualties among the most basic of such concrete items."[24] The Greeks must have been aware of the importance of the topography of a battlefield as they always fought their hoplite battles on level ground, and yet Herodotus includes no topographical information on the plain of Marathon. So the first item to be examined will be the topography of Marathon.

The plain of Marathon is about six miles in length and about one mile in width. It is surrounded by mountains, ranging in height from Mt. Agrieliki in the southwest at 1,827 feet to Mt. Drakonera in the northeast at 794 feet to the Kynosoura Peninsula at 164 feet.[25] It is an alluvial plain, and the major waterway that formed it was the Charadra waterway that was often a torrent when rain fell, and along with smaller torrents carried vast amounts of material to form the plain.[26] In 1955 Pritchett followed the channel from end to end and observed banks as high as 18 feet in some places, and almost level at other areas.[27] Soteriades claimed that based on sherds he found on either bank of the Charadra, the waterway had not changed course since the fifth century BCE. Pritchett explored the Charadra again in 1956, accompanied by Professor Turner, department chair of geology at UCLA, who stated that "we have no indication where the riverbed ran in 490 BCE."[28] Pritchett returned to the Charadra again in 1959 with Professor C. Higgins of the University of California at Davis, who observed that the Charadra had flooded at times against two different mountains and that "lines of depression in the plain prove the existence of earlier channels different from the present one," one of which may have drained into the Great Marsh.[29] Hammond concluded that the course of the Charadra in 490 is unimportant as it would have been dry in September, and it was a minimal obstacle for either an advancing or retreating army.[30]

There is a large marsh at the northeast end of the plain. Pausanias describes it as "a mere" (small lake or pond), most of which is marshy. After their defeat, many Persians ignorant of the terrain were pushed into the mere during their flight, and it is said that "many died there." A river flows out of the mere, and near the mere the water of the river is good to drink, but as it gets close to the sea it becomes salty and full of sea fish.[31] Today, the marsh is 1.25 to 1.9 miles wide and 6 to 7 miles in circumference.[32] Did the marsh exist in 490, and if so what was it like? As a result of some recent work by geologists, we now have some answers. Citing work by Kosmos Pavlopoulos, who drilled boreholes in the western part of the marsh, Krentz claims that the marsh oscillated between freshwater and saltwater, but by 550 BCE the area was no longer "inundated by saltwater." Krentz goes on to refer to work by

Richard Dunn, who did drillings across the marsh while he was at the American School of Classical Studies in Athens in the 1990s. Based on his drillings, Dunn concluded that in 490 the marsh was actually a "shallow lake or lagoon open to the sea." Krentz explains that it is "uncertain whether in 490, the connection to the sea was wide enough and deep enough to permit Persian ships to enter the lake." Pointing out that the replica trireme (Olympia) has a draft of only 3.9 feet fully loaded, he speculates that some of the Persian ships may have anchored in the lake.[33]

In addition to the Great Marsh in the northeast, Leake in 1828 also identified a small marsh in the southwest part of the plain below Valaria, which was dry during the summer. In 1934, the Rockefeller Foundation drained the marsh to help control malaria. Soteriades claimed to find a harbor at the outlet of the marsh, archaic remains in the area and also an ancient road. From this he concluded that there was no marsh in the area of the small marsh in 490 BCE. Pritchett inspected the area in 1959 and found "what seems to be a tumulus, or possibly two adjacent tumuli, of perhaps the sixth century BCE." He goes on to say that only an excavation could prove that a tumulus existed, but in any case he concludes, "I think it is safe to accept the conclusion that there was no marsh in antiquity."[34]

After examining the arguments against a marsh existing in 490, Hammond disagrees with the prevailing opinion and believes a marsh did exist in 490. He believes that "the strength of the springs and the lie of the ground make it almost certain that in the fifth century BCE there was a marsh in the area."[35] Van der Veer believes "a better explanation of this phenomenon [powerful springs] can be given by taking into account the rising sea level, which forced back the water of the local spring."[36] An adequate water supply is obviously essential to any army, but especially to one on campaign during the hot, dry Greek summer. In the northeast part of the plain of Marathon, the powerful Macaria spring is found at the western corner of the Great Marsh. Leake, in 1825, describes the existence of several springs below which were "deep stagnant pools, fed by other subterranean sources."[37] In the southwest part of the plain, there were several springs near the camp of the Greeks, so both armies had good water sources. General Maurice adds that the Persians could also draw water from the Charadra, although most assume that the Charadra was dry in September when the battle took place. Van der Veer believes the Persians "probably dug wells along the north-east coast into which freshwater was pushed back by the saltwater from the sea." Scott and van der Veer believe both armies had adequate water supplies; however, Lacey estimates that the Persian forces needed about 60,000 gallons of water each day for men and horses and thinks it unlikely the Persians could meet their needs, as the Greeks probably damned up any streams that might have been available to the Persians.[38]

Herodotus tells us that the Athenians took up "their position in the precinct of Heracles" when they arrived at Marathon; however, he does not identify exactly where it was located, so historians and archaeologists have come up with a variety of possible locations over time without any one receiving universal acceptance. In 1846, Leake located the Herakleion "at the foot of Mount Agrieliki about three-quarters of a mile southeast of Vrana." In 1876 Lolling placed the Herakleion at a stone enclosure called "the old woman's sheepfold" in the narrow valley of Avlona. In 1934, Soteriades placed Herakleion near the chapel of St. Demetrius on the lower slope of Mt. Agrieliki. In his summary of archaeological work done in Greece during the years 1933–1934, H. G. G. Payne of the British School of Athens stated,

"The excavation at Marathon has been conducted by Soteriades, who identified beyond dispute the site of the sanctuary of Heracles, in the immediate neighborhood of a spring by the chapel of St. Demetrius."[39] Pritchett initially accepted the claim of Soteriades, "albeit reluctantly," but later in 1965 no longer accepted the evidence put forth by him.[40]

In 1966, Eugene Vanderpool, of the American School of Classical Studies in Athens, rejected Lolling's location because the ruins were found to be from the second century CE. He also rejected Soteriades' location of the Herakleion because of a lack of "positive evidence." Vanderpool found an inscription just north of the Small Marsh in an area known as the Valaria which referred to the Herakleion Games held at Marathon. As Vanderpool examined the area around where the inscription was found, he discovered numerous "traces of antiquity, including large marble blocks." He concluded that while he may not have found the exact spot for the Herakleion, he thinks he did find an approximate location. He supports his viewpoint by pointing out that the location was a good one militarily speaking, since its location on the main road would have allowed the Athenians to block any attempt of the Persians to march on Athens.[41]

Pritchett questioned Vanderpool's conclusion, since the inscription was not found "in situ," and he had found no sherds in the Valeria clay beds.[42] Vanderpool responded to this criticism by explaining that for Pritchett to dismiss the inscription as evidence because the stone may have been transported seems foolish. He says that some "wandering stones" have been found, but it is up to Pritchett to prove the stone had been moved. Regarding the lack of sherds, Vanderpool points out that the excavations Pritchett referred to were over 150 m from the place where the stone had been found and were thus "quite irrelevant."[43]

In 1992 a second inscription was found near the "find spot" of the first inscription. This second sign has led van der Veer to state that he believes the Herakleion definitely was located in the area where Vanderpool made his two finds. He goes on to say that A.R. Burn has changed his view of the location of the Herakleion to Vanderpool's location and judges it the most satisfactory location from a "tactical point of view as it blocks the south end of the plain and coastal road more directly."[44] Scott, writing in 2005, and Krentz, writing in 2010, concur that "the best choice based on current evidence is Vanderpool's site."[45]

Vegetation on the plain of Marathon in 490 is uncertain. Probably there were green fields and some scattered trees. On the day of the battle, there was no grain left in the fields as the harvest had taken place earlier.[46] Grundy points out that south of the Charadra, vines were cultivated. He suggests that if vines were also cultivated in 490, they would impact the battlefield as the Greeks allowed the vine tendrils to grow along the ground, which makes the vineyards "troublesome, if not dangerous obstacles to the passage of a mounted man going at more than a slow pace."[47] If that were the case, it might help explain why the cavalry appear to have had little impact upon the battle.

There were two roads leading from the plain of Marathon to Athens. Leake found traces of an ancient road that led from the Macaria spring to the foothills of Mt. Kotroni and into the Vrana valley for a distance of approximately 22 miles. It also had a branch that ran north past the modern city of Marathon and then bent west-southwest through the hills toward Athens by way of Kephisia, a distance of about 25 miles. Grundy describes the tracks as rugged, "though not very difficult."[48] The coastal road was a much easier road to travel.

It had no steep grades and left the plain by the narrow passage between the Small Marsh and Mt. Agrieliki and its distance was about 25 miles to Athens.[49]

Why Did the Persians Land at Marathon?

Herodotus tells us that the Persians landed at Marathon because this "region of Attica was most suitable for cavalry as well as the one closest to Eretria."[50] Some scholars criticize Herodotus' reasons as being wrong, while others accept his reasons but consider them inadequate to explain the Persian decision to land at Marathon. J. B. Bury explains that Herodotus is simply wrong as he points out that "Marathon is not the part of Attica nearest to Eretria, and the Cephesian plain was much better for cavalry."[51] Other areas suggested where the Persians might have landed include Oropus, located straight across the Euripus straits from Eretria; Phaleron, the harbor of Athens; and Araphen. When Lazenby considered these alternative locations that the Persians might have chosen, he states,

> After all, what were the alternatives? A landing at Oropus? The nearest point in Attica to Eretria would have left the Persians with a comparatively long and difficult road to Athens. A landing at Phaleron would have been nearest to Athens, but it was a long way from Euboea, or any other place of safety, should things go wrong, and although the Persians probably did not fear that a landing there would be contested, it was bound to have led to a battle within a short time. A landing at Rafina (the ancient Araphen), finally, though nearer to Athens would not have provided a terrain which suited Persian strength as well as Marathon, in the event of a battle. Marathon was, thus, probably the best place for a beach-head for anyone coming from Euboea, and wishing to take Athens, as Peisistratus, too, seems to have thought.[52]

Munro asks why the Persians landed 25 miles from Athens when there were places suitable for cavalry much closer to Athens, and he sees no advantage to being close to Eretria.[53] How and Wells in their *Commentary on Herodotus* react to Herodotus' reasons for the Persians landing at Marathon by stating,

> The reasons alleged by Herodotus (6.102) that it was near Eretria and good ground for cavalry are inadequate. Nearest to Eretria would not compensate the Persians for remoteness from Athens, and the plain of Athens (not to speak of the Thracian plain) is more suitable for the operations of cavalry; nor is it likely the Persian leaders doubted their power to force a landing on or near Phaleron.[54]

It has been suggested that Hippias guided the Persians to Marathon because of his past history with the location. In 546 BCE Hippias had accompanied his father, Peisistratus, when he landed at Marathon and gained local support as he marched on Athens and took power. While much had changed in Athens while Hippias was in Persia, he may have hoped that the former center of Peisistratid power and the location of his ancestral home would still rally people to his cause.[55] When dealing with this point, Doenges suggests that the Persians were seeking the political objective of restoring Hippias and hoped to accomplish it peacefully, if possible. Thus it was decided to land at Marathon rather than Phaleron in an effort to gain time to accomplish their political objective and still be able to use military force if necessary rather than immediately using military force by landing at Phaleron.[56] Lazenby comments that it is not inconceivable to think that treachery on Hippias' behalf was a possibility, as even Miltiades referred to the possibility in his speech to Callimachus. Lazenby states,

> At the very least, there were probably many Athenians who were in favor of what would now be called "appeasement." It was presumably such men who had secured the withdrawal of aid to Ionia, and possibly the condemnation of Phrynichos for his play "The Capture of Miletus." Athens would have been almost unique among Greek states if her citizens had been completely unanimous, and the example of Eretria will have reinforced Persian convictions that they would find allies in all Greek cities.[57]

Scott, in his *Historical Commentary on Herodotus, Book 6,* reinforces Lazenby's view when he says that Hippias may have convinced the Persians that he could persuade the Athenians to surrender without a battle. He states,

> It is doubtful if many in Attica as a whole would welcome his return, but he may have been in touch with potential supporters; he probably had adherents bound by ties of family or cult, e.g. from family estates, in Brauron or amongst the people in the area to the north. It is just possible that he had also support in the Marathon area itself: there is evidence that resistance to synoecism first persisted in some areas of Attica, including the tetrapolis of Marathon, with traditions and practices continuing which reflected their former independence; Hippias may have tried, or hoped to exploit that. Any such support presumably evaporated when the Athenian army assembled at Marathon, and could later be hidden behind the accusations against the Alcmaeonidae.[58]

Another logical reason for landing at Marathon is that the Persians could land unopposed. Munro raised this point in 1899 but did not declare it overly important, while Hammond simply mentions it in the *Cambridge Ancient History*, vol. 4, in 1988 with no comment.[59] Scott in his 2005 commentary on Herodotus explains that Marathon is approximately 40 km (24.8 miles) from Athens while the Phaleron is approximately 5 km (3.1 miles) from Athens, "but it was a long sail from Eretria, and he could fear that the Athenians would see his armada en route and resist his landing."[60] Jim Lacey, a 12-year active military officer and professor of strategy, war and policy at the Marine War College, explains the importance of an unopposed landing best. He states, "Even a modern amphibious landing is a scene of almost unparalleled chaos. Unloading thousands of men, tons of supplies, and possibly 8,000 horses from unsteady wood ships beached or lying in the shallows would have been a nightmare."[61] Attempting to land at the Phaleron facing the Athenian phalanx would have been a disaster. Lacey goes on to describe his own experience with amphibious landings as a marine. In the Marine Amphibious School, he found carrying off amphibious landings to be difficult and confusing. He says that eventually the confusion was worked out, but had they been facing an enemy force they would have "been slaughtered." He then says that some ancient historians with no battlefield experience seem to think that ancient armies could easily force a landing facing an enemy army. He specifically mentions Munro's assertion that the Persians would not have had a problem forcing a landing at Phaleron where they would have faced the Athenian army. He concludes his argument saying that he could not imagine a "greater nightmare" than to be unloading ships as a hoplite phalanx attacked.[62]

In addition to the above reasons for landing at Marathon, the location also provided excellent anchorage and defensible positions at both the springs of Macaria and the Schoenia beach. At the Macaria springs the pass between the base of Mt. Stavrokoraki and the Great Marsh was barely wide enough for two horses to pass each other, and the entrance to the

Schoenia beach at the southern end was very narrow and easily defended.[63] Pritchett says that the seas are much rougher near Marathon than in the Saronic Gulf and that fishermen in that area told him that often they did not put out from this area at the mouth of the present Charadra; however, the Kynosoura Peninsula would have provided the Persian anchorage along the Schoenia beach protection from the northeast winds. The Schoenia beach is about two miles long and would have provided about three miles of protected anchorage if the ships started at the rocky base of the Kynosoura Peninsula. At 30 feet each abeam, the 600 ships mentioned by Herodotus would have required at least three and a half miles if they anchored in a single file; however, they could have anchored two ranks deep.[64] In addition, if Richard Dunn is correct and the Great Marsh was really a shallow lake or lagoon in 490 BCE some of the Persian ships could have anchored in the lake\lagoon, which would have given them even better protection and put them closer to the springs of Macaria, which would have made it easier to disembark and re-embark the horses.[65]

Landing at the Schoenia beach not only provided the Persians with well-defended sites for their camps and protected anchorage for their ships, but it also helped them with logistical issues. The Macaria spring and farmers' wells supplied adequate water, and the area by the marsh/lake was one of the few areas in Greece with green pasturage in September. In addition, "overland roads for supply from northern Attica and Southern Boeotia" were available. Finally, Persian bases at Eretria and Carystus were close enough for purposes of supply.[66]

Size of the Persian and Greek Forces

In 1920, Norman Whatley, headmaster of Clifton College, presented a paper to the Oxford Philological Society titled, "On the Possibility of Reconstructing Marathon and Other Ancient Battles." While it was not published at that time, it was in private circulation and highly regarded. Whatley was finally convinced to publish it in 1964. In this paper he talked about the difficulty of reconstructing battles, as so many things happen in a battle at once and changes quickly occur. He explains that the participants are under great stress, which means that usually they do not view events objectively or put them into the proper perspective. He describes the difficulty in distinguishing what was foreseen from what was unforeseen and good generalship from a lucky break. He goes on to say that it is especially hard to know what was going on in the minds of generals. He adds that often generals themselves may be unsure what happened and tend to conveniently forget mistakes if they did not cause a disaster and to take credit even if the result came about because of luck or a fluke. In addition, outsiders tend to think that every part of the battle is carefully planned, which is not always the case.[67] Whatley explains that military historians are fortunate to have "war diaries, field messages, written orders, the order of battle, strength of the units involved, memoirs of officers and participants and staff members, training routines, normal strategy and tactics used by the participants"; however, historians dealing with ancient battles seldom have such resources available to them. He then adds that the ancient historians that we depend upon were also lacking such resources.[68]

Whatley says it is difficult to reconstruct battles unless one has accurate numbers as to how many troops are involved or at least the type and numbers of units involved such as legions, divisions, and so forth on both sides. He suggests that there are three methods for dealing with numbers in ancient battles. The three methods with an evaluation of each follows:

1. The historian may accept the numbers given by ancient sources. Some of the numbers given by ancient sources such as Herodotus' figure of 1,700,000 infantry for Xerxes are simply too absurd to even be considered. In addition, figures given by ancient sources often contradict each other. Many modern historians pick and choose which numbers to accept, but with little reason to back up their choices. Whatley concludes that one cannot depend on Greek historians for accurate figures.
2. Historians may "argue from probabilities and possibilities." This approach is very helpful in eliminating absurd numbers but is not much help in determining exact numbers. He uses Munro as an example. Munro suggests that Persian forces at Marathon were 20,000 based on the fact that 6,400 Persians were killed and the center of the Persian force was annihilated. He bases his conclusion on the fact that the center was one-third of the Persian army and that 6,400 times 3 equals 19,200, or a force of about 20,000. But his approach faces problems. Was the entire center wiped out? What about casualties of the wings that were decisively defeated? Were all of the Persian forces committed to the battle? Is the number of 6,400 Persian dead accurate? Munro's conclusion may be correct, but there are too many variables for one to be too positive about it.
3. A historian may reach a figure based upon what he knows concerning the command structure and the organization of an army. Whatley says that this approach looks good on paper, but upon closer examination conclusions cannot be accepted with much certainty. He says that numbers such as 10,000 and 60,000 seem to fit the Persian military organization, but yet he claims one could equally argue for 60,000, 180,000 or even 300,000. In addition he adds that we still remain uncertain as to which units and how many of the units were with the army.[69]

While Whatley has identified key difficulties in determining numbers in ancient battles, Marathon presents even more difficulty in that Herodotus does not include the number of the Persian forces or the Greek forces involved in the battle. The only number he includes is the size of the Persian fleet. Herodotus states,

> So, the newly appointed generals left the King and set out on their journey. They went first to the plain of Aleion in Cilicia, bringing along a huge and well-equipped land army. As they camped there, all the ships that had been levied from the various districts arrived to join their forces, as well as the horse-transport ships, which Darius had ordered his tribute-paying peoples to prepare the year before. [Verse 2] After putting the horses on board the ships, the land army embarked, and the expedition sailed to Ionia with a fleet of 600 triremes.[70]

Since the size of the fleet is the only number Herodotus gives concerning the Persian forces, it has come under greater scrutiny by historians who utilize the three methods identified by Whatley in their work. A major concern regarding Herodotus' figure of 600 triremes is that it seems to be "a conventional" number as it is also used for the fleet during the

Scythian campaign, and at the Battle of Lade during the Ionian Revolt. As a result, Cawkwell believes Herodotus is "hardly to be trusted," and is in effect "worthless." How and Wells conclude that the number of 600 triremes "cannot be safely used as a basis for calculating the Persian force at marathon."[71]

Just because the number of 600 triremes occurred twice previously does not mean it is incorrect or inaccurate. Perhaps 600 ships was the normal complement for the Persian fleet. Many historians appear to utilize Whatley's first method for dealing with ancient numbers by accepting the number that is given by the ancient historians. Grundy states, "Assuming it to be correct, the numbers of the expedition were extraordinarily small for a Persian enterprise." Lazenby says that "it is not impossible that Herodotus' figure for the number of triremes is about right." He goes on to say that an army of about 24,000 that could be carried by 600 triremes "was clearly not large enough to conquer Greece, but it would have been large enough to settle the score with Naxos, punish Eretria and reinstate the tyrant Hippias, probably the three primary objectives of the expedition." Lacey seems willing to accept Herodotus' figure of 600 triremes, although he sees them being used for different purposes than just as combat ships. He includes the horse transports in the total of 600. He addresses the concern that Persia could not provide 600 triremes after the disaster at Mt. Athos by claiming, "They could easily have been replaced in the interval before the invasion." He adds that Darius could draw ships from "every Ionian city along with everything the ports of Ionia and Phoenicia could produce."[72]

Wallinga accepts Herodotus' figure of 600 triremes although he believes most were used for transport, with crews "not necessarily larger than 50 to 60 oarsmen on average."[73] While 170 oarsmen are generally stated as the crew of a trireme, Wallinga claims that "there can be no doubt that the manning of ships in ancient fleets was not uniform. He believes that the degree of manning was dependent on a variety of factors such as the number of rowers available, the money available, and the goal of the operation. He believes that troop transports and horse transports could operate with 60 rowers.[74] He goes on to say that the Persians could concentrate their crews and come up with 200 to 300 battle triremes, which would be more than adequate to defeat any fleet which the Greeks could possibly come up with. Athens had 50 to 70 ships with few triremes, and Corinth and Eretria about the same with more triremes; however, no alliance was created and no Greek fleet was sent to challenge the Persian fleet.[75]

Other historians have used Whatley's second method of dealing with ancient numbers in military history and argue from probabilities and possibilities. Munro rejects Herodotus' number of 600 triremes as "highly improbable." He points out the slight resistance expected from Athens and Eretria, who had only sent 25 ships during the Ionian Revolt and who had virtually no triremes, and considers Plato's estimate of 300 triremes as more reasonable, but "of dubious authority, and still too large to be accepted." He does not suggest an acceptable number.[76]

Doenges rejects Herodotus' number concerning the fleet because in order to carry the number of troops and supplies, the size of the fleet would be enormous and difficult to coordinate. He adds that the Marathon expedition was the first amphibious expedition ever recorded and would have required "precise" planning and coordination. He claims that based upon the limited ships Athens and Eretria had sent to Ionia, the Persians expected little naval resistance. As a result, he believes that 100 triremes would have been more than adequate to overcome any naval resistance by Athens and Eretria. He also believes that because of the difficulty of transporting horses and supplies as well as guarding the fleet, the Persians would have wanted to keep the size of the fleet as low as possible.[77]

Billows also rejects Herodotus, because "basic practicalities of cost, logistics, and need suggest very much smaller numbers." He points out that in 480 after Athens had built 200 new triremes, the mainland Greeks altogether could only come with about 400 triremes, while in 490 Athens only had 50 ships with a couple of triremes. He concludes, "A more plausible number for the Persian fleet adapted to the actual scale of operations would be 200 or fewer."[78]

Ray, in his *Land Battles in Fifth Century Greece*, believes that the 600 triremes may have referred to "total Persian potential" or been a "generic number," but either way he believes 300 triremes "is a much more realistic figure." He explains that "assembling the fleet of even this lesser size was very demanding and required all that could be gathered from the empire's naval contingents (Phoenicia) plus an Ionian levy." He adds that Ionian losses at Lade precluded any sizable naval contribution from Ionia.[79] Krentz considers Herodotus' number of 600 triremes to be either a "stock figure meaning nothing more precise than a large number," or perhaps Herodotus used the term *triremes* loosely and really included all ships. He suggests that perhaps the Persian fleet consisted of 300 triremes, as Plato says, and 300 supply ships which Herodotus included under *triremes*. He also points out that between 478 and 331 the Persian fleets were usually made up of about 300 triremes.[80]

Finally, we come to F. Maurice, an army general in World War I, and N.G.L. Hammond, an operative for British Special Operations in occupied Greece during World War II. They apply Whatley's third method which is to deduce the numbers from what they know of command and organization. General Maurice deduces the size of the Persian fleet from the size of the Persian troops, which is certainly unusual since Herodotus gives no number concerning Persian troops. Maurice assumes the Persian "expeditionary force was composed of organized units." He then suggests that Datis and Artaphernes were each in command of one division of 12,000 troops and states that one division could be carried in 200 ships, thus concluding that the fleet consisted of 400 vessels. At no point does he explain how 200 vessels could carry 12,000 troops, nor does he explain how he determined the divisions that would be used.[81] Hammond also works from the estimated number of Persian troops to determine the size of the Persian fleet. Using knowledge of the Athenian expedition to Syracuse and adjusting the scale to an estimated 25,000 Persian troops, Hammond determined that the Persian fleet "needed 376 triremes, 280 merchant men, 400 small craft and an unknown number of horse transports."[82] He gives no evidence to support his conclusion.

Number of Persian Infantry and Cavalry

Herodotus does not give a number for the size of the Persian army at Marathon; however, other ancient authors have given figures. Simonides, a contemporary of Herodotus, suggests 90,000 troops, while Plato gives the number of 500,000. Cornelius Nepos, writing in the first century BCE, writes that the Persian force was made up of 210,000 foot soldiers, along with 10,000 cavalry, of which 110,000 participated in the battle. Plutarch writing in the first century CE sets the Persian force at 300,000, and Justin writing in the third century CE talks of a Persian force of 600,000. Needless to say modern historians have rejected the above figures as being absurdly exaggerated, but while they seem to agree that it is "impossible to establish accurately" the Persian force, modern historians have suggested numbers ranging from 6,000 to 40,000.[83]

Ray rejects Herodotus' figure of 600 ships because a fleet of 300 triremes would be "a much more realistic figure for the sort of punitive expedition being attempted here." He claims that each Persian trireme could carry 226 men, including 173 rowers, 16 sailors, 10 marines and 30 passengers. This would allow 500 to 600 horsemen and their mounts to be carried in 100 ships. In the other 200 ships he suggests that they carried "four *hazaraba* (1,000) of Medean *sparabara* (spearmen), one of Persian *sparabara* and another of Sakae bowmen," for a total of 6,000 infantry, 3,000 marines and 500 to 600 cavalry. Later he suggests that Herodotus' claim that 6,400 Persians died might have actually represented the size of the Persian army. To reach this figure, he adds 40 Ionian ships to his total and concludes the army had 4,000 Medes, 1,000 Persians, 1,000 Sakae, and 400 Ionians (10 per ship). He then eliminates the 3,000 marines and cavalry saying they did not participate in the battle.[84] At this point his numbers do not seem to have attracted many supporters.

Doenges quotes Evans' estimate of "no more than 200 cavalry," carried in 40 ships, but he thinks even that figure may be too high. He also recognizes that modern historians estimate the number of Persian infantry to be between 20,000 to 25,000, but he again thinks that figure is too high. He points out that 600 triremes would be required to carry that number of troops at 30 to 40 soldiers per ship and states that the idea that "some 90,000 men, including rowers and support troops, were disembarked on the plain of Marathon to confront roughly 10,000 Athenians and Eretrians boggles the mind. Even more boggling is the prospect of evacuating all those men in the chaos following the defeat of the Persian military. With that in mind, he suggests that a Persian force of 12,000 to 15,000 infantry is more realistic, as a much larger force, no matter how poorly led and equipped, would have been able to overwhelm the Greeks. Finally he states that the Persians would not have been able to logistically support such a large amphibious operation in 490 BCE.[85]

Munro proposes an estimate of 25,000 infantry, which he calls "half a Persian army corps," which he claims would meet the needs of the expedition. He says that 5,000 cavalry would represent a "proper quota" but says that it is not credible for a sea expedition, so instead he suggests 1,000 horsemen.[86] Grundy believes that there was no rational reason to estimate that the Persian troops numbered above 20,000, and in fact he seems to believe the number might have been smaller and claims the ratio between Persian troops to Greek troops was not 2:1 but rather the armies might have been close to even.[87] Hignett uses the number of 6,400 Persian casualties to suggest a total of 20,000 Persian troops. He bases this number on his belief that the Persian center was close to being wiped out and that it represented about one-third of the Persian forces. From that belief he concludes that the total Persian forces were about 20,000 and that they were all present at Marathon at the time of the battle.[88] Whatley also places the Persian forces at about 20,000 as he believes it would have been difficult if not possible to transport such a large number of troops by ship. He adds that few cavalry were present.[89]

Wozniak, writing in 2011, agrees that the Persian force was probably made up of two *baivarabam* units of 10,000 soldiers each for a total of 20,000 soldiers. He points out that they could have been transported in 500 triremes, leaving 1,000 cavalry to be transported by the remaining 100 triremes. He adds that the expeditionary force was made up of Persians, "well-reputed Medes" and "Saca, who were "highly skilled mercenaries."[90]

Using 40 soldiers per trireme, Krentz suggests that the Persian forces ranged between 12,000 using 300 triremes and 24,000 as an outside limit using 600 triremes. He recognizes that some scholars give higher estimates, but goes on to mention that General Maurice thought that the water supply at Marathon could have sustained a force of 16,000 for one week. Krentz calls 16,000 troops "as good a figure as any." Regarding cavalry, he believes that the Persians had horse transports that "carried a handful of horses each."[91]

Maurice put forward the idea that Datis and Artaphernes each commanded a division of troops of 12,000 carried in 200 ships for a total of 24,000 troops and 400 ships in the expeditionary force; however, he also advances the theory that Datis took 3,000 to 4,000 troops to attack Eretria while Artaphernes landed at Marathon with the remaining 16,000 to 17,000 troops.[92] From a military commander's point of view, Maurice's theory probably makes a lot of sense, but there is certainly no mention that Datis and Artaphernes split their forces in Herodotus, and few if any modern historians give any support to this theory.

Scott recognizes that coming to an accurate figure on the number of Persian troops is impossible. But as a guesstimate he suggests "it is not unrealistic that the actual Persian soldiers numbered 20,000 to 30,000, and outnumbered the Greeks by at least 2 to 1."[93]

Hammond proposes that the Persian infantry numbered at least 25,000 as the Persians knew that Athens, Eretria and Sparta had more than 20,000 hoplites between them, and the Persians had to make their plans assuming they might have to face a united Greek force. Also he points out that the Persians planned to land at Phaleron after their defeat at Marathon in which they lost 6,400 soldiers. They certainly would not have sailed to Phaleron to again face the Athenians with a diminished force if they had started with only 20,000 troops. Hammond adds that personally he feels the Persian force numbered at least 30,000 troops.[94]

Lazenby bases his troop totals on the Persians' 600 triremes carrying 24,000 troops and horse transports carrying 1,000 cavalry. He believes that such a force was certainly inadequate to attempt to conquer Greece but that it would be adequate to "settle the score with Naxos, punish Eretria and reinstate the tyrant, Hippias, in Athens, probably the three primary objectives of the expedition."[95]

Cawkwell agrees that there is no way to accurately come up with a number for the Persian forces, and he also states that Herodotus' number of 600 triremes is not to be trusted, so therefore it is useless to try to determine the total of Persian troops. He also rejects the idea that the number of Persian casualties would be of any use in determining the number of Persian troops. Instead he simply sets the number of Persians at 30,000 because that figure would allow the Persians to deal with any combination of Greek forces that they faced.[96]

Tuplin in 2010 explained that the Greeks faced an Iran-Sacan force raised over a period of 12 to 18 months and that "their number is unknown." He recognizes that the prevailing view of most modern historians is that the force was between 20,000 and 30,000, but adds,

"None of this is any more scientific than simply speculating that the Persians brought forces at least twice as numerous as the army of any individual adversary." He also reminds us that the point of "earth-and-water diplomacy was, of course, to diminish the chances of any collective opposition."[97]

Finally, Jim Lacey, our most experienced military expert, writing in 2011, proposes that Datis would have wanted at least 300 combat triremes to be available to meet the 150 to 170 Greek vessels that would be available if the Greeks unified and met them at sea. In addition he suggests the Persians had 50 horse transports carrying 20 horses each, for a total of about 1,000 cavalry. Finally he puts forward the idea that the remaining 250 triremes could use their sails since they would not be needed to fight, and as a result they could carry up to 100 soldiers on each trireme, as fewer rowers would be necessary. The resulting Persian force would equal about 35,000 infantry and cavalry. While he admits his figures are open to debate, he claims that they fairly represent what Persia "was capable of accomplishing in 490 BCE."[98]

At this point what can be concluded after examining the various proposals put forward by modern historians? First of all, it is obvious that they all reject the exaggerated numbers given by ancient sources. Secondly, they seem to recognize that it is impossible to come up with an accurate figure of the Persian forces or even a figure accepted by all historians. It does appear that there is some agreement that the Persian forces numbered between 20,000 to 30,000 troops and cavalry; however, as Tuplin points out, "None of this is any more scientific than simply speculating that the Persians brought forces at least twice as numerous than any individual adversary."[99] But then one could ask why they brought twice as many. What about the conventional rule of thumb of the need to have a three-to-one ratio when one side attempts to break through an opponent?[100] So it appears it will have to be left up to the reader to determine whether or not the size of the Persian force can be determined, and if so how to do it and what to conclude.

Numbers of Greek Forces

Our ancient sources are in more agreement on estimating the number of the Greek forces. Herodotus does not give a figure for the number of Greek troops at the Battle of Marathon; however, there is less controversy among modern historians concerning the estimated number of Greek troops, and even among the ancient sources, the number quoted is closer and less exaggerated. Cornelius Nepos claims that the Athenian force supported by 1,000 Plataeans equaled 10,000.[101] Justin on the other hand claims that there were 10,000 Athenians supported by 1,000 Plataeans.[102] Pausanias claimed that there were less than 10,000 Athenians at Marathon.[103]

Modern historians appear willing to accept the above estimates concerning the number of Greek forces at Marathon as appropriate, although there is some disagreement on exact totals. Grundy points out that the Athenians had 8,000 hoplites and 8,000 light-armed troops at the Battle of Plataea while also supplying troops to serve on its fleet, so he sees 9,000 to 10,000 Athenian troops at Marathon as a reasonable figure. In fact, he believes that "the number 10,000 at Marathon is probably an understatement, though not one of gross character."[104] Whatley thinks that it is reasonable to accept 10,000 Athenians and Plataeans as being fairly accurate.[105]

Billows believes that the Athenian force plus the Plataean force equaled 10,000 men. He bases his conclusion on an estimate that there were perhaps 30,000 Athenian adult male citizens in 490, of whom less than 50 percent were able to financially "equip themselves as hoplites." He sees the 9,000 hoplites as representing "essentially a full call-up of all able-bodied Athenians of military age and about one-third of the total citizen body." In addition he thinks "thousands of light infantry" were also present at Marathon.[106]

Krentz suggests that the Greeks had "at least 18,000 Athenians at Marathon and perhaps as many as 22,000." To get to 22,000 Krentz adds the 4,000 cleruchs from Chalcis and 1,000 Plataeans, of which about half were hoplites and half were light armed. Of the 22,000 Athenians, Krentz believes that there were 9,000 hoplites and an equal number of attendants.[107] Scott seems willing to accept the figure of 1,000 Plataeans but believes that the Plataean contingent may have been filled out with "Boeotians from adjacent settlements such as Hysai."[108] Hignett believes that 9,000 was "not an excessive estimate" of the Athenian hoplites who fought at Marathon but believes that 1,000 Plataeans was an overestimate; however, he is willing to accept 600 Plataeans. He believes that all of the hoplites had attendants with them, which would have added approximately 10,000 additional people. He believes that the attendants may have been used as light-armed troops but feels that "their military value was probably slight." He states that the wealthiest citizens served in the cavalry, as they could afford the expense of maintaining a horse; however, he thinks that they probably dismounted and fought as hoplites.[109]

Glenn Bugh, in his book *The Horsemen of Athens,* feels that the Athenians had no cavalry at Marathon because the Greeks felt that their number of cavalry was too small to be effective against Persian cavalry; however, he believes that they may have been stationed elsewhere.[110] Gaebel, in his book *Cavalry operations in the ancient Greek World*, agrees that Athens had cavalry but that it was not at Marathon because it would contribute little to a hoplite battle. He goes on to say that Greek cavalry played "no important" role during the Persian Wars.[111]

Hammond believes that the number of 9,000 Athenians was included "for rhetorical effect" and that the number of 10,000 troops is the best answer. He also believes that the hoplites were "unsupported by cavalry or archers." He explains that a "small force of hoplites, cavalry and light armed" were left at Athens, "in case of treachery or a sudden attack." In the number of 10,000 Athenians, Hammond includes the 4,000 cleruchs that had left Eretria before it fell.[112]

Concerning the 4,000 cleruchs from Chalcis, Thomas Figueira, in his article "Khalkis and Marathon," doubts that all of the 4,000 cleruchs were hoplites. He points out that in 479, only 400 Chalcidian hoplites were at Plataea. He thinks that about one-half of the cleruchs may have been hoplites and that they would have served in a separate unit had they all fought at Marathon; however, there is no record that such a unit fought at Marathon. As a result, Figueira concludes that cleruchs who "once belonged to the tribal regiments had rejoined them." He does not, however, suggest a number for the cleruchs at Marathon but rather suggests that many may have filled other roles such as protecting Athens, protecting the Phaleron, serving on some ships that had been mobilized, and/or some may have returned to Chalcis.[113]

After the Athenians learned of the Persians landing at Marathon, Miltiades, one of the 10 Athenian generals, introduced a proposal to the assembly calling for the Athenians to take action against the Persians, and the proposal also included "that a number of slaves were to be given their liberty in order to fight against the Persians."[114] This was an extraordinary proposal as it was generally accepted that slaves were not allowed to fight as soldiers. In fact after Marathon there are only two other instances in which the Athenians emancipated slaves because of their desperate need for soldiers—the Battle of Arginusa in 406 and the Battle of Chaeronea in 338. Some historians have rejected the idea that slaves were freed to fight at Marathon as Herodotus mentions in his account; however, Sargent points out that Herodotus left out many important details and the fact that Herodotus was writing at a time when Marathon had already become a legend. She believes that "the vanity of the Athenians concerning this remarkable victory" would have made them much more interested in listening to a history read to them that emphasized that the freedmen were responsible for the defeat of the Mede, and yet Herodotus mentions the slaves which seems to give credence to his statement.[115]

There is little doubt that slaves were part of every army raised in Athens. Previous to Marathon, Sargent describes their duties as to "help prepare the food, act as guides, rescue wounded men, serve as attendants to generals, carry important messages, carriers of baggage, shield bearers, and caretakers in general of the armor of hoplites.[116] Hunt, in his article "Slaves, Warfare, and Ideology in the Greek Historians," believes that at Marathon the slaves probably fought as hoplites. He asks, "why else would they have been freed?" He argues that "an individual hoplite attendant might be freed after a battle at his master's discretion for some particular act of valor, but attendants would not have been released *en masse* before a battle." He goes on to answer why the slaves were freed rather than arming the *thetes*, citizens who could not afford the hoplite equipment. He states that arming the slaves instead of the *thetes* may have resulted from the fear of the hoplite class that if the *thetes* were to gain any power they might threaten the "hoplite and aristocratic supremacy."[117] However, neither Sargent nor Hunt gives an estimate of the number of slaves that might have been involved.

While there appears to be a general consensus among modern historians that the Greek army at Marathon was made up of 9,000 to 10,600 hoplites, including the Plataeans, Ray concludes that we can "reasonably project that the Athenian army at Marathon probably had 5,000 spearman (up nearly 40 percent since Solon's day) within 10 tribal units and that Plataea added a further 600 spearman (per their strength in 479 BCE)." He supports his conclusion by stating that Solon in 594 BCE gave "each clan 30 war bands of 30 men each," for a total army of 3,600. He believes that population growth by 500 BCE had been such as to allow a tribal muster of 500 for each of the 10 tribes created by Cleisthenes' so that the Athenian army in 490 had 5,000 men. He adds that in addition to the 5,000 spearman there would also have been "a crowd of attendants, with perhaps 500 to 600 serving as javelin men; however, there seems to have been no horsemen or archers." He does say that Athens had 96 riders at the time, but that they did not go to Marathon because "the marching route required a climb unsuitable for horses."[118] Ray's conclusion about the number of Greek forces does not appear to have gained any adherents.

The Athenian March to Marathon

Peter Green suggests that once Eretria fell to the Persians a series of debates took place concerning the response of Athens.[119] Some in Athens believed that the best policy to follow would be to stay in Athens and defend its walls while others believed that the army should march to Marathon and confront the enemy. R. M. Berthold questions whether Athens even had walls in 490 to defend.[120] Winter, in his book *Greek Fortifications*, concludes,

> In short, Athens must have had a city circuit in 480. When it was built, we cannot say; I believe the third period of Peisistratus' rule to be a likely date. In any case, perhaps as early as the time of Cleisthenes, and certainly by the time of the Persian wars, Athens had spread so far outside this defensive line (which may not have included the whole city even at the time of its construction) that it was not considered worth defending in 490 and 480.[121]

Scott believes that "most of Athens itself was unwalled (the walled area was probably limited to the Acropolis and a small area to the north)." He goes on to point out that J. M. Camp in his book *The Archaeology of Athens* limited the wall of Athens to the Acropolis.[122] Lazenby raises the question of how long the Athenians would be able to defend the walls. The Persians were well known for their ability to take cities by siege as demonstrated when they took Miletus to end the Ionian Revolt.[123]

Another problem that Athens faced was the threat of internal treachery. Graf, in his analysis of Medism in Greece, states,

> Personal rivalry was the norm of political life, and the polis was essentially the arena for entering competition and obtaining success over rival aristocrats and factions.... The factional politics and partisan loyalties of the archaic period are substantial enough to suggest that treason in behalf of individual loyalties was a constant problem and destructive feature of political life.[124]

With the example of what happened in Eretria before them, Green asks, "Could a city such as Athens, one that had been rife for a decade with rumors of treachery, fifth columnists, and profiteers from the great King's gold for a decade really hope to hold out during a siege?"[125] Regarding their decision to march to Marathon, Lazenby points out that it was the normal reaction for the Athenians to march out to confront invaders.[126] Hignett adds that Athens' hope for Spartan aid must have depended on Athens' willingness to take the field.[127]

Recognizing the above concerns, Miltiades made a proposal to the assembly which it passed calling for the Athenian soldiers "to provide themselves with provisions and set out."[128] While Herodotus does not mention this decree, Aristotle and Demosthenes do, and most modern historians accept it as true with Miltiades as its author.[129]

Munro presents a totally different view of when the decree of Miltiades was passed and the objective of the decree. He claims that the day Artaphernes landed his troops east of Eretria, Eretria appealed to Athens for help. Munro sees the decree of Miltiades being passed in order to send the Athenian army to aid Eretria. He says that the Athenian army was on its way to Eretria by the shortest route, which was through "Decella and Oropus"; however, the army was still in the plain of Cephisus when word was received that Artaphernes had landed his division of troops at Marathon. Callimachus quickly turned his troops eastward and marched to Marathon, along the hills that skirt Mt. Pentelicus. He claims that the landing at Marathon was part of Persia's strategy to take Eretria by making a "thrust on the right flank, which was designed to intercept" the Athenian army and prevent it from going to Eretria's aid.[130]

As pointed out in the topography section of this chapter, there were two roads leading to Marathon from Athens. The southern road running along the coast was about 25 miles to Marathon, while the northern road was only 22 miles; however, the last few miles of the northern road runs through the more rugged "foothill country which was probably forested in 490."[131] While the northern road was more rugged, it was a shorter distance, and Grundy claims it was "not very difficult, and is certainly that which was used by the Athenians in their advance on Marathon."[132] Hammond agrees with Grundy when he says that the Athenians would have taken the fastest and safest route to Marathon, which would have been the northern route through Kephisos and the hills to the Vrana valley.[133]

Burn agrees with Grundy and Hammond that the route through Kephisos was the shortest and quickest route "for a messenger or small party, but thinks it was no way to take a large body of troops to a battlefront. He claims that narrow passages along the route would lead to congestion and that with a large body of troops, the congestion "is multiplied by the number of men in the column, divided by the number of who can move abreast, and the delay to the rear thousands becomes appalling." He points out that Hammond worked with guerrilla forces in World War II but wonders if Hammond would have chosen "to take a regular infantry division that way."[134]

Doenges, writing in 1998, agrees with Grundy and Hammond because the northern route is three miles shorter than the southern route, but he rejects Burn's argument about troops being delayed by the terrain. He agrees that a modern army dependent upon vehicles to carry troops and supplies would have found the terrain a problem but does not think that the Greeks who were used to walking in mountainous terrain would have been slowed or stalled as they moved along familiar mountain trails. He goes on to explain that if the Athenians took the southern route to Marathon, they would have allowed the Persian cavalry and light armed to exploit the northern route. He also asked for an explanation of how an experienced commander like Datis would allow the Athenians using the northern route to move to a better defensive position in the Vrana valley when his cavalry could have hindered their movement.[135] Part of Doenges' argument depends upon the Herakleion being located at the mouth of the Vrana valley, and as pointed out earlier in this chapter, it appears that Vanderpool's evidence locating the Herakleion near the small marsh in the Valaria area is accepted by many historians as the definite location.[136]

Berthold adds to Burn's criticism of using the northern route, stating that the rough conditions would slow down the movement of the Athenian army as the attendants accompanying the hoplites would have doubled the size of the force that had to move through narrow areas. In fact he claims that if the Athenians were concerned about saving time, taking the southern route was actually the best route. In addition he points out that if the Persians were to march on Athens, the southern route would be the route they would take due to the size of the Persian force and its accompanying cavalry. The Athenians would want to prevent the Persian army from leaving the plain, and thus they would take the southern route. He agrees that the southern route was more dangerous for the Athenians to take as it could expose them to the Persian cavalry, but he thinks they had little choice as taking the northern route might allow "a fast squadron of horse and light armed troops" to make a quick strike on Athens while the Athenian army was strung out along the northern route. If that occurred, the war would come to an end without the Athenian army being involved.[137]

On this same point, Green says that the most obvious reason for the Athenians to take the southern route is that if they took the northern route,

> Such a move would leave the coast-road—the only approach to Athens easily negotiable by cavalry—wide open, a bonanza Datis and Artaphernes could not possibly have missed. Miltiades' dash to Marathon was designed to forestall, or block, such an attack. This end would hardly be achieved by struggling over the hills (where cavalry could not operate) and totally ignoring the coastal gap. Nor would any commander in his right mind have first stripped Athens of defenders, and then obligingly left the front door open, as it were, while he led his troops up the back lane. One alert Persian scout on the hills, and Datis's squadrons could have ridden into Athens while Miltiades' hoplites were still stumbling down the track above Vrana.[138]

Krentz finds Green's argument compelling and agrees that the Athenians would have taken the southern route.[139] Scott on the other hand seems to think that both routes were utilized. He suggests that those soldiers living in Athens would have used the southern route, and probably arrived at Marathon first. Those soldiers living in other parts of Attica would have waited for messengers to inform them where to meet the army. For many the northern route would have been more convenient for them to take in order to meet up with the rest of the army. As a result, soldiers would arrive over a period of time using both routes to Marathon.[140]

Billows agrees with Scott that the Athenian force did not march as one force to Marathon. He believes that the *Hippeis,* wealthy Athenians who could afford to own horses, arrived first, some hundreds in number.... They likely secured the position in the southern foothills as an advance force, to be joined later by some thousands of hoplites marching from Athens. He points out that about half of the Athenian hoplites lived in Athens, with the other half spread out over Attica. He claims that they would have arrived in various-sized contingents over the next few days; however, he does not comment upon the route that they might have taken.[141] Burn would appear to support Scott and Billows when he implies that the Athenians did not call all the other soldiers together in Athens, as feeding the army would have created "an economic strain; and until the sea-born enemy's intentions were known, it was impossible to say where to march."[142]

Philippides and Sparta

After the Persian forces landed at Marathon, Herodotus tells us that "the first thing the generals did, while still in the city, was to send a messenger to Sparta by sending Philippides, who was an Athenian long-distance runner and a professional in this work." At times historians refer to Pheidippides instead of Philippides, which is supported by some manuscripts. Macan calls Pheidippides a "corruption" and says that Aristophanes "would never have made 'Pheidippides' the son of Strepsiades, if the name had been consecrated in the Athenian traditions of Marathon."[143] How and Wells agree with Macan, saying, "Philippides is a common Athenian name, whereas Pheidippides is a witticism of Aristophanes, which he certainly would have not dared to use had the name been consecrated in the tale of Marathon."[144] Burn claims manuscripts are evenly divided but says, "It will not do to say 'Pheidippides' is excluded because it appears as a comic compromise in Aristophanes' *Clouds* for the name Phidippos occurs in the *Iliad* (II, 678) and, since this existed, Pheidippides is also possible."[145] Frost says that "the best class of Herodotus' manuscripts has the reading Pheidippides; however, he goes on to state, "the weight of ancient testimony is certainly on the side of the reading Philippides. Almost every writer who mentioned the run to Sparta seems to have read Philippides in his text of Herodotus." After stating that Pheidippides "appears only as the comic name of Strepiadus' son addicted to horse racing," he points out that the spelling "Philippides" is found in four other manuscripts of Herodotus and concludes that "*Pheidippides*, therefore, is probably to be seen as a copyist's error, although one can never be certain."[146]

Philippides arrived in Sparta "on the day after he had left Athens." He appealed to the magistrates in Sparta by saying, "Lacedaemonians, the Athenians beg you to rush to their defense and not look on passively as the most ancient city of Hellas falls into slavery imposed by barbarians. For in fact Eretria has already been enslaved, and thus Hellas has become weaker by one important city." The Spartans replied to Philippides' request by saying that they would send help but that according to their law they could not "march out to war, but must instead wait until the moon was full."[147]

Later when Philippides had returned to Athens he claimed that during his run he had met the god Pan who told him to "ask the Athenians why they were paying no attention to him, although he was well disposed toward them, had already and often been of service to them and would serve them further in the future." After the crisis in Athens had passed the Athenians set up a "shrine to Pan below the Acropolis, and in response to his request to them, they propitiated Pan with sacrifices and a torch race every year."[148]

Since Herodotus has the Persians landing at Marathon in book 6.102 and has the generals send Philippides to Sparta in book 6.105, it seems that Philippides was sent after the Persians landed at Marathon; however, on a closer reading of book 6.105, Herodotus does not clearly say that Philippides was sent after the Persians had landed at Marathon. Scott says that it is possible that Philippides was sent after the fall of Eretria but before the Persians landed at Marathon. He points out that while Philippides, in his appeal to the Spartans, says that Eretria has fallen, he does not mention that the Persians had landed at Marathon. Scott also points out that when the Spartans marched to the aid of Athens, they were heading to Athens when they were met at the border of Attica and told of the Athenian victory. Scott adds that it was possible that Philippides had been sent to Sparta "by the assembly or perhaps the Boule rather than by the generals." He thinks that Herodotus may have been influenced by the mid-fifth century viewpoint when the generals had gained more importance than in 490 BCE.[149]

To the average person, the fact that Philippides arrived in Sparta, which was 140 miles from Athens, on the day after he had left Athens seems to be impossible, or at least an incredible accomplishment, especially considering the rough terrain and the mountain passes that lay between Athens and Sparta. Victor Matthews points out that Philippides is called a *hemerodromes*, "day-runner," and adds that the word "is usually employed to denote ultra-long distance runners." Matthews states that there is little doubt but that this class of runners could achieve the run to Sparta as described by Herodotus. He estimates the distance to Sparta at about 136 miles and estimates that Philippides covered it certainly in less than 48 hours, and probably in less than 40 hours.[150] Grote points out that the Persian foot messengers routinely covered 60 to 70 miles for several successive days.[151] Krentz adds that in 1982 two officers from the Royal Air Force "ran from Athens to Sparta in 34 and 35.5 hours." In Greece an annual Spartathlon race is held in Athens in September to trace the run of Philippides. The run covers 152.85 miles and the elevation goes from sea level to 3,937 feet. The modern record for the run is an unbelievable 20 hours and 29 minutes, and in 2007, 157 runners finished under 36 hours, which makes it clear that Philippides reaching Sparta the day after leaving Athens is a very reasonable expectation.[152]

A more difficult story for modern readers to accept is Herodotus' description of the god Pan joining Philippides during his run and asking him why the Athenians did not pay attention to him; however, to Philippides and the Athenians "the experience was a very real religious experience."[153] The shrine of Pan described by Herodotus was located on the northwest slope of the Acropolis and was excavated in 1897. It seems that there was no earlier worship of Pan in Athens, so it appears that the Athenians believed Philippides' account, and probably believed that Pan had spread panic among the Persians at Marathon.[154]

Herodotus does not tell us whether Philippides met Pan on his way to Sparta or on his return trip, but in either case he did experience an epiphany of the god Pan.[155] Green says that "we can explain this as a hallucination induced by exhaustion and lack of sleep."[156] Scott gives a detailed explanation of how this might have occurred. He states,

> Philippides' story is intrinsically feasible as a hallucination. Whether it occurred on the outward or return journey (if we assume that he returned immediately), his physiological state would be one in which the brain typically malfunctions: he was performing a remarkable physical feat with little sleep, probably little food; if not dehydrated, at least his blood chemistry would be impaired, and he would have become hypoglycemic: stream water would not replenish salts and sugar. If he was on the outward leg, he will have been running for some 25 to 30 hours, and it would be twilight or dark in the second day, which would enhance the possibilities for hallucinating. If on the return journey, even after a quick meal, but probably no sleep, and perhaps 3 to 4 hours on his way, it would still be dark; in addition, he might be upset, even clinically depressed, if he felt that he had failed in his mission to get immediate Spartan help, and he would be open to persuading himself that he had secured divine help.[157]

When Herodotus says that Philippides appealed to the magistrates, he was probably referring to one or more of the Ephors or perhaps the Ephors plus the Gerousia. The Spartans responded that they would support the Athenians with troops, but they could not march until the next full moon because of a religious festival. This reason is often read as an excuse, but "in reality, the situation may have been more complex." Scott suggests that there are three possible reasons for the delay of the Spartans to march, which include the religious festival, possible internal political tension and anti–Athenian sentiment, and a possible helot disturbance in Messenia.[158] The three possible reasons will be examined in order.

1. Did Sparta have a general ban on military action before marching out of Sparta before the first full moon of the month, or did the ban only apply to certain festivals? Scott says that ancient authorities are divided on the subject, so we do not know; however, Macan states, "It seems well-nigh incredible that the Spartans should have put up with such a hin-

drance to military operations every month."¹⁵⁹ While it may be uncertain if a ban on military action before the full moon applied to every month, there is little doubt but that the festival of Carneia, which was going on when Philippides arrived, did impose "military restraint amongst Dorian states."¹⁶⁰

Holland describes the scene Philippides might have found when he arrived at Sparta during the Carneia Festival. He states,

> The whole of Lacedaemon was *en fete*. Phillipides had arrived while one of the Spartans' holiest festivals, the Carneia, was in full swing, and all across the city young men were resting after a day spent playing brutal games of tag, while their elders feasted in field tents set up in deliberate imitation of a battlefield encampment. Far from signaling the Spartans' readiness to leap up and march off to war, this parody of their conventional campaigning style in fact displayed the precise opposite: the Carneia was a time of peace. There could be no question, the Spartans informed Philippides, regretfully, of breaking such a sacrosanct period. Only once the moon climbed full in the silver-lit August sky would they be able to March to Marathon. On the evening of Philippides' arrival in Sparta, that was still a week away. Add the marching time, and the Athenians could not expect to see a Spartan Army for at least another 10 days.¹⁶¹

Holland goes on to claim that if Cleomenes was still at Sparta, he would have ignored the taboo on marching and would have led an army against Persia which he despised.¹⁶² This raises the question of whether the Spartans were sincere in their beliefs, or if they were using the religious festival as an excuse for not taking immediate action.

M. D. Goodman and A. J. Holladay, in their article "Religious Scruples in Ancient Warfare," state that if a Greek state breached the peace of a festival, there was usually a financial penalty; however, if they paid the penalty and were penitent the was matter was resolved. They go on to explain that festivals caused few problems for the early Greeks as their campaign season took place before the festivals began, but it was impossible to maintain this practice during the Persian Wars, as the Persians did not plan their campaigns around Greek festivals. They add that although "all Greek states would have preferred to respect the festivals, if possible, not all of them were renowned for willingness to sacrifice, or even jeopardize, their interest in order to do so." They point out that Argos once moved the dates of a festival in the hope of stopping a Spartan invasion. They also point out that Thebes had attacked during local festivals; however, they further claim that "Sparta was the one Greek state, which held the reputation of being willing on occasion to sacrifice her own and her allies' interests in fulfilling her duty to the gods."¹⁶³

Macan, How and Wells and Krentz accept the view that Sparta was sincere in refusing to march because of the Carneia festival.¹⁶⁴ Billows agrees that the "Spartans were admittedly a people given to religious scrupulosity, and this reason deserves some respect; but he adds that the Spartans "didn't seem to have had difficulty overcoming religious scruples when their own vital interests were at stake."¹⁶⁵ Green believes that "we have no right, without strong supporting evidence, to accuse them of practicing religious hypocrisy for political ends. Yet it is undeniably curious how often such taboos happen to fit their practical plans."¹⁶⁶

2. While it certainly appears that the Spartans were very scrupulous about their religious obligations, another factor that may have influenced the Spartan decision to delay marching to the aid of Athens was internal political tension and anti–Athenian sentiment. Scott thinks that "public opinion may have been divided as to whether to become involved outside the Peloponnese, despite the Persian threat." He says that some may have had resent-

ments concerning Sparta's defeat in 508 by Athens, while others might have had concerns that Athens' dispute with Aegina had led to Demaratus being deposed. He adds that "while few, if any, Spartans would have accepted submission to Persia for themselves, some would see it as poetic justice if Persia beat Athens." Finally, he suggests that "Sparta's close ties with Delphi may have made her cognizant of Delphi's policy not to resist Persia."[167] Holland points to factionalism in Sparta, explaining that the "bitterness between Leotychides and Demaratus, in particular, was continuing to poison public life, with the new king jeering at his predecessor as a commoner at every turn. With Spartans embroiled in such turmoil, it would hardly do to anger the gods further."[168]

3. Did a helot revolt influence Sparta's decision to delay sending troops to the aid of Athens? In his *Laws*, Plato wrote,

> Datis, with his many myriads, captured by force the whole of the Eretrians; and to Athens he sent on an alarming account of how not a man of the Eretrians had escaped him: the soldiers of Datis had joined hands and swept the whole of Eretria clean as with a drawn net. This account—whether true, or whatever its origin—struck terror into the Greeks generally, and especially the Athenians; but when they sent out embassies in every direction, to seek aid, all refused, except Lacedaemonians; and they were hindered by the war they were then waging against Messene, and possibly by other obstacles, about which we have no information, with the result that they arrived too late by one single day for the battle which took place at Marathon.[169]

Krentz states that "for all his brilliance Plato was not a very good historian" and adds that many scholars reject his view as there is no other literary evidence to support it.[170]

Guy Dickins, writing in 1912, believes that "the evidence seems strong enough to prove that there was a helot rising in 490, and it is inevitable to associate the rising with the plot of Cleomenes." He goes on to explain that when it became obvious that Persia was planning an attack on Greece, Cleomenes intervened on Athens' part in Aegina, which had given "earth and water" to Persia. In addition, Cleomenes succeeded in getting rid of Demaratus, his co-king, who opposed his policy; however, in order to accomplish the overthrow of Demaratus he had to bribe the oracle at Delphi, and when the bribe became public knowledge he fled to Thessaly and then to Arcadia to avoid prosecution. In Arcadia, he organized an anti–Spartan league and got them to sign an oath to "follow him wherever he led them," and in return he swore to follow the constitution. In addition to forming an anti–Spartan league, it appears Cleomenes also offered the helots "some measure of enfranchisement" to get them to rise up against Sparta. To stop the threat, Sparta recalled Cleomenes and restored him to power; however, shortly after his return he went mad and killed himself. Many historians question the validity of the account of his death and believe that he was murdered in Sparta.[171]

W.P. Wallace agrees that Cleomenes organized an anti–Spartan league and was also involved in causing a helot revolt, and he concludes, "The threat to their security is a more likely reason than religious scruples for the Spartans' unwillingness to leave the Peloponnesus at a moment's notice when Athens sent her urgent request for help." He also agrees that "the story of his death conceals a murder which the Ephors had arranged and hushed up."[172]

Ageladas, an Argive sculptor living in the late sixth and early fifth centuries, made a statue of Zeus for the Spartans, which served as a thanks offering for a victory over the

Messenians. It may provide evidence of a helot revolt in 490. The lettering on the inscription on the pedestal could be as late as 464 BCE but the construction of the pedestal suggests an earlier date, perhaps 490 BCE.[173] Additional evidence may be provided by Anaxilas, the tyrant of Rhegium in southern Italy. Around this time he changed the name of the city of Zankle to Messene to honor his Messenian heritage. Numismatic evidence appears to confirm a date of around 489 for the name change. Pausanias and Strabo state that Anaxilas made the name change because so many refugees living in the area were from the Peloponnesus. Hunt wonders where these refugees came from if the last Messenian defeat was in the seventh century. He suggests they may have been refugees from the helot uprising in 490.[174] Peter Hunt says, "There is nothing surprising about Herodotus ignoring a helot revolt. In his neglect of Messenians, Herodotus is typical of Greek historiography."[175]

Duncan Campbell, writing in 2011, describes Cleomenes as having great antipathy toward Persia and working hard to prepare Sparta and Athens to be ready to face the Persian threat. He says that first Cleomenes had to eliminate Demaratus, as he was a Persian sympathizer who might have persuaded the Spartans to give in to their demands. Then he had to make sure to "prevent Argos from taking advantage of the Persian threat. He also took hostages from Aegina as he saw that Aegina might serve as a base for Persia to take action against Athens, Aegina's great enemy. But he felt that Cleomenes did not work with Messene, which could cause trouble.[176]

Campbell then asks why the Spartans delayed their march to Athens. He says that the Spartans were very evasive when it came to any actions that might reflect badly upon Sparta. He claims that Sparta was in crisis in 490, whether from a helot revolt or from the death of Cleomenes. He says that if Cleomenes was indeed assassinated in Sparta or even if Cleomenes fell in battle against the helots, there should be little doubt but that the Spartan sources of Herodotus would be silent on the topic. He concludes that the lack of evidence means we probably will never know for sure why the Spartans arrived after the Battle of Marathon was over.[177]

Philippides returned to Athens with the good news that Sparta would send aid along with the bad news that it would be about 10 days before the Spartan help arrived. Most historians seem to be convinced of Sparta's desire to help as evidenced by their rapid march to Athens once they were able to leave Sparta; however, despite their effort they arrived too late to have any impact on the battle. Why were they late? Was it religious scruples, factionalism, divided public opinion, or because Sparta faced a crisis at home? Theories abound, but there is insufficient evidence to reach a conclusive answer.

Styles of Fighting

Persia successfully expanded its power through the use of a combination of military power and diplomacy. Cyrus was aided in his defeat of the Medes by the defection of Astyages' commanding general. Against Babylonia, Cyrus used diplomacy to appeal to minority populations within the Babylonian Empire such as the Jews and used raids against frontier provinces to convince the people that the king of Babylonia had forsaken them. Cambyses gained important knowledge and help from a key mercenary leader in Egypt, who defected to the Persians. During the Ionian Revolt the Persians used diplomacy to convince Samos to desert the Ionian fleet, which caused others to follow and led to a great Persian victory.

Once the Ionian Revolt was put down, Persia renewed its expansion into Europe and sent Mardonius to punish Athens and Eretria. Mardonius' disaster at Mt. Athos, where his fleet was destroyed by a storm, caused Darius to rethink his campaign against Greece. In 490 Darius decided to send an amphibious expedition across the Aegean, through the islands to avoid Mt. Athos, in order to punish Athens and Eretria and probably to establish a base in central Greece from which to attack the rest of Greece. In preparing for the campaign Darius used diplomacy in an effort to isolate Athens and Eretria by sending heralds to the islands and neighbors of Athens demanding "earth and water." The Persian diplomacy appears to have been successful, as Herodotus states, "On the mainland, many of the Hellenes visited by the heralds gave what the Persians asked, as did all the Islanders to whom the heralds had come with the request."[178] Against Eretria, Persia continued its strategy of using its military and diplomacy to achieve its goal. It used its military to force the Eretrians to defend their walls and diplomacy to convince some Eretrians to open the gates to the Persians. The Persian decision to land at Marathon seems to reflect the same strategy, as it is generally accepted that the Persians landed at Marathon for military reasons, such as good logistics and good terrain for cavalry, but also for the diplomatic reason which was to draw the Athenian army away from Athens so that Persian diplomacy could create conditions similar to Eretria and have Persian sympathizers take over the city.

The Persian style of fighting was dramatically different from the Greek style, which is to be expected as they developed their styles of fighting in two different environments. Both How and van der Veer point out that different physical environments lead to different styles of fighting and the development of different weapons and armaments.[179]

The main strategy of the Persian army was to defeat the enemy before hand-to-hand combat was reached. On the broad plains of Asia this was a practical strategy since there was plenty of room for the cavalry and infantry to maneuver. The Persians would open a battle with the slow initial advance by the infantry, which would plant their wicker shield in the ground and release their arrows when the enemy came within archery range. At this same time the light-armed troops would be releasing their missiles over the infantry, and the cavalry would be swarming around the advancing enemy lines discharging arrows and throwing javelins, trying to put the enemy infantry into confusion. For successful implementation of the strategy, the Persians depended primarily on superior numbers and cavalry, which enabled them to outflank, surround, envelop, and defeat the enemy before hand-to-hand combat was necessary. If the Persian strategy was successful, the surrounded enemy would be so reduced in numbers and so confused that the Persian infantry could advance and easily defeat them. If, however, the Persian plan failed and their army was defeated, the Persians responded by simply putting more armies into the field in order to wear down and defeat their enemy.[180]

The Persian cavalry played a major role in the strategy used by the Persians. It was not a heavily armed cavalry that used shock tactics like Alexander the Great's cavalry, but rather was a light cavalry, which was extremely quick and maneuverable. The principal weapon of the cavalry was the bow, although javelins were also used. On the broad Asian plains the cavalry could hang around the advancing (or retreating) enemy, assailing, retreating, rallying, and attacking again and then retreating if the enemy infantry tried to make contact, and even while it was retreating the Persian cavalry was a formidable force as they were trained to accurately shoot even as they rode away.[181]

The strategy of Athens was to face the Persians on the field of battle rather than to defend Athens, face a siege and risk internal betrayal by Persian sympathizers.[182] The style of fighting for the Greeks was to utilize a phalanx of heavily armed infantry, which used frontal attacks, hand-to-hand combat and shock tactics to defeat the enemy as opposed to the Persians' use of distance weapons, light infantry, archers and highly maneuverable cavalry. While the Persians were dependent upon archers and cavalry, the Greeks used neither at Marathon.[183] The Greeks knew that their phalanx was almost impervious to cavalry attacks; however, they were also aware, from intelligence gathered during the Ionian Revolt, that the phalanx if caught on open ground was vulnerable to attacks on their flanks by cavalry, and if gaps were opened by casualties from archers the cavalry would exploit them.[184]

Why the Delay?

There is no general agreement concerning the date of the Battle of Marathon, nor even the month in which it took place; however, there is agreement that six to nine days passed between the Persian and Greek armies arriving at Marathon and the day of the battle.[185] Herodotus tells us that when the 10 generals of the Athenian army met to discuss their next action they were split evenly between those who felt "their own numbers were too few to engage the forces of the Mede" and those who "urged that they should fight." Since they were evenly split, Miltiades, who voted to fight, went to Callimachus, the *polemarch*, who had been selected by lot, and who held the eleventh and deciding vote, and appealed to him to support the position to engage the enemy.[186] Callimachus was convinced to vote with Miltiades, after which the other generals in favor of going to battle "each in turn, ceded their day of command to Miltiades when the day came around for each to be in charge"; however, Miltiades chose to wait to attack the Persians until it was his normal day to command.[187]

Herodotus' comment that Callimachus was chosen by lot has caused problems for scholars, as according to Aristotle's *Constitution of Athens,* archons were elected by the assembly, and only after 487–486 were they chosen by lot.[188] To deal with this inconsistency between sources, Scott suggests that perhaps "the archons were elected as a group, but the three main officers (eponymous archon, baseleus archon, *polemarch*) were allocated by lot." Kurt Von Fritz and Ernst Kapp in their introduction to Aristotle's *Constitution of Athens* claim that Herodotus is simply wrong. Others claim that Herodotus was guilty of "an anachronism," which was not rare in his work.[189] Scott adds that whichever view of the *polemarch* is correct, Marathon is the first test of the new army created under the reforms of Cleisthenes. He believes that Marathon was such a major crisis that the entire army and all 10 generals were deployed, and he thinks that a rotating command of the army on a daily basis was very feasible.[190]

The Athenians certainly had good reasons for not attacking the Persian army upon arriving at Marathon. They were aware that the Spartans had promised help but that it would not arrive for six to nine days. It would certainly make sense to avoid battle until the best army in Greece came to their aid. In addition, the Athenian generals did not want to be drawn into the plain where the Persian cavalry would be able to play a role in harassing their flanks and rear. Finally, the Greeks knew that the Persians could not stay at Marathon indefinitely, as the food, water and fodder for soldiers, sailors and horses would eventually run short. In addition, Lacey points out that the issue of sanitation, while seldom discussed, would present a major problem. He adds that "the amount of fecal material an army can produce in a very short time (on full or half rations) is, to put it mildly, amazing." He claims that a Persian force of about 80,000-plus cavalry would create unlivable conditions in a short time, and that disease could quickly wipe out an army if it developed and spread.[191] If a battle was to take place before the Spartan army arrived, the Greeks wanted to make sure that the Persians would have to attack the Greeks at a location chosen by the Greeks and not out on the open plain.

While the Persians marched out and offered battle to the Greeks on the plain of Marathon on a daily basis, they also had reasons to delay if the Greeks refused to be drawn out onto the plain. Probably the primary reason for the Persian delay was to gain time for treachery to work in Athens, as it had at Eretria. There is little doubt but that factionalism existed in Athens. Graff pointed out "that rivalry and strife were a permanent and inherent aspect of Greek politics," and he added that during the archaic period, "treason in behalf of individual loyalties was a constant problem."[192] How and Wells claim that "Athens was at this time honeycombed with intrigue, and that a faction within her walls was in communication with Hippias."[193] Another reason for the Persian decision to delay a battle was their desire to draw the Greeks onto the plain where the terrain was advantageous to the Persian style of fighting. Hignett suggests that the Persians had simply made a mistake in not occupying the pass at Marathon and allowing the Athenians to arrive without a fight.[194] Berthold, on the other hand, claims that it would have been easy for the Persian cavalry to have given advance warning of the Greek approach and for the Persians to meet them; however, he claims the Persians intentionally did not advance to the passes because they wanted to fight on the plain. He adds that if the Greeks refused to advance onto the plain, the Persians could land troops behind them and force them to enter the plain.[195] The problem with his argument is that the Persians did not land a force behind the Greeks. Since both the Persians and the Athenians had reasons for delaying battle, why then did the Athenians decide to attack the Persians before the Spartans arrived?

The Decision to Attack

The generals who voted with Miltiades turned the days they were to command the army over to Miltiades, and "while he accepted this, he would not make the attack until it was his day to command."[196] Scott calls Herodotus' explanation the simplest of why the Greeks attacked the Persians before the Spartan army arrived. He explains this action by saying that Miltiades "wanted the glory, and took action on his prytany instead of prudently waiting for the Spartans." He adds that perhaps the "troops were getting restless" and perhaps they began to worry that the Spartans might not arrive in time before the Persians attacked. Some may have spoken out about retreating to the safety of Athens to await the Spartans.

Also it was possible that one of the generals who had voted with Miltiades might change his vote if pressured by his men, and if the resulting vote was changed to six to four, Miltiades would lose no matter what Callimachus favored. So in order to prevent either of the above from occurring, Miltiades ordered the attack.[197]

Most historians, however, have not accepted Herodotus' explanation for the timing of the Greek attack. How and Wells comment, "The change in the strategy of Miltiades from the defensive to the offense ... must have been occasioned by some more serious motive than the supposed prytany of Miltiades."[198] With little direct evidence to work with, historians have speculated widely about why the Greeks attacked before the Spartans arrived. Three viewpoints have emerged, although details have varied. The three viewpoints are (1) the Persians split their forces which caused the Greeks to attack the weakened Persian Army, (2) the Persians initiated the action and the Greeks responded by attacking, or (3) the Persian cavalry was not immediately available and the Greeks attacked before the cavalry could play a major role.

Macan presented a hypothesis in 1895 which stated that "the Persians at last decided to make a movement upon Athens with fleet and infantry at once." He suggested that the fleet and infantry could keep in touch as the infantry moved down the main road toward Athens and then the fleet could sail to Phaleron to attack Athens.[199] In 1899 Munro developed the hypothesis in more detail in an article in the *Journal of Hellenic Studies*. According to Munro the Persians planned that half to two-thirds of the army would stay at Marathon to keep the Athenian army occupied. The rest would sail to Phaleron to attack Athens. The Athenians, however, could not afford to split their army, as superior Persian numbers required the entire Athenian army to meet the Persian army at Marathon. If the Athenian army chose to return to Athens rather than face the Persians at Marathon, the Athenian army would be vulnerable from the rear as they marched toward Athens. If that was the Persian plan why did they delay implementing it? Obviously they were waiting for Persian sympathizers to take control in Athens. Hippias could not only depend upon his old family connections, but there is also evidence that Hippias had a "secret understanding with a powerful party in the city." It appears his ally was the Alcmaeonidae, and Herodotus' apology for them is "very damning" according to Munro. Miltiades was well aware of the political machinations taking place in Athens, and he knew that "in attacking a superior force the half is better than the whole." When the attack would take place would be determined by the Persians, so Miltiades had to make sure that the Greeks would be ready for it.[200]

Anticipating the criticism that Herodotus makes no mention of a division of the Persian forces, Munro claims that if anything was to be forgotten in the Athenian tradition, the story of the Persian army splitting would qualify, as it reduced the magnitude of the Athenian victory at Marathon. He claims a trace of evidence of the split may be seen in Cornelius Nepos when he says 100,000 out of the 200,000 Persian troops took part in the battle. Finally he claims that "patriotism and Alcmaeonidae influence" would combine to omit mention of the fact that the Greeks fought only a portion of the Persian troops.[201] Grundy agrees with Munro but adds an explanation of why the cavalry was sent on the fleet rather than remaining to aid in fighting the Athenian army. He claims that the difficulty of transportation had greatly limited the amount of cavalry that Datis had brought to Marathon, and it would have been of little use in pursuing the Greek army if it took the northern route to Athens. Also the small number of cavalry meant it would be ineffective against a Greek phalanx, whereas if it went with the fleet it could be "of immense value for a dash on Athens immediately upon arrival at Phaleron."[202]

Writing in the first edition of the *Cambridge Ancient History* in 1926, Munro stuck with his hypothesis that the Persians split their forces, but he made a major change in how it was done. In his 1926 article he claimed that the Athenian army was not marching to Marathon but rather was marching to the aid of Eretria; however, the Persians anticipated the move by Athens and "landed at Marathon in order prevent the Athenian army from going to the aid of Eretria by occupying them at Marathon. When the Persian expedition reached Greece, Datis had split his forces, with one division led by Artaphernes attacking Eretria and the other division led by Datis landing at Marathon. When informed of the action of Datis, the Athenian army turned toward Marathon and made camp in the Avlona valley. Regarding the five- to eight-day delay before the battle took place, Munro says the Persians were content to keep the Athenian army occupied while waiting for Artaphernes to defeat Eretria and make his force available to go to Phaleron or provide reinforcements for Datis at Marathon. The Athenians could not return to Athens because "the moral effect of the retreat would decide the issue in favor of Hippias." Hesitant to attack the Persian army in the open plain, the Athenians were content to wait for the Spartans to arrive; however, when word came that Artaphernes was leaving Eretria, it was coincidentally the day of Miltiades' command, and he chose to attack before Artaphernes either arrived at Marathon or sailed to Phaleron.[203] Why the cavalry was with Artaphernes and not with Datis, Munro does not address.

General Maurice essentially accepts Munro's hypothesis, but adds some different details. He believes that Artaphernes did not need 12,000 men at Eretria, so 4,000 were sent to Datis, giving him a total of 16,000 at Marathon. He claims that water was in short supply for the Persians and uses that as an additional support to prove that the entire Persian force was not at Marathon.[204] While many historians appear convinced by the argument that the Persians split their forces, it seems that Munro and Maurice are not supported by most historians regarding when the split occurred.

Examining articles and books concerning the Battle of Marathon, the hypothesis that the Persians split their forces appears to be the most widely accepted viewpoint. While many accept the theory, there are some minor differences, such as Sekunda claiming that there was a 50–50 split in Persian forces, while Green says 15,000 were at Marathon and 10,000 were sailing to Athens. Burn simply says the bulk of troops remained at Marathon, but some infantry and cavalry embarked on the ships.[205] The fact that the cavalry was sent with the navy to attack Athens seems accepted by most of those accepting the split forces theory.[206]

Evidence in support of the hypothesis that the Persians split their forces includes the *Suda* in which some Ionians warned the Athenians that the cavalry was away; Cornelius Nepo's statement that only 100,000 of 200,000 troops participated in the battle; the fact that only seven ships were captured by the victorious Athenians, proving most of the ships had departed; the absence of cavalry in Herodotus' account of the battle, showing that the cavalry was with the ships; the Greeks rushing back to Athens after the battle to face the Persian fleet; and the length of time required to sail to the Phaleron.[207]

Billows, writing in 2010, believes that the Athenians were concerned about being significantly outnumbered by the Persians, and were especially worried about the Persian advantage in archers and cavalry. While they waited for the Spartan army, the Athenians cut down trees "and laid them, untrimmed, into a so-called abatis; lines of untrimmed trees with their branches toward the enemy forming an anti-cavalry obstacle on each flank. Each night they extended the abatis preparing a secure advance into the plain for when the Spartan reinforcement should arrive and the battle would take place."[208]

Billows believes that the Persians were unwilling to attack the Greek camp and were waiting for Hippias' supporters to betray Athens to them. He adds that if their supporters in Athens should fail, Persia still had the option to attack Athens by sea. In addition Persian intelligence was aware of when the Spartans were to arrive. When the Spartan's arrival was imminent and Hippias' supporters had not succeeded in Athens, the Persians decided to move on Athens by sea and embark "a substantial part of their army, importantly, including most of their cavalry force" to sail to Phaleron and attack Athens.[209] The Greeks also had sources of information in the Persian camp, and they reported the Persian plans to the Athenians. Some Greek generals argued to return to Athens to defend the city, but Miltiades pointed out the negative impact such a move would have on the morale of the army. He also called attention to the fact that many of the hoplites did not live in Athens and "would be tempted to peel away from the march from Marathon to Athens to head for their own home towns and villages in Attica, to secure their families and homes." Also, a concern existed as to whether the Plataeans would follow the army to Athens or simply return to Plataea. Finally, a Greek retreat from Marathon might embolden the Greek supporters of Hippias to follow Eretria's lead.[210]

When the Persians split their forces, Miltiades recognized that the Persian army at Marathon was much weaker and that it had little or no cavalry. Miltiades believed that the Greeks could attack early in the morning, defeat the weakened Persian army and still have time to return to Athens before the Persian fleet could complete its voyage to Phaleron. Miltiades' plan won the support of the generals, and the decision to attack was made.[211]

While the theory that the Persians split their forces has won many adherents, critics remain. Whatley in his article thinks it absurd to believe that the Persians would re-embark their cavalry, because militarily it made no sense. He adds that the cavalry was the only force that could have been effective in preventing the Athenians from returning to Athens from Marathon. It would have been very dangerous for the Athenians to attempt to march back to Athens with the Persian army and cavalry in a position to harass them and attack their rear.[212]

Whatley has little respect for the *Suda* as a source. He says most agree that the author must have lived around 1000 CE which means that he was chronologically closer to Macan and Munro than he was to the Battle of Marathon. He goes on to question whether it is probable that the source used for the *Suda* had not been seen or used by Cornelius Nepos, Pausanias or the author of *The Malice of Herodotus*, since the last author was particularly hostile to Herodotus and would certainly have included the story as it would make Herodotus look bad.[213]

Krentz agrees that the *Suda* is a poor source. He includes a translation of the pertinent passage in the *Suda* by J.A.S. Evans:

When Datis invaded Attica, men say that the Ionians, when he had withdrawn (or gone away), came up inland to a wooded area (or climbed trees) and told (or signaled) the Athenians that their horses were apart (or away or brigaded by themselves, or possibly off on a separate mission). And Miltiades, who took note of their departure (or understood what they were up to), attacked and won a victory. Thus the aphorism said of those who break up (or destroy) battle order (or an Army detachment, or possibly even an army).[214]

Krentz then proceeds to evaluate the *Suda* as a source. First of all he points out the late date of the source and the fact that the author is unknown. He next says that there is no explanation of where the horses were or why they were gone. He goes on to point out that the hills in the area allowed the Athenians to view the Persian camp, and they would have been able to see for themselves that the cavalry was gone and there was no need of a message from the Ionians. Finally he says, "The story reeks of Ionian propaganda." He adds that the Ionians are the only beneficiaries of the story and suspects that the "story was first told somewhere in Ionia."[215]

Whatley continues his assault on the split Persian forces theory when he says the evidence in support of it is so weak that it is not worth discussing and adds that Nepos is totally unreliable, especially concerning the numbers he includes. He rejects Munro's view that the Persians landed at Marathon to lure the Athenians away from Athens, as they could have forced a landing at Phaleron rather than 25 miles away at Marathon. Whatley points out that in ancient and even modern history amphibious landings are made away from the defending army if possible. He continues saying Marathon was "a good landing-place, fairly near Eretria and more or less on the direct route to Athens, and where the Persians could disembark their cavalry and stores undisturbed." Munro claimed that the Persians would have occupied the passes if they meant to march on Athens; however, Whatley says that he does not know what "occupy the passes" means, as there is "no Thermopylae between Athens and Marathon." He goes on to say that even if there was a pass, a small cavalry force would not have been able to hold it. He concludes, "The language of an age of machine guns is inapplicable to an age of bows and arrows."[216]

Hignett rejects the view that the Athenians attacked because the Persians were beginning to re-embark some of their troops and cavalry. He says this view, "so frequently at variance with the implications of Herodotus' narrative, rests on no ancient evidence worthy of the name." He also says that if 20,000 Persians fought at Marathon, then 40,000 must have accompanied the mission, as half had re-embarked, and this total number is too high. Finally he wonders why the Persians did not withdraw north of the Charadra, as it was the strongest position if their only goal was to hold the Athenians at Marathon.[217]

In an article in 1968, Hammond claims that the Persians had probably offered battle often to the Greeks who chose to wait for the Spartans or to wait for the Persians to put themselves into a weak position. While the Persian infantry stayed on the plain, the horses were sent to the Macaria springs for water and fodder. During the waiting, the Greeks cut down trees to set up obstructions to the Persian cavalry and extended them out on the plain in order to draw closer to the Persians without engaging them. The Persian groomsmen returned the horses from Macaria by moonlight so that the cavalry would be ready at dawn; however, as the days passed, the moon was setting earlier and there was a period of darkness before sunrise which made it more difficult for the Persian groomsmen to get the horses back to Marathon by sunrise. Hammond accepts the *Suda* version of the Ionians telling the Greeks that "the cavalry was away." When Miltiades was informed, he already had his troops in position, so he decided to attack into the plain before the horses returned.[218]

Avery, writing in 1972, claims that the Persians, who had attacked and taken the walled city of Eretria, should have been willing to attack the Greek camp, and yet they delayed. He thinks that they did not attack because they were lacking cavalry. Where was the cavalry? He says that we do not know, and in fact he thinks that perhaps the Persians also did not know.[219]

Lazenby, writing in 1992, rejects the fact that Herodotus does not mention cavalry in the battle and the fact that only seven Persian ships were captured by the Greeks as being evidence that the Persians had split their forces and re-embarked their cavalry. He says that there is a simpler explanation for the fact that the battle took place before the Spartans arrived. He claims that the Persians made a move against the Greeks, and while the Greeks were happy to wait for the Spartans, it did not prevent "them from seizing the tactical initiative, once battle was forced upon them."[220]

Doenges in 1998 suggests that Datis hesitated to attack the Greeks because he "lacked a sufficient numerical superiority." One may assume that Datis deployed his forces each morning in an attempt to draw the Greeks out of their defensive position into the plain where the Persians would have the advantage; however, the Greeks refused to respond. Doenges concludes by stating, "At last, after five days of this *sitzkrieg* Datis must have decided to act. He chose to attack because he had to break the deadlock or else he would 'have to evacuate Marathon.'"[221]

Ray, in 2009, says, "The confrontation at Marathon opened as something of a standoff. The Greeks clearly had no intention of risking a cavalry attack by advancing into the coastal plain, while their foe was equally unwilling to charge into the hills." In addition, there were scattered trees by the Greek camp, and they added to their defense by building an abatis. While the Greeks could draw unlimited supplies from Athens and the surrounding area, the Persian supplies were running low. So the Persians decided to attack before the Spartan reinforcements arrived. Ray says that the Persians marched into the Vrana valley, thus precipitating the Greek attack.[222]

Writing in 2010, Krentz rejects the Persians splitting their forces theory, but suggests that the battle was caused by the Greeks attempting to block all exits from Marathon. The Greeks at Valaria blocked the coastal road to Athens, but to block the Stamata route, "the Greeks had to advance not only in front of the Vrana valley, which would cut off one entry to the Stamata route, but also to Mt. Stavrokoraki in order to cut off the other entry to the pass between Mt. Kotroni and Mt. Stavrokoraki." The problem was that to accomplish this task would require the Greek army to cross into the plain, which would expose their army to the Persian cavalry and archers, so Miltiades needed a plan to deal with the cavalry and archers. As the Persians deployed on the plain daily in an attempt to draw out the Greek army, Miltiades and Callimachus had time to observe the Persian deployment and search for weaknesses. They observed that the grooms took the horses of the cavalry to the Macaria springs each night for water and fodder. They were also aware that the road that ran between the springs and Mt. Stavrokoraki and the battle site was very narrow at the springs, so it would take about 50 minutes to an hour and 40 minutes for the horses to return from

Macaria. Miltiades determined that if the Athenians attacked early enough, they had the opportunity to cross the plain before the cavalry could be fully deployed. So the attack was planned.[223]

Christopher Tuplin, in an article entitled "Marathon in Search of a Persian Dimension," suggests that the Persians may not have intended to fight at Marathon but rather to march on Athens. He thinks that they may have been surprised by the Greek army marching to Marathon, but that the Persians also felt that it was to their advantage as it took the Greek army "further from sources of outside help, and denied them easy refuge within the city in the event of the expected defeat." Tuplin explains the delay before the Persians attacked as a Persian attempt to see if "Athenian solidarity might falter," and he points to the battles of Lade, Thermopylae and Plataea as other examples of Persian delays. What happened during this delay is unknown, but Tuplin suggests that perhaps the Persians attempted to put psychological pressure on the Athenians by ravaging some land around Marathon. He says, "Herodotus presents the battle as an Athenian choice, but has them conform their battle line to that of the Persians."[224]

Johan Henrik Schreine, of the University of Oslo, presents the most original and unique theory concerning the Persians and Greeks at Marathon. He contends that there were two battles at Marathon rather than the one battle as described by Herodotus. He suggests that the Greeks marched to Marathon and established a camp in the Vrana valley. He then states that the Persians immediately attacked the Greek camp, which was in a strong defensive location, and the Greeks defeated the Persians in the battle but Callimachus was killed. After their defeat in the first battle, the Persians retreated, and Datis embarked part of his army and his cavalry in order to attack Athens from the sea. Meanwhile, Miltiades moved the Greek camp to the Herakleion located in Valaria. From that camp Miltiades led the Greek army out to attack and defeat the Persian forces led by Datis.[225] Schreiner rejects much of Herodotus and bases most of his conclusions on the *Suda,* Cornelius Nepos and Polemon, a sophist in the second century AD. Most historians question the value and validity of Nepos and the *Suda*, and there is no evidence that Schreiner's thesis has gained any adherents.

After examining the wide range of viewpoints concerning the decision of the Greeks to attack the Persian army before the Spartans arrived, can we draw any conclusion? The only literary evidence comes from Herodotus and some later sources such as Cornelius Nepos and the *Suda*, and views on their credibility vary. It appears that perhaps the best approach is to accept the minimal information provided by Herodotus and attempt to fill in the details with speculation based upon probabilities, possibilities and what we know of command and organization; however, it appears that the majority viewpoint of most historians is that the Persians split their forces, even though Herodotus makes no mention of it.[226] Most of the historians present rational, logical, reasonable and convincing arguments for their viewpoints, so how is one to determine the "correct" or the "best" or at least the most reasonable viewpoint? At one point while describing the Persian deployment on the day of the battle, Krentz states, "You'll recognize that I'm making this up."[227] Aren't all the authors doing the same thing—making up the details to fill in the information missing in Herodotus' account? Ultimately it's up to the reader to determine which is the "best" viewpoint based upon the criteria that the reader establishes.

Deployment of Armies

Once the plan of Miltiades had been finalized, the deployment of the army was set. Callimachus, as *polemarchon*, was placed in command of the right wing, and the rest of the tribes "were posted next to one another in succession, according to their numerical order and the Plataeans were posted at the end of the line, holding the extreme left wing."[228] Regarding the deployment of the Persian army, Herodotus only mentions that the Saka and Persians were deployed in the center of the Persian line. Wozniak suggests that the Medes might also have been present as some claim Datis was the satrap of Media. In addition, as the generals passed through northern Mesopotamia on their way to Cilicia, they may have recruited local troops. It is probable that Lydian soldiers also may have been involved since the father of Artaphernes was the satrap of Lydia; however, the only thing that we can be certain of is that the Persians had their best troops in their center while their weaker troops were on the wings. Where the cavalry was is uncertain.[229]

Van der Veer has done the most comprehensive examination of possible locations that the Greek and Persian armies may have taken as they prepared for battle. Herodotus tells us that the distance between the Greeks and the Persian armies was eight stades, or about one mile.[230] Van der Veer feels that the Soros (grave of the Athenians at Marathon) can be used as a reliable point of reference since it must have been the area in which the charging hoplites came under fire from Persian archers. He thinks that the Persians lined up within 150 m of the Soros, which meant that the Greeks were about 1,415 m (1,565–150 m) from the Soros.[231] Based upon the above figures, van der Veer believes that militarily speaking there are three locations in the neighborhood of the Herakleion which qualify for possible Greek battle positions. The three possible locations are as follows:

1. In the Vrana Valley.
2. Along the northeastern slope of Mt. Agrieliki.
3. In the southern entrance to the plain.

The Persian battle position would be about 150 m beyond the Soros with the direction determined by the Greek battle position. The first possible location is supported by those who believe the Greek camp in the Herakleion was located in the Vrana valley. Using that Location as their camp, the Greeks probably lined up "across the face of the Valley between Mt. Kotroni and Mt. Agrieliki." The opening between the mountains was about 1,500 m and about 1,415 m from the Soros. From the Greek perspective this position offered good defensive and offensive possibilities and included a good water supply. There was also reliable communication with Athens using the northern route which was available and three miles shorter than the southern route. Also another route through the Avlona valley north of the Deme of Oinoe and through Kephisia to Athens was also available, although this final route was "rough and narrow in many places," which hindered any swift movement.[232]

If the Greeks took the above position, the "corresponding Persian position stood within 150 m South-East from the Soros, front facing North-West, parallel to the south coast." A good water supply was available for the Persians; however, that position caused a problem for the Persians, as "only a narrow slanting corridor was available in case of retreat to the ships at Schoenia beach." As a result, How and Wells as well as Hammond believe that the

Persians anchored their ships behind the Persian army in case of retreat or defeat to facilitate loading of the troops; however, such a positioning of the Persian ships would have exposed them to the fierce northeast winds (the so-called Etesians), which blew in the summer.[233]

Finlay, Meyer, Kromayer, Schachermeyr, Hignett and Pritchett have suggested another possible position of the Greek army which ran along "the foot of Mt. Agreiliki," with the left wing "close to the Herakleion at St. Demetrius" and the right wing near the small marsh. The line of troops would "extend for about 1500 m in a South-Eastern direction along the base of Mt. Agreiliki; front facing NE, at about eight stades from the Soros." In that position, Mt. Agrieliki would cover the flanks and rear of the Greek army, and the position also enabled the Greeks to "command the highway between Marathon and Athens, an important road of supply and communication with the political center." Water was available at this position, and the Valley of Maki-Dionysos could supply a retreat if necessary. With this Greek position, the Persian army would have been located within 150 m, northeast from the Soros, front facing southwest, nearly at right angles to the coast. Water supply in that location is less certain as the Mati spring near Breccias was controlled by the Greeks, so they would have been dependent upon wells on the surrounding farms.[234]

In 1970 Vanderpool discovered a "second Herakles inscription in the locality of Valaria which seemed to settle the location of the Herakleion where the Greeks set up their camp. Using this location as their camp, van der Veer describes the position of the Greek and Persian armies. He believes the Greek battle line would have lined up between Mt. Agrieliki and the seacoast at about a right angle to the sea facing north-northeast. The distance between Mt. Agrieliki and the coast is about 1,500 m. The Persians would have lined up north of the Soros, and the Charadra would have been at their back. Both armies would have had adequate water supplies in those locations.[235] Van der Veer feels that each of the above three locations could be used to help explain the battle that took place; however, since the third location is the only one based upon archaeological evidence, he feels it is the best choice.[236]

Writing in 1988 in the *Cambridge Ancient History*, Hammond accepts Vanderpool's location of the Herakleion, and as a result essentially accepts the location of the Greek and Persian armies as described by van der Veer's location C.[237] Ray, writing in 2009, seems to be unaware of Vanderpool's conclusion concerning the Herakleion or simply dismisses it, as he has the Persians attacking the Greeks into the Vrana valley.[238] Billows, writing in 2010, also seems to ignore Vanderpool's conclusion, as he sets the Herakleion "near the present-day Chapel of St. Demetrius" in the Vrana valley, and thus supports positions described in van der Veer's first location in which the Greek and Persian lines were parallel to the sea.[239] Krentz in 2010 believed that Vanderpool's Herakleion is "the best choice based on current evidence," and as a result he has the Greek and Persian armies face each other at right angles to the sea and includes a map similar to van der Veer's location number three.[240] Lacey, writing in 2011, says that the "grove of Heracles was a matter of great dispute for a number of years, but it has now been definitively located by Eugene Vanderpool in the South East corner of the plain, so he would also agree with van der Veer's third location.[241]

In describing the deployment of the Greek army, Herodotus tells us that "the line of the Athenian army was equal in length to that of the Medes, but the center of the Athenian line was only a few rows deep, and thus the army was at its weakest there; each wing, however, was strong in numbers."[242] While it would seem that the Athenians weakened their center in order to lengthen their line and make it equal to the Persian line, Macan suggests that the numbers were not very unequal and that Miltiades weakened the center in order to "strengthen the wings" or because "the nature of the ground" required the change.[243] How and Wells believe that the center was weakened to prevent being outflanked, but they also suggests that the center "was obstructed by plantations of olives and vines."[244] Both commentaries, of course, were written long before Vanderpool's archaeological work identified the location of the Herakleion.

Scott, in his 2005 commentary on Herodotus, thinks that the Persians were already drawn up for battle in a line about 1,600 m long. The Greeks had to adjust their deployment to meet the longer line of the Persians. He also points out that the Greek term referring to the Greek wings meant "to be strong," and not "to be strengthened" as Macan claimed. He believes the redeployment meant the center was four men deep, while the wings remained the conventional eight men deep.[245] Lazenby would agree with Scott that the Athenian center was four men deep and the wings eight men deep, and he used 10,000 hoplites to calculate the Athenian frontage. He says if "we allow about 90 cm per man, we would get the following frontages: left wing 315 m, center c. 1,000 m, right wing c. 300 m, total 1615 m." He also claims that the center was weakened only for defensive purposes and not to accomplish a double envelopment.[246] Krentz in 2010 claims that the Athenian army had 18,000 men, including 10,000 hoplites and 8,000 light armed. He believes that Miltiades observed the Persians deploying their troops during the delay before the battle. As a result he could estimate the length of their front line so that he knew the length required of his front in order to avoid being outflanked. He says 18,000 with eight deep on the wings and four deep in the center would cover about "1.5 miles with a file width of 3 feet," which would prevent his army from being outflanked.[247]

Billows, writing in 2010, agrees that Miltiades weakened his center to extend the line, but he thinks with the hope "that the two strong wings would be able to defeat the two wings of the Persian army opposing them, drive the Persian wings backward into flight and then turn inward to envelop the Persian center."[248] Lacey in 2011 agreed that the Athenians extended their battle lines to avoid being outflanked, but he suggests similar to Billows that the weakened center was to draw the Persian center into a trap, which the wings would spring after defeating the Persian wings which were made up of inferior groups compared to the center; however, Lacey believes it was the brilliant plan of Callimachus rather than Miltiades.[249]

The Charge

Herodotus describes the actual Greek attack on the Persian army and the resulting battle in about 30 lines, so needless to say many details are lacking and many questions are left unanswered. One question that has attracted a lot of attention is whether or not the Greek army actually ran the entire mile between the two armies at Marathon.

George Grote, who wrote his multivolume *History of Greece* between 1846 and 1856, takes Herodotus literally and believes that the Greek army ran the entire distance, claiming that the run succeeded "in rendering the Persian cavalry and archers comparatively innocuous"; however, he also states that it "disordered the Athenian ranks, and that when they reached the Persian front, they were both out of breath and unsteady in that line of presented spears and shields which constituted their force." As result he thinks it explains why the weakened center was defeated while the eight-ranks-deep wings were less disordered and thus were able to decisively defeat the flanks of the Persian army.[250] In his commentary on Herodotus, Macan says the claim that thousands of hoplites in full armor advanced the best part of a mile at a rapid run without breaking ranks seems incredible; however, he adds, "on the other hand, that a rapid advance was one of the characteristic memories of Marathon, and need not be doubted."[251] W. Watkins Lloyd, in 1881, says that in reading Herodotus' account of the battle, "we may be prepared to assume a large alloy of inaccuracy and considerable incompleteness." He goes on to say that at times Herodotus is "guilty of a little extravagance" and that the Athenians "did not start at a run for a charge of near a mile." He agrees with Grote that the run occurred in order to cut down losses to the Persian archers and to bring the hoplites to hand-to-hand combat as soon as possible. He implies that the run began as they came within range of the Persian archers.[252] How and Wells in their commentary on Herodotus also weigh in on the issue. They state,

> on the other hand, an orderly and effective charge after a mile run in full armour would be beyond the power of any large body of soldiers, however well-trained. The mile, however, is probably an inference from the distance between the Athenian position near Vrana and the place where they charged the Persians near the Soros. No doubt the advance was rapid, but only for the last 200 yards, when within bowshot would the Attic hoplites charge at full speed.[253]

There has been some debate about whether translating the Greek term that Herodotus uses should be "to run" or "at the quickstep." In an article in the *Classical Quarterly*, How examines how the term was used by other Greek historians such as Thucydides and Xenophon, and he concludes that in comparing the same term as used at the Battle of Plataea, it is certain that at Marathon the term used by Herodotus means "at the run."[254] Grundy says that the "Athenians advanced at the quickstep upon the barbarians." Grundy prefers to translate the Greek term that Herodotus uses as "quickstep" rather than "at the run." He claims that the "Greek hoplite seems to have been incapable of rapid movement." He says that the hoplite was the product of his culture in which citizens of each polis had "to fight on behalf of their annual produce." The hoplites from all poleis were similarly equipped, so slow-moving heavily armed hoplites was the norm in archaic Greece. So an advance at the "quickstep" would have been considered extraordinary. He goes on to say that for the Greeks to advance at a run for a mile would have been a "physical impossibility"; however, he says that "Herodotus may have ascribed to the whole length of the advance a form of movement, which was only adopted when the Greeks came within range of missiles."[255]

Writing at the turn of the century, Hans Delbruck simply rejects Herodotus' version of the Greeks running for a mile to engage the Persians, saying it "is a physical impossibility: a heavily equipped unit can cover at the most 400–500 feet (120–150 m) at a run without completely exhausting its strength and falling into disorder." He goes on to say that individuals trained as runners and primitive peoples "are of course capable of covering great distances at the run, even when burdened," but he also points out that the Athenians were neither primitive people nor trained runners but rather were regular citizens who had little or no training. He says that even in the highly respected Prussian army, "running with full field equipment is not permitted for more than two minutes or 330–350 m." He gives an example from the Danish war in 1864, where a larger Danish force attacked a weaker Prussian unit that was in a defensive position. Lieutenant General von Quistorp described the Danish charge as follows:

> A body of troops cannot continue for 400 paces at forced speed that spontaneously develops into a full run, in a situation leading to hand-to-hand combat with the enemy. The individual runs out of breath, and after 100 paces the company is forced to halt. The ensuing minutes until they can again move forward are most painful.[256]

Munro, in the first edition of the *Cambridge Ancient History,* agrees with Delbruck when he states, "Herodotus, indeed understood that the Athenians doubled over the whole mile interval between the two armies. He says that a mile run might be possible, but it "would at least be senseless, and is to be regarded as a misapprehension."[257] Whatley questions whether the Greek term translated as "to run" really means to actually run, but regardless of the translation, Whatley says that the mile run is not acceptable as a mile run by hoplites in full panoply would mean that the hoplites would be in no condition to fight at the end of the run.[258] Maurice, writing in 1932, also rejects the mile run by the hoplites. He says that perhaps during the charge the Greeks ran some of the time, but he says that Herodotus' story of running "eight furlongs" is no longer credible. He goes on to say that the goal of Miltiades was to bring his men into close contact with the Persian infantry as quickly as possible to minimize the exposure of his men to the Persian archers, so the charge "at the double" was probably for less than 300 yards.[259]

Hignett, in 1963, says that the "timing and speed" of the Greeks may have taken the Persians by surprise, but he also declares Herodotus' statement that the Athenians "charged at the double" for eight stades is an exaggeration, as such a charge was "a feat which no phalanx of citizen militia could have performed." Rather, he says the Athenians probably "advanced at a quick march to the attack, but did not break into its double until they came within range of the Persian archers."[260] Hammond, on the other hand, writing in 1968, basically agrees with Grote and calls Herodotus' account "completely unimpeachable."[261]

Walter Donlan and James Thompson, professors at Pennsylvania State University, recognized that there were two conflicting viewpoints concerning the Greek charge at Marathon. They state, "There can be no doubt, however, about Herodotus' intent; he meant his audience to believe that the Athenians charged the Persians at a run for eight stades and that this was a most notable achievement deserving special mention." They add that to their knowledge, they were unaware of anyone actually measuring "the physical requirements of a mile run in full panoply." Therefore, they decided to do a series of experiments (two in the field and one in the human performance laboratory) "to simulate the charge to test the validity of Herodotus' statements." They had 10 young physical education majors carrying a total of 15 pounds and a nine-pound shield on their left arm run in pairs over uneven terrain. They were told to hold their shield chest high as they ran 1,600 yards (1,760 m). In the first test, they found that none of the runners could hold their shield chest high after 75 yards and that the formation broke up after 300 yards. Only one runner, a varsity long-distance runner, was able to complete the 1,600-yard run. In the second field test the following year, the results were similar, except that not one of the PE majors completed the run. In the laboratory tests the participants carried 15 pounds along with the nine-pound shield and ran on a treadmill for 8.5 minutes at seven miles per hour.

Using data from the runs, Donlan and Thompson calculated that it would take 90 to 95 percent of the runners' "maximum capability" to complete the test. They claim that the participants were above average in fitness; however, most of them would have been so fatigued by the end of the run that they would have been incapable of fighting an opponent in hand-to-hand combat with any effectiveness. The one exception was a long-distance runner on the varsity track team at Penn State, as he would have had sufficient energy to fight. They also point out that if the participants had carried the shield chest high for the entire distance, their energy expenditure would have been 28 percent higher. They then point out that the average Greek male in 490 BCE was approximately 5'6" tall and weighed about 145 pounds, while the participants in the test averaged 5'11" in height and weighed about 164 pounds, which meant that the weight being carried would have been an even greater percentage of their body weight for the ancient Greeks. Extrapolating from their data, using the generally accepted viewpoint that the hoplite's panoply weighed between 50 to 70 pounds, Donlan and Thompson "conclude with some confidence that the maximum distance for a phalanx-charge at double time, maintaining formation and arriving fit for close engagement, was no more than one stade, approximately 200 yards."[262]

Writing in 1988, Hammond appears to have been familiar with Donlan and Thompson's research, as he changed his position concerning the mile run from the position he took in 1968. Hammond now suggested that the Athenians moved fast over the first few stades, but only "ran through the barrage of arrows for the last 140 m."[263] Lazenby in 1992 suggested that the Athenians probably ran for part of the charge, and "by the time Herodotus heard the story, it might well have been extended to the full eight stades in the popular imagination, whereas in reality, it had only been over the last part of the distance"; or perhaps Herodotus heard that the distance between the Greek and Persian armies was eight stades, and he may have "mistakenly assumed the Greeks had run the full distance." Lazenby goes on to say that the Persian archers would become effective at about 175 m, so it was at that point that the Greeks would have probably broken into a run.[264]

The Twenty Five Hundredth Anniversary of the Battle of Marathon was celebrated in 2010, and three new books were published on the battle. Billows writing in 2010 accepts the consensus view that the Greeks advanced at a fast pace but did not break into a run until they came within bow shot of the Persians. He claims it is "almost impossible for thousands of men running forward to maintain formation properly." He says that the differences in stamina and running ability "would tend to make lines ragged" but that over a shorter distance, the lines while ragged would hold together as opposed to how the lines might disintegrate if they ran for the full mile.[265]

Krentz in 2010, however, disagrees with what appears to have become the consensus view that the hoplites could not run a mile and still be able to defeat the Persians. First he examines the experiments of Donlan and Thompson and finds their value questionable. He claims that "mistaken assumptions vitiate these experiments." He believes that they should not have used 7 mph in their experiments but rather 4.5 mph, as he says that is the point when a fast walk turns into a run. Secondly he rejects the weight of the hoplite's panoply and states that it was not as heavy as the weights used in the calculations by Donlan and Thompson. He also challenges Donlan and Thompson's projection of the hoplite's panoply as weighing between 50 to 70 pounds, which he estimated weighing between 30 to 50 pounds. He goes on to say that even if the correct figures had been used, he still questions whether it is possible to compare college students with ancient Greek farmers. He claims that one cannot compare college students who eat a high-sugar, high-sodium diet, who drive cars and who work out for a limited time each day with Greek farmers who did physical labor all day, ate a lean diet with little meat, sugar or salt and who walked wherever they went. Krentz then proceeds to say, "We ought to look at soldiers in the field rather than students in a lab." He also takes issue with Delbruck's comments that the director of the Military Central Physical Training School told him that a column with field equipment would only be able to run for two minutes, or about 400 to 500 feet, and still be able to fight.[266]

Krentz counters Delbruck by telling of a French captain who had an infantry platoon "that covered 12.7 miles in 106 minutes, a pace of 7.2 mph." In another instance, the platoon "carried field equipment for 6.8 miles in 80 minutes, a pace of 5.1 mph, and proceeded to target practice in which they bested all their rivals." Delbruck rejects these claims because he believes that they had used carefully selected, well-trained soldiers to accomplish them, while the Greek army was made up of amateur soldiers who were unwilling to take the time to train. Krentz decided to test Delbruck's assertion that only selected specially trained troops could achieve the results claimed by the French captain. In order to test the claim he e-mailed all the ROTC graduates from Davidson College concerning their ability to run a long distance carrying a heavy pack. He received back 50 replies, and "with one exception, they were all confident that troops caring 35 pounds could run a mile and then fight." Krentz included 10 comments from his respondents. He quotes Maj. David Taylor, class of 1991, who made the following comment: "Present-day U.S. infantry troops are trained to move 12 miles with a 35 to 50 pound load in less than three hours (4 mph) and fight upon arrival.[267] Krentz then comments that "if our soldiers today can manage 12 miles at 4 mph, ancient Greeks, carrying a comparable load could have done 1 mile at 4.5 mph." He adds that "we should not underestimate the work capacity of farmers accustomed to doing hard physical labor all their lives"; however, he says that if one is unwilling to believe that Greeks could have jogged one mile, they could have jogged to just outside arrow range, stopped briefly to recover and then made their final charge."[268]

Regarding comments that the Greeks had no need to charge the entire mile at a run as the effective range of Persian arrows was only about 175 yards, Krentz claims that it was necessary for the Greeks to run (jog) the entire distance because the purpose was to make contact with the Persian infantry before the Persian cavalry could be deployed, not to avoid Persian arrows. Krentz also deals with the argument that the Greek phalanx could not have held its formation over a mile run. He claims that the Greek word used by Herodotus concerning the formation is too often translated as "close order" when it is better understood as "all together." He says that the phalanx did not advance in close order, but rather "hoplites and light armed and dismounted horsemen, all with spears and swords," charged at the Persians in loose order, and thus the concern for holding their formation together was not an issue.[269]

Lacey, writing in 2011, examines the idea of the Greek hoplites running a mile. He says that Herodotus was not an eyewitness at Marathon, so he must have depended on conversations with veterans of the battle for details of what occurred. Lacey raises a question concerning the reliability of "battlefield memories." He says that work by James L. McGaugh, a research professor in neurobiology, has shown that a "rush of adrenaline imprints a clear memory of events that will last a lifetime," and then Lacey comments that going into combat with the enemy definitely releases a surge of adrenaline; however, he adds that perhaps the memory might not be correct. He describes his own experience in interviewing participants in the invasion of Iraq in 2003. His interviews took place about 18 months after the actual events occurred; however, in many cases he had access to what soldiers had said immediately after the event and so was able to compare them. When he compared the accounts immediately after the events and the accounts 18 months after the events, he found that there was little difference between the two interviews concerning events in which the soldiers had actually participated. He concludes his discussion on the reliability of Greek battlefield memories by stating,

> Given the imperative to close the distance before the Persians could fully prepare to meet the attack, and the extra impetus of getting through the kill zone of the archers as rapidly as possible, it is clear the Athenians had every reason to run. It should therefore be judged a certainty that if 10,000 hoplites "remembered" running toward the Persians, they did.[270]

Lacey, like Krentz, rejects the conclusions of Donlan and Thompson that a hoplite could not run a mile and still be able to fight when they made contact with the enemy. He says that you cannot compare physical education majors with soldiers because "exercise is specific." He says that hours in the gym would not prepare a person to compete with a soldier in the field. As a military veteran, he uses his personal experience to rebut Donlan and Thompson's claims. He tells of reporting to the 82nd Airborne and serving under a commander who thought it was great fun to take his officers on long runs with full rucksacks and then have them run the steps in the local stadium after the run. He adds that after running "10 or more miles, day after day," it is certainly possible for soldiers carrying heavy loads to run five miles, and as for carrying a shield, he says that he "often witnessed units running in close order carrying rifles at port arms for mile after mile." After saying a mile run by hoplites is possible, he adds, "I will relent on one matter: a mile sprint, while just barely possible, would wreck the cohesion of the phalanx, and leave the hoplites too winded for immediate combat. What Athenians remembered as a run was probably a double time for most of the distance, followed by a real run once they were within archery range."[271]

While it appears that the viewpoint that a mile run by hoplites was unrealistic and that the experiments of Donlan and Thompson had pretty well decided the question, Krentz and Lacey have certainly brought new arguments to the question; however, just as they question the work of Donlan and Thompson, so their work must also face questions. Between Krentz and Lacey, they provide many examples of soldiers carrying heavy loads advancing at rates up to 7.2 miles an hour for distances greater than the one mile that the Greeks had to run. Their examples come from the 19th century up to the present day. Their examples seem conclusive, but do they really relate to Greek hoplites in 490 BCE? Even Lacey admits that perhaps the Greek hoplites advanced at a "real run" only when they came within the range of Persian archers. Krentz requires the hoplites to run the entire mile since they were running to prevent the Persian cavalry from becoming a force in the battle, but even he is willing to allow the hoplites to stop to catch their breath. The biggest question that must be answered is, are their examples relevant to Marathon? The answer appears to be that they are not because all of the examples that they provide are from well-trained soldiers. Regarding the Athenians, Lacey says we must remember that the Athenians had been involved in fighting for the past ten years against other Poleis such as Aegina and Corinth, so they obviously "took training seriously." This statement, however, does not appear to be correct concerning the Greek hoplites in the late archaic period, because at that time it appears that the hoplites had little training and were often unwilling to take any time for training. Krentz says "not to underestimate the work capacity of farmers accustomed to doing hard labor all their lives"; however, Lacey points out that "exercise is specific." That raises the issue that all the hard work in the fields and all the walking done by the farmers would not prepare them to run a mile in full panoply carrying a shield even if Krentz is correct that the hoplite's panoply only weighed 30 to 50 pounds instead of the 50 to 70 pounds quoted by other authors. Finally, after all the examples that Krentz includes, he seems to hedge on his conclusion when he says, "Anyone who doubts that the Greeks at Marathon could have jogged 8 stadia is free to believe that they stopped "just out of missile range, caught their breath, and made their final charge." Here the key word is "jogged." The debate has been about whether the hoplite can "run" a mile not whether he can "jog" a mile. Lacey also seems to back off on his claims when he says that the Athenians probably did double time until they came under fire from the Persian archers, at which time they broke into a full run. Later the Athenians probably remembered it as a full run, as it made them appear more impressive.[272] So, in spite of their criticisms of Donlan and Thompson's research, the views of Krentz and Lacey may not be all that different from the consensus viewpoint that claims a mile "run" by hoplites is unrealistic.

Where Was the Persian Cavalry?

There can be no doubt that the Persians had cavalry at Marathon. Herodotus specifically states that Darius ordered that horse transports be built (Hdt. 6.48), that the horse transports were built and used (Hdt. 6.9, 5.2), that the Persian cavalry was used at Eretria (Hdt. 6.101), and that the Persians chose Marathon because of its suitability for cavalry (Hdt. 6.102), and yet when Herodotus describes the Battle of Marathon, the only mention he makes of cavalry is that the Greeks had none (Hdt. 6.11, 2.2). Since the cavalry played such an important role in Persian battle tactics, the question must be asked, where was the Persian cavalry during the Battle of Marathon?

In his article "Herodotus 6.11 2.2," Harry C. Avery states, "Neither those who claim the cavalry was present, nor those who claim the cavalry was absent have been able to produce arguments sufficiently compelling to convince the other side." He goes on to argue that there must be some reason that the Persian army did not attack the Greeks, and he believes that reason is because "their cavalry was not present to support their attack"; however, he does not present an explanation of where it was, nor why it was not present.[273]

Those historians that claim that the Persian army split their forces at Marathon explain that Herodotus does not mention the Persian cavalry at the Battle of Marathon because the cavalry did not participate in the battle; rather, they were on the ships that were going to sail against Athens, as the cavalry would be very useful on the plain at Phaleron. They use the story from the *Suda* that the Ionians told the Greeks that the cavalry was away as evidence to support their viewpoint.

Delbruck and Cawkwell point out that the re-embarkation of cavalry must have been a difficult and time-consuming procedure, so they suggest that the Persians may have withdrawn their cavalry early in the battle or perhaps even before the battle started in order to re-embark them on the ships. As evidence they point out that in spite of their great victory the Greeks only captured seven ships and that Herodotus makes no mention of captured horses, "which as a prized possession would certainly have been worthy of mention and would necessarily have been long remembered by the Athenian people by virtue of their offspring."[274]

In spite of the above viewpoints, most historians appear willing to accept as fact that the Persian cavalry was present at the Battle of Marathon, even though Herodotus does not specifically mention it as participating in the battle. In 1980, Gordon Shrimpton, in his article "The Persian Cavalry at Marathon," argues that the Persian cavalry was present at the Battle of Marathon and explains why its impact was limited. He rejects the notion that the Greeks attacked because the "cavalry was away." He argues that there was no way for Miltiades to know anything but to expect the cavalry to be present, so Shrimpton thinks Miltiades must have developed a plan to counter the Persian cavalry or else he would not have been able to convince Callimachus to support him and those who voted with him. Shrimpton then says that Miltiades took advantage of the delay before the battle to prepare his plan and to train his troops. Once his troops were prepared, Miltiades simply waited for the right opportunity to attack. He claims that Miltiades needed to get his troops deployed and attack at least 15 to 20 minutes before the Persians were prepared for battle.[275] He goes on to explain that Miltiades was able to catch the Persians by surprise for three reasons: (1) Hippias had convinced the Persians that the Athenians were demoralized and divided in loyalty, (2) the Persians had become "accustomed to Athenian inactivity during the delay before the battle," and (3) the Persians were not expecting an attack before the Spartans arrived.

Herodotus tells us that the Persians and Sacae occupied the center of the Persian line, and it is usually assumed he meant Persian and Sacae infantry; however, Shrimpton says using Sacae, who were the best cavalry troops, as infantry makes little sense. Instead he suggests that the Sacae were cavalry and that they were stationed in the center to support the Persian infantry. He then goes on to describe the Persian camp as having been set up with the infantry camped in front and the cavalry camped behind them near water and fodder for their horses. Their horses were hobbled to avoid them wandering off.

If the Greeks attacked, the role of the cavalry was to charge the Greeks as early as possible, harass them with javelins and arrows in order to slow them down, and cause confusion and breaches in the enemy formation; however, on the day that the Greeks attacked the Persians were not ready to fight. Shrimpton believes that Miltiades must have found some way to deploy and advance some distance before the Persians could see them and realize that they were under attack. He translates Herodotus' statement that "they were preparing themselves" or "they began to prepare" as evidence that the Persians were not prepared to fight. He says that the infantry quickly got into ranks, but that the cavalry, "bivouacked behind the line of infantry, would have to respond by doing ... the following, depending on the degree of surprise: waking up and donning armor, mounting, forming up and riding around or through the line of scurrying infantrymen." How much time that action would take the cavalry is uncertain, but he also points out that the greater the number of cavalrymen, the more time it would take them to prepare; and while fewer cavalry could deploy more quickly to respond to the Greek attack, they would also have less impact upon the battle. Once prepared the cavalry would advance, but the Greeks with their earlier start would be nearing the archer's range, at which point the cavalry would have to withdraw to avoid being hit by their own arrows. Thus the impact of the cavalry would be minimal as the Greeks had advanced too quickly and too far for the normal cavalry tactics to work. When the cavalry saw the battle was going against them, they would have withdrawn in order to begin re-embarking their horses.[276]

In 1985, Arthur Ferrill pointed out that "Herodotus' account strongly implies that it [cavalry] was involved, and a Roman historian, Cornelius Nepos, states categorically that it was." He argues that the Persian cavalry was considered light cavalry made up primarily of lightly armored cavalrymen whose main weapon was the bow. He goes on to state that light cavalry could not breach a phalanx and was primarily used to attack the flanks and harass the phalanx with arrows, but the Greeks had extended their line so it was difficult to outflank them.[277]

Doenges in 1998 stated that "the *Stoa Poikile* painting, the Brescia Sarcophagus, and Herodotus all indicate that the cavalry, in fact, was present at the battle." He suggests that Herodotus does not mention the cavalry because it did not play a significant role in the battle. He argues that the battle lines were only about a mile apart and when the Greeks advanced "on the double," "there was neither time nor opportunity for the cavalry to harass or to disrupt the hoplite formation." He goes on to say that once the cavalry saw they would have little impact upon the battle, the cavalry began to withdraw and when they battle was turning against them, the cavalry "must have been the first of the Persian forces to reach the ships and embark."[278]

In his 2002 book, *Cavalry Operations in the Ancient World*, Robert Gaebel says that the Greek phalanx was "incomparable for direct frontal attack, but it lacked versatility and was not self-sufficient when facing an enemy with a strong cavalry arm"; however, he points out the key was for the phalanx to protect its flanks with topographical features such as the foothills of Mt. Agreiliki and the sea as the Greeks did at Marathon. In addition, the cavalry were primarily javelin throwers and archers whose "effectiveness would have been severely reduced by the rapid charge of the Greeks, and it would come as no surprise if they played no further role in the battle, being neither experienced in nor armed for hand-to-hand combat."[279]

Lacey, writing in 2011, agrees that "archaeological evidence tilts the balance in favor of the cavalry being present." He believes that Herodotus does not mention the Persian cavalry because "his audience was well aware of the fact" and did not need to be reminded of it. His explanation as to why the cavalry was ineffective is different than the previous authors. He suggests that the Persians had decided to withdraw from Marathon and that the Greeks attacked as the Persians were in the process of re-embarking their cavalry and infantry. He suggests that the cavalry, not yet re-embarked, took time to organize, and by the time they entered the battle the Persian flanks had already collapsed and the numbers of cavalrymen were too small to stem the tide of the Greek victory.[280]

Hammond in the second edition of the *Cambridge Ancient History* seems to accept the *Suda* story of the Ionians telling the Athenians that the cavalry was away. He says that each night the Persian horses were taken to the Macaria spring for water and fodder. They returned to the Persian line by moonlight in order to be ready for battle the next morning. Hammond claims, the "night of the 16th to the 17th, for the first time that lunar month, the moon now waning set after dawn and that "may have caused the grooms to miscalculate the timing of their return." As a result, the Greeks were able to attack and reach the Persian infantry before the cavalry could intervene. Thus, while technically the cavalry was present, it played no role in the battle.[281]

Krentz, writing in 2010, rejects the idea that the cavalry had re-embarked and that the Ionians had told the Greeks that the cavalry was away. He dismisses the value of the *Suda* as a worthy source, but at the same time he is not willing to accept that the cavalry played a role in the battle. Rather, like Hammond, he believes that the Greeks were successful because they were able to engage the Persian infantry before the cavalry could become involved. He argues that Miltiades observed the Persians and recognized that they sent the horses for water and fodder each night, which opened a small window of opportunity for a surprise Greek attack. He explains that the road running between Mt. Stavrokorki and the Macaria spring was very narrow and formed a bottleneck for the horses to pass through. He says that 600 horses would need 50 minutes if it took five seconds for each horse to pass through the bottleneck and one hour and 40 minutes if it took 10 seconds for each horse to pass through the bottleneck. If there were more cavalry, the time would naturally have been greater. He then suggests that the Greeks observed the process and timed their attack prior to the return of the horses. He also suggests that the Athenians ran the entire eight stades at double time as they might have observed the horses returning. Due to luck, brilliant planning or both the Greeks were able to engage the Persian infantry without the cavalry interfering and won a great victory.[282]

In 2010 Christopher Tuplin of the University of Liverpool wrote two articles concerning the Achaemenid Persian military. In "All the King's Horse: In Search of Achaemenid Persian Cavalry" he raised some points that seem to go counter to commonly accepted viewpoints concerning the Persian cavalry. He says that the Greeks did not seem to think that there was "anything radically unusual in the way in which Persians used cavalry," and he seems to question the importance of the Persian cavalry when he claims there was "an unwillingness on the part of Persian commanders of that era to build battle plans around cavalry." He also calls into question the viewpoint that the bow was the main weapon of the cavalrymen and instead states that "text and pictures agree that horsemen predominantly used spears or swords rather than bows."[283] In his second article, "Marathon in Search of a Persian Dimension," he agrees with those claiming the cavalry participated in the battle. He argues that the fact Herodotus does not mention the cavalry means little. He says Herodotus' narrative does mention arrows, but he says this does not prove that there were not any arrows. Rather it simply means that they did not play a crucial role in the battle because of the fact that the Greeks ran across the battlefield before the archers could fire enough arrows to play an important role. By the same token the cavalry being at the battle made no crucial difference. He claims the simplest explanation is that the number of cavalrymen was too small to have a major impact, so Herodotus does not even mention it. While he is certain the cavalry was at Marathon, Tuplin claims that "it does not seem to occur to anyone to use them to attack the sides and rear of the Greek force during the encounter." In fact, Tuplin suggests that the cavalry may have been stationed in the middle of the Persian line, and says it may have contributed to the initial success of the Persians in pushing back the center of the Greek phalanx.[284]

Duration of the Battle

Herodotus tells us that "they fought in the battle at Marathon for a long time." What is a long time? He gives no indication. Munro in the first edition of the *Cambridge Ancient History* says, "The battle from first to last was a brief affair, a morning's work before luncheon." He goes on to say that Herodotus' "long time" refers to hand-to-hand combat only, and in this context "is to be measured in minutes, not hours." Pritchett in *The Greek State at War, Part IV* has drawn together ancient references to the length of ancient battles. In the six battles that Herodotus covers between 493 and 479, Herodotus describes five of them as taking "a long time," with the sixth, the Battle of Himera, lasting "from dawn until late evening." While Pritchett offers little help in defining "a long time," he does quote the Roman historian Vegetius who says "that a battle was commonly decided in 2–3 hours."[285]

Cawkwell, in his article "Orthodoxy and Hoplites," starts from the premise "that battles were not short in duration" and thanks Pritchett for tabulating the evidence upon which his premise is based; however, he attempts to be more precise as to what a "long time" means. He says, "We know what the Greeks knew as a long battle" and refers to the Battle of Himera described by Herodotus as lasting "from dawn to late evening," as well as the Battle of Sphacteria which Thucydides described as going on for "most of the day." In addition to the above examples, he says that Diodorus tells us that the Battle of Oenophyta between Athens and the Boeotians city-states in 457 lasted all day, and he also tells us of a battle in Egypt in 351 that also lasted all day. Cawkwell concludes by saying, "If one follows Vegetius' 2 to 3 hours, one is probably not far wrong."[286]

James Holoka, writing in 1997, believes hoplite battles were generally short, and victory was usually achieved in two to three hours or even less. But he also claims there are exceptions, and he thinks the Battle of Marathon is certainly an exception since the Greeks were not fighting another hoplite phalanx and thus had to adjust to the a new style of fighting. He also points out that the battle took place over an unusually large battleground that extended from the Soros to the Great Marsh about three miles away and to the Shoenia beach up to Cape Cynosura, which was about four miles from the Soros. After advancing one mile to make contact with the Persians, many of the hoplites covered about six miles in full panoply while facing heavy opposition. He concludes that if the battle started around 7:30 a.m. the fighting probably ended about 1:30 p.m.[287]

Rawlings in 2007 says "it is difficult to imagine how men could fight continuously under the hot Mediterranean sun for minutes, let alone hours at a stretch. He goes on to say that those fighting in the front ranks must have found some way to "temporarily withdraw out of the range of the spear."[288]

Wheeler in 2007, in referring to the typical "for a long time" quote concerning ancient battle, raises the issue of when one starts timing the battle. He asks how much time should be included for deployment and prebattle rituals and how much time should be included after the enemy is routed and chased. While the question cannot be answered with our available sources, he does take issue with the idea that there may have been lulls in the battle while the exhausted hoplites caught their breath. He says, "It is difficult to imagine once hand-to-hand combat commenced how someone called for a timeout."[289]

In his book *Reinstating the Hoplite: Arms, Armor and Phalanx Fighting in Archaic and Classical Greece* in 2009, Adam Schwartz devotes 22 pages to an examination of the question concerning the length of hoplite battles and concludes that Cawkwell is incorrect when he says they "were not short in duration." He begins by examining the battles Cawkwell used to reach his conclusion and states that the sources for the battles are suspect. Two of the battles are from Diodorus, and Schwartz calls him "notoriously untrustworthy" and claims that Diodorus is very repetitious, and as an example of this point Schwartz explains that Diodorus uses the phrase πολύν Χρόνον (long time) 31 times in connection with battles. Also he says that Diodorus uses formulaic language throughout his work. Schwartz quotes Jane Hornblower concerning Diodorus. She says,

> Diodorus made up his own clichés and applied them everywhere mechanically, even when they were actually inappropriate to the context.... Formulaic language was more suited to epic than to history; and, in his efforts to silhouette the general moral truth behind the historical situation, Diodorus took out much of the color of the narrative he drew upon. His main purpose being instructive, it did not matter if battles were standardized or individuals stereotyped: rather, this message facilitated his didactic aims.[290]

While Schwartz considers Herodotus a far superior source compared to Diodorus, he also questions Herodotus' description of the Battle of Himera in 480 in which Herodotus claims the battle lasted all day. He even suggests that Herodotus himself may have doubted the account he received from the Carthaginians concerning this battle. Diodorus also describes the Battle of Himera, and Schwartz says that in both Herodotus and Diodorus "everything about this battle seems to be larger-than-life," which probably reflects the impact of the epic tradition in Greek literary developments. As a result Schwartz concludes that it is not possible to completely trust Herodotus or Diodorus when they describe "long battles." He thinks that they have exaggerated aspects of the battle in order to "give the reader an impression of the mighty deeds done."[291]

After rejecting the accounts of long battles in Herodotus and Diodorus as acceptable evidence, Schwartz examines the Battle of Sphacteria as described by Thucydides. Thucydides describes the battle as lasting most of the day, and Schwartz does not question his description concerning the length of the battle as he did with those descriptions by Herodotus and Diodorus; rather he claims it was a unique event as it was not really a hoplite battle. The Athenians used light-armed troops that avoided Spartan efforts to engage them and constantly harassed the Spartans until they ultimately were able to surround the Spartans with their superior numbers. They then offered the exhausted Spartans terms which were accepted. Schwartz concludes that

Thucydides was trying very hard to convey to his audience the unusual nature and uncommon duration and, most of all, the excessive stress it put the soldiers under. If it was not so much the usual physical pressure from phalanx fighting which exhausted the Spartan hoplites, then it seems that the duress and suffering Thucydides is trying to express resulted precisely from the extraordinary length of the battle, which in turn aggravated the corollary sufferings of combat: those of heat and dehydration.

Everything thus seems to point to the logical conclusion that hoplite battles, or, to be more precise hoplite battle *fighting*, were in reality very short in duration. The frequent references to long battles are at best ambiguous, as designation such as long and short are impossible to define in the absence of definite criterion.[292]

Schwartz next takes up the issue of what one means by the term "long battle." Does it include the preparation, deployment, prebattle rituals, hand-to-hand combat, the *othismos*, the pursuit, caring for the wounded and recovering bodies, or does it only refer to the actual combat phase? The answer, obviously impacts the description concerning the length of the battle. For example, it is estimated that at the Battle of Kunaxa described by Xenophon it took between two and a half to four hours for the 10,600 mercenary Greeks to deploy. It is suggested that the fighting phase lasted from 2 p.m. to possibly 8 p.m. but that also includes the pursuit of the defeated enemy for five km and a return march of five km, which must have taken at least several hours as the hoplites were certainly tired from the combat phase of the battle. And after the pursuit and return, the bodies still had to be recovered and all the wounded collected. The battle may have lasted most of the day, but how much time was actually spent fighting?[293]

Schwartz also considers the physical limitations of the hoplites in fighting unusually long battles. How long were hoplites capable of fighting? Cawkwell, who claims hoplite battles were "not of short duration," also made the following comment which does not seem to fit his viewpoint:

> If battles lasted for a couple of hours, that is an improbably long time to be pushing, and one may add, for a man to be fighting. Fifteen three-minute rounds with rests, exhaust the fittest pugilists in the world, and those who have had experience of scrummaging and forward play generally in the Rugby game of football must be skeptical about how long such intense efforts could have been maintained without the rest provided by "line outs," "half-time" and injury time.[294]

While most of the hoplites in an army were farmers who did hard physical labor every day which gave them great stamina and toughness, it still must be remembered that they were not used to wearing the hoplite panoply, carrying a spear and a 10- to 17-pound shield.[295] Also, they were under tremendous nervous strain as they were about to come into contact with other hoplites whose goal was to kill them.[296] Schwartz concludes that phrases such as "a long time" or "fighting until darkness" are too vague to be useful. He says that the weather conditions, the weight and discomfort of the hoplite panoply and the *othismos* all influenced the length of time a battle took. He believes that the actual fighting was over relatively quickly. He also suggests that the idea of battles taking a long time may have been influenced by the epic tradition in which "superhuman (and indeed, divine) feats were performed." However, ultimately he says we lack conclusive evidence to reach a conclusion, but he suggests that the existing evidence and the physical demands placed upon hoplites "mitigate against an assessment of hoplite battles as drawn out."[297]

Greek and Persian Casualties

Herodotus tells us, "In the Battle of Marathon, about 6,400 of the barbarians died, and of the Athenians, 192." The number of 192 Athenian deaths is generally accepted as accurate since Pausanias, in the second century CE, visited Marathon and described seeing the Soros and a list of the Athenian dead organized by tribes.[298] The number of Persian dead is not as easily accepted as accurate. In *The Landmark Herodotus,* the editor suggests that the number of Persian deaths "was probably a wild guess, but Billows claims that the Athenians made a careful count "of the Persian dead since they had made a vow to the goddess Artemis, if she helped bring them victory, to sacrifice to her one goat for every enemy warrior slain.[299]

Since the exact number of Persian troops at Marathon is uncertain, it is difficult to determine whether 6,400 Persian dead would be a plausible estimate. Modern historians' estimates of Persian troops range from 15,000 to 40,000, with most estimates falling between 20,000 to 30,000 troops. Accepting the last two figures, the percentage of dead would be 21.3 percent if there were 30,000 and 32 percent if there were 20,000.[300] Krentz analyzed 17 battles and found a pattern in which 10 to 20 percent of the defeated phalanx were killed with about 3 to 10 percent of the victorious phalanx being killed. Comparing these estimates with the casualty rates at Marathon, we find the Persian casualty rate much higher and the Athenian casualty rate much lower; however, we also must remember that Marathon was not a battle between two similar phalanxes, but rather a heavily armored and armed phalanx against a lightly armored enemy whose major weapon was the bow.[301]

Gabriel and Metz analyzed 14 battles and determined that the defeated army averaged 37.7 percent killed while the victorious side averaged about 5.5 percent. These percentages would certainly be more in line with the numbers at Marathon, but they are based mostly upon battles in Hellenistic and Roman times, so they may not be applicable to Marathon.[302]

Ray reaches the most provocative conclusion about the Persian casualties at Marathon. He claims that the number of 6,400 killed "more reasonably reflects the size of the total force engaged." He claims that the "Persians' ability to seriously pose a threat after Marathon shows that their losses could not have been as high as claimed by Herodotus. He then gives a guess of 2,000 to 3,000 losses for the Persians, which would be about 40 percent of their total. His argument that Persia could not have lost 6,400 troops as they would continue to pose a threat to Greece makes little sense as estimates for the population of the Persian Empire range from a low figure of 17 million to a high figure of 35 million. Even taking the low figure of 17 million, the Persian Empire would have had no trouble absorbing the loss of 6,400 men and still being able to attack Greece. Ray is more willing to accept the Athenian dead as he notes that Pausanias observed a list of their names.[303]

Avery, while willing to accept the figure of 192 dead for Athens, expresses a strong suspicion of the 6,400 dead figure for the Persians. He says that if you divide 6,400 by 192, you get 33.33, or to put it another way, you get 6,400 if you multiply 192 by 33.33. He then goes on to explain that the number three has a "mystical significance" in Greek religion; however, he does point out that he has found nothing significant about 33.33, except that it has "an infinite series of threes." While he cannot explain the numerical connection between the number of Greek dead and the number of Persian dead, he feels it does "cast some doubt on the historicity of the number of Persian dead.[304]

In 1976 Professor William F. Wyatt of Brown University reacted to Avery's article in *Historia*. He begins by claiming that Avery's article leads to two different options concerning the number of the 6,400 Persian dead. One may either see 6,400 "as an accurate tradition concerning Persian losses, perhaps based upon a battlefield count or one may believe that the number 6,400 was derived from 192 in some way." He goes on to say he will not try to prove which option is best, but rather to "lay out conclusions which must inevitably follow" from Avery's observations. His first step was to "convert his [Avery] observations from theoretical to practical arithmetic."[305] Wyatt goes on to suggest that there were a variety of traditions concerning the numbers of Persian dead at Marathon. One was that 100 Persians were killed for each Athenian killed, which seems an extreme exaggeration, but there were probably other estimates that were more reasonable. Wyatt then suggests that Herodotus had to make a choice as to what to include as his number and that he might have divided the exaggerated numbers such as 19,200 (100 Persians × 192 Athenians) by three, which would give him a more reasonable number, and still "incorporate the data of the conflicting reports."[306] Wyatt then concludes that there are two possibilities concerning the number of Persian dead. The first is that the number of Persian dead is based upon an actual count of the Persian dead after the battle. The second possibility it is that there was no official count and Herodotus simply made his decision concerning the various estimates "available to him on the basis of the Athenian dead."[307] Pausanias tells a story that the Persians fleeing the Greeks got confused as they neared the Great Marsh, and as a result, many got lost and died in the Great Marsh and this "was the cause of most of the carnage."[308] If Pausanias' statement is accurate it is then doubtful that there was an official count of the Persian dead, as it is not likely that the Greeks would be willing to retrieve Persian bodies from the marsh in order to get an accurate count.

Why Were Only Seven Ships Captured?

After the Greek wings had defeated the Persian flanks and come together to defeat the Persian center, the Greeks pursued the Persians and "cut them down until they reached the sea, where they called for fire and started to seize the ships," but they only managed to capture seven ships, while losing Callimachus; Stesilas, one of the 10 generals; and Kynegeiros, the brother of Aeschylus, whose hand was chopped off as he was seizing the "sternpost of a ship."[309] With such an overwhelming victory, why did the Greeks only capture seven ships?

To answer the question, one must look at the topography around the Persian camps. Herodotus does not tell us the location of the Persian camps, but it appears that their naval camp may have been set up on the Schoenia beach where there was sufficient space to moor the 600 Persian ships under the protection of the Kynosoura Peninsula, which provided protection from the dangerous northeast winds.[310] While we have no literary evidence, it would seem logical for the naval camp to be on the Schoenia beach and the infantry and cavalry camp to be at the Macaria springs, as both areas were easily defended because they would be protected by the narrow entrances to each location. As already mentioned, the road from a Macaria that passed between Mt. Starokoraki and the Great Marsh was so narrow that the cavalry had to go single file on the road.[311] The entrance to the Schoenia beach was also narrow with the Great Marsh on one side and the sea on the other side.[312] A limited number of men would be able to slow up the enemy at both bottlenecks as the rest of the troops re-embarked on their ships. Once the Greeks broke through, most of the ships had already pushed off.

Obviously, if one accepts the split forces theory, it is even easier to explain the few ships taken, as a great number of troops and cavalry had re-embarked before the battle began, so fewer troops had to be re-embarked while the Greeks were attempting to break through the troops guarding the entrance to the naval base. Even if one rejects the split forces theory, the same scenario should hold true. When the Greek wings defeated the Persian wings, the Greek wings, allowed the defeated Persians to escape as the two Greek wings drew together to help the Greek center to defeat the Persian center, which had been victorious up to that point. Herodotus tells us that the Persians fought well, so while the Greeks were fighting the Persian center, the fleeing wings had time to escape and re-embark on their ships. Also, when the Persian center was finally defeated, the Greeks probably took some time to reorganize to pursue the defeated center and to attack the Persian camps. Even if the Greeks did not take time to reorganize, the Persians would have had time to organize a rear guard to defend the Persian camps. It must be remembered that the Persian army was a well-organized army with a clear command structure so that even though the wings had been defeated and fled the battlefield, the officers would have had sufficient time while the Greeks were fighting against the center to establish an effective rear guard at the entrances to their two camps. In addition, there is another possible addition to the above scenario that might help explain the Persian's ability to re-embark their troops and cavalry and escape with only seven ships being taken. Krentz points to the geological work done by Richard Dunn, in which he says that the Great Marsh was probably a lake in 490 with an outlet to the sea which may have allowed ships to enter the lake for shelter. Again there is no evidence that this occurred, but it was certainly a possibility as the Persian triremes had a shallow draft of about 3.9 feet fully loaded so they could have operated in a shallow lake.[313] If that did occur, the Persians would have been able to re-embark their troops and cavalry from several locations, which would have speeded up the operation, leaving fewer ships for the Greeks to attempt to seize once they had broken through the Persian rear guard.

The Shield Signal

Herodotus refers to a shield signal two different times in his account of the Battle of Marathon. In 6.115 he states, "At Athens, the Alcmaeonidae were later blamed for having contrived a scheme whereby a shield would be displayed to send a signal to the Persians aboard their ships." In 6.124 he goes on to defend the Alcmaeonidae, claiming they would not do such a thing. He then states, "a shield was certainly displayed—that is a fact that is impossible to deny, since it did happen—but as to who was responsible I can say no more than I already have."[314] Since Herodotus gives little specific information concerning the shield signal, it leaves his passages open to a wide variety of theories and speculation.

George Grote, in 1856, said, "the bright shield uplifted on Mount Pentelikus, apprising the Persians that matters were prepared for them at Athens, was intended to have come to their view before any action had taken place at Marathon." He goes on to explain that the signal would let Datis know that he could send a portion of his force by sea to Phaleron where they would be joined by "treacherous Athenians" and they could gain control of Athens. That action would cause the hoplites at Marathon to be so distracted by fear for their wives and children that unanimous action by the army at Marathon would be impossible, as the army would end up being divided and unable to win.[315]

In his commentary on Herodotus, Macan claims that Herodotus "failed to obtain satisfactory evidence" on the shield episode and was led astray by "sophistic apologies and fallacious anecdotes" that were meant to defend the Alcmaeonidae against accusations of treachery. He claims that an understanding of the shield episode is necessary if one is to gain a rational understanding of the Battle of Marathon. He then proceeds to point out that the spot from which the signal was sent is not identified, and while the time of the signal is unclear, as is the message of the signal, it is implied that it relates to a quick return of the Athenian army to Athens after the battle; however, he says that the message may have been different, and it could have referred to a variety of things. He also points out that the Alcmaeonidae are accused but absolved by Herodotus, but no alternative sender is mentioned. He reports that some believe the entire episode may have been a later interpolation into Herodotus' work. Finally, Macan states,

> to conclude, however, that no shield was raised at all with treacherous intent, no signal given, and to rationalize away the episode into pure fiction dictated by malignity, or see no more historic basis for the anecdote than an unintended flash of shield, or other shining surface, in sight of Greeks and Barbarians at Marathon, misinterpreted by the suspicious and heated imagination of a political partisan; to reduce, in short, the shield-episode to the level of the vision of Epizelos, is to be too benevolently skeptical in regard to Athenian disaffection, and defeats the very object which the skeptic may be supposed to have at heart. The presence of traitors in Athens exalts not diminishes the heroism of the patriotic majority. The splendor and the wonder of the victory at Marathon were enhanced by the magnitude, not of the battle, but of the danger; a danger more than doubled by the presence of traitors within.[316]

J. B. Bury believes that the Persian strategy was to re-embark their cavalry and send them by ship to land south of mount Agreiliki to cut off the road to Athens, either to oppose the Greeks attempting to return to Athens or to intercept Greeks fleeing after the Persian victory. He claims that the signal referred to by Herodotus was sent "before" the battle as a signal for the ships with the cavalry to sail. In addition, he says the signalmen could observe the battle and signal the result, which, if it was a Persian defeat, they would send the signal to the Persian cavalry to return to the shore to re-embark on their ships.[317]

How and Wells in their commentary on Herodotus say it is clear that the purpose of the shield signal was to let the Persians know the "conspiracy in Athens was ripe" and took place from a spot on Mount Pentelikus; however, Herodotus also states that the Persians "were already on board when the signal was made." They think the Persians waited for the signal before sailing, fearing that the Spartans could have arrived and spoiled their plan.[318]

P. K. Baillie Reynolds examined the "shield episode" in his article "The Shield Signal and Marathon" in 1929. First he states that the only signal that could be sent had to have a yes or no answer because the five-mile distance from Mt. Pentelicus to Datis' ships made any other message impossible, as at that distance only a flash could be seen. He feels the message was sent by the "pro–Peisistratid" party in Athens, which had opened discussions with the

Persians at Marathon. When Datis had not heard about a successful conspiracy from Athens, he began to worry about the imminent arrival of the Spartans, so he decided to split his force and sail to Phaleron; however, he still needed to know if he would be welcomed. Baillie Reynolds claims that the signal the Persians received was that the conspiracy had failed; however, Datis, expecting a Persian victory at Marathon, still sailed to Phaleron. When he discovered his forces had been defeated at Marathon and arrived at Phaleron to find the Athenian army waiting, he gave up on his plan and sailed back to Persia.[319]

General Maurice takes a very different approach to the shield signal. He says that Herodotus' story about a shield signal and the accusation against the Alcmaeonidae is one which "I find difficult to swallow." He says that too often there is a "tendency to imagine or invent spy stories" during wartime, and he considers Herodotus' story to be one of those imaginary stories. He goes on to say that after the battle there were hoplites all over the battlefield with shields and asks how the Persians would be able to identify one particular shield. He says that a better explanation would be that Miltiades had sent observers up on the high ground where they could observe the Persian fleet and Persian army. He then suggests that when the Greek observers sent signals to Miltiades, some of the Greek troops saw the signal and "jumped to the conclusion that spies were at work."[320]

Harris Gary Hudson, in his article "The Shield Signal at Marathon" in 1937, advanced a another theory concerning the shield signal. He claims that the signal was "from an Athenian outpost informing Miltiades of the Persian movements and indicated to him the opportunity to attack." He accepts Herodotus' contention that a shield signal did occur and points out that Lysander used a shield signal to mark the "critical moment for attack" at the Battle of Aegospotami in which he decisively defeated the Athenian fleet in the Peloponnesian War as an example that shield signals were used. He claims that Datis mistakenly thought that the inactivity of the Greeks and their refusal to fight reflected timidity, and as a result Datis believed he could split his force and attack Athens without being concerned with the Greek army at Marathon as being a major threat. He then claims that Miltiades "had set outposts on the heights ... with instructions to report instantly any sign that the Persians were about to move by land or sea." He rejects any signal to the Persians at Marathon because if the signal was negative, why would the Persians sail to Phaleron? He also says that the signal could not have been favorable or the Persians would have attempted to land at Phaleron. Rather he claims that in spite of the defeat of his forces at Marathon, Datis still sailed to Athens, hoping to receive a signal that the pro–Persian conspirators had succeeded. When he failed to receive the signal at Phaleron he sailed back to Persia.[321]

Hammond, writing in 1968, accepts the viewpoint that a shield signal was sent to the Persian fleet, was observed by the Athenians and resulted in the Persian fleet setting sail for Phaleron. Based upon personal experience, Hammond believes it took the Athenians eight to nine hours to return to Athens after the battle at Marathon, which meant that they had to leave Marathon by 9 or 10 a.m. in order to get to Athens by nightfall. As a result he says the shield signal had to be sent by 9 a.m. as he claims that at that time the sun was well east of south and had a proper angle to send the signal to the Persian fleet from either Mt. Agreiliki or Mt. Pentelikus. He says that the signal must have been sent from the Athenian side of the plain as those at other locations would not know the situation in Athens. In a footnote, he changes the means of sending the signal from a hoplite shield to a "round, flat polished disk."[322]

In 1992 Lazenby points out that Herodotus simply refers to raising a shield and does not make any reference to signaling by flashing a shield. That being said he explains that the signal must have been given much closer to the ships, as a shield could not be seen if it was raised up in the mountains. But if it had to be close, he asks how the person giving the signal avoided detection, or even more importantly, how the Persians would pick it out of the many shields on the battlefield. He then explains that it would have to be a simple message like yes or no or sail or don't sail. He then asks, if the signal was meant to convey the message that the conspiracy either succeeded or failed, why they waited to send it until after the defeat at Marathon. Finally he asks, what would the message mean coming after the battle? He goes on to say that since the message had to be simple, it would have to have been preconceived as to what it would mean. If the message was meant to say to the Persians after their defeat that they should sail to Athens anyway because the conspiracy was becoming successful, how could it have been preconceived since the Persians expected to win the battle? As a result of the above points, Lazenby concludes, "All in all, it seems unlikely that there was such a signal and that it was one of the rumors used to discredit the Alcmaeonidae and their associates in the early 480s."[323]

J.A.S. Evans points out that Herodotus was convinced there was a shield signal that led to the Persians sailing to Phaleron and that the Alcmaeonidae were blamed for the signal; however, he then states, "The flashing signal of Marathon is a modern myth, which originated with Colonel Leakey." He explains that the flashing shield could not have occurred because a hoplite shield, no matter how brightly it polished, could not be used to send a signal over a long distance because the convex side of the shield would diffuse the light and the concave side would focus the beam of light too narrowly for anyone to see it at a distance. He then claims that if there was a signal, the person sending it stood "on a house top or ruined wall in the deme of Marathon," since that would have put the signal close enough for the Persians in the fleet to observe. He then asks why the leader of the pro–Peisistratid party was not accused of treason instead of the Alcmaeonidae. He concludes by saying, "We can hardly ask for a better indication that the tradition surrounding the shield signal owes more to politics than historical fact."[324]

Holoka sees a major problem concerning the postbattle shield signal. He cannot imagine how the Persians in the fleet would be able to see a single raised shield on the shore. He seems to agree with Lazenby's assessment that there was probably no shield signal given. He quotes Busolt, a German historian who blames "the story on the imagination of some overexcited combatant."[325] His view of no signal is reinforced by A. Trevor Hodge in an article published in 2001 but based upon research done during the 1970s. It seems to conclusively prove that a hoplite shield could not have been used to flash a message over a great distance to the Persian fleet. He begins by examining four cases where a shield was used as a signal during ancient times and says that in all the cases, "we are simply told a shield was lifted or waived as a semaphore signal." He defines "flash" as a "bright light of such intensity that it is clearly seen at a distance where the object admitting it is itself invisible." Using the basic laws of optics, which say that an angle of incidence equals the angle of reflection, he concludes that optically it is simply not possible to use a curved surface such as a shield to create a flash. The surface does not have to be large, but it does have to be flat. The reason for this is that on a curved surface "every point on the surface is set at a different angle to the light source," and as a result the reflected light will be so defused that the flash will be so weakened that it will not be seen.

He explains that at 100 m a flash off a curved surface would be diminished by 1/10,000 of its intensity. He figures that at the distance from its source to the Persian fleet, 99.9999993 percent of the strength of a flash would be lost, which means it could not possibly be seen.[326]

It appears that Hammond became aware of Hodge's work, as he changed his hoplite shield signal to a signal using a round flat polished disk; however, Hodge says that using a flat disc also presents major problems.[327] He states that he successfully flashed a signal over 5.5 km using a tin lid of 9 cm in diameter; however, the problem is aligning the signal with the person who is to receive it. He says that beyond 100 m, alignment is very difficult, and "at a range of 3 to 4 km, even if one could accurately identify the spot to be aimed at, the most one could hope for would be one or two split-second flashes, visible at the other end out of five or 10 minutes of steady transmitting." How would the person who sent the signal ever know that his message was received?[328]

Scott, the latest commentator on Herodotus, questions whether a "shield would be seen by Persian officers on a ship or be distinguishable among the many men now moving south." He then asks why did the signaler send the message and what did it mean. After raising possibilities he finally concludes, "The probability is that there was no such signal, and it either grew as a rumor out of some innocent incident, or it was invented as a piece of political malice."[329]

Billows says that Herodotus refers to a signal from someone who raised a shield, but he also points out that "there were thousands of shields being raised and lowered around the plain of Marathon." He rejects the idea that the signal was sent from Mt. Pentele by flashing a signal, since Herodotus "doesn't say anything like that." Finally, he says "the entire shield episode seems dubious, especially as this supposed signal was reported to Herodotus in the context of alleging treason by the powerful and controversial Alcmaeonidae family. The whole story of the shield may be a fabrication by enemies of the Alcmaeonidae."[330]

After summarizing various views of the shield incident over the past 100 years, Krentz seems to feel that since Herodotus is so certain a shield signal had occurred, we should not reject it simply because Herodotus does "not identify the signaler." He does reject the idea of using a shield to flash a light signal and calls it a modern myth. He also agrees that a shield signal from the battlefield was impossible because of "all the other shields being waived by jubilant soldiers." He suggests the signaler could have been on a roof "in the village of Marathon." He agrees the signal would have to have been kept simple, but also says that a series of signals could be worked out, such as "a white flag if the collaborators had taken over the city, a red cloak if the Spartans had reached Athens and a shield if the city was still defended." He says that some type of signal may have occurred as Datis would want to know what he was going to find. He also suggests that the Alcmaeonidae may have been responsible for the signal in spite of Herodotus' denial that they were guilty. He explains that the Alcmaeonidae may have been willing to support Datis if he promised to guarantee democracy for Athens.[331]

A Messenger Sent to Athens

The Marathon race in the modern Olympics can be traced back to the Battle of Marathon. The story goes that Baron Pierre de Couberton agreed to add a "Marathon race" to the first modern Olympics held in 1896 in Greece at the suggestion of a friend who was a philologist.[332] It is thought that the suggestion had been influenced by Robert Browning's poem, "Pheidippides." After describing the Athenian victory, the poem includes the following lines:

> Unforeseeing one! Yes, he fought on the Marathon day:
> So, when Persia was dust, all cried, "To Acropolis!
> Run, Pheidippides, one race more! The meed is thy due!
> 'Athens is saved, thank Pan,' go to shout!" He flung down his shield,
> Ran like fire once more: and the space twixt the Fennel-field
> And Athens was stubble again, a field which a fire runs through,
> Till in he broke: "Rejoice, we conquer!" Like wine thro' clay,
> Joy in his blood bursting his heart, he died—the bliss![333]

While it is a wonderful, inspiring story, it is more legend than history. Herodotus tells of Philippides running to Sparta to seek aid from the Spartans but makes no mention of him at Marathon, nor any messenger being sent to Athens after the battle.[334] The first mention of a messenger is in Plutarch, who says that Heraclieides Ponticus, who lived about 340 BCE said that Thersippus of Eroeadae brought the message to Athens, but Plutarch claims that "most historians declare it was Eucles who ran in full armor, hot from battle, and, bursting in at the doors of the first men of the state, could only say, "'Hail! we are victorious!' and straightaway expired."[335] The name of Philippides enters the picture in the second century CE, when Lucian writes,

> Philippides the hemerodromos, reporting the victory from Marathon to the archons, who were seated anxiously awaiting the result of the battle, said, "rejoice, We have won," and saying this, died at the same time as his report, expiring with the salutation. *Pro lapsu inter salutandum*.[336]

While questioning the historicity of Philippides' run to Athens with his message of the Athenian victory, Frost says that there probably was a messenger who took news to Athens in spite of Herodotus' silence on the matter. In fact, he thinks that there were probably multiple runners who hoped to gain glory as the first runner to inform Athens of the great victory over the Persians; however, he adds that "someone in one of the many villages along the route undoubtedly jumped on a horse and swiftly outdistanced those on foot."[337]

Lacey agrees that there probably was a messenger sent to Athens to announce the victory and that it was probably a professional runner like Philippides who ran the entire distance; however, while Lacey says that we will never know the name of the runner for sure, he adds that Philippides had had plenty of time to recover from his run to Sparta, so perhaps he was "given the honor of reporting the great victory to awaiting Athens."[338]

Billows calls the supposed run by Philippides the "most famous legend" about Marathon, but then says that "the truth is, in this case, much more impressive than the legend." He writes,

> Philippides ran, not a paltry 25 or so miles from Marathon to Athens, but roughly 140 miles from Athens to Sparta, and then the same distance back again. To this super-fit 'all day runner' the run from Marathon to Athens would have been a pleasant little training exercise. But it was in fact the majority of the Athenian army, those who were still fit and able after the battle, who traveled that afternoon of August 11, 490 BCE from Marathon to Athens, after fighting the most desperate battle of their lives in the morning. And they traveled, not in running gear, but in full armor, with shields and spear.[339]

March Back to Athens

After the Battle of Marathon ended, Herodotus tells us that the Persians sailed away from Marathon and picked up the captive slaves from Eretria, who had been held on the island of Aigilia, and sailed around Sounion toward Phaleron, "hoping to arrive at the city of Athens before the Athenians could march there." He goes on to say that when the Athenians saw the Persians sailing toward Athens, the Athenians marched back to Athens "as fast as they could to defend their city, and they managed to arrive there in advance of the barbarian fleet." He then comments that the Athenians had left their camp at the sanctuary of Heracles at Marathon and made camp in another sanctuary of Heracles at Athens called Kynosarges. When the Persian fleet arrived, they anchored for a time, but observing that the Athenian army had already arrived and was ready for battle, the Persians sailed back to Asia.[340]

While Herodotus implies that the Athenian army marched back to Athens on the same day as the battle, he does not explicitly say that. He says that the Persian fleet first sailed to Aigilia to pick up the Eretrian prisoners and then sailed around Sounion at which time the Athenians were marching back to Athens. Thus he ties the march of the Athenians to the time when the Persians were sailing around Sounion and does not tell the time or day that the fleet rounded Sounion. Plutarch, however, does mention the exact day of the march. In "Aristides," he writes,

> But after they had beaten the barbarians back to their ships, and perceived that they sailed not for the Isles, but were driven in by the force of sea and wind towards the country of Attica, fearing lest that they should take the city, unprovided of defense, they hurried away thither with nine tribes, and reached it the same day.[341]

While Plutarch wrote about 500 years after the Battle of Marathon, he did have access to literary sources not available today and preserved some fragments of information that can be used to supplement Herodotus.[342] This passage would seem to provide confirmation that the Athenians marched back to Marathon on the same day as the battle; however, Plutarch, in an essay titled "Were the Athenians More Famous in War or in Wisdom?" wrote, "For Miltiades set forth to Marathon, joined battle the next day, and returned victorious with his army to the city." This again seems to support the idea that the Greek army returned to Athens on the day of the battle; however, Krentz explains that Plutarch's statement can be read as, "Miltiades, having joined battle at Marathon on the next day, returned to the city with his army," depending on whether the translator takes "'on the next day' with the participle or the main verb." He then points out that "if we take it with the participle, Plutarch contradicts Herodotus in denying a delay before the battle; however, if we take it with the main verb, Plutarch contradicts himself."[343]

Once again we are back to uncertainty about an aspect of the Battle of Marathon, so some modern historians have concluded that the Athenians marched back to Athens immediately after the battle, while others claim that they rested after the battle and returned the next day. We will proceed to examine the arguments and evidence for each view and attempt to reach a conclusion as to which is most probable.

Macan and How and Wells seem unwilling to take a strong position on whether or not the Athenians marched back to Athens on the day of the battle. Macan, in his commentary, states, "The other nine tribes returned to Athens, but surely not the same day." He goes on to argue that before the Athenians could even think of returning to Athens, they had to be sure that it was a crushing victory and that the entire fleet was indeed clearly on the way to Athens in order to be sure that no vessels could return to Marathon and embark troops at the back of the Athenians returning to Athens; however, he then wavers on his view, saying if the fleet had sailed early toward Athens, he could understand the need for a rapid return to the city. How and Wells state that whether the Athenians took the road to Athens, which was 25 miles, or traveled 22 miles to Athens by Kaphesia, it was too much to expect of an army, that had just fought a tough battle, to return the same day. Also, they say, the Athenians could not leave Marathon until they were certain that the Persian fleet was sailing to Athens. They also add that the Persians' trip around Sounion would take longer and conclude, "Hence both the march and voyage, placed on the same day as the battle, should probably be assigned to the following day." But they also waver saying that the army might have had to march back to meet "a flying squadron, which set sail before the battle."[344]

Grote believes that Miltiades saw the shield signal as an effort to get the Persian fleet along with its cavalry to Athens, so that the Persians with or without the aid of pro–Persian Athenians could take the city before the Athenian army could return to Athens, since the Phaleric wall had not yet been built. So Miltiades immediately marched his army back to Athens "on the very day of the battle," and they arrived just prior to the Persian fleet. He adds that if they had arrived slightly later they might have found "the Persians with the partisans of Hippias" in control of Athens. When Datis arrived and did not find a "friendly movement to encourage him," but rather found the Athenian army waiting for him, he made no move to land his troops but instead sailed away.[345]

According to Grundy the distance from Marathon to Phaleron is about 90 miles, and he says that "even under the most liberal computation of speed and even under the most favorable circumstances," the voyage from Marathon to Phaleron would take at least 9 to 10 hours; however, he adds that the Persian vessels "were heavily laden with troops, horses and baggage," so their speed would have been cut by about 50 percent, which meant that the trip would take about 18 hours. This would mean that if the Persian fleet left immediately after the battle, around 10 a.m. it would not arrive at Phaleron until the following day, so there would have been no reason for the Athenians to rush back to Athens immediately after the battle; but, being a believer in the split forces theory, he suggests that part of the fleet left at daybreak or earlier, meaning they would arrive at Phaleron on the same day as the battle, so the Athenians had to march in a hurry back to Athens immediately after the battle.[346]

Munro explains that while Artaphernes' squadron sailed on Athens, Datis and his squadron picked up the Eretrian prisoners off the island of Aigilia so as to not slow the rest of the Persian fleet's voyage to Athens. Miltiades, recognizing the danger to Athens, immediately marched his army to Athens. While troops may have been tired from the battle, they had won a great victory, so they were willing to rush back because of the threat to Athens.[347]

Burn and Hammond agree that the Athenian army marched back to Athens on the day of the battle, fearing that traitors at Athens might help the Persians gain control of the city. Hammond explains that Phaleron is about 58 nautical miles from Marathon and believes that the Phoenician ships of the Persian navy could have reached Phaleron in eight hours if the conditions were right and if they could maintain an average speed of over seven knots.

He then says that the Phoenician fleet actually arrived in about nine hours, averaging about 6.5 knots.[348]

Green thinks that the Battle of Marathon ended by about 9 a.m. and then the Athenian army rushed back to Athens, arriving about four in the afternoon with the Persian fleet arriving "an hour or less later." He then says,

> Yet, that hour made all the difference, in more ways than one. The re-appearance of the Marathon warriors—grim, indomitable, caked with dust and sweat and dried blood—not only gave Datis pause for thought; it also, obviously, came as an unexpected shock to the Alcmeonidae and the pro–Persian party. A lot of people in Athens must have silently switched sides in a hurry.

Datis, recognizing that he would receive no help from within Athens, shortly thereafter sailed off back to Persia.[349]

Holland says that after observing the signal to the Persians, the Greeks realized that their families were in Athens, which was undefended. So the army immediately headed back to Athens "as fast as their legs could take them." He goes on to say that "in an outstanding display of toughness and endurance" they reached Athens before the Persian fleet appeared. When the Persian fleet arrived they "lay stationary for a few hours ... then, as the sun sets at last on that long and fateful day," they sailed back to Persia.[350]

Billows believes that it would have taken the Persian fleet under 12 hours to "row as directly as possible" to Phaleron at their best speed. He points out that triremes could achieve six to eight knots (seven to nine mph) for short sprints and that they would have pressed their rowers "to make an extreme effort." He believes that the faster ships promptly passed ahead, leaving the transports to follow by sail. The rowers certainly could not maintain seven knots for 70 miles but he thinks they could have maintained perhaps six knots, and thus the fleet could appear at Phaleron "before dusk."[351] In order for the Athenians to reach Athens before the Persian fleet, Billows believes they split their forces, sending the younger men to take the shorter northern route, which was 22 miles but which also included a steep climb of three to four miles at the beginning, but concluded with a downhill path of about 18 miles to the city. The older men would take the longer southern route of 25 miles but on a "flatter and therefore physically last tiring route." No matter which route they took, Billows believes they should all be admired, for "they traveled, not in running gear, but in full armor, with shields and spear." Would this be physically possible? Billows believes it would have been possible for the Greeks and reminds us that we must remember that the ancient Greeks "were used to walking everywhere, often for hours at a time and on hilly dirt roads, so this will have seemed much less extreme to an ancient Greek" than to a person today; however, he does admit that there would be differences in "fitness, stamina and running ability" among the Greeks, so they would be strung out over long distances, with the younger, fitter men arriving in six to seven hours, and the others straggling in over time. He also states that it would not be necessary for the entire army to be at Phaleron to cause the Persians consternation when they saw the Greek army on their arrival. Since the Persians had left Marathon before the battle, they would have been shocked and wondered where these troops had come from, but they must have realized as they observed more hoplites arriving that this was the army from Marathon, which obviously had been victorious. After discussions the Persians decided not to try "to force a landing in the face of a large, determined, and victorious force of hoplite warriors."[352]

Lacey claims that after the battle, the Athenians "looked out to the sea in horror," as they saw that the Persian fleet was headed toward Athens and they realized Athens was undefended. He then says that the "exhausted hoplites steeled themselves for one more great effort" and "set off on a race against time" in an effort to arrive at Athens before the Persians. When the Persians anchored off Phaleron, Datis "saw that through an almost super human effort, the Athenian hoplites had beaten him there."[353] Lacey then asks why the Persians sailed to Phaleron. He says that even if Datis took Athens he would "have found himself locked up in Athens" facing the victorious Greek army "with blood and vengeance on its mind," and the Spartans would have arrived soon possibly along with reinforcements from other poleis. Lacey concludes that taking Athens would make no sense. So Datis must have had a different goal. Lacey thinks that Datis had had a successful campaign up until the Battle of Marathon and that he hoped to offset his loss at Marathon by landing troops at Phaleron, making "a lightning march to seize Athens, burn as much as possible and return to their ships. Datis then would be able to tell Darius that Naxos and the Cyclades had been added to his empire, Eretria had been punished and Athens had been burned in retaliation for the destruction of Sardis; however, seeing the Athenian army waiting for him at Phaleron, Datis realized that he could not accomplish his final goal and ordered the fleet to sail back to Persia.[354]

Due to the lack of conclusive evidence concerning when the Athenians marched back to Athens, other historians have argued that a same-day march back to Athens was unreasonable and that they did not return to Athens on the same day of the battle. In 1951 Lionel Casson published an article titled "Speed under Sail of Ancient Ships," which included a great deal of data and information that could be applied to the Persian voyage to Phaleron. First, Casson challenged the method used to determine the average rate of speed for ancient ships in the past. Up to that point, most authors had taken "a list of various miscellaneous voyages and from it deduced what the average speed of ancient ships was." He claims that conclusions reached by such an approach are "worthless" as "they ignore the fundamental fact that the speed of a sailing ship depends first and foremost on the direction of the wind." In order to more accurately determine the rate of speed for voyages, it required knowing whether the voyages were made under fair or foul winds, knowing if the ship was fast or slow, and knowing the strength of the wind. He then looked at 22 different voyages that were made with the wind and determined that ships could log between four and six knots on the open sea, but only three to four knots while sailing among islands or along the coast. After analyzing 10 voyages against unfavorable winds, Casson concluded that the average speed for ancient ships with unfavorable winds would be "from less than two to 2½ knots." Since the above voyages were made by single ships, Casson then looked at speeds that ancient fleets could maintain. He examined 15 voyages by fleets that ranged from 55 miles to 340 miles and explained that the fleet speeds were determined by their slowest vessels. He concluded that fleets with a favorable wind could maintain speeds of two to three knots while with unfavorable winds they could only attain 1 to 1.5 knots.[355]

In 1974–1975, A. Trevor Hodge wrote two articles concerning the Persian voyage to Phaleron incorporating Casson's conclusions. Hodge first gives reasons for the different estimates for the length of the voyage from Marathon to Phaleron that range from 66 to 90 miles. He explains that distances can vary according to "how close a course was laid to round

Sounion and whether the ship had to tack." He also states that a "straight line is not always the best or fastest route between two points, and calculations based on direct distance may sometimes turn out to be very misleading."[356] Hodge then listed five factors that would influence the voyage from Marathon to Phaleron. Obviously the most important factor is the wind, but he also includes the composition of the fleet, heaviness of the sea, the course of the voyage, and the urgency of the situation. He then proceeds to explain that the winds in the summer and early September were called the Etesian winds and were quite regular, although they generally fell off "every evening to a windless calm." He then gives a technical description of a sailing voyage and the problems that the "U-shaped course" to Phaleron would involve. He states, "A north wind, for example, blowing on a heading of 180 degrees, will be very favorable, as far as Sounion but very adverse (in fact, 37 degrees forward of the beam) from then on." He concludes, "Marathon to Phaleron, in short, was not a particularly difficult voyage; it was only difficult to do it fast."[357]

Hodge then considers the issue of whether the Persian fleet sailed as a single unit or sent their fastest ships ahead to get to Phaleron more quickly. While it would seem logical to send the faster ships ahead, the problem was that the horses for the cavalry were carried on horse transports, which could not sail fast, and the cavalry was essential to the Persian plan to land at Phaleron; thus it appears that the fleet would have had to sail as a single unit. If they sailed as a single unit, their speed would have been 2 to 3 knots with favorable winds and 1 to 1.5 knots in unfavorable winds. He applies these speeds to the Persian voyage and comes up with the Persians needing 10 to 15 hours to reach Sounion with favorable winds but an additional 20 to 30 hours to reach Phaleron with unfavorable winds for a total of 30 to 45 hours for the entire voyage.[358] He then examines Hammond's estimate that the Persians could average 6.5 to 7 knots and reach Athens in eight hours. Hodge concludes that it would have been impossible for the Persians to maintain such an average speed based on the fact that they were sailing a U-shaped course and would face adverse wins for at least 50 percent of it. To make his point further, he says that in the 1967 America's cup, the winning American racing yacht, *Intrepid,* averaged 6.5 knots over the entire course. It would seem absurd to think that the Persian fleet could maintain an average speed of 6.5 knots when an American yacht built for racing could only average 6.5 knots.[359]

Writing in 1993, Evans appears to accept the conclusions of Hodge as he wonders why the Athenians would have immediately returned to Athens as the Persian fleet could not have reached Athens in less than 30 hours even if it sailed straight to Phaleron with the best possible sailing conditions. He goes on to say that Datis had sailed to Athens, perhaps in the hope that somehow the machinations of the pro–Persian conspirators would benefit him; however, he adds that in actuality they probably sailed to Athens "because they had to report to the great King, and it would go better for them if they left nothing untried in their effort to carry out their mission."[360]

In 1997 James P. Holoka published an article entitled "Marathon and the Myth of the Same-Day March." In the article, he begins by rejecting the idea that the Battle of Marathon began about 5:30 to 6:00 a.m. and was over by 9 to 10 a.m. because the argument for the early start of the battle is based upon the need for the battle to begin that early because of the need for the army to be able to reach Athens before dusk.[361] Rather, Holoka claims there is more evidence to indicate that the battle began later. He says that it is unreasonable to think that the Athenian hoplites went into battle without having a meal. After the meal the generals would have to meet their religious obligations, "by consulting omens and paying homage to the gods by sacrifice." He adds that the omens could be consulted in camp, but that the "supplementary and propitiating sacrifices" had to be performed immediately before the action began. He then claims that the Greeks could not have taken the field before the Persians took the field because Miltiades made adjustments in how he arrayed his troops in order to extend his line to cover the Persian front. Finally, Miltiades had to deploy his forces to the battlefield, and this in itself was a lengthy procedure. Holoka claims that the above actions would have required at least two hours, meaning the battle could not have started until 7:30 a.m. at the earliest.[362]

Holoka then addresses the length of the battle. He says that the fighting occurred over "an unusually large battleground" ranging from the initial battle lines up to the Great Marsh and also to the 3,000-yard Schoenia beach all the way to Cape Cynosura. He claims that the Greek hoplites moved over a distance of up to six miles while facing armed resistance with 70 pounds of armor and weapons during a hot summer day and then after the battle they had to march back at least three miles to their camp. He claims that just marching the distances involved would take four hours, but on that day, much longer, because they were fighting against armed opponents. Next he estimates two hours to fight and kill the defeated enemy, and concludes that the battle took at least six hours. Finally he gives a conservative estimate of one hour for the scattered Greeks to reorganize their forces, concluding that the Athenians were not ready to consider marching back to Athens until 2:30 p.m. which left only four hours of daylight for them to march to the city as dusk fell at 6:30 p.m.[363]

Holoka next took up the Athenian march back to Athens. He believes that the Athenians would have taken the southern route along the coastal road, which measured about 25 miles; however, he says, it is necessary to add the approximate 10 miles that they marched during the battle, to end up with a total of about 35 miles that the Athenians would have had to march if they returned to Athens on the same day that the battle took place. He then adds the three miles that the Athenians would have to march from the Herakles sanctuary at Kynosarges to reach the beach at Phaleron where they confronted the Persian fleet and says this means that the Athenians would have had to march a total of 38 miles in one day. In addition, he adds that the Athenians were wearing their armor and had to carry their own food and water, which added at least four more pounds to the 70 pounds of armor and weapons they already were carrying. He claims that having armor bearers and/or wagons drawn by oxen or mules would have added too much confusion and slowed down the army, which was "marching back as fast as they could to defend Athens." Obviously, given the title of his article, Holoka considers a same-day march back to Athens a myth, as it would have been physically impossible.[364]

Holoka is willing to accept that Hammond as a young man in 1930 walked round trip to Marathon in one day, a total of 45 miles in 13 hours, but he points out that Hammond was not wearing armor and carrying a shield and spear and had not fought in a four-hour battle under the hot sun. While the cuirass and the Corinthian helmet offered excellent protection to the Athenian hoplites, they also brought added problems. The bronze cuirass acted as a solar collector, forcing the hoplites to wear felt or linen undergarments to keep from being, burned and these undergarments quickly became soaked with sweat as the cuirass allowed for little ventilation or evaporation. The Corinthian helmet also conducted the heat of the sun and concentrated the heat around the face nose and eyes and made breathing difficult in the hot, humid and dusty summer battlefields. As a result of those two factors, heat prostration and dehydration were constant problems on Greek battlefields.[365] To add further support for his conclusion that a same-day march back to Athens was not possible, Holoka states that there is no record of any ancient army marching 38 miles on the day of a battle. He points out that the fastest rate ever achieved by the Macedonian army was 19.5 miles per day, while the Roman armies averaged no more than 18 miles per day, and the Byzantine armies marched an average of 16 miles per day at most. He says armies have marched over 25 miles on foot, but at a very high price as demonstrated when the Duke of Marlborough's infantry marched 36 miles in 16 hours. When that army reached their destination, they had barely 50 percent of their original number and scores had died during the march.[366] Holoka says that the Athenians marching at 1.5 miles per hour would require 14 hours of steady marching after fighting a major battle in order to reach Athens. He says that no Athenian general would be willing to put his hoplites into such a dangerous situation. He adds that even if they had done so, the force that arrived at Phaleron would have been so exhausted and depleted that it probably could not have prevented a landing of Persian forces. He concludes,

> The same-day version of the battle and the march, if it existed in some source earlier than Plutarch, likely resulted from the tendency of battles perceived to be turning points in history to inspire romanticizing and mythologizing retellings and of victorious commanders like Miltiades to undergo concomitant lionizing.[367]

As pointed out earlier in the chapter, Krentz says that Plutarch's statement about a same-day march is open to interpretation as to how it is to be read. He then states, "I think it is preferable to interpret Plutarch charitably, so that he contradicts neither Herodotus nor himself, which means it should be read as the Athenians hurried all the way back to Athens on the day after the battle. He seems to agree with the work of Casson and Hodge, as he goes on to say that looking realistically at ship speeds, the Persian fleet could not have reached Phaleron in less than 30 to 45 hours, and thus came to anchor at Phaleron the day after the battle. He also agrees with Holoka's work when he says that the Athenians "would have been in no condition to march back to Athens, the same day after fighting a long battle under the hot summer sun, which had them moving over 10 miles while fighting and returning to their camp."[368]

After examining scholarship in English on the topic of the same-day march over the last 162 years, what conclusion can be drawn? References to patriotism, a sense of urgency, an astounding sense of toughness, superhuman effort, great stamina, and Greeks used to marching all day are made in support of the same-day march, but little data or evidence is included. Casson, Hodge and Holoka have all presented facts and data that would seem to settle the question in favor of the argument that the same-day march did not occur; however, two of the last three books written on the Battle of Marathon in 2010–2011 have still concluded that the Athenian army heroically marched back on the day of the battle to save Athens from the Persian fleet. So, once again, there is no consensus on an issue, and readers must draw their own conclusion.

Burial

When the Athenians marched back to Athens, they left Aristides and his tribe at Marathon to guard the battlefield and plunder taken from the Persians. While Herodotus is silent on the issue, Plutarch writes that Aristides

> did not disappoint the opinion they had of him. Amidst the profusion of gold and silver, all sorts of apparel, and other property, more than can be mentioned, that were in the tents and the vessels which they had taken, he neither felt the desire to meddle with anything himself, nor suffered others to do it; unless it might be some who took away anything unknown to him.[369]

Krentz suggests that while the rest of the army marched to Athens, Aristides and his tribe gathered the Greek dead and prepared them for cremation, in addition to gathering the plunder from the Persian corpses and guarding it.[370] Normally, the funerals for Athenian soldiers took place on the second day after the battle; however, that would seem to have been impossible at Marathon since the army was certainly in Athens the day after the battle, and possibly longer if they did not march back to Athens until the day after the battle. When the army returned to Marathon, the Athenians were cremated as quickly as it could be accomplished as the bodies must have been in terrible shape after lying out in the hot sun for several days. They were placed upon "a brick-lined cremation-tray, about 3 feet wide and 16 feet long," and then the Athenians built a funeral mound over their cremated bodies.[371]

Pausanias claims to have seen the grave of the Athenians and describes tombstones which included the names of the 192 Athenian dead listed by their tribes.[372] Grote quotes Colonel Leake, who described a mound of about 30 feet with a circumference of about 200 yards at Marathon. Hammond adds that the mound had a diameter of 45 meters.[373] Most historians seem to believe that the burial took place where the Athenians lost the most men. The mound was excavated in 1890 by a Greek archaeologist, and human remains were found which would seem to prove it is the burial mound of the Athenians.[374] Krentz describes a second brick-lined tray on the outer face of the mound upon which he claims the Athenians continued to make offerings "to the heroized dead" 600 years after the battle.[375]

Pausanias claims also to have seen a second grave for the Plataeans and the slaves that fell at Marathon; however, this time the grave's location has not been agreed upon. In the 19th century, E. D. Clark and Colonel Leake claimed to have seen "a small artificial elevation of the surface at a short distance from the Soros"; however, in 1970 S. Marinatos excavated "a tumulus in the necropolis near Vrana" and found 11 burials, and he then claimed that he had found the grave of the Plataeans. With the location of the Herakleion near Valaria being generally agreed upon, it seems unlikely that the Plataeans would have been buried near Vrana. While the elevation referred to by Clark and Leake is no longer visible, van der Veer believes it was probably "due to a rising of the ground level at this point," which may have amounted to up to three feet.[376] Pausanias says that he was told that the Persians had been buried, but he said he could not find any trace of a grave; instead, he claims that the Greeks simply "carried them to a trench and flung them in pell-mell."[377]

Regarding the monuments and tombstones referred to by Pausanias, Vanderpool in 1966 found evidence of a monument in the ruins of a medieval tower which he claims was the white monument described by Pausanias.[378] Krentz refers to a find by Theodorus Spyropoulos, a Greek archaeologist, who has found one of the tombstones inscribed with the names of the Athenian dead that had been taken to the Peloponnese. It may be an original or a copy, but it includes 25 names "cut in letters that look late archaic." For some reason he has not published on his find.[379]

Why the Greeks Won

In 490 BCE Athens, with a population estimated at 140,000 citizens, took on the Persian Empire with a population estimated at 17 million people on the low side to 35 million people on the high side. Over a period of 70 years the Persians had conquered much of the known world and created the greatest empire up to that time in history. It had a huge army, a large navy, unbelievable wealth and had defeated the Greeks in Ionia and had added them to the Persian Empire. There seems to have been little doubt as to what would happen when the Persian expeditionary force landed at Marathon after defeating Eretria; however, the Athenians with the aid of Plataea won a great victory over the Persian army at Marathon. How did Athens, with a small population and small army, defeat Persia, the superpower of Asia, at the Battle of Marathon? The main factors that enabled Athens to win the battle will be examined.

Superior Generalship

Grundy claims that "the Greek generalship during the brief campaign was in respect to strategy and tactics, the best of the century."[380] The Greek generals were divided on their best course of action, but Miltiades convinced Callimachus, the *polemarchon*, to cast the deciding vote to take an offensive strategy rather than a defensive one. According to Herodotus, Miltiades waited for his regular day to command the army and then ordered an attack on the Persian army. Before he ordered the attack, Miltiades and Callimachus had probably studied the Persian army as it deployed each day and challenged the Athenian army to fight. During their observations they saw the length of the Persian front and possibly recognized that the Persian wings were less capable and less disciplined then the Persian center, where the Persians traditionally placed their best troops. Miltiades recognized that he would have to make changes in his deployment if he was to avoid being outflanked by the longer Persian front. To avoid the problem he weakened his center to perhaps four ranks while keeping his wings at the original strength of eight ranks. In addition, he gave an order to his wings to halt their pursuit of enemy soldiers if they defeated the Persian wings until they saw if the weakened Athenian center required their assistance. Finally he ordered his men to attack at a run when they came within range of the Persian archers, or another possibility is that he ordered his infantry to trot the entire distance in order to engage the Persian infantry before the cavalry could intervene effectively. Thus, Miltiades made tactical adjustments based upon the circumstances facing the Greeks.[381] Lacey agrees that the Greek changes to their normal deployment and tactics helped them win the battle, but he gives credit for the plan and adjustments to Callimachus, rather than to Miltiades. He claims Miltiades was able to step forward and claim to be the hero because Callimachus died in the battle.[382]

Ineffective Persian Tactics

While the Greeks studied their Persian opponents and made adjustments to their normal formation and tactics, it seems the Persian generals were perhaps overconfident and planned to use their normal tactics, even though they were fighting on a battlefield that was quite different from the open plains of Asia where their tactics had developed. How claims that countries develop "a style of fighting suitable to the nature of the country in which it dwells," and as a result the Persians were at a great disadvantage since they were fighting in the narrow confines of mountainous Greece and not on the open plains of Asia where their fighting style developed.[383] The Persians "relied on the coordinated action of its combined arms, centered on mass archery to inflict sufficient losses to shatter the enemy's cohesion." As the archers on foot poured arrows into the enemy forces, the cavalry would attack the flanks, also shooting arrows into the enemy forces both as they rode at the enemy and as they retreated away from the enemy to avoid contact with the infantry. The Persians never expected to fight an organized army at close quarters, as the archers and cavalry would break the enemy's cohesion; only then would the infantry charge the disorganized enemy. Lacey adds that "the Greek phalanx possessed an overwhelming advantage on a narrow front fought in a box—a perfect description for the plain of Marathon." Perhaps if the Persian generals had made adjustments as Miltiades had, the outcome might have been different; however, Christopher Tuplin says that the Persians showed little "tactical inventiveness."[384]

We know that their cavalry played a huge role in Persian tactics and we also know that the Persians brought cavalry to Marathon, and yet Herodotus makes no mention of it in the battle. There have been many explanations for its absence or lack of impact on the battle. Some claim it had been re-embarked on the Persian ships in order to sail to attack Athens while her army was occupied at Marathon; however, others believe that the cavalry was at the battle but that they were simply too few in number to have any impact. Krentz and Hammond claim that the cavalry was at Marathon but that on the day of attack the grooms were late in returning the horses to the battlefield after watering them at the springs at Macaria and that Miltiades, when he saw that the cavalry was going to be late, ordered his army to run/trot to engage the Persians before the cavalry could enter the battle. Evans on the other hand claims that the cavalry might have been on another mission and thus not at the battlefield when the Greeks attacked. Finally, some suggest that the cavalry was at the battle but was stationed at the center and helped the center to push back the weakened Greek center but did little to help the Persian wings. Shrimpton thinks that the cavalry was bivouacked behind the infantry and was simply too slow in deploying to blunt the Athenian charge since the Athenians were running for all or part of the charge and caught the Persians by surprise as they had never seen such an attack.[385] Whatever the reason, the cavalry simply did not play its intended role in the battle, thus making it easier for the Greeks to win.

Superior Greek Armor and Weapons

Since the Persian army depended so heavily on archers, both on foot and on horse, one must examine the effectiveness of Persian arrows against the Greek armor and shields. The Corinthian helmet, the bronze or linen cuirass, and bronze greaves provided excellent protection for the hoplite. Using a 5'8" Greek soldier weighing 165 pounds as an example, Gabriel and Metz conclude that the soldier had 515 square inches left vulnerable to arrow penetrations after putting on his panoply. They then state that an arrow fired from 250 yards would have a 22 percent chance of hitting a soldier and a 10.8 percent chance of hitting him in a vulnerable area. They project that if 1,000 arrows were fired in a salvo, 120 arrows would hit a soldier at a vulnerable spot, of which 3.1 percent would be fatal with the rest causing wounds of various degrees of severity, some of which could result in death at a later point but certainly would put the soldier out of the battle. Thus, while the armor provided good protection, losing about 10 percent of their force to one salvo of arrows would be devastating to them; however, Gabriel and Metz explain that adding the hoplite shield to the protection of their armor totally changes the outcome, as the shield would protect most of the vulnerable areas not covered by armor. They conclude, "Unless a lucky shot struck a particularly inattentive or poorly trained soldier," the hoplites had little to fear from the Persian archers. They do add that while they were physically protected, massive archery fire on an infantry "could provide very high rates of combat stress and paralyzing fear, especially among newer, untrained soldiers."[386]

Blyth, in his 1977 study "The Effectiveness of Greek Armor against Arrows during the Persian Wars, 490–479," says that the Persian arrows were inadequate to perforate Greek armor because the Persians had been more interested in developing bows with range than in increasing the penetrating power of their arrows. He states that the arrows may have had 35 J of kinetic energy when they were fired, but upon striking their target "the energy was 30 J at 50 m, 26 J at 100 m and 20 J at 200 m." The tests that Blyth ran show that it would take between 31.4 and 41.2 J to perforate the curved bronze armor of the Greeks, so it is obvious that the Greeks' armor would protect them from most arrows, unless they were shot at a very close range of less than 50 m. In addition the arrowheads usually used by the Persians were designed for flesh cutting rather than for penetration and would usually bend as they hit the armor. Blyth concludes that the Greek hoplites could depend on their helmets, cuirass and greaves to protect them from Persian arrows; however, even with the armor and shield the Greek hoplite was still vulnerable to arrows around his eyes, arms and thighs, which could not all be protected at the same time.[387] Blyth's conclusion is supported by Gabriel and Metz, as they add that an arrow fired at a speed of 197 fps produces 47 foot-pounds of energy, but they also point out that 76 foot-pounds of energy were required to penetrate bronze armor.[388]

Christopher Matthews, an experimental archaeologist, decided to test the hypothesis that relatively few Athenians were killed by Persian arrows at the Battle of Marathon. At the Australasian Historical Conference in 2009, Matthews conducted a series of tests. He used 20 people fully equipped as hoplites and 16 archers using rubber tipped arrows and had the hoplites advance under fire from the archers. In the tests, 672 arrows were shot in salvos over a period of time simulating a hoplite attack in formation. As they advanced, each hit by arrow in an unarmored spot was recorded, and the results showed that of the 672 arrows fired, only three hoplites were hit in vulnerable places. One was hit in the right arm, one was hit on the right hand and a third not wearing greaves was hit on the left shin. The rest of the arrows hit the shield the helmet, the cuirass or simply hit nothing. Matthews claims his test validates the work of Blyth and suggests that the hypothesis that the Greeks charged the Persians at a run in order to avoid the Persian arrows should be dismissed or revised.[389]

What happened when the Greek phalanx was not broken or stopped by the archers but rather smashed into the Persians in a cohesive unit well accustomed to close-quarter fighting? The Persians were unprepared for close-quarter fighting with a phalanx, as their main strength, archers and cavalry, were designed for long-distance battle, and they never anticipated fighting against well-ordered heavy infantry. The Persians had spear bearers who were to protect the archers, but their weapons were meant to be used against a demoralized, disorganized and defeated enemy. Their spear was 6 to 6.5 feet long compared to the Greek spear which was 7 to 9 feet long, and the Persians carried a dagger/sword, which was about 15 to 16 inches compared with the Greek sword that was 24 to 29 inches long. Their shield was made of wicker and was about as tall as a man, but it was designed to be stuck in the ground to protect against enemy arrows. The Greek shield, on the other hand, was made of wood faced with bronze and was designed both for offense and defense, and could even be used as an additional weapon in close-quarter fighting. The extra length of the Greek spear and sword would keep the Persians at bay, but even if they got in close, their weapons could not overcome the Greek shield and armor. If a Persian soldier did manage to get past the spear and the shield and deliver a blow to the head of a Greek hoplite, the Greek's Corinthian helmet and horsehair crest absorbed blows with little impact to the head. While some of the Persian and Sacae troops may have had scaled armor, most of the archers and troops on the wings had little if any armor and no metal helmets.[390]

With little training for hand-to-hand combat, little or no experience with close-quarter fighting, inferior weapons, inadequate shields and little or no armor or protective clothing or helmets, one should not be surprised that the Greek wings quickly smashed through the wicker shields and spearmen and archers as they routed the Persian wings; rather, one must recognize the bravery and discipline which allowed the Persian center to drive back the weakened Greek center until they were attacked by the victorious Greek wings and annihilated. Certainly few Persians from the center would have survived. Also, even after the rout of the wings, the Persians held out at the Schoenia beach allowing most of their troops and cavalry to re-embark on their ships and escape with only the loss of 7 ships.

Freedom Versus Despotism

In 1898, Edward Crecy in his book, *Decisive Battles of the World,* describes the Athenians in 490 as follows:

> Versatile, restless, enterprising, and self-confident, the Greeks presented the most striking contrast to the habitual quietude and submissiveness of the Orientals. And, of all the Greeks, the Athenians exhibited these national characteristics in the strongest degree. This spirit of activity and daring, joined to a generous sympathy for the fate of their fellow Greeks in Asia, had led them to join in the last Ionian war, and now mingling with their abhorrence of the usurping family of their own citizens, which for a period had forcibly seized on and exercised despotic power at Athens, nerved them to defy the wrath of King Darius, and to refuse to receive back at his bidding the tyrant whom they had some years before driven from their land.[391]

Does the above statement seem outdated and biased toward the Greeks and prejudiced against the Persians? It certainly seems to be, but did the spirit of the Athenians and their desire for freedom have an influence on the outcome of the battle? For at least some modern historians, the answer appears to be yes.

Hammond, while giving credit to Miltiades, says, "But the victory was won by the indomitable courage of the Athenians and Plataeans, and of the liberated slaves who fought beside their masters in the line." He goes on to say that the Athenians saw the victory as due to "the courage of free men pitted against an Oriental despotism." In addition, he says that the popular belief was that the gods had intervened on the part of the Athenians. They believed Artemis Agrotera and Apollo had answered their prayers while Athena answered the appeal of Callimachus. Supernatural heroes, such as Marathon and Echetlus, were seen on the battlefield, and Athena, Herakles, and Theseus were depicted in the *Stoa Poikile* painting as present at the battle. Every year, 500 goats were given to Artemis Agrotera as a partial payment for the 6,400 goats they owed her, as the Athenians had promised to sacrifice one goat to her for every enemy killed if Athens was victorious. Also a bronze statue of Athena was dedicated on the Acropolis, and at Delphi a treasury to Apollo was built with the plunder taken from the Persians after the battle.[392]

Green agrees that the tactics of the Greeks were important but adds that the best reason for their victory was that "they were not Imperial conscripts, but free men fighting to preserve their freedom."[393] Lazenby, on the other hand, rejects Green's viewpoint, saying that "Imperial" conscripts can fight for their master with courage and loyalty as "Indian soldiers repeatedly demonstrated in the days of the Raj." He adds, however, that "to argue that the battle was not won by highly trained and disciplined professionals through brilliant strategy or tactics, but by militiamen through sheer guts and chance, enhances the quality of the victory, and makes it all the more astonishing."[394] After examining various factors that contributed to the Greek victory, Krentz adds, "But praise should also go to the Athenians who elected him [Miltiades], who voted to take the field, who made the run, who fought to defend their land, their families and their freedom."[395]

8

The Importance of the Battle of Marathon

Creasy describes the importance of the Battle of Marathon as follows:

> The day of Marathon is the critical epoch in the history of the two nations. It broke forever the spell of Persian invincibility which had paralyzed men's minds. It generated among the Greeks the spirit which beat back Xerxes, and afterwards led on Xenophon, Agesilaus, and Alexander, in terrible retaliation through their Asiatic campaigns. It secured for mankind the intellectual treasures of Athens, the growth of free institutions, the liberal enlightenment of the Western world, and the gradual ascendancy for many ages of the great principles of European civilization.[1]

From the Persian point of view Creasy's statement is pure hyperbole. The Persian expedition under Datis and Artaphernes had been a great success in adding Naxos and the Cyclades to the Persian Empire and defeating and punishing Eretria for its interference during the Ionian Revolt. True, they had suffered a defeat, but the defeat at Marathon had no impact outside the area of Greece. Pierre Briant explains,

> Certainly the Greeks of Asia minor, who had barely survived a terrible repression, saw no sign of the weakening of Persian domination in the battle of Marathon. On the contrary, they understood perfectly well that Darius' power had never been greater. The only hint of insubordination is mentioned in the article already are ready cited in the *Suda*: the Athenians were supposedly kept abreast of Datis' tactical dispositions by Ionians in the Persian army. If this information is true, it obviously refers only to a small group acting in the utmost secrecy. Nothing is ever said about anti–Persian activities among the Ionian or Aeolian contingents that Datis brought with him.[2]

In fact, the defeat even had little influence on the delay of 10 years that occurred before the Persians invaded Greece; rather, the delay was caused by the death of Darius in 486, leaving it up to Xerxes who had to subdue the Egyptian revolt and perhaps a revolt in Babylon, as well as completing preparations for the invasion of Greece, which included digging the canal at the Mount Athos Peninsula.[3] If the Persians had been able to invade earlier than 480, the outcome might have been different, as the rich vein of silver in the mines at Laurium found in 483/482 and the Athenian fleet which was expanded to 200 ships and paid for with the silver from Laurium was not available until 481. If the Persians had invaded prior to that date, the mighty Athenian fleet would not have been available, and one can wonder how the lack of an adequate fleet would have affected the outcome of the Persian invasion since the victory of Plataea occurred only after the victory at Salamis and the departure of Xerxes with part of his army back to Persia.

Irrespective of the above viewpoint, many modern historians seem to agree with much of what Creasy describes. It is emphasized by some that while it may not have been a decisive defeat it was a defeat for Persia, and it was the first time that the Greeks had beaten the Persians in the field. It showed the rest of Greece that the Persian army was not invulnerable and that the best soldiers in Asia could be defeated by a Greek army. And it was not even the best Greek army, which was the Spartan army, that had defeated the Persians, but rather the army of Athens, "a little state, possessed of no military reputation worth speaking of that had defeated a superior force of the conquerors of a continent."[4] This victory gave the rest of Greece hope and supplied them "with a resolution for the greater actual sacrifices which they cheerfully underwent 10 years afterwards."[5]

Suddenly the Greeks realized that defeat "at the hands of the superpower was not inevitable."[6] When the Athenians returned to Marathon to bury the dead, they must have realized that they had achieved something great when they counted the 6,400 enemy dead, and that feeling was reinforced when the Spartans, the greatest warriors in Greece, "praised them for their achievement." The Athenian victory "gave an enormous boost to Athenian morale," and from a psychological viewpoint the "legend" that grew up around the victory was probably more important than the actual battle.[7]

The Battle of Marathon also had important political consequences for Athens as it saved democracy in the polis. A defeat at Marathon would have resulted in Hippias being installed as a tyrant and Persian puppet. In their commentary, How and Wells say that "Marathon made tyranny and Medism impossible at Athens. The blood of the heroes buried there was the seed of Greek liberty." While some members of the Delian League may have questioned the above statement, it is definitely true that the victory at Marathon and the following victories during Xerxes' invasion convinced the Athenians of their ability to successfully govern themselves democratically.[8] The victory at Marathon was the turning point for Athens, which prior to 490 was simply one polis among many poleis; however, after its victory at Marathon, Athens began its rise to "the position of Hellenic protagonist."[9]

Just as the Ionian Revolt had given Greece some breathing room before Persia began its move to incorporate mainland Greece into its empire, so Marathon gave the Greeks additional time to prepare to meet the large-scale Persian invasion by land and sea in 480. During this time Athens discovered a rich vein of silver and used it to build its 200-ship fleet that played such an important role in the defeat of Xerxes. Ray sums up the importance of Marathon when he says,

> Without Marathon, there would have been no free Athens to build a fleet and bring the Persians down at Salamis, and no Athenian phalanx to hold the left flank at Plataea or fight to victory at Mycale. Without these later triumphs on sea and land, Greece might have become just another Persian satrapy, with all the consequences for western history that implies. The battle of Marathon saved Athens to fight another day and, in so doing, rightfully earned its lasting fame.[10]

Lacey concludes his book on the Battle of Marathon by extending the importance well beyond its impact upon Greece and Persia to its impact upon all of Western civilization. He writes,

> At Marathon, Athens saved itself, Greece, and by extension all of Western civilization. Some have proposed that Marathon made little difference in the creation and development of a unique Western civilization. After all, this argument goes, Pericles, Aristotle, Plato, and Socrates still would have been born. They still would have been brilliant, and their achieve-

ments would have been as great. One is hard-pressed, however, to think how these great minds and independent spirits would have soared as slaves to a despotic empire. In truth, Western civilization owes its existence to a thin line of bronze encased "men as hard as Oak" who went bravely forward against overwhelming odds, to victory and never ending glory.[11]

Billows also concludes his book on Marathon with an even stronger statement concerning the impact that a Persian victory would have had on Western civilization. He writes,

> In short, we can see that, beyond any reasonable doubt, the impact of an Athenian defeat at Marathon, not just on Athenian history, not even just on classical Greek history, but on the history and culture of all of Western civilization would have been huge: everything would have been different. Of course, it might be argued that even without classical Athens and the contributions of the great Athenians, the Greeks might have somehow managed to keep the Persians at bay under Spartan leadership, and some form of classical Greek culture might have arisen under the leadership and inspiration of other Greeks. Perhaps the Greeks of the West, of Sicily and Italy, would have played a bigger role. Perhaps the Syracusans or Tarentines would have pioneered political and intellectual development, drama and historiography, philosophy and art. Perhaps they might have. Or perhaps not: Greek culture might just as well have gone into a decline and faded away under the depressing impact of Persian predominance.
>
> Whatever might have come about, it undoubtedly would have been radically different than what did happen, even without the seminal contributions of the Athenians, such as Themistocles and Pericles, Aischylus, Sophokles, and Euripides, Aristophanes and Menandros, Thucydides and Socrates, Plato and Aristotle, Isocrates and Demosthenes, Iktinos and Pheidias, and all the rest. As unfashionable as it is to say it, the battle of Marathon really was a decisive turning point in Western civilization; the 10,000 Athenians who made their stand that day really did, in a very meaningful sense, "save Western civilization."[12]

This completes the examination of 162 years of scholarship on the Battle of Marathon. What can be concluded? During the journey we have found some limited consensus, lots of controversy, fascinating characters, colorful stories, lots of speculation, some unusual theories, and impressive scholarship. Because of the lack of true primary sources from Greece, the varying views on Herodotus, and the lack of Persian sources, the topic is open to many interpretations and wide speculation. Perhaps that is one of the reasons it is such a popular topic. Many interpretations and theories can be put forward, and most cannot be conclusively proven or disproven. Thus at this point, with the sources available today, it appears that no single acceptable conclusion can be reached on any of the issues or questions considered. Even when hard data becomes available, such as the sailing times required for the Persian fleet to reach Phaleron or new archaeological evidence concerning the location of the "precinct of Heracles," highly regarded historians continue to advance viewpoints seemingly contradicted by the new data and evidence.

About all that can be said for certain is that in spite of the vast amount of research done over the past 162 years, there is no agreement or consensus on the accuracy, usefulness or honesty of the account of the battle by Herodotus, our most complete ancient source. In addition, no matter how one views Herodotus, all agree that the incompleteness of his account along with the absence of any narrative Persian sources has led to a great many questions concerning the Battle of Marathon about which there are many conflicting answers. But perhaps it is not so bad to leave it to the readers to reach their own conclusions after reviewing the available sources, research and interpretations concerning the battle. Is that not the job of each generation of historians to reinterpret the evidence and historical viewpoints of the past utilizing new evidence, new historical tools and the values of their culture?

Chapter Notes

Chapter 1

1. Ily Gershevitch et al., eds., *The Cambridge History of Iran* (Cambridge: Cambridge University Press, 1985), 20; Pierre Briant, *From Cyrus to Alexander: A History of the Persian Empire* (trans. Peter Daniels (Winona Lake, IN: Eisen braus, 2002), 5.
2. Duncan Head, *The Achaemenid Persian Army* (Stockport, England: Montvert Publications, 1992), 7.
3. Ibid., 8.
4. J.M. Cook, *The Persian Empire* (New York: Schocken Books, 1983), 12; Gershevitch, 5.
5. Cook, 14.
6. Briant, 7.
7. Hdt. 1.1, trans. Aubrey de Selincourt. In 2007 Andrea Purvis translates it as, "so that human events do not fade with time. May the great and wonderful deeds—some brought forth by the Hellenes, others by the barbarians—not go unsung; as well as the causes that led them to make war on each other." Robert B. Strassler, ed., *The Landmark Herodotus*, trans. Andrea L. Purvis (New York: Pantheon, 2007), 3.
8. Carolyn Dewald and John Marincola, *The Cambridge Companion to Herodotus* (Cambridge: Cambridge University Press, 2006), 30.
9. Arthur Ferrill, "Herodotus and the Strategy and Tactics of the Invasion of Xerxes," *American Historical Review* 72 (1966): 113.
10. C. Hignett, *Xerxes' Invasion of Greece* (New York: Oxford University Press, 1963), 25. He suggests 484 for Herodotus' birth date. George Rawlinson, *The Five Great Monarchies of the Ancient World*, vol. 3 (New York: Dodd, Mead, 1881). He suggests 484. Aubrey de Selincourt, *The World of Herodotus* (Boston: Little, Brown, 1962), 28. He suggests between 490 and 480.
11. Cook, 15.
12. George Cawkwell, *The Greek Wars: The Failure of Persia* (Oxford: Oxford University Press, 2004), 4.
13. Detliv Fehling, *Herodotus and His "Sources": Citation, Invention and Narrative Art* (Leeds: Francis Cairns, 1990), 240–241.
14. Robert Drews, *The Greek Account of Eastern History* (Cambridge, MA: Harvard University Press, 1973), 41.
15. Hdt. 8.88.3; Cook, 17.
16. Cook, 17; Gershevitch, 202.
17. Cook, 17; J. Wells, "The Persian Friends of Herodotus," *Journal of Hellenic Studies* 27 (1907): 38; Hignett, 31.
18. Wells, 38–47. Many historians feel that Herodotus' story on the siege of Babylon, which supposedly he got from Zopyrus, is incorrect, and his story of the "self-devotion of Zopyrus is rejected as a fable." After a long discussion of the criticisms, Wells concludes, "It is quite possible to accept the view that Herodotus derived important information from the younger Zopyrus, even if we feel ourselves to convict Herodotus of undue credulity in accepting the whole of his stories." See Dewald, 34–36, for why "many historians question its basic factual content."
19. Hdt. 3.139; Cook, 17; Gershevitch, 202.
20. Cook, 19; Hignett, 3.1.
21. Cook, 19.
22. De Selincourt, 30.
23. J.F. Lazenby, *The Defence of Greece, 490–479* (Warminster, England: Aris and Phillips, 1993), 3, 13.
24. W.W. How and J. Wells, *A Commentary on Herodotus, II* (Oxford: Clarendon Press, 1912), 357; R.W. Macan, *Herodotus: The Fourth, Fifth and Sixth Books* (New York: Macmillan, 1985), 174.
25. Cook, 205.
26. Lazenby, *Defence*, 13.
27. John Boardman, N.G.L. Hammond, D.M. Lewis, and M. Ostwald, ed., *The Cambridge Ancient History*, vol. 4, *Persia, Greece and the Western Mediterranean* (Cambridge: Cambridge University Press, 1988), 89.
28. Hignett, 23; Lazenby, *Defence*, 9.
29. Dewald, 3; Hignett, 32; Lazenby, *Defence*, 13.
30. Cawkwell, 10.
31. C. Behan McCullagh, "Bias in Historical Description, Interpretation and Theory," *History and Theory* 39, no. 1 (February 2000): 60–66.
32. Dewald, 33.
33. Hdt. 9.62.
34. Hdt. 9.62.
35. Lionel Scott, *A Historical Commentary on Herodotus Book 6* (Leiden: Brill, 2005), 28.
36. Fehling, 1–2.
37. Ibid., 10.
38. Ibid., 240–243, 258.
39. Kimball O. Armayor, "Did Herodotus Ever Go to the Black Sea?" *Harvard Studies in Classical Philology* 82 (1978): 62; O Kimball Armayor, "Catalogues of the Persian Empire in Light of the Monuments and Greek Literary Traditions," *American Philological Association* 108 (1978): 2–8.
40. Armayor "Black Sea," 49–62. See W. Kendrick

Pritchett, *Studies in Ancient Greek Topography, Part IV: Passes* (Los Angeles: University of California Press, 1982), 234–242, for countering Armayor's view with a discussion of how Herodotus used a conventional means of measuring distances.

41. O. Kimball Armayor, *Herodotus: Autopsy of the Fayoum; Lake Moeris and the Labyrinth of Egypt* (Amsterdam: Gieben Publisher, 1985), 25–32.

42. Ibid., 34–38.

43. Ibid., 116.

44. Stephanie West, "Herodotus' Epigraphical Interests," *Classical Quarterly*, new series, 35, no. 2 (1985): 302–304. She says that Herodotus used as many Oriental inscriptions as he did Greek inscriptions, and she is impressed that he is evenhanded since there are many more Greek inscriptions. He appeared to be satisfied with those he took on trust as with those that he had verified himself. She is concerned that he failed to differentiate between the two. She claims that his description of the serpent column, which is of great importance to his theme, is "inaccurate and perfunctory."

45. Stephanie West, review of *Herodotus' Autopsy of the Fayoum: Lake Moeris and the Labyrinth of Egypt*, by O. Kimball Armayor, *The Classical Review* 37, no. 1 (June 1987): 639.

46. J.A.S. Evans, review of *Herodotus' Autopsy of the Fayoum: Lake Moeris and the Labyrinth of Egypt*, by O. Kimball Armayor, *American Historical Review* 92, no. 3 (June 1987), 639. Concerning the labyrinth, Dr. Sarah Parcat of the University of Alabama at Birmingham has done some work in which she used infrared satellite imaging to search for potential archaeological sites in Egypt. She discovered one site in the Fayoum which could possibly be an intricate temple that could have been thought to be a labyrinth.

47. W. Kendrick Pritchett, *The Liar School of Herodotus* (Amsterdam: J.C. Gieben Publisher, 1993), 176.

48. Fehling, 131.

49. W. Kendrick Pritchett, *Studies in Ancient Greek Topography, Part IV: Passes* (Los Angeles: University of California Press, 1982), 258–262.

50. West, "Epigraphical," 293.

51. Ibid., 297.

52. Quoted in Pritchett, *Liars*, 174.

53. Ibid., 174–175.

54. Ibid., 175.

55. Ibid.

56. Hugh Bowden, review of *Herodotus and His Sources: Citation, Invention and Narrative Art*, by D. Fehling, *Journal of Hellenic Studies* 112 (1992): 184.

57. Lazenby, *Defence*, 10–11.

58. Robert L. Fowler, "Herodotus and His Contemporaries," *Journal of Hellenic Studies* 116 (1996): 81–82.

59. Oswyn Murray, "Herodotus and Oral History," in *Achaemenid History II: The Greek Sources*, ed. Heleen Sancisi-Weerdenburg and Amelie Kuhrt (Leiden: Nederlands Instituut Voor Het Nabije, 1984), 101 note 12.

60. Ferrill, "Herodotus," 103. Ferrill lists the views of the following concerning Herodotus as a military historian: R.W. Macan, *Herodotus: The Seventh, Eighth, and Ninth Books*, vol. 2 (London, 1908), lxxxii–lxxxiii. He treats Herodotus more harshly than the others and suggests that he was "just not the right man" for military narrative. G.B. Grundy, *The Great Persian War* (New York: Scribner, 1901), 291; Amedee Hauvette, "Herodote, historien des guerres mediques" (Paris, 1894), 499–500; How and Wells, vol. 1, 45; vol. 2, appendix 21, 378–379; W.W. How, "Arms, Tactics and Strategy in the Persian War," *Journal of Hellenic Studies* 43, no. 2 (1923): 128; Joseph Wells, *Studies in Herodotus* (Oxford, 1923), 162–163; T.R. Glover, "Herodotus" (Berkeley, CA, 1924), 228–229; F.E. Adcock, *The Greek and Macedonian Art of War* (Berkeley, CA, 1957), 99; A.R. Burn, *Persia and the Greeks* (New York, 1962), 4–5; Ferrill, 2.

61. F.E. Adcock, *The Greek and Macedonian Art of War* (Los Angeles: University of California Press, 1962), 99.

62. Lionel Scott, *A Historical Commentary on Herodotus Book 6* (Leiden: Brill, 2005), 17–18.

63. Hignett, 37–39.

64. Lazenby, *Defence*, 13–14.

65. Ferrill, "Herodotus," 108.

66. Ibid., 102–115.

67. Lazenby, *Defence*, 15.

68. Hignett, 39–40.

69. Macan, *Fourth, Fifth and Sixth Books*, I, 10.

70. Ibid., 9–11.

71. Drews, 103.

72. Ibid., 105.

73. Ibid., 107; J.T.M. Bigwood, "Ctesias as Historian of the Persian Wars," *Phoenix* 32, no. 1 (Spring 1978): 36. Bigwood concludes, "Whatever Ctesias' sources were, and whatever Photius' methods of summarizing, there is exceedingly little in this whole account of the Wars which could be right and nothing that suggests concern for the truth or careful investigation. Instead we have all the ingredients which one associates with Ctesias—reckless army statistics, misidentified characters, simplifications, astounding confusions, chronology which is muddled, some degree of anachronism, and a certain amount of bias."

74. J.B. Bury, *The Ancient Greek Historians* (New York: Dover Publications, 1958), 1951.

75. Head, 17, 19, 22, 34–36, 40–41; Nicholas Sekunda, *The Persian Army, 560–330 BC* (Oxford: Osprey Press, 1992), 7–13, 17–19, 22–28, 48, 54, 60.

76. Macan, *Fourth, Fifth and Sixth Books*, I, 27–28.

77. Hignett, 15–16.

78. Diodorus, *The Persian Wars to the Fall of Athens: Book 11–14.34 (480–401 BCE)*, trans. Peter Green (Austin: University of Texas Press, 2010), intro., 2.

79. Bury, *The Ancient Greek Historians*, 236.

80. Diodorus, intro., 6.

81. Cornelius Nepos, trans. John Carew Rolfe (Cambridge: Harvard University Press, 1929).

82. Macan, *Fourth, Fifth and Sixth Books*, I, 82; W.W. How, "Cornelius Nepos on Marathon and Paros," *Journal of Hellenic Studies* 39 (1919): 48.

83. How, *Nepos*, 52.

84. Macan, *Fourth, Fifth and Sixth Books*, I, 83.

85. Peter Krentz, *The Battle of Marathon* (New Haven, CT: Yale University Press, 2010), 178.

86. S. Casson, "Cornelius Nepos: Some Further Notes," *Journal of Hellenic Studies* 40, pt. 1 (1920): 43–44.

87. Macan, *Fourth, Fifth and Sixth Books*, I, 84.
88. Hignett, 20–21.
89. Ibid.
90. Plutarch, *The Malice of Herodotus*, trans. Anthony Bowen (Warminster, England: Aris & Phillips, 1992), intro., 3.
91. Hignett, 22.
92. Plutarch, intro., 5–13.

Chapter 2

1. Duncan Head, *The Achaemenid Army* (Stockport: Montvert Publications, 1992), 8.
2. Nick Sekunda, "The Persians," in *Warfare in the Ancient World*, ed. John Hackett (New York: Facts on File, 1989), 84.
3. C. Hignett, *Xerxes' Invasion of Greece* (Oxford: Clarendon Press, 1963), 5; J.F. Lazenby, *The Defence of Greece, 490–479* (Warminster: Aris & Phillips, 1993), 21.
4. Nicholas Sekunda, *The Persian Army, 560–330 BC* (New York: Osprey Publishing, 1992), 5.
5. Hdt. 1.136.
6. Pierre Briant, "The Achaemenid Empire," in *Warfare & Society in Ancient and Medieval Worlds: Asia, The Mediterranean, Europe, and Mesoamerica*, ed. Kurt Raaflaub and Nathan Rosenstein (Washington, DC: Center for Hellenic Studies Trustees for Harvard University, 1999), 115.
7. Strabo 15.3, 18.9.
8. Briant, "Achaemenid Empire," 114.
9. Sekunda, *Persian Army*, 5.
10. Briant, "Achaemenid Empire," 115–116.
11. Head, 10.
12. Lazenby, *Defence*, 39.
13. Hdt. 1.136.
14. Kaveh Farrokh, *Shadows in the Desert: Ancient Persia at War* (New York: Osprey Publishing, 2007), 39.
15. Sekunda, *Persian Army*, 5.
16. George Cawkwell, *The Greek Wars: The Failure of Persia* (Oxford: Oxford University Press, 2004), 238–239; Head, 12.
17. Farrokh, 39; Head, 13–14.
18. Josiah Ober et al., "Persia at the Crest," in *TimeFrame, 600–400 BCE: A Soaring Spirit*, ed. Time-Life (Alexandria, VA: Time-Life Books, 1987), 27.
19. Hdt. 3.91; J.M. Cook, *The Persian Empire* (New York: Schocken Books, 1983), 111.
20. Ober et al., 27.
21. Head, 15.
22. Ibid., 16.
23. Cawkwell, *Greek Wars*, 243.
24. Lazenby, *Defence*, 29.
25. Hdt. 1.135; Sekunda, *Persian Army*, 13; Head, 20. Head believes that the Persians always wore the tunic and trousers in battle and only used the robe which they borrowed from their Elamite neighbors for ceremonial purposes.
26. Hdt. 3.12.4, 7.61; Head, 21; see Sekunda, *Persian Army*, for excellent colored plates illustrating Persian military dress.
27. Hdt. 7.61.1.
28. Sekunda, *Persian Army*, 9–10; Head, 21.
29. Sekunda, "The Persians," 84–85.
30. Ibid., 85.
31. Hdt. 1.136.
32. Ann Hyland, *The Horse in the Ancient World* (Westport, CT: Praeger, 2003), 120–121.
33. Peter Krentz, *The Battle of Marathon* (New Haven, CT: Yale University Press, 2010), 24; J.A.S. Evans, "Cavalry about the Time of the Persian Wars: A Speculative Essay," *Classical Journal* 82, no. 2 (December 1986–January 1987): 99.
34. Evans, "Cavalry," 102–103; Gordon Shrimpton, "The Persian Cavalry at Marathon," *Phoenix* 34, no. 1 (Spring 1980), 31 note 23.
35. Shrimpton, 31 note 23; Evans, "Cavalry," 103.
36. Shrimpton, 31 note 23.
37. Sekunda, "The Persians," 85.
38. Hdt. 7.84; Evans, "Cavalry," 99.
39. Sekunda, "The Persians," 85.
40. Cook, 102.
41. George Rawlinson, *The Five Great Monarchies of the Ancient Eastern World, III* (New York: Dodd, Mead, 1881), 178; See Head, 37, for excellent illustrations of early art showing cavalry without shields. Gordon Shrimpton, 29. Shrimpton says that "they carry no shield; they do not apparently have heavy protective head-gear, nor any protective body weaponry, such as a breast-plate."
42. Evans, "Cavalry," 100. Phil Sidnell, "Press Home the Charge," *Ancient Warfare* 6, no. 3 (2012): 8. Sidnell disagrees with Evans on the importance of stirrups. He says that the Numidians were considered to have exceptional cavalry and they rode without a saddle, stirrups or a bridle as they had only a rope around the horse's neck. "Firstly, the Numidians were considered by ancient writers to be among the most skilled cavalry around, and they rode not only without stirrups or saddles but also without any bridle or tack other than a rope around the horse's neck. He says that they only served as light cavalry, but throwing a javelin and making quick turns with their horse required "a firm seat." He then points out that thee Assyrian reliefs show heavy cavalry attacking infantry when they only used blankets with a strap on their horses. Finally he says that the Romans considered the Celts effeminate for using saddles. He concludes by saying that "horsemanship and élan" are the most important for cavalry.
43. Evans, "Cavalry," 100; Cook, 103; Rawlinson, 179–183.
44. Rawlinson, 183–184.
45. Sidnell, 7.
46. Shrimpton, 34.
47. Head, 62.
48. Evans, "Cavalry," 100–107.
49. Christopher Tuplin, "All the King's Horse: In Search of Achaemenid Persian Cavalry," in *New Perspectives in Ancient Warfare*, ed. Garrett Fagan and Mathew Trundle (Boston: Brill, 2010), 149, 158–159; Christopher Tuplin, "Marathon: In Search of a Persian Perspective," in *Marathon: The Battle and the Deme*, ed. Kostas Buraselis-Katerina Meidani (Athens: Institut Du Livre—A. Kardamitsa, 2010), 251–271.
50. Tuplin, "King's Horse," 178–181.
51. Sekunda, "The Persians," 85.

52. Hdt. 3.4.
53. H.T. Wallinga, "The Ancient Persian Navy and Its Predecessors," in *Sources, Structures and Synthesis: Proceedings of the Groningen 1983 Achaemenid History Workshop*, ed. Heleen Sancisi-Weerdenburg (Leiden: Nederlands Instituut voor het Nabije Oosten, 1987), 48; Lionel Scott, *Historical Commentary on Herodotus Book 6* (Leiden: Brill, 2005), 489.
54. Hdt. 3.19.3.
55. Cawkwell, *Greek Wars*, 256.
56. Hdt. 6.6.
57. Hdt. 7.89–99.
58. Rawlinson, 194.
59. Wallinga, "Persian Navy," 47–53; H.T. Wallinga, *Ships and Sea-Power before the Great Persian War: The Ancestry of the Ancient Trireme* (Leiden: Brill, 1993), 118.
60. H.T. Wallinga, *Xerxes' Great Adventure: The Naval Perspective* (Leiden: Brill, 2005), 117–118. Wallinga goes on to say that in his description of Persian naval forces, Herodotus suggests that the naval organization of the Persians was analogous to the auxiliary system that the Romans employed before 260 BCE as a reinforcement of their own rudimentary navy. He makes the maritime subjects of the Persians "furnish ships," called Ionia, Cilician, Phoenicians, etc., as the case may be (Hdt. 7.89). "Are these and similar formulas, seemingly massive evidence, sufficiently unambiguous to controvert Ephoros' testimony? It seems to me that they are not. It is significant in the first place that the Herodotean formula also occurs in Ephoros and his dependents: the ships described by Diodorus as furnished by the King in 480 are never-the-less called Greek, and the Royal Navy mobilized in 449 is described as consisting of Phoenician and Cilician ships. This usage is not unnatural in the context of an organization as is implied in Ephoros' testimony as a whole. If the naval service imposed on subjects was sufficiently compensated by good pay, or privileges, these subjects may well have been proud of the squadrons they served in and have considered them their own. And some of them may well have been more 'own' than others: if, as I believe, the Persian Navy organization included peacetime patrols such as are known in the tradition about the Delian league, the Persian subjects involved in the maintenance of these patrols really would have had their own ships to furnish. Sidon and Halicarnassus are most likely to have been in that position."
61. Wallinga, *Ships and Sea-Power*, 120–121.
62. Scott, 480–481.
63. J.S. Morrison, review of *Ships and Sea-Power before the Great Persian War: The Ancestry of the Ancient Trireme*, by H.T. Wallinga, *Journal Of Hellenic Studies* 114 (1994): 206–208; Anthony Graham Keen, review of *Ships and Sea-Power before the Great Persian War: The Ancestry of the Ancient Trireme*, by H.T. Wallinga, *Scholia Reviews* 3 (1994): 5; F.J.A.M. Meijer, review of *Ships and Sea-Power before the Great Persian War: The Ancestry of the Ancient Trireme*, by H.T. Wallinga, *Mnemosyne*, 4th series, 47, no. 5 (November 1994): 109–117.
64. Hdt. 6.48.2, 7.89–7.97.
65. Rawlinson, 197; Lionel Casson, *Ships and Seamanship in the Ancient World* (Princeton, NJ: Princeton University Press, 1971), 93.
66. Wallinga, *Ships and Sea-Power*, 118, 131, 159.
67. Casson, *Ships*, 94–95; Rawlinson, 195; Cook, 105–106.
68. J.S. Morrison and R.T. Williams, *Greek Oared Ships, 990–322 BCE* (Cambridge: Cambridge University Press, 1968), 256.
69. Hdt. 7.184.1.
70. Wallinga, *Ships and Sea-Power*, 170 note 2.
71. Cook, 106.
72. Hdt. 7.96; Cook, 106.
73. Cook, 106. He points out that the Persian fleet would perform much better in "calm waters with plenty of sea room" in which to maneuver. In the narrow waters around Salamis, the Persian advantage in maneuverability was negated. Wallinga, *Xerxes' Adventure*, 2, 5, explains that it should not be a surprise that the Persian triremes were better sailing ships as they had 50 years in which to improve their ships and crews, while the Greeks had only turned to triremes three years before the Battle of Salamis. Ian Whitehead, "What Constitutes a Better Sailing Ship?," in *The Trireme Project: Operational Experience in 1987–90, Lessons Learnt*, ed. Timothy Shaw (Oxford: Oxbow Books, 1993, 91–94. Whitehead examined the speed of "dried out" triremes compared to "waterlogged" triremes and found that the loss of speed "due to roughness and water logging would be about 12%" but adds that there is no evidence that the Greek triremes had rough bottoms and were waterlogged. He agrees that Persian triremes were built lighter than the Greek triremes but says that "was not the most important reason for their better sailing qualities." He concludes that it "was mainly the performance of the crew that would have determined whether or not an oared warship was regarded as a good or bad sailor."
74. Aeschylus, *Persians*, 342–348.
75. H.J. Rose, *A Commentary on the Surviving Plays of Aeschylus*, vol. 1 (Amsterdam: Noord-Hollandsche Uitgevers-maatschappij, 1957), 116–117.
76. Hdt. 7.89–96.
77. George Grote, *Greece*, vol. 4 (New York: Peter Fenelon Collier & Son, 1900), 36.
78. Reginald Walter Macan, *Herodotus: The Seventh, Eighth and Ninth Books*, vol. 2 (London: Macmillan, 1908), 150.
79. W.W. How and J. Wells, *A Commentary on Herodotus*, II (Oxford: Clarendon Press, 1912), 364.
80. W.W. Tarn, "The Fleet of Xerxes," *Journal of Hellenic Studies* 28 (1908): 202.
81. J.B. Bury, *A History of Greece* (New York: Modern Library, 1913), 256.
82. J.A.R. Munro, "Some Observations on the Persian War Continued," *Journal of Hellenic Studies* 22 (1902): 300.
83. Hans Delbruck, *Warfare in Antiquity*, vol. 1, trans. Walter J. Renfroe (Lincoln: University of Nebraska Press, 1975), 99.
84. Tarn, 204–206. He claims all four admirals were equal in authority. Two of the admirals were brothers of Xerxes, one of which commanded the Ionians and Carians, while the other controlled the Egyptians, for a total of 370 ships between them. Megabogos and Preaspes, two unknown men, controlled the other 837 ships. He says this makes no sense whatsoever. Therefore he concludes that Herodotus was incorrect about the four di-

visions. Rather, he states there were five divisions—the fifth being commanded by Xerxes himself. He lists the five divisions as (1) Egypt; (2) Phoenicia; (3) Cyprus, Cilicia, Pamphylia and Lica; (4) Ionia; and (5) Aeolis and the Hellespont. He calls each division a separate fleet that contained 120 ships. He goes on to say, "I think we shall see every reason for believing this to be correct. Six Hundred would be the paper strength on a general mobilization; but in 480 BCE if ever, the fleets were at paper strength."

85. Ibid., 206.
86. A.T. Olmstead, *History of the Persian Empire* (Chicago: University of Chicago Press, 1948), 246; Cook, 116.
87. Hignett, 347.
88. A.R. Burn, *Persia and the Greeks: The Defence of the West, C. 546–478 BCE* (Stanford, CA: Stanford University Press, 1984), 331–332. He believes that the 1,207 number may have come from raw material that combined figures of standing armies and ships being built and that the Greeks believed all of the ships could be manned. Finally, he says, "Men of letters after the war from Aeschylus onward were delighted to feel justified in saying they had fought at sea or on land against overwhelming odds."
89. Cawkwell, *Greek Wars*, 260–263. He gives the following figures: when Artaxerxes II invades Egypt in 343, he had according to Diodorus 300 triremes and 500 supply ships; 300 ships were raised but never used in the Ionian War; 300 ships for invasion of Egypt in the 370s; 300 in fleet of Memnon in 333.
90. Ibid., 260–267.
91. Wallinga, *Xerxes' Adventure*, 6, 32. In note 1, p. 32, he lists Lysias, two citations of 1,200 and 1,000 ships; Isocrates, two citations of 1,200 and 1,000 ships; Diodorus Siculus, more than 1,200 ships; Cornelius Nepos, 1,200 ships; Aeschylus, 1,000 ships; Plato, 1,000 ships and more; Ktesias, 1,000 ships.
92. Wallinga, *Ships and Sea-Power*, 136. In note 17 he adds, "The fear ascribed to the Persians may also be a speculation brought up to explain the delay of the Persian attack: this delay, which is implied in Herodotus' report (6.9.2ff, 6.11.1ff) may have well been caused by Persian hopes that the Ionian fleet would disintegrate for want of sufficient finance, which it eventually did.
93. Wallinga, *Ships and Sea-Power*, 170. As an example he points out that Phoenicia would be expected to contribute "60,000 men, including 51,000 rowers. Even if we put the population of the Phoenician cities at a total of 300,000, this would imply the mobilization of about all the able-bodied men."
94. Ibid., 172–177. He goes on to explain that triremes were also used as troop transports and were converted into horse transports. "From the naval accounts it appears that horse transports carried 120 oars and so were rowed by 60 men at most, and it may be presumed that troop transports were rowed by comparable crews although in this case the number may have been more variable."
95. Wallinga, *Xerxes' Adventure*, 38–45. He also explains why 1,200 ships were in the Persian fleet. He believes that the reconnaissance ordered by Darius and led by Demokedes brought back information that worried the king (Hdt. 3.136ff). Darius had to be concerned with a Greek fleet that would have 400 triremes but could also grow to over 600 triremes with possible help from Corcyra's 60 triremes and Cyprus' 200 triremes and perhaps other ships from other western areas. By bringing 1,200 ships, Darius would have spare ships which could fill in for any lost due to storms or battles and still have enough to meet the possible 600 to 660 ships of Greece and its potential allies.
96. Peter Green, *The Greco-Persian Wars* (Los Angeles: University of California Press, 1996), 61. See Wallinga, *Xerxes' Adventure*, 43–45.
97. Green, *Greco-Persian Wars*, 161.
98. Wallinga, *Ships and Sea-Power*, 125–126. He explains how he reached the figure as follows. Firstly the building, maintaining, and finally replacing of the ships: if the cost of construction of one trireme is put at half a talent (as it was in Athens in 483), and upkeep over 20 years assessed (arbitrarily) at the same amount, 450 talents would be needed. Secondly, the infrastructural works (slipways, ship sheds, gear stores etc. and above all defensive works): Isokrates put the cost of the fifth-century Athenian ship sheds alone at no less than 1,000 talents (7.66). As the Persians had to build far more (on virgin soil and not near a great harbor!), this item in their accounts will have run into at least something like double this amount. Thirdly defense: in this connection we must think of the cavalry division that was stationed in Cilicia, no doubt to guard the naval base, at a cost of 140 talents a year, or 2,800 or 20 years. I feel certain that these troopers were only the outer ring of a more elaborate system of defense, but I shall try not to specify the other elements; for this reason the 2,800 talents must be considered an absolute minimum. Fourthly: as argued earlier, there is reason to assume that permanent patrols, such as are known in the Delian League, were a feature of the Persian naval organization as well; assuming the same aggregate strength for both units—60 triremes—and putting the pay of the Persian cruise (120 men per trireme on an average) at two-thirds of the half-drachma rate of the mid–fifth century, we may assess the yearly cost for eight months' active service at $60 \times 240 \times 120 \times 1/3$ drachmas equals 96 talents, or 1,920 in 20 years. Finally, large-scale actions like the attack on Egypt must have been foreseen and the cost involved estimated, however roughly: six months' service for 300 ships as just described would amount to 360 talents, and 720 if two such actions were foreseen for the whole. Taken together, these items amount to 7,890 talents, some 400 talents a year, that is, a very large part of what was to be the empire's money income under Darius I's tributary regime. These figures may be inexact estimates, but they do at least give us a rough estimate of the huge costs of maintaining a navy for the Achaemenid Empire. The costs make clear how radical Cambyses' decision to create his navy was, given the lack of a stable system of finance. Its implementation must have entailed measures amounting to little short of a revolution, and though this revolution is not precisely recognizable in the tradition, traces of the concomitant crisis (or crises) are evident in the traditions about Cambyses' madness and the revolt of Bardiya/Gaumata.
99. Wallinga, "Persian Navy," 70.

100. Ober et al. 27.
101. Hdt. 3.89–90.
102. Pierre Briant, *From Cyrus to Alexander: A History of the Persian Empire*, trans. Peter Daniels (Winona Lake, IN: Eisenbrauns, 2002), 390–392.
103. Ibid., 392–400.
104. J.F. Lazenby, "The *Diekplous*," *Greece and Rome* 34, no. 2 (October 1987): 169. Michael Jameson, "The Provisions for Mobilization in the Decree of Themistocles," *Historia: Zeitschrift fur alte Geschichte* 12 (1963): 394; Casson, *Ships and Seamanship*, 92–94; Wallinga, *Ships and Sea-Power*, 124.
105. A.W. Gomme, *The Population of Athens in the Fifth and Fourth Centuries BCE* (Chicago: Argonaut, 1967).
106. Ian Morris and Walter Scheidel, *The Dynamics of Ancient Empires from Assyria to Byzantium* (Oxford: Oxford University Press, 2009). Morris claims the population of the Persian Empire was between 17 and 30 million. Walter Scheidel, Ian Morris, and Richard Saller, *The Cambridge Economic History of the Greco-Roman World* (New York: Cambridge University Press, 2007), 45. Scheidel says that "the Persian Empire of the Achaemenid dynasty stretched from Egypt and the Aegean to the Indus Valley and may have comprised 20 to 25 million subjects. Walter Scheidel, "Demography," in *The Cambridge Economic History of the Greco-Roman World*, ed. Walter Scheidel, Ian Morris, and Richard Saller (New York: Cambridge University Press, 2007), 45. Scheidel estimates the population of the Persian Empire as between 30 and 35 million. Peter R. Bedford, "The Persian Near East," in *The Cambridge Economic History of the Greco-Roman World*, ed. Walter Scheidel, Ian Morris, and Richard Saller (New York: Cambridge University Press, 2007). Bedford agrees with Scheidel's estimate. In *The Dynamics of Ancient Empires from Assyria to Byzantium*, 77, Joseph Wiesehofer of the University of Kiel gives a high estimate of the population of the Persian Empire as 35 million and a low estimate of 17 million.
107. Hdt. 6.61.
108. Macan, *Seventh, Eighth and Ninth Books*, vol. 1, 168; Rawlinson, 174; Lazenby, *Defence*, 24; Head, 27.
109. Marek Wozniak, "The Achaemenid Army at Marathon: The Army of All Nations," *Ancient Warfare, Special Issue 2011: The Battle of Marathon*, 80; Head, 27.
110. Rawlinson, 73.
111. Head, 28.
112. Marouchehr Moshtagh Khorasani, *Arms and Armor from Iran: The Bronze Age to the End of the Qajar Period* (Tubingen: Legat Verlag, 2006), 74–75. See page 407 for colored plates of the famous Golden Akenakes. See Sekunda, *Persian Army*, 56, for a similar *akenakes* from the New York Metropolitan Museum that was made out of gold and was 43 cm long; Head, 28.
113. Khorasani, 287.
114. Christopher Zutterman, "The Bow in the Ancient Near East: A Reevaluation of Archery from the Late 2nd Millennium to the End of the Achaemenid Empire," *Iranica Antiqua* 38 (2003): 122. He explains that the basic design for a bow was "a wooden core with a horn-lined front and backed with sinew, all glued together.

115. Simon Anglim et al., *Fighting Techniques in the Ancient World, 300 BCE to AD 500* (New York: St Martin's, 2001), 82; C.A. Bergman, E. McEwen, and R. Miller, "Experimental Archery: Projectile Velocities and Comparison of Bow Performances," *Antiquity* 62 (1988): 661.
116. Zutterman, 122; Anglim et al., 660.
117. Khorasani, 288; Head, 24–26.
118. Delbruck, 78 note 6.
119. Wallace McLeod, "The Range of the Ancient Bow," *Phoenix* 19, no. 1 (Spring 1965), 8–13.
120. N.G.L. Hammond, "The Campaign and Battle of Marathon," *Journal of Hellenic Studies* 88 (1968): 17 note 27.
121. McLeod, "Ancient Bow," 12.
122. Krentz, *Battle of Marathon*, 27.
123. Wozniak, 80; Head, 22–23; Sekunda, *Persian Army*, 17.
124. Wozniak, 81–82.
125. Hdt. 9.62.
126. Head, 27–28. Sekunda, *Persian Army*, 18, seems to agree when he says some wore cuirasses, "but by no means all."
127. Rawlinson, 189; Head, 60.
128. Head, 24, 61.
129. Farrokh, 40; Lazenby, *Defence*, 32; Head, 61; W.W. How, "Arms, Tactics & Strategy in the Persian Wars," *Journal of Hellenic Studies* 43, no. 2 (1923): 123.
130. Jim Lacey, *The First Clash: The Miraculous Greek Victory at Marathon and Its Impact on Western Civilization* (New York: Bantam, 2011), 133–134.

Chapter 3

1. F.E. Adcock, *The Greek and Macedonian Art of War* (Los Angeles: University of California Press, 1962), 3. See J.F. Lazenby and David Whitehead, "The Myth of the Hoplite's Hoplon," *Classical Quarterly*, new series, 46, no. 1 (1996): 27, for a list of historians agreeing with Adcock.
2. Lazenby and Whitehead, 29.
3. Ibid., 28–33.
4. Hans van Wees, *Greek Warfare: Myths and Realities* (London: Duckworth, 2004), 48, agrees, saying the literal meaning of *hoplites* is those who were equipped, and that is where the name comes from rather than their shield. Adam Schwartz, *Reinstating the Hoplite: Arms, Armour and Phalanx Fighting in Archaic and Classical Greece* (Stuttgart: Franz Steiner Verlag, 2009), 25–27, argues that at times "hoplon does mean precisely shield, and no other specific weapon or piece of armour, to my knowledge, can claim this." He goes on to say, "It is thus not wholly inconceivable that the hoplite's shield could be casually spoken of as 'the tool,' the piece of equipment which defined him above all."
5. Adcock, 3.
6. Peter Connolly, *Greece and Rome at War* (London: Greenhill Books, 1998), 37.
7. John Salmon, "Political Hoplites," *Journal of Hellenic Studies* 97 (1977): 87–88.
8. H.L. Lorimer, "The Hoplite Phalanx with Special Reference to the Poems of Archilochus and Tyrtaios," *Annual of the British School at Athens* 42 (1947): 76, 128.

9. Ibid., 76, 128. She points out, "Unless exceptionally large, the single-grip shield was easily maneuverable, and could be used to cover practically any part of the owner's person." The hoplite shield on the other hand was only useful in phalanx tactics and not in individual duels; Paul Cartledge, "Hoplites and Heroes: Sparta's Contribution to the Technique of Ancient Warfare," *Journal of Hellenic Studies* 97 (1977): 20.

10. A.M. Snodgrass, "The Hoplite Reform and History," *Journal of Hellenic Studies* 85 (1965): 110.

11. Victor Davis Hanson, "Hoplite Technology in Phalanx Battle," in *Hoplites: The Classical Greek Battle Experience*, ed. Victor Davis Hanson (New York: Routledge, 1991), 64–65. See Victor Davis Hanson, *The Other Greeks: The Family, Farm and the Agrarian Roots of Western Civilization* (Los Angeles: University of California Press, 1999), 228–229; Schwartz, 13–17. Schwartz writing in 2009 examines other viewpoints including several German sources not available in English.

12. Schwartz, 20–22. Schwartz cautions about the usefulness of iconography as it is "fundamentally difficult to interpret." He believes we lack the ability to interpret scenes "that may have been perfectly logical to contemporary Greeks but are a bit enigmatic to us." In addition, he says that "we have no way of knowing whether battle scenes are intended to show contemporary reality or a mythical battle scene."

13. A.M. Snodgrass, *Arms and Armour of the Greeks* (Ithaca, NY: Cornell University Press, 1967), 53.

14. Schwartz, 28–29; Connolly, 53–54; Paul Bardunias, "The Aspis: Surviving Hoplite Battle," *Ancient Warfare* 1, no. 3 (October–November, 2007), 13.

15. Victor Davis Hanson, *The Western Way of War* (New York: Oxford University Press, 1989), 68.

16. Christopher Matthew, *A Storm of Spears: Understanding the Greek Hoplite at War* (Philadelphia: Casemate, 2012), 42–43.

17. Schwartz, 32.

18. Bardunias, "Aspis," 13.

19. Schwartz, 31.

20. Peter Krentz, *The Battle of Marathon* (New Haven, CT: Yale University Press, 2010), 49. Estimates by other authors follow: Connolly, 53—13 pounds; Schwartz, 31—quotes A. Reith's estimate as 7–8 kg (14–17.6 pounds); P.H. Blyth, "The Effectiveness of Greek Armour against Arrows during the Persian Wars, 490–479" (PhD diss., University of Reading, 1977), 16—6.2 kg (13.7 pounds); Peter Hunt, "Military Forces," in *The Cambridge History of Greek and Roman Warfare*, vol. 1, ed. Phillip Sabin, Hans Van Wees, and Michael Whitby (New York: Cambridge University Press, 2007), 113–16 pounds; Hanson, *Western Way*, 65—16 pounds; Van Wees, *Greek Warfare*, 48—7 kg (15 pounds). Krentz seems to base his low weight figure on the fact that a bronze exterior added 6.6 pounds, and this unfaced shield would only weigh 7.1 pounds. He also quotes a modern armorer in Australia, who produced a poplar shield of 33 inches in diameter that weighs 9.5 pounds. He contacted the Hoplite Association in London and quotes a 35.8-inch pine shield faced with brass and lined with leather at 19.8 pounds but claims that in poplar it would be at most 15 pounds. It is unclear how he concludes that most hoplite shields in late archaic would be less than 11 pounds or even 10 pounds based on the evidence he presented.

21. Schwartz, 34. See page 33 for illustrations of the concave shield. See Van Wees, *Greek Warfare Myths*, 168, for illustrations from iconography illustrating the concavity of the shield; Tyrtaios in describing the protection the shield offered stated that the hoplite's body was "nearly absorbed and became a human battery ram with both his chest and shoulders in the belly of the hollow shield."

22. Schwartz, 34–35.

23. Hanson, *Western Way*, 66.

24. Ibid., 65–67; Schwartz, 34–38. See note 104 on page 35 for opposing viewpoints on the awkwardness of the two-handled hoplite shield.

25. Hanson, *Western Way*, 65, 70.

26. Snodgrass, *Arms and Armour*, 56; Nicholas Sekunda, *Greek Hoplite, 480–323 BCE* (New York: Osprey Publishing, 2000), 10. He goes on to point out that the Spartan general Brasidas was wounded when his shield was pierced and how Leonymos, the Lakonian, died when a spear pierced his shield.

27. J.K. Anderson, *Military Theory and Practice in the Age of Xenophon* (Los Angeles: University of California Press, 1970), 17; Sekunda, *Greek Hoplite*, 10.

28. Blyth, 193.

29. Ibid., 194.

30. Snodgrass, *Arms and Armour*, 6.

31. Aristotle, *Constitution of Athens*, 42.4.

32. Cartledge, "Hoplites and Heroes," 14; Hans Delbruck, *Warfare in Antiquity*, vol. 1, trans. Walter J. Renfroe (Lincoln: University of Nebraska Press, 1975), 55. Delbruck says that the spear pushed the bow to the background in ancient Greece. Richard Gabriel and Karen S. Metz, *From Sumer to Rome: The Military Capabilities of Ancient Armies* (New York: Greenwood Press, 2002), 55. Gabriel and Metz claim that the spear was the dominant weapon for close-order fighting and that the spear produced the phalanx. Anderson, *Military Theory*, 2. Anderson agrees that the "Hoplite" weapon was the spear. Hanson, *The Other Greeks*, 245–246. Hanson writes that the spear required little expertise and that the spear depended upon muscle rather than technique, which the untrained farmer/hoplite was able to provide.

33. J.K. Anderson, "Hoplite Weapons and Offensive Arms," in *Hoplites: The Classical Greek Battle Experience*, ed. Victor Davis Hanson (New York: Routledge, 1991), 22–23.

34. Sekunda, *Greek Hoplite*, 13–14. He quotes an experiment conducted by the Royal Society in 1663 in which laths of fir, oak and ash were compared: 200 pounds broke the fir, 250 pounds the oak and 325 pounds the ash, which proved the superiority of ash over the others. He also explains how the logs were split into shafts of a couple of inches in diameter and then formed with a whittling knife, a rasp and finally a spokeshave until they were round and smooth.

35. Schwartz, 81–82.

36. Anderson, *Hoplite Weapons*, 23; Sekunda, *Greek Hoplite*, 14; Schwartz, 82; Blyth, 22. Blyth includes an excellent drawing of a typical spearhead. Blyth claims the length of the spearhead ran from 14 to 20 inches. *Snodgrass, Arms and Armour of the Greeks* (New York:

Cornell University Press, 1967), 96. Snodgrass mentions a resurgence of bronze spearheads in the sixth and perhaps fifth centuries BCE. Matthew, *Storm of Spears*, 146–149.

37. Schwartz, 83; Anderson, *Hoplite Weapons*, 24; Blyth, 28, includes an excellent drawing of a butt-spike; Matthew, *Storm of Spears*, 12.

38. Ibid., 12–13.

39. Hanson, "Hoplite Technology," 72; Blyth, 29.

40. Paul Bardunias, "The Aspis: Surviving Hoplite Battle," *Ancient Warfare* 1, no. 3 (October–November, 2007): 14.

41. Hanson, *Hoplite Technology*, 72–74; Blyth, 21, 29; Anderson, *Hoplite Weapons*, 24; Schwartz, 83; Sekunda, *Greek Hoplite*, 14–16.

42. Sekunda, *Greek Hoplite*, 14.

43. Matthew, *Storm of Spears*, 146–149. He adds that the *sauroter* failed to penetrate the bronze armor "due to the larger impacting area of the point (4 mm) compared to that of the spearhead (0.7 mm).

44. Matthew, *Storm of Spears*, 6–8.

45. Sekunda, *Greek Hoplite*, 12–13; Anderson, "Hoplite Weapons," 22. Anderson gives 7.3 to 8 feet for the length of the spear. Minor M. Markle, "The Macedonian Sarissa, Spear and Related Armor," *American Journal of Archaeology* 81, no. 3 (Summer 1977). Markle gives 8 feet for the spear. Hanson, *Western Way*, 84. Hanson gives 6 to 8 feet for the spear. Blyth, 22. Blyth gives 7 to 8 feet for the spear. Hunt, 115. Hunt gives 8 feet for the spear.

46. Matthew, *Storm of Spears*, 11–12; Schwartz, 83.

47. Schwartz, 90; Gabriel and Metz, *From Sumer*, 59–60. Gabriel and Metz's experiments show that the overhand thrust could produce 70.8 foot-pounds of impact energy while the underhand thrust could produce only 13.5 foot-pounds.

48. Matthew, *Storm of Spears*, 15–17.

49. Blyth, 21; Gabriel and Metz, *From Sumer*, 59–60. They point out that the force required for a spear to penetrate 2 mm of bronze armor enough to kill an opponent was 137 foot-pounds. They found that an overhead thrust of a 1.5-pound spear could produce 70.8 foot-pounds of energy, and an underhand thrust could only produce 13.5 foot-pounds. While neither could produce a killing blow, the overhead thrust could break the breastbone or rib, which required 67 foot-pounds of energy.

50. Schwartz, 92.

51. Blyth, 22; Hanson, *Western Way*, 85; Schwartz, 88–92.

52. Matthew, *Storm of Spears*, 151–152.

53. Hanson, *Western Way*, 85–86; Schwartz, 91.

54. Eero Jarva, *Archaiologia on Archaic Greek Body Armour* (Rovanie mi: Pohjois-Soumen Societas Historica Finlandiae Septentrionalis, 1995), 25–51.

55. Jarva, 25.

56. Gabriel and Metz, *From Sumer*, 59–60. In doing their experiments they utilized a formula from the U.S. Army ballistics laboratory in Aberdeen, Maryland, to make their calculations (page xix). Blyth, 16. Blyth projects that a soldier in close combat could produce 30 J of energy with a spear or sword. The larger the diameter of the projectile, the more energy would be required to penetrate the armor. Blyth estimates the spearhead cut between 1 and 2 cm and calculates the kinetic energy required to penetrate .62 mm of bronze and 1 mm of bronze with a sharp object with a diameter of 12.7 mm and 14.3 mm as ranging from 31 to 42 J.

57. Jarva, 24.

58. Jarva, 32; Schwartz, 68.

59. Jarva, 135; Krentz, *Battle of Marathon*, 34–46.

60. The temperatures are taken from the National Meteorological Service in Greece. The average day temperature in the shade for the Peloponnese (measured at Corinth) in the period May–September is as much as 28.5°C (83.3°F). Similar data for Kalamata show 29°C (84.2°F). On any individual day, the temperatures may of course be far higher and certainly are around noon: absolute maximum temperatures measured are 38.8°C (101.8°F) and 42.6°C (108.6°F), respectively. Schwartz, 73–74; Hanson, *Western Way*, 79–80.

61. Jarva, 158.

62. Snodgrass, *Early Greek Armour*, 61–90.

63. Jarva, 33–40.

64. Connolly, 58.

65. Krentz, *Battle of Marathon*, 34–47.

66. Jarva, 158–160.

67. Connolly, 60–61. He includes 20 excellent illustrations of 20 different helmets showing how they changed over the years as they developed. Jarva, 111.

68. Snodgrass, *Early Greek Armour*, 51. He adds that the technology to produce a helmet from a single bronze piece was very advanced. In fact he explains that in the 17th century, armorers could not do it and that in 1939 modern skilled Greek metalworkers were unable to produce an exact replica.

69. Anderson, *Hoplite Weapons*, 28; Sekunda, *Greek Hoplite*, 11; Schwartz, 60; Cartledge, "Hoplites and Heroes," 14.

70. Snodgrass, *Early Greek Armour*, 93–94; Schwartz, 55–63. See page 53 for excellent drawings that illustrate the changes in the Corinthian helmet over time. Jarva, 141.

71. Jarva, 134. See note 919 for more specific examples. He also states that late Corinthian helmets were "thinner so the weight could be below 1 kilogram." Hanson, *Western Way*, 72; Schwartz, 63. Schwartz also quotes Franz who believes that 25 percent should be added to the weight of helmets that were found in order to compensate for deterioration of metal and padding. Krentz, *Battle of Marathon*, 46.

72. Schwartz, 64.

73. Blyth, 106, 224, 232.

74. Ibid., 84.

75. Ibid., 189.

76. Ibid., 195.

77. Gabriel and Metz, *From Sumer*, 57–59.

78. Victor Davis Hanson, *Wars of the Ancient Greeks* (London: Cassell, 1999), 75; Hanson, *Western Way*, 71.

79. Hanson, *Western Way*, 72.

80. Translated and quoted in Schwartz, 61.

81. Schwartz, 61.

82. Hanson, *Western Way*, 72; Schwartz, 65. Both Schwartz and Hanson comment on how the long hair and beards of the Greeks added to the problems of heat and breathing when wearing the helmet. Close-cropped hair would have helped; however, close-cropped hair was

commonly regarded as a mark of slavery, and thus no free Greek would be willing to cut his hair.

83. Hanson, *Western Way*, 73; Schwartz, 60–61.
84. Schwartz, 65.
85. Anderson, *Military Theory*, 29.
86. Connelly, 61. He includes an excellent illustration of an Attic helmet along with the Corinthian helmet to show the dramatic difference.
87. Jarva, 81–96. They started at about 35 cm and a few exceeded 47 cm, but the average was about 41 cm. Snodgrass, *Early Greek Armour*, 52.
88. Schwartz, 76; Hansen, *Western Way*, 76. Both wonder why a tie system was not developed for the greaves to hold them in place and make them more comfortable.
89. Schwartz, 71.
90. Ibid., 142–143.
91. Jarva, 79–84.
92. Ibid., 105.
93. Connolly, 60.
94. Anderson, *Hoplite Weapons*, 25.
95. Ibid., 25; Schwartz, 85; Connolly, 63. Connolly includes an excellent illustration of a recovered sword from the ninth century and one from about 500 BCE
96. Anderson, *Hoplite Weapons*, 26; Schwartz, 86.
97. Schwartz, 93. He quotes the Roman historian Vegetius, who said that "a stroke with the edges, though made with ever so much force, seldom kills as the vital parts of the body are defended both by the bones and armor. On the contrary, a stab, though it penetrates but 2 inches, is generally fatal. Besides, in the attitude of striking, it is impossible to avoid exposing the right arm and side; but on the other hand, the body is covered while a thrust is given, and the adversary receives the point before he sees the sword."
98. Ibid., 95.
99. Peter Krentz, "War," in *The Cambridge History of Greek and Roman Warfare*, ed. Phillip Sabin, Hans van Wees, and Michael Whitby (Cambridge: Cambridge University Press, 2007), 151; Hanson, *The Other Greeks*, 225; Stephen Mitchell, "Hoplite Warfare in Ancient Greece," in *Battle in Antiquity*, ed. Alan B. Lloyd (London: Duckworth, 1996), 89–90.
100. Jarva, 143.
101. Van Wees, *Greek Warfare*, 49–50. He bases his reasoning on Jarvis' numbers of the various parts of armor found at Olympia—350 helmets, 280 shields, 33 breastplates and 225 greaves.
102. Jarva, 125.
103. Schwartz, 96–97; Hansen, *Western Way*, 204. Hanson suggests that the victors replaced their own damaged armor from their booty and also sold captured armor on the open market.
104. Jarva, 133–139. He even includes an unbelievable figure of 52 kg for Alkimos' two-talent panoply mentioned by Plutarch. The figure is reached if one uses the Attic standard where one talent was 26.196 kg, and he also includes figures from Rostow-Kochly, 26kg; Hanson, 31 kg; and Blyth, 12–13 kg. Schwartz, 95, quotes JFC Fuller's 32.73 kg and Franz's 29.1 kg.
105. Jarva, 138; Schwartz, 96; Krentz, *Battle of Marathon*, 50.
106. Peter Hunt, "Military Forces," in *The Cambridge History of Greek and Roman Warfare*, ed. Phillip Sabin, Hans van Wees, and Michael Whitby (Cambridge: Cambridge University Press, 2007), 109.
107. W. Kendrick Pritchett, *The Greek State at War, Part II* (Los Angeles: University of California Press, 1974), 209.
108. Van Wees, *Greek Warfare*, 91.
109. Hanson, *Western Way*, 31.
110. Van Wees, *Greek Warfare*, 91–92.
111. Hanson, *Western Way*, 31.
112. Van Wees, *Greek Warfare*, 90–91.
113. Pierre Ducrey, *Warfare in Ancient Greece* (New York: Schocken Books), 69–70.
114. Van Wees, *Greek Warfare*, 62; Everett Wheeler, "The General as Hoplite," in *Hoplites: The Classical Greek Battle Experience*, ed. Victor Davis Hanson (New York: Routledge, 1991), 125.
115. Peter Hunt, "Military Forces," in *The Cambridge History of Greek and Roman Warfare*, ed. Phillip Sabin, Hans van Wees, and Michael Whitby (Cambridge: Cambridge University Press, 2007), 131; Hanson, *The Other Greeks*, 261. Hanson states, "Theoretically, the seer who accompanied the army may have had as much authority in directing the time and occasional battle as the general himself, for if the sacrifice revealed unfavorable omens, the battle might be delayed and in rare instances postponed altogether."
116. Wheeler, "The General," 203.
117. Hanson, *Western Way*, 109–114; Schwartz, 180–181. Schwartz reinforces how dangerous the right wing was by listing 59 generals who died in battle between 490 and 352 BCE Connolly, 40–41. While the typical hoplite army was made up of amateur fighters and was poorly organized, Sparta was the exception. It was a military state with a professional army and an educational system designed to turn out well-trained hoplites. Beginning at age seven, Spartan boys trained solely to be a soldier and entered the professional army at age 20. Being a professional army, it was well organized, with officers at every unit. Connolly describes the organization of the Spartan army as follows: (1) The smallest unit of the Spartan army, the *enomotia*, composed of three files of 12 men or six half files each of six men. It was commanded by the *enomotarch*. The *enomotiae* were coupled to form *pentekostyes*, each commanded by a *pentekonter*. (2) A *lochos*, the basic unit of the phalanx. It was composed of two *pentekostyes* (four *enomotiae* and was commanded by a *lochagos*. (3) A *mora* composed of four *lochoi* (576 men) and commanded by a *polemarch*. The entire Spartan army was made up of six *morae* and was commanded by the king. He bases his organization on Xenophon's description but suggests that in archaic Sparta, there may have been five "super *lochoi*" commanded by a *lochagos*, each of whom served in a council of war under the king. He believes the smaller units were similar.
118. A.H. Jackson, "Hoplites and the Gods: The Dedication of Captured Arms and Armour," in *Hoplites: The Classical Greek Battle Experience*, ed. Victor Davis Hanson (New York: Routledge, 1991), 229–230. Thirty drachmas would be the equivalent of about six fine oxen in Solon's time. Van Wees, *Greek Warfare*, 55; Kurt Raaflaub, "Archaic and Classical Greece," in *War and So-*

ciety in the *Ancient and Medieval Worlds: Asia, the Mediterranean, Europe and Mesopotamia*, ed. Kurt Raaflaub and Nathan Rosenstein (Cambridge, MA: Center for Hellenic Studies Trustees for Harvard University, 1999), 149 note 30. Plutarch equates one drachma with one sheep.

119. Raaflaub, "Archaic and Classical Greece," 136; Hanson, *Other Greeks*, 297.

120. Delbruck, 63.

121. Raaflaub, "Archaic and Classical Greece," 34.

122. Schwartz, 12.

123. Quoted in Michael Sage, *Warfare in Ancient Greece: A Source Book* (New York: Routledge, 1996), 34.

124. Hanson, *Other Greeks*, 330.

125. Anderson, *Military Theory*, 6. Hanson comments that, "logistically, it was critical that the farmer-hoplite fight in person, briefly and decisively on the battlefield, free from obstacles and encumbrances. That way he would neither squander his year's produce nor surrender control over the conduct of the war" to professionals who might lead them on costly campaigns. Hanson, *Other Greeks*, 251–252.

126. Quoted in Krentz, *Battle of Marathon*, 44.

127. Victor Davis Hanson, *Warfare and Agriculture in Classical Greece* (Los Angeles: University of California Press, 1998), 2.

128. Everett Wheeler and Barry Straus, "Battle," in *The Cambridge History of Greek and Roman Warfare*, ed. Phillip Sabin, Hans van Wees, and Michael Whitby (Cambridge: Cambridge University Press, 2007), 202.

129. Anderson, *Military Theory*, 5; Hanson, *Warfare and Agriculture*, 7.

130. Hanson, *Warfare and Agriculture*, 7; Anderson, *Military Theory*, 5; Hanson, *Other Greeks*, 250–251.

131. Wheeler and Straus, 197–199.

132. Hanson, *Other Greeks*, 235–237.

133. Van Wees, *Greek Warfare*, 61–64. Van Wees believes that "admiration for the bravery of citizen hoplites may have led Greek historians to develop something of a blind spot for other kinds of troops." He claims that there were also poor light-armed citizens who fought. A bow and arrows would cost about two or three weeks' wages and a javelin about three days' wages, which were much cheaper than a hoplite panoply. If they could not even pay that much, they were able to throw stones, which could cause confusion for the enemy hoplites. Krentz, *Battle of Marathon*, 59. Krentz points out that as late as 640–600 BCE, Tyrtaios wrote, "You light-armed men, wherever you can aim, from the shield-cover pelt them with great rocks and hurl at them your smooth-shaved javelins, helping the armored troops with close support. Wheeler and Straus, 199. Rejecting the views of van Wees and Krentz, Wheeler states, "The combination of hoplites, archers and horsemen on late archaic vases reflected colonial warfare in the northern Aegean, as Greeks expanded into Chalcidice, Thrace and the Black Sea. Colonial warfare did not follow the agonal concept of set-piece heavy infantry clashes."

134. Anderson, *Military Theory*, 7; A. J. Holladay, "Hoplites and Heresies," *Journal of Hellenic Studies* 102 (1982): 94; James Lacey, *The First Clash* (New York: Bantam, 2011); Delbruck, 53.141.

135. Adrian K. Goldsworthy, "The Othismos, Myths and Heresies: The Nature of Hoplite Battle," *War in History* 4 (1997): 5–8; Connolly, 37–38.

136. Delbruck, 54; Sekunda, *Greek Hoplite*, 8. Sekunda tells how Xenophon compared the phalanx to building a house. You use the best materials for the foundation and the roof "while mud bricks and timber are fillers and placed in the middle."

137. Thucydides 5.71.1.

138. Schwartz, 157. For the quote from Asklepiodotos, see note 642 which also includes other views that are similar. W. Kendrick Pritchett, *The Greek State at War, Part I* (Los Angeles: University of California Press, 1974), 151. After examining the literary and archaeological sources, Pritchett concludes that Polybius was correct when he said *synsaspismos* and *pyknosis* were synonymous and that there were only two battle orders—marching, in which the intervals were six feet, and compact, in which the intervals were at three feet—and that the three-foot interval was the norm for the phalanx. Goldsworthy, 17; Richard A. Gabriel, *The Great Armies of Antiquity* (Westport, CT: Praeger, 2002); Sekunda, *Greek Hoplite*, 8; Lacey, *First Clash*, 141.

139. A.D. Fraser, "The Myth of the Phalanx-Scrimmage," *Classical Weekly* 36, no. 2 (October 12, 1942): 15–16.

140. Louis Rawlings, *The Ancient Greeks at War* (Manchester: Manchester University Press, 2007), 56–58; Krentz, "War," 52–54; G.L. Cawkwell, "Orthodoxy and Hoplites," *Classical Quarterly*, new series, 39, no. 2 (1989): 379–386. Cawkwell asks, "Where in the traditional view can the individual distinguish himself?" Van Wees, *Greek Warfare*, 169–185.

141. Schwartz, 122.

142. Paul Bardunias, "Storm of Shields and Press of Spears: The Mechanics of Hoplite Battle," *Ancient Warfare, Special Issue 2011: The Battle of Marathon*, 62–63.

143. Bardunias, "Storm of Shields," 62–64; Bardunias, "Aspis," 13.

144. Bardunias, "Storm of Shields," 67–68; Matthew, *Storm of Spears*, 220. Matthew rejects Bardunias' conclusions concerning the ability of the *aspis* to protect hoplites from the pressure generated by crowds pushing against each other. Citing Xenophon's description of the Battle of Coronea in which he describes shattered shields littering the battlefield, Matthew suggests that "the hoplite shield could not stand up to the pressures of a mass push." In addition he explains that the casualty rates for victorious hoplite armies are relatively low and states that "references to crushing or asphyxiating deaths during fighting are nonexistent." He concludes that despite Bardunias' claims, "a mass, crowded, push was not a common aspect of hoplite engagement, nor was a hoplite shield designed to be an instrument of such a mass push.

145. Matthew, *Storm of Spears*, 213, 222–223.

146. Paul Cartledge, "Hoplites and Heroes," 12.

147. Schwartz, 129. See pages 123–129 for examples of different interpretations of the same iconographic material.

148. Krentz, *Battle of Marathon*, 52.

149. Schwartz, 129–130. He adds, "The contention that there are few specific portrayals of recognizable phalanx fighting from the Archaic period can in fact be extrapolated to encompass the entire antiquity: with the

Nereid monument as a possible exception, there are scarcely any representations from the Classical period either."

150. Ibid., 135.

151. Ardant Du Picq, *Battle Studies: Ancient and Modern Battle* (New York: Macmillan, 1921), 46.

152. Hanson, *Western Way*, 101. See Richard A. Gabriel, *No More Heroes: Madness and Psychiatry in War* (New York: Hill and Wang, 1987), 94–95. He includes two tables: table 1, "Psychiatric Symptoms Reported by Israeli Soldiers in the 1982 Lebanon War," and table 2, "Symptom Clusters in Various Wars—World War I, World War II, Arab-Israeli War, 1973, Arab-Israeli War, 1982."

153. Hanson, *Western Way*, 103; Gabriel, *No More Heroes*, 48. Gabriel states that, "Herodotus records that as the battle for the pass of Thermopylae was about to begin, two soldiers of the handpicked elite Spartan unit of 300 reported to the surgeon and claimed that they were suffering from an 'acute inflammation of the eyes.' That two soldiers should acquire the same ailment at the precise point when fighting was about to start is, to say the least, suspicious. The soldiers asked for permission to retire to the rear. When the battle began one of the Spartan soldiers, Aistdemis 'finding his heart failed him' remained safely in the rear and did not join the fight, although the other soldier did."

154. Du Picq, 46.

155. S.L.A. Marshall, *Men against Fire: The Problem of Battle Command* (Norman: University of Oklahoma Press, 1947), 150.

156. Ibid., 141.

157. Hanson, *Western Way*, 117–124.

158. Krentz, *Battle of Marathon*, 59–60; van Wees, *Greek Warfare*, 170–173.

159. Van Wees, *Greek Warfare*, 170.

160. Ibid., 173.

161. Hanson, *Other Greeks*, 234.

162. Delbruck, 55; Hansen, *Other Greeks*, 236–237. Hanson states, "My point is not to deny that horsemen and missile troops—through their mobility, speed, rates of fire, and power—enhanced infantry, but simply to assert that in Greece proper, until the Peloponnesian war, landed infantrymen developed a system that deliberately made missiles and mounted warriors incidental to success in battle. The system reflected contemporary social economic and political aspects of agrarianism."

163. W. Kendrick Pritchett, *The Greek State at War, Part IV* (Los Angeles: University of California Press, 1985), 51.

164. Wheeler and Straus, 188–189; Krentz, "War," 147; W.R. Connor, "Early Greek Land Warfare as Symbolic Expression," *Past & Present* 119 (1988): 11; Josiah Ober, "Classical Greek Times," in *The Laws of War: Constraints on Warfare in the Western World*, ed. Michael Howard, George Andreopoulos, and Mark R. Shulman (New Haven, CT: Yale University Press, 1994), 13. Ober believes that while there were no formal laws regarding hoplite warfare there were "neoformal rules and practices conditioned largely by practicality." He lists the unwritten conventions in hoplite warfare as follows: (1) The state of war should be officially declared before commencing hostilities against an appropriate foe; sworn treaties and alliances should be regarded as binding. (2) Hostilities are sometimes inappropriate: sacred truces, especially those declared for the celebration of the Olympic Games, should be observed. (3) Hostilities against certain persons and in certain places are inappropriate: the inviolability of sacred places and persons under protection of the gods, especially heralds and suppliants, should be respected. (4) Erecting a battlefield trophy indicates victory; such trophy should be respected. (5) After a battle it is right to return enemy dead when asked; to request the return of one's dead is tantamount to admitting defeat. (6) A battle is properly prefaced by a ritual challenge and acceptance of the challenge. (7) Prisoners of war should be offered for ransom rather than being summarily executed or mutilated. (8) Punishment of surrendered opponents should be restrained. (9) War is an affair of warriors; thus noncombatants should not be primary targets of attack. (10) Battles should be fought during the usual (summer) campaigning season. (11) Pursuit of defeated and retreating opponents should be limited in duration. Ober believes most of the above were followed in intra–Greek warfare from 700 to 450 BCE but that numbers 5 through 11 broke down between the years 450 and 350. See Connor, 19.

165. Wheeler and Straus, 203; Peter Krentz, "Fighting by the Rules: The Invention of the Hoplite Agon," *Hesperia: The Journal of the American School of Classical Studies at Athens* 71, no. 1 (January–March 2002): 35–37. Krentz agrees that "the idea of agonistic warfare matters," but he rejects the notion that it applied to hoplite warfare during the archaic period; based upon his contention that the archaic phalanx fought in a loose order, he concludes that "Greeks invented the hoplite *agon* in the mid fifth century" and that it never existed in archaic times.

166. Doyne Dawson, *The Origins of Western Warfare: Militarism and Morality in the Ancient World* (Boulder, CO: Westview, 1996), 55; Wheeler and Straus, 204; Antonio Santosuosso, *Soldiers, Citizens, and the Symbols of War: From Classical Greece to Republican Rome, 500–167 BCE* (Boulder, CO: Westview, 1997), 21. He uses the example of Pausanias refraining from battle at Plataea until sacrifices were favorable.

167. Wheeler and Straus, 203–204; Sage, 98–100; Dawson, 55–56. Connor observes that Walter Burkert has provided a useful key to understanding this ritualization in Greek antiquity and quotes Burkert as saying "war may almost appear like one great sacrificial action." Connor goes on to state "This is not mere simile. Many of the elements in such warfare are correlatives of those in ritual sacrifice among the Greeks: the sequence of procession, the violent blow, the spilling of blood, the burning of flesh and the pouring of libations that stands at the center of the sacrificial ritual is paralleled by the sequence in the land battle: the march into battle, the blood spilled in fighting, the funeral pyres and the truce (call the *spondai*, the libations). Furthermore the cry of the women at the moment of sacrifice, the *ololugmos*, has its echo in the soldiers' battle cry, the *alalagmos*. The garlanding after the battle adapts to warfare another practice from sacrificial ritual." Connor, 22.

168. Hanson, *Western Way*, 129–131. Sekunda, *Greek Hoplite*, 21.

169. Van Wees, *Greek Warfare*, 192; Wheeler and Straus, 203; Mogens Herman Hansen, "The Battle Exhortation in Ancient Historiography: Fact or Fiction?" *Historia: Zeitschrift fur Alte Geschichte* 42, no. 2 (1993): 163–165. Hansen claims that if speeches before battles actually took place, then one must be able to find the same types of speeches in rhetorical literature. Since he found no such examples he concludes that "battlefield exhortations ... are fiction. He is willing to concede that the general may have made a brief exhortation by unit since his voice could not carry to all the hoplites in the army. For a counter viewpoint see W. Kendrick Pritchett, *Essays in Greek History* (Amsterdam: J.C. Gieben, 1994), 24–109. Regarding Hansen's conclusion concerning generals' speeches and rhetoric, he states, "I find this nonsense," and he calls himself the "chief exponent of veracity" and proceeds to state his case in an 85-page essay. M.C. Clark, "Did Thucydides Invent the Battle Exhortation?," *Historia: Zeitschrift fur Alte Geschichte* 44, no. 3 (3rd Qtr., 1995), 375–376. Clark rejects Hansen's view that "a general's voice could not carry far enough to be intelligible to more than a small fraction of his troops." He refers to Benjamin Franklin's statement in his *Autobiography* that he had heard an itinerate preacher and said, "I computed he might well be heard by Thirty-Thousand. This reconciled me to the Newspaper Accounts of his having preach'd to 25000 People in the Fields."

170. Hanson, *Western Way*, 144; Wheeler and Straus, 204; Sekunda, *Greek Hoplite*, 26; Krentz, *Battle of Marathon*, 53.

171. Hanson, *Western Way*, 141; Sekunda, *Greek Hoplite*, 3.

172. Krentz, *Battle of Marathon*, 53.

173. Fuller, 148; Hanson, *Western Way*, 139–140.

174. Hanson, *Western Way*, 144. Hanson suggests about two minutes to collision. Van Wees, *Greek Warfare*, 87. Van Wees suggests 35 to 40 seconds to collision if they approached at 5 to 6 mph, their underhand grip hoping to thrust under their adversary's shield at the his unprotected groin or legs above the greaves which would disable him.

175. Hanson, *Western Way*, 162; Krentz, "War," 53.

176. Hanson, *Western Way*, 161–164; Robert Luginbill, "Othismos: The Importance of the Mass-Shove in Hoplite Warfare," *Phoenix* 48, no. 1 (Spring 1994): 57–58; Sekunda, *Greek Hoplite*, 27; Santosuosso, 14; Van Wees, *Greek Warfare*, 188–189.

177. Van Wees, *Greek Warfare*, 188.

178. Wheeler and Straus, 209; Krentz, *Battle of Marathon*, 53. Krentz claims that "no conclusive evidence shows that Greek armies collided on the run."

179. Hanson, *Western Way*, 172; Schwartz, 183.

180. Hanson, *Western Way*, 174. Hanson states, "From reconstructions of the hoplite shield, evidence of vase painting, and suggestions in Greek literature, we know that the lip of the top rim of the hollow Greek model was ideal for precisely that steady pushing; the hoplite supported the shield on his shoulder as he drove against the backs of his friends ahead. That way the weight was distributed over the entire body rather than the left arm alone, while the shield's broad surface ensured that such pressure would be distributed evenly across the back of the man in front, neither tripping him nor forcing him off balance." Santosuosso, 15. Santosuosso claims, "There is no doubt that pressure on the back would have resulted in a fall for most troops on the line. Yet if the soldiers lined up sideways with their left shoulders ahead and if their companions in the rear ranks lined up in the same manner, then pressure would be exerted not on the center of a man's back but only on his shoulder.

181. Marshall, 41–42, 141, 150.

182. Hanson, *Western Way*, 179. Hanson gives three examples from Thucydides when such a retreat took place and one from Xenophon. Two of the four examples involve the Spartans who were professional soldiers and the other two involve classical phalanxes which included trained hoplites as opposed to the archaic phalanx which had little or no training.

183. Santosuosso, 16.

184. Krentz, *Battle of Marathon*, 61.

185. Schwartz, 188–189. Using material from the German historian J. P. Franz's book *Krieger, Bauern, Burger, Untersuchungen zu den Hopliten der archaischen*, Schwartz concludes that the pressure generated in the *othismos* on the front ranks, while great and inhibiting, would "not be impossible to resist." See notes 796 and 797 in Schwartz for excerpts from Franz's book translated by Schwartz.

186. Fraser, 15–16.

187. Goldsworthy, 21–23.

188. Van Wees, *Greek Warfare*, 191; Wheeler and Straus, 211. Wheeler states that the "theory that psychological pressure in the rear ranks of massed formations induces collapse cannot be supported by ancient Greek evidence."

189. Goldsworthy, 20; Cawkwell, 15–16; Peter Krentz, "Continuing the *Othismos* on *Othismos*," *Ancient History Bulletin* 8 (1994): 47; Krentz, *Battle of Marathon*, 146–151. Krentz also argues that Greek farmers "ate a lean diet with little meat, and walked almost everywhere they went and did hard physical labor all their lives" and should be compared with soldiers in the field, and he concludes they could run a mile with the hoplite panoply. If the Greeks could run a mile with the hoplite panoply and still be able to fight, does it not seem possible that the same Greek hoplites could push in the *othismos* for a long period of time? Schwartz, 189–190. Schwartz claims that "Cawkwell's assertion that descriptions of 'long battles' means hours worth of fighting, is unfounded." Schwartz includes Franz's explanation of crowd pressure (translated by Schwartz) and explains that the pressure "was not constant, but fluctuating, allowing the pushed and pushing hoplites a little respite at short intervals." Luginbill, 56. Luginbill explains how hoplites could sustain *othismos* for a prolonged period. He says if the initial collision between the charging lines did not achieve a breakthrough, a struggle would occur in which the two lines pushed and relaxed similar to a "tug-of-war except that the front lines would still be fighting." He says that the terrain, casualties, skill, courage, cowardice and fatigue would all combine until one "side literally pushed the other side to the breaking point."

190. Van Wees, *Greek Warfare*, 168; Gabriel and

Metz, *From Sumer*, 20; Krentz, *Battle of Marathon*, 19–20.

191. Goldsworthy, 19.

192. Krentz, *Battle of Marathon*, 56; van Wees, *Greek Wars*, 300.

193. Krentz, *Battle of Marathon*, 56; Krentz, "Continuing the *Othismos*," 46; Peter Krentz, "The Nature of Hoplite Battle," *Classical Antiquity* 4, no. 1 (April 1985): 55–57; Schwartz, 185 rejects Krentz's view and states, "Of the 41 battles in the inventory, 12 contained explicit references to othismos, making up for 29.27% of the battle narratives." He adds that "three more battles, Thermopylae 480, Peiraieus 403/2, and Olympia, which are not listed in the inventory, also describe the phenomenon."

194. Schwartz, 185. See note 779 for a complete list of the battles he examined.

195. The orthodox include Victor Davis Hanson, Robert Luginbill, John Lazenby, J.K. Anderson, W. Kendrick Pritchett and Jim Lacey. The heretics include Hans van Wees, A.D. Fraser, A.K. Goldsworthy, A.J. Holliday and Peter Krentz.

196. Goldsworthy, 19; Krentz, *Battle of Marathon*, 56; Hanson, 172. Hanson states, "It is surprising how many ancient authors saw the crucial phases of hoplite battle as 'the push,' where each side sought desperately to create the greater momentum to the superior 'weight' or 'mass.'" Cf. Xen. Hell. 2.4.34; 6.4.14; 7.1.31; Ages. 2.12; Cyr. 7.1.33; Thuc. 4.96.2; 6.70.2; Hdt. 7.224–225; 9.62.2; Polb. 18.30.4; Arr. Tact. 12.10.20; 14.16; Paus. 4.7.7–7; 13; Plut. Ages. 18.2. In Aristophanes' *Wasps*, the veterans are made to say, "After running out with the spear and shield, we fought them.... Each man stood up against each man.... We pushed them with the gods until evening" (1081–85). At Koroneia, Xenophon wrote, the Spartans "crashed against the Thebans face to face, and throwing up their shields, they pushed, fought, killed, and died" (Hell, 4.3.19).

197. Wheeler and Straus, 211.

198. Cawkwell, "Orthodoxy and Hoplites," 376.

199. Schwartz, 200.

200. Lacey, *The First Clash*, 141.

201. Wheeler and Straus, 211.

202. Schwartz, 185.

203. Peter Krentz, "Casualties in Hoplite Battles," *Greek, Roman and Byzantine Studies* 26 (1985): 19.

204. Gabriel and Metz, *From Sumer*, 86–87. They suggest that a modern conventional army could expect 17.6 percent killed in action and 41.6 percent wounded. These numbers are similar in wounded, but their killed in action of 37.7 percent for ancient armies is quite high; however, if you take Krentz's combined total of 19 percent killed in action, they are quite similar. This probably reflects Krentz's analysis of battles in classical Greece while Gabriel and Metz's figures are the result of battles of Alexander the Great and Roman battles.

205. Hanson, *Western Way*, 210.

206. Gabriel and Metz, *From Sumer*, 91.

207. Hanson, *The Other Greeks*, 309–312.

208. Gabriel and Metz, *From Sumer*, 95. They think that fractures were probably the most common wound suffered by hoplites. The reason was that "on average 67.7 ft./lbs. of impact energy will produce a fracture in any bone in the body," and both the spear with the overhand thrust which produces 70.8 foot-pounds and the sword which produces 77.5 foot-pounds will easily cause fractures.

209. Hanson, *Western Way*, 209–215.

210. Wheeler and Straus, 213.

211. Gabriel and Metz, *From Sumer*, 97–99.

212. Hanson, *Western Way*, 2–3.

213. Ibid., 223–224.

214. Gabriel and Metz, *From Sumer*, 131.

215. Ibid., 131–132.

216. Hanson, *Western Way*, 217.

217. Ibid., 241; Wheeler and Straus, 212.

218. Sekunda, *Greek Hoplite*, 30.

219. Hanson, *Western Way*, 202.

220. Sekunda, *Greek Hoplite*, 30.

221. Ibid., 30; Hanson, *Western Way*, 204.

222. Jackson, 244–245. Jackson states that the estimate that Olympia received 100,000 helmets over the seventh and sixth centuries was not overly exaggerated. He also points out that Delphi once received 2,000 shields from one battle and was probably not far behind Olympia in the equipment and weapons that were dedicated. W. G. Runciman, "Greek Hoplites, Warrior Culture and Indirect Bias," *Journal of the Royal Anthropological Institute* 4, no. 4 (December 1998): 739–740. Runciman writes about the "Dedicate Spoils to the Gods" meme. He states that "it is commonplace in many societies for victorious warriors to take the weapons, standards, uniforms, armor or even heads of their fallen enemy and place them on display." He mentions that when the Phocians killed 4,000 panicked Thessalians, they dedicated half the captured shields to Aboe and the other half at Delphi. He concludes that it is difficult to determine whether dedications were motivated by giving thanks to the gods or by the desire for self-glorification. No matter which, the duty to dedicate part of their spoils was strongly felt by the Greeks.

223. Jackson, 243.

224. Krentz, "War," 173. Krentz lists several rare cases when the victors refused to allow the defeated hoplites to recover their dead. He also mentions that there were instances "when the Greeks mutilated their enemy's corpses. Pamela Vaughn, "The Identification and Retrieval of the Hoplite Battle-Dead," in *Hoplites: The Classical Greek Battle Experience*, ed. Victor Davis Hanson (New York: Routledge, 1991), 41. She says that the practice of mutually returning the battle dead was a tradition attributed "variously to Theseus or Herakles."

225. Vaughn, 44–57.

226. Krentz, "War," 175; Vaughn, 57. Vaughn feels that the rationale for the above practice "is nicely summarized in the following passage from Onasander in his *Strategikos* (36:1–2) which may have applied to the archaic period. "The general should take thought for the burial of the dead, offering as a pretext for delay neither occasion nor time nor place nor fear, whether he happened to be victorious or defeated. Now this is both a holy act of reverence for the dead and also a necessary example for the living. For if the dead are not buried, each soldier believes that no care will be taken of his own body, should he chance to fall, observing what happens before his own eyes, and thereby judging of the future, feeling that he,

likewise, if he should die, would fail of burial, waxes indignant at the contemptuous neglect of burial."
227. Krentz, "War," 175–176.
228. Sekunda, *Greek Hoplite*, 32; Pritchett, *Greek State at War, Part IV*, 139–153. Pritchett provides all the casualty lists in Athens, outside of Athens and those reported by Pausanias.
229. Krentz, "War," 175.
230. Sage, 104.
231. Krentz, "War," 181.
232. Ducrey, 236.
233. W. Kendrick Pritchett, *The Greek State at War, Part V* (Los Angeles: University of California Press), 238. See pages 226–234 for tables showing 173 battles that ended in enslavement.

Chapter 4

1. Richard Billows, *Marathon: How One Battle Changed Western Civilization* (New York: Overlook Duckworth, 2010), 110–113.
2. Ibid., 114.
3. Hdt. 1.108.
4. Ibid., 1.08–1.113.
5. Ibid., 1.14–1.120.
6. Ibid., 1.121–1.123. Ctesias claims that Cyrus was the son of a brigand and as a poor boy attached himself to a palace worker. Because of his dedication he eventually was attached to Artembares, the king's chief cupbearer. Later, Cyrus succeeded Artembares as the king's chief cupbearer, and when Artembares died, "King Astyages gave him, as befits a son, all Artembares' goods and many other presents so that he became a great and renowned man." Ctesias, *Persica*, in *The Persian Empire: A Corpus of Sources from the Achaemenid Period*, ed. Amelie Kuhrt (New York: Routledge, 2010), 97–98.
7. Hdt. 1.123.
8. Xenophon, *Cyropaedia*, 2.6–2.12.
9. Hdt. 1.123–1.124.
10. Hdt. 1.125–1.130.
11. Hdt. 1.24–1.26, 1.7.
12. David F. Graf et al., "Persia at the Crest," in *A Soaring Spirit Time Frame, 600–400 BCE* (Alexandria, VA: Time-Life Books, 1987), 15.
13. Hdt. 1.53, 1.69–1.70.1.
14. James Lacey, *The First Clash* (New York: Bantam, 2011), 4.
15. Hdt. 1.76.4.
16. Hdt. 1.79–1.80.
17. Hdt. 1.80–1.81.
18. Hdt. 1.84; Crawford H. Greenwalt describes a fascinating archaeological find at the base of the cliff under the fallen remains of the wall at Sardis. The skeleton of a 22- to 26-year-old soldier was found. This skeleton showed defensive wounds and a knife wound in his back. Carbon 14 dating places the skeleton possibly within the time of the attack on Sardis. Was he perhaps a Lydian sentry at that weak point in the defense of Sardis? The article includes outstanding illustrations. Crawford H. Greenwalt Jr., "When a Mighty Empire Was Destroyed: The Common Man at the Fall of Sardis," *Proceedings of the American Philosophical Society* 136, no. 2 (June 1992), 247–271.

19. Poem by Bacchylides in Amelie Kuhrt, *The Persian Empire: A Corpus of Sources from the Achaemenid Period* (New York: Routledge, 2010), 65–66.
20. Hdt. 1.88.
21. J.A.S. Evans, "What Happened to Croesus?," *Classical Journal* 74, no. 1 (October–November 1978), 39.
22. Ctesias, *Persica*, in Kuhrt, *Persian Empire*, 68.
23. Evans, "What Happened to Croesus?," 40.
24. Ibid., 39–40.
25. Hdt. 1.141.1.
26. Hdt. 1.153.
27. Hdt. 1.155–1.57.
28. Hdt. 1.152.2–1.169.
29. Lacey, *First Clash*, 16.
30. Ibid., 17.
31. Ibid., 15 note 2.
32. Hdt. 1.178–1.181.
33. Lacey, *First Clash*, 19; Billows, 118–119.
34. Lacey, *First Clash*, 19. An example can be found in Isaiah 44:28- 45:7. "Thus says Yahweh.... Who says to Cyrus: you shall be my shepherd to carry out my purpose that Jerusalem may be rebuilt and the foundations of the Temple may be laid. Thus says the Lord the Cyrus is anointed, Cyrus whom he is taken by the hand undue nations before him and undo the might of Kings before whom he'd shall be opened and no doors closed."
35. Billows, 20–21.
36. Lacey, *First Clash*, 20.
37. Hdt. 1.190–1.192.
38. Berossus, *Babyloniaca*, in Kuhrt, *Persian Empire*, 81–82.
39. *Cyrus Cylinder*, in Kuhrt, *Persian Empire*, 70–71.
40. Kuhrt, *Persian Empire*, 82.
41. Graf, *Persia at the Crest*, 17.
42. Hdt. 1.205–1.214.
43. Kuhrt, *Persian Empire*, 101.
44. Xenophon, *Cyropaedia*, in Kuhrt, *Persian Empire*, 102.
45. Hdt. 2.1. According to Herodotus, Cyrus, upon making his decision to invade the territory of the Massagetai, "placed his son Cambyses, whom he intended to be heir to his kingdom, into the hands of Croesus, ordering his son to honor Croesus and treat him well in the event that his crossing over into Massagetai territory did not succeed." Hdt. 1.208.
46. Hdt. 3.1–3.5. He also tells an Egyptian version which was that "Cambyses was one of their own kinsmen.... Cyrus, not Cambyses, they say sent the request to Amasis for his daughter but they are incorrect." He also tells another story in which Cassandane, Cambyses' mother, complained that "Cyrus scorns me and has placed this creature from Egypt above me in the esteem.... Then Cambyses said: when I am grown up mother, I will turn the top of Egypt to the bottom and the bottom to top. He is supposed to have said this when he was 10 years old.... But he remembered the words when he grew up and became king and so made war on Egypt." He then states that he did not consider this story reliable.
47. Ctesias, *Perica*, in Kuhrt, *Persian Empire*, 109.
48. Billows, 120.
49. Hdt. 3.4.2–3.4.3.
50. Hdt. 3.19.

51. Lacey, *First Clash*, 26.
52. Hdt. 3.9. Herodotus also gives a less "credible version" in which the king of Arabia made a pipeline of stitched together "untanned cow hides and other skins and extended them out into the desert" to fill cisterns that were a 12-day journey from the river being used to fill the source cisterns.
53. Hdt. 3.13.
54. Hdt. 3.14–3.15.
55. Hdt. 3.28–3.38.
56. Kuhrt, *Persian Empire*, 104.
57. Ibid., 104–105.
58. Ibid., 116 note 1.
59. Strabo XVII 1.5, in Kuhrt, *Persian Empire*, 116.
60. Diodorus Siculus I.34.7, in Kuhrt, *Persian Empire*, 116.
61. Lacey, *First Clash*, 28.
62. Ibid., 28–29.
63. *Autobiography of Udjahorresne*, in Kuhrt, *Persian Empire*, 118.
64. Egyptian hieroglyphic stella, in Kuhrt, *Persian Empire*, 122–123.
65. Egyptian hieroglyphic inscription, in Kuhrt, *Persian Empire*, 124.
66. Hdt. 3.61–3.66; Ctesias *Persica* in Kuhrt, *Persian Empire*, 164. Ctesias claims that Cambyses was in Babylonia and "was carving some wood with a knife, it struck his thigh up to the muscle and he died after 11 days. Justin I, 9.4–13, in Kuhrt, *Persian Empire*, 165. Justin claims that "his sword slipped out of its sheath and seriously wounded him in his thigh. As a result he died."
67. Hdt. 3.67–3.69.
68. Hdt. 3.70; Kuhrt, *Persian Empire*, 169 note 1. Kuhrt points out that the Behistun Inscription confirms that Herodotus had access to Persian documents as the inscription confirms five of the six names that Herodotus states were in the conspiracy against Smerdis.
69. Hdt. 3.72–3.75.
70. Hdt. 3.76–3.7. Aspathines was wounded in the thigh, and Intaphrenes lost an eye.
71. Hdt. 3.85–3.88. Herodotus includes two different stories. In the first, Oibares, Darius' groom, took a mare outside the city and tied it up. During the night he took Darius' stallion out to the mare and let him mount her. The next morning when the stallion approached the spot where the mare had been, he whinnied first. In another story, Herodotus was told by the Persians that Oibares rubbed the genitals of the mare with his hands and kept it in his trousers. When sunrise came, he held his hand to the stallion's nose and the stallion whinnied.
72. Kuhrt, *Persian Empire*, 151 note 1.
73. See paragraph 68 of the Behistun Inscription as quoted in Kuhrt, *Persian Empire*, 149; Briant, *From Cyrus*, 108.
74. Hdt. 3.70.2, 3.78–3.79; paragraph 13 in Behistun Inscription in Kuhrt, *Persian Empire*, 143.
75. Briant, *From Cyrus*, 63.
76. Cook, 52.
77. Briant, *From Cyrus*, 100.
78. Hdt. 3.66.
79. See Briant, *From Cyrus*, 101–106.
80. Ibid., 101.
81. Lacey, *First Clash*, 30.
82. Behistun Inscription, paragraphs 1 and 14, in Kuhrt, *Persian Empire*, 141–143.
83. Briant, *From Cyrus*, 111. He goes on to explain, "It is not because he wasn't Achaemenid (in the clan sense) that Darius achieved power; it was his accession to royalty that allowed him to redefine the reality of what it meant to be 'Achaemenid.' At the same time, this redefinition did not wipe out the earlier understanding; it seems clear that the documented clan continued to function as in the past. But it is also clear that membership in this clan was not enough to claim any sort of right of succession. This decision remained solely in the hands of the 'head of the family'—in other words, the reigning king. It was thus the very bases of dynastic reality that Darius modified from top to bottom, as well as the special themes of dynastic ideology, which he did more to manipulate than to restore. It is therefore entirely pointless to judge Darius' candidacy for the throne in terms of a right of succession that he in fact redefined *after* his accession."
84. Hdt. 3.88. He goes on to state that among them, "the first were Atossa and Artystone, both daughters of Cyrus. Atossa had earlier been the wife of her brother Cambyses and then had been left to the Magus while Artystone was a virgin. In addition, Darius married the daughter of Smerdis, son of Cyrus, whose name was Parmys, and also the daughter of Otanes who had revealed the identity of the magus.
85. Behistun Inscription, paragraph 52, in Kuhrt, *Persian Empire*, 148.
86. Billows, 124–125.
87. Hdt. 4.97–4.98.
88. Hdt. 4.143–4.144, 5.18.
89. Hdt. 5.11.
90. Hdt. 5.23.2–3.
91. Hdt. 5.24.
92. A. Blamire, "Herodotus and Histiaeus," *Classical Quarterly*, new series, 9, no. 2 (November 1959): 144; George Harris, "Ionia under Persia: 547–477—a Political History" (PhD diss., Northwestern University, 1971), 169. Harris agrees with Blamire pointing out that Darius "knew the use of good intelligence sources" and was aware "of both the strategic and economic assets of the area and of its potential importance to his Empire."
93. Harris, 169; J.A.S. Evans, "Histiaeus and Aristagoras: Notes on the Ionian Revolt," *American Journal of Philology* 84, no. 2 (April 1963): 117.
94. Blamire, 143; David Frank Graf, "Medism: Greek Collaboration with Achaemenid Persia" (PhD diss., University of Michigan, 1979), 90.
95. Harris, 174.
96. Blamire, 145. Graf, "Medism," 91, suggests that "difficulties encountered in controlling Thrace and the Hellespontine revolt perhaps provide better reasons for the abandonment of Myrcinus and the promotion of Histiaeus."
97. Pericles B. Georges, "Persian Ionia under Darius: The Revolt Reconsidered," *Historia: Zeitschrift fur Alte Geschichte* 49, no. 1 (1st Qtr., 2000), 14.
98. Briant, *From Cyrus*, 144.
99. Billows, 128–129.
100. Hdt. 3.89.
101. Hdt. 3.90–3.97.
102. Billows, 130.

103. Hdt. 3.97.
104. Briant, *From Cyrus*, 338–345.

Chapter 5

1. J.A.S. Evans, "Herodotus and the Ionian Revolt," *Historia: Zeitschrift für Alte Geschichte* 25, no. 1 (1st Qtr., 1976): 31–32; Donald Lateiner, "The Failure of the Ionian Revolt," *Historia: Zeitschrift für Alte Geschichte* 31, no. 2 (2nd Qtr., 1982), 130–131.
2. G.B. Gray and M. Cary, "The Ionian Revolt," in *The Cambridge Ancient History*, vol. 4, ed. J.B. Bury, F.E. Adcock, and S.A. Cook (Cambridge: Cambridge University Press, 1960), 215.
3. Barry Baldwin, "How Credulous Was Herodotus?," *Greece and Rome* 11, no. 2 (October 1964): 167.
4. Lateiner, "Failure," 129.
5. George Cawkwell, *The Greek Wars* (Oxford: Oxford University Press, 2006), 61–67; Pericles Georges, "Persian Ionia under Darius: The Revolt Reconsidered," *Historia: Zeitschrift für Alte Geschichte* 49, no. 1 (1st Qtr., 2000), 2. Georges takes issue with Cawkwell's third criticism as he states, "Herodotus' account is consistent with what we know about Persian Ionia with the politics of the Persian Empire under Darius, and with the motives of the leading actors."
6. See Evans, "Herodotus and the Ionian Revolt," 33. He states, "We can't take it as very probable that the Alcmeonids did support Athens' withdrawal of assistance to the revolt, and there is a modern tendency, which I cannot share, to treat Herodotus as a 'house historian' of the Alcmeonids."
7. Oswyn Murray, "The Ionian Revolt," in *The Cambridge Ancient History*, vol. 4, ed. John Boardman, N.G.L. Hammond, D.M. Lewis, and M. Ostwald (New York: Cambridge University Press, 1988), 470–472.
8. W.G. Forrest, "Motivation in Herodotus: The Case of the Ionian Revolt," *International History Review* 1, no. 3 (July 1979): 311–313; K.H. Waters, "Herodotus and the Ionian Revolt," *Historia: Zeitschrift für Alte Geschichte* 19, no. 4 (November 1970): 506.
9. Peter Krentz, *The Battle of Marathon* (New York: Yale University Press), 69; Waters, "Ionian Revolt," 506. On this issue Waters says that the "stories about individuals" were most important and none mentioned economic causes. He goes on to ask why shouldn't individuals be at the center. No single action reason can be given for the Ionian Revolt that is more important than the role of Aristagoras.
10. A.T. Olmstead, "Persia and the Greek Frontier Problem," *Classical Philology* 34, no. 4 (October 1939): 306.
11. Waters, "Ionian Revolt," 506.
12. J. Neville, "Was There an Ionian Revolt?" *Classical Quarterly*, new series, 29, no. 2 (1979): 273–274.
13. Evans, "Herodotus and the Ionian Revolt," 34.
14. H.T. Wallinga, "The Ionian Revolt," *Mnemosyne*, 4th series, 37, nos. 3/4 (1984): 401–402.
15. B.M. Mitchell, "Herodotus and Samos," *Journal of Hellenic Studies* 95 (1975): 75.
16. Lateiner, "Failure," 153–157.
17. Neville, 275.
18. G.A.H. Chapman, "Herodotus and Histiaeus' Role in the Ionian Revolt," *Historia: Zeitschrift für Alte Geschichte* 21, no. 4 (4th Qtr., 1972): 47.
19. Mabel Lang, "Herodotus and the Ionian Revolt," *Historia: Zeitschrift für Alte Geschichte* 17, no. 1 (January 1986): 24. She states that "because Herodotus is our only even halfway respectable source, we are forced to make use of his materials." Cawkwell, 61. He states, "Unfortunately, for knowledge of the course and for understanding of the Ionian Revolt, we have to rely almost entirely on Herodotus."
20. Chapman, 549.
21. "Guest-friendship served as a device for the promotion of the material and political interests of the elites engaged in it. Individuals integrated into politically separated communities exchanged substantial amounts of wealth and performed significant services for each other.... It becomes apparent that the elites of the ancient world were not confined to the boundaries of their immediate communities (whether this be a city, a tribe, a petty kingdom or a Persian satrapal court). On the contrary, they participated at one and the same time both in these networks and in their immediate communities. Power, prestige and resources that could be acquired through one system could readily be transferred to the other, and at times the horizontal ties of solidarity which link together the elites of separate communities were stronger than the vertical ties which bound them to the inferiors in their own communities." Gabriel Herman, *Revitalized Friendship in the Greek City* (New York: Cambridge University Press, 1987), 19.
22. P.B. Manville, "Aristagoras and Histiaios: The Leadership Struggle in the Ionian Revolt," *Classical Quarterly*, new series, 27, no. 1 (1977): 83.
23. Hdt. 5.3–5.35.
24. Hdt. 5.31–5.32.
25. Hdt. 5.33.
26. Hdt. 5.34.
27. Wallinga, "Ionian Revolt," 427–429.
28. Lateiner, "Failure," 132.
29. Arthur Keaveney, "The Attack on Naxos; A Forgotten Cause of the War," *Classical Quarterly*, new series, 38, no. 1 (1988): 76.
30. Ibid., 76–77.
31. Ibid., 778–781; Forrest, "Motivation," 78–81. Forrest states, "Megabates' punishment of Skylax need not show more than ill tempered contempt for Greek dignity. But the quarrel with Aristagoras which brought out the real question, who is the master now, and Aristagoras' straight answer is more than enough to explain Megabates' betrayal of the expedition to the Naxian's, and extreme reaction perhaps but by no means as incredible as it has seemed too many."
32. Harris, 187–188; A.R. Burn, *Persia and the Greeks: The Defense of the West* (New York: Minerva Press, 1962), 196. Burn claims that the "leakage" of news about the Naxian expedition may have taken place through the Naxian exiles.
33. J.A.S. Evans, "Histiaeus and Aristagoras: Notes on the Ionian Revolt," *American Journal of Philology* 84, no. 2 (April 1963): 119.
34. Georges, "Persian Ionia," 16 note 63.
35. Lang, 82–83.
36. G.B. Grundy, *The Great Persian War and Its Pre-*

liminaries: *A Study of the Evidence, Literary and Topographical* (London: John Murray, 1901), 86.
 37. Hdt. 5.35–5.36.
 38. Hdt. 5.36.4–5.37.
 39. Gray and Cary, 218.
 40. Ibid., 476–478.
 41. Harris, 95–96, 104–106.
 42. Ibid., 137.
 43. Ibid., 95–96, 116, 137–139.
 44. Georges, "Persian Ionia," 3, 7, 9–10.
 45. Krentz, *Battle of Marathon*, 69–70.
 46. Cawkwell, *The Greek Wars*, 73–74.
 47. Hdt. 4.137.2.
 48. J.B. Bury, *A History of Greece* (New York: Modern Library, 1913), 231.
 49. Gray and Cary, 218; A. Andrews, *The Greek Tyrants* (New York: Harper Torch, 1963), 127.
 50. Blamire, 146.
 51. Harris, 96–97.
 52. J.M. Cook, *The Persian Empire* (New York: Schocken Books, 1983), 67–79; Pierre Briant, *From Cyrus to Alexander: A History of the Persian Empire* (Winona Lake, IN: Eisenbrauns, 202), 388–412.
 53. David Frank Graf, "Medism: Greek Collaboration with Achaemenid Persia" (PhD diss., University of Michigan, 1979), 88–89.
 54. Harris, 98–101.
 55. Graf, "Medism," 86.
 56. Harris, 144.
 57. Ibid., 190.
 58. Cawkwell, *The Greek Wars*, 72–73.
 59. Evans, "Histiaeus," 118; Harris, 176. Harris claims the Scythian expedition showed the Ionians "the formidable strength that they could muster when they joined together in a common effort." He also points out that Persian coercion brought them together.
 60. Graf, "Medism," 94.
 61. Evans, "Histiaeus," 9; Cawkwell, *The Greek Wars*, 74–76.
 62. Hdt. 5.37.2–5.38.
 63. Harris, 192–193.
 64. Hdt. 5.48–5.51.3.
 65. Lateiner, "Failure," 137.
 66. Jakob A.O. Larsen, "Sparta and the Ionian Revolt: A Study of Spartan Foreign Policy and the Genesis of the Peloponnesian League," *Classical Philology* 27, no. 2 (April 1932): 149–150.
 67. Cawkwell, *The Greek Wars*, 76.
 68. Hdt. 5.97.
 69. Lateiner, "Failure," 141; Grundy, *The Great Persian War and Its Preliminaries*, 93.
 70. Hdt. 5.99–5.102. For a fuller discussion of the battle, see Fred Eugene Ray, *Land Battles in 5th Century BC Greece: A History of 173 Engagements* (Jefferson, NC: McFarland, 2009), 32–36.
 71. Hdt. 5.105.
 72. Lateiner, "Failure," 142–144.
 73. Grundy, *The Great Persian War and Its Preliminaries*, 98.
 74. Plutarch, *The Malice of Herodotus*, 24.B–C.
 75. Grundy, *The Great Persian War and Its Preliminaries*, 96–97.
 76. Ibid., 96–97.
 77. Gray and Cary, 221–222.
 78. Georges, "Persian Ionia," 25.
 79. Harris, 201–202.
 80. Lang, 33.
 81. Grundy, *The Great Persian War and Its Preliminaries*, 98.
 82. Harris, 203.
 83. Murray, 483; Burn, 201–202; Grundy, *The Great Persian War and Its Preliminaries*, 99–100.
 84. Hdt. 5.106.2–5.107.
 85. Reginald Walter Macan, *Herodotus: The Fourth, Fifth and Sixth Books*, vol. 2 (London: Macmillan, 1895), 69–70; Gray and Cary, 223; Chapman, 560.
 86. Chapman, 560–571.
 87. Harris, 222.
 88. Blamire, 147–148.
 89. Gray & Cary, 23.
 90. P.B. Manville, "Aristagoras and Histiaeus: The Leadership Struggle in the Ionian Revolt," *Classical Quarterly*, new series, 27, no. 1 (1977): 84–85.
 91. Murray, "Ionian Revolt," 483.
 92. Grundy, *The Great Persian War and Its Preliminaries*, 105.
 93. Hdt. 5.108.
 94. Hdt. 5.109.
 95. Hdt. 5.110–5.112.
 96. Gray and Cary, 233.
 97. Hdt. 5.115.
 98. Murray, "Ionian Revolt," 484. For an illustration of the plan of the siege mound and tunnels at Old Paphus, see page 485.
 99. Hdt. 5.116–5.117, 5.122–5.123.
 100. Hdt. 5.126.
 101. Grundy, *The Great Persian War and Its Preliminaries*, 111.
 102. Hdt. 5.118–5.119.
 103. Hdt. 5.119–5.121.
 104. Grundy, *The Great Persian War and Its Preliminaries*, 114–115.
 105. Harris, 217–218.
 106. Hdt. 6.5.1.
 107. Hdt. 6.1–6.5.
 108. Grundy, *The Great Persian War and Its Preliminaries*, 133.
 109. Gray and Cary, 225; Harris, 226. Harris agrees with Cary and Gray but adds, "Although some of the Carian cities had to be reduced after Lade, it is clear that Caria was reduced to a negligible quantity at the time when the great attack on Miletus was planned."
 110. The Panioniian was a "hilltop shrine of Heliconian Poseidon which became the federal sanctuary and festival center of the 12 leading Ionian cities" and the place where the Ionian League met to make important political decisions. Michael Grant, *A Guide to the Ancient World: A Dictionary of Classical Place Names* (New York: Barnes and Noble, 1986), 410–411; Hdt. 6.7.
 111. Harris, 227.
 112. Hdt. 6.7.
 113. Lateiner, "Failure," 148.
 114. Harris, 229.
 115. Harris, 229; C. Hignett, *Xerxes' Invasion of Greece* (Oxford: Clarendon Press, 1963), 348; Grundy, *The Great Persian War and Its Preliminaries*, 129, 219.

116. Lateiner, "Failure," 146.
117. Harris, 228.
118. Hdt. 6.11–6.12.
119. Hdt. 6.9.
120. Hdt. 6.9.2–6.1- 3.1 Hdt. 6.13
121. Lateiner, "Failure," 158.
122. Graf, "Medism," 6.
123. Harris, 146; Burn, *Persia*, 212.
124. Hdt. 6.14.
125. Hdt. 6.14–6.15.
126. Hdt. 6.16–6.17.
127. Harris, 229 note 58.
128. Hdt. 6.18.
129. Daniel Gillis, *Collaboration with the Persians* (Wiesbaden: Franz Steiner Verlag GMBH, 1979), 22.
130. Hdt. 6.19.3–6.21.
131. Grundy, 84–88.
132. Lang, 25–29.
133. Harris, 185–186.
134. Chapman, 559. See Evans, "Histiaeus," 123.
135. Blamire, 147.
136. Georges, "Persian Ionia," 19 note 69.
137. Manville, 84–85.
138. Hdt. 5.34–5.35, 5.99, 5.124.
139. Grundy, *The Great Persian War and Its Preliminaries*, 97, 115–116.
140. Evans, "Histiaeus," 121–122.
141. Lang, 27–33.
142. Manville, 82–86.
143. Georges, "Persian Ionia," 19.
144. Cawkwell, *The Greek Wars*, 76.
145. Michel Austin, Jill Harries, and Christopher Smith, *Modus Operandi: Essays in Honor of Geoffrey Rickman* (London: Institute of Classical Studies, 1998), 303; Graf, "Medism," 98.
146. Manville, 86–87; Harris, 223; Chapman, 562.
147. Chapman, 62; Blamire, 149. Blamire believes that at this "stage Artaphernes felt insufficiently secure to murder the King's favorite."
148. Georges, "Persian Ionia," 29–30.
149. Evans, "Histiaeus," 123.
150. Hdt. 6.4.
151. Hdt. 6.5.
152. Blamire, 150.
153. Hdt. 6.5.
154. Grundy, *The Great Persian War and Its Preliminaries*, 135–136.
155. Lang, 35.
156. Blamire, 151.
157. Harris, 303; Burn, 208.
158. Hdt. 6.26–6.28.
159. Blamire, 150–152.
160. Grundy, *The Great Persian War and Its Preliminaries*, 137–139.
161. Hdt. 6.28–6.31.
162. Harris, 310.
163. Hdt. 6.31.
164. Blamire, 154.
165. Grundy, *The Great Persian War and Its Preliminaries*, 141–142.
166. Manville, 91.
167. Hdt. 6.25, 6.31.
168. Hdt. 6.19.3, 6.32–6.33, 6.41.
169. Hdt. 6.42–6.43.
170. Georges, "Persian Ionia," 34. Gray and Cary, 227, called it "a better distribution of the tax burden." Murray, "Ionian Revolt," 489, called it a "new and fair taxation at the same level as before."
171. Hdt. 6.42–6.43.
172. Austin, 306.
173. Murray, "Ionian Revolt," 490.
174. Gray and Cary, 228.
175. Cawkwell, *The Greek Wars*, 80.
176. Harris, 292–293.

Chapter 6

1. Hdt. 6.43–6.44.
2. Pierre Briant, *From Cyrus to Alexander: A History of The Persian People* (Winona, IN, Eisenbrauns, 202), 157; G.B. Grundy, *The Great Persian War and Its Preliminaries; A Study of the Evidence, Literary and Topographical* (London: John Murray, 1901), 145.
3. Grundy, *The Great Persian War and Its Preliminaries*, 153.
4. G. B. Gray and M. Cary, "The Ionian Revolt," in *The Cambridge Ancient History*, vol. 4, ed. J.B. Bury, F.E. Adcock, and S.A. Cook (Cambridge: Cambridge University Press, 1960), 230; N.G.L. Hammond, "The Expedition of Datis and Artaphernes," in *The Cambridge Ancient History*, vol. 4, ed. John Boardman, N.G.L. Hammond, D.M. Lewis and M. Ostwald (Cambridge: Cambridge University Press, 1988), 496.
5. Hdt. 6.44–6.45.
6. Grundy, *The Great Persian War and Its Preliminaries*, 152–153.
7. Ibid., 152–153.
8. Hdt. 6.46; Michael Grant, *A Guide to the Ancient World: A Dictionary of Classical Place Names* (New York: Barnes and Noble, 1986), 1.
9. Hdt. 6.133, 6.49; Robert Strasser, ed., *The Landmark Herodotus: The Histories* (New York: Pantheon, 2007), 549 note 7.133.1d. Strasser explains that criminals that Athens had condemned to death were thrown into a pit. Peter Krentz, *The Battle of Marathon* (New York: Yale University Press, 2010), 83. Krentz adds that later sources claim that Miltiades wanted to execute the heralds and that Themistocles even wanted to execute the interpreter.
10. Grundy, *The Great Persian War and Its Preliminaries*, 153.
11. C. Hignett, *Xerxes' Invasion of Greece* (Oxford: Clarendon Press, 1963), 87.
12. Raphael Sealey, "The Pit and the Well: The Persian Heralds of 491 BCE," *Classical Journal* 72, no. 1 (October–November, 1976), 15–20.
13. Sealey, 15–20. On Sparta' decision see, James Holladay, "Medism in Athens 508–480 BCE" *Greece and Rome* 2nd Series 25#2 (October 1978), 175–176.
14. David Franklin Graf, *Medism: Greek Collaboration with Achaemenid Persia*. Ph.D. dissertation, University of Michigan, 1979., 144–145; Hdt. 6.91–6.99.
15. Graf, *Medism*, 145–146.
16. Ibid., 148–151.
17. Hdt. 6.94–6.98.
18. Jack Martin Balcer, "The Persian Wars against Greece: A Reassessment," *Historia: Zeitschrift fur Alte*

Geschichte 38, no. 2 (2nd Qtr., 1989): 129; A.R. Burn, *Persia and the Greeks: The Defence of the West, c. 546–478 BC*, 2nd ed. (Stanford, CA: Stanford University Press, 1984), 236.
   19. Krentz, *Marathon*, 89–90.
   20. Ibid., 90.
   21. Burn, *Persia*, 236; D.M. Lewis, "Datis the Mede," *Journal of Hellenic Studies* 100 (1980): 194–195. Lewis says that the Lindian Temple Chronicle "describes an undated attack by Datis on the island of Rhodes." He says that it is difficult to correlate the attack with Herodotus but that there "is some temptation to use it as evidence that he was fleet commander in 494.
   22. Amelie Kuhrt, *The Persian Empire: A Corpus of Sources from the Achaemenid Period* (London: Routledge, 2007), 236.
   23. Lewis, "Datis," 195.
   24. Balcer, 129; Krentz, *Battle of Marathon*, 90.
   25. Grundy, *The Great Persian War and Its Preliminaries*, 159.
   26. Gray and Cary, 233.
   27. A complete discussion regarding the size of the fleet and number of troops will be found in Chapter 7.
   28. Hdt. 6.95–6.100.
   29. Murray, 503. Murray states that transportation of a large force by sea requires specialized skills which the Phoenicians had probably learned from their colonists in Carthage who staged a large-scale sea invasion of Sardinia.
   30. Krentz, *Battle of Marathon*, 96–97.
   31. Hdt. 6.100–6.101.
   32. Hdt. 6.100–6.102.
   33. Lionel Scott, *A Historical Commentary on Herodotus Book 6* (Leiden: Brill, 2005), 351.
   34. Grundy, *The Great Persian War and Its Preliminaries*, 162.
   35. Scott, 353. Cleruchs were a special kind of colonist from Athens who maintained their original citizenship, and their colony was not autonomous. *The Oxford Classical Dictionary*, 202.
   36. Gray and Cary, 237; Scott, 353.
   37. Gray and Cary, 237.
   38. Scott, 352.
   39. Murray, 505.
   40. Scott, 354–355.
   41. Murray, 505.
   42. Scott, 353–355.
   43. Murray, 505.
   44. Krentz, *Battle of Marathon*, 100; Scott, 355.
   45. Graf, *Medism*, 371.
   46. Krentz, *Battle of Marathon*, 100; Scott, 356.
   47. N.G.L. Hammond, "The Expedition of Datis and Artaphernes," in *The Cambridge Ancient History*, vol. 4, ed. John Boardman, N.G.L. Hammond, D.M. Lewis and M. Ostwald (Cambridge: Cambridge University Press, 1988), 506.
   48. Ibid., 506.

Chapter 7

   1. Hdt. 6.102–103.
   2. Hdt. 6.108. Originally the Plataeans had approached Cleomenes and the Lacedaemonians, but Cleomenes had refused support due to the distance between their cities; he suggested that they approach Athens for help. Cleomenes offered his suggestion to Plataea in an effort to create "trouble for the Athenians by provoking them into active hostilities against the Boeotians." When Thebes learned of Plataea's submission to Athens, the Theban army marched against Plataea. The Athenians went to the aid of Plataea, and Corinth intervened in an effort to prevent a battle and offered to serve as arbitrator. "The Corinthians reconciled the parties by defining the boundaries of their respective territories on the condition that the Thebans should leave anyone alone who did not wish to be classified as members of the Boeotian League." In spite of Corinth's efforts a battle between Athens and Thebes still took place after the Corinthians left and Athens defeated Thebes and "extended the boundaries of the Plataeans."
   3. Hdt. 6.109.3–109.6.
   4. Hdt. 6.110–111.
   5. "A stade equaled 600 Greek feet (equivalent to approximately 583 feet on the Attic standard, or approximately 630 feet on the Olympic standard). The term stade is derived from the ancient Greek term for stadium (*stadion*) and it was a standard distance for a footrace in Greek athletic competitions." Thomas Martin, "Ancient Greek Units of Currency, Weight and Distance," in *The Landmark Herodotus*, ed. Robert B. Strassler (New York: Pantheon, 2007), 775.
   6. Hdt. 6.111–112.
   7. Hdt. 6.115–6.116.
   8. Hdt. 6.120.
   9. Hdt. 6.117–121.1.
   10. C. Hignett, *Xerxes' Invasion of Greece* (Oxford: Clarendon Press, 1963), 39–40.
   11. A.W. Gomme, "Herodotus and Marathon," *Phoenix* 6, no. 3 (Autumn 1952): 77.
   12. Reginald Walter Macan, *Herodotus: The Fourth, Fifth and Sixth Books*, vol. 2 (London: Macmillan, 1895), 149.
   13. Ibid., 148–169.
   14. J.B. Bury, "The Battle of Marathon," *Classical Review* 10 (1896): 95.
   15. W.W. How and J. Wells, *A Commentary on Herodotus*, vol. 2 (New York: Oxford University Press, 1912), 354.
   16. Gomme, "Herodotus," 81.
   17. N.G.L. Hammond, "The Campaign and Battle of Marathon," *Journal of Hellenic Studies* 88 (1968): 14.
   18. Ibid., 47.
   19. J.A.S. Evans, "Herodotus and the Battle of Marathon," *Historia: Zeitschrift fur Alte Geschichte* 42, no. 3 (3rd Qtr., 1933): 279, 303–307.
   20. Norman A. Doenges, "The Campaign and the Battle of Marathon," *Historia: Zeitschrift fur Alte Geschichte* 47, no. 1 (1st Qtr., 1998): 2.
   21. Kurt Raaflaub, "Herodotus, Marathon and the Historian's Choice," in *Marathon: The Battle and the Ancient Deme*, ed. Kostas Buraselis-Katerina Meidani (Athens: Institut Du Livre- A. Kardamitsa, 2010), 221–223.
   22. Peter Krentz, "How Did the Battle Go Down?" *Ancient Warfare, Special Issue 2011: The Battle of Marathon*, 34–35.

23. F. Maurice, "The Campaign of Marathon," *Journal of Hellenic Studies* 52, pt. 1 (1932): 14.
24. Fred Eugene Ray, *Land Battles in 5th Century BC Greece: A History and Analysis of 173 Engagements* (Jefferson, NC: McFarland, 2009), 5.
25. Krentz, *Battle of Marathon*, 113.
26. Ibid.
27. W. Kendrick Pritchett, *Marathon*, University of California Publications in Classical Archaeology 4, no. 2 (1960): 156.
28. Ibid., 156–157.
29. Ibid., 157.
30. Hammond, "Campaign," 23.
31. Pausanius 1.32.7.
32. Hammond, "Campaign," 21; Scott, 600.
33. Krentz, *Battle of Marathon*, 116–117.
34. Pritchett, "Marathon," 153–154; J.A.G. van der Veer, "The Battle of Marathon: A Topographical Survey," *Mnemosyne* 35 (1982): 306.
35. Hammond, "Campaign," 24.
36. Van der Veer, 306.
37. Hammond, "Campaign," 21.
38. Van der Veer, 308; Lacey, *The First Clash: The Miraculous Greek Victory at Marathon and Its Impact on Western Civilization* (New York: Bantam, 2011), 159; Hammond, "Campaign," 20; Maurice, "Campaign," 20.
39. H.G.G. Payne, Archaeology in Greece, 1933–34," *Journal of Hellenic Studies* 54, pt. 2 (1934): 189.
40. Van der Veer, 294.
41. Eugene Vanderpool, "The Deme of Marathon and the Herakleion," *American Journal of Archaeology* 70, no. 4 (October 1966): 323.
42. W. Kendrick Pritchett, *Studies in Ancient Greek Topography, Part II: Battlefields* (Los Angeles: University of California Press, 1969), 90–91.
43. Vanderpool, "The Deme," 323.
44. Van der Veer, 296–297.
45. Lionel Scott, *Historical Commentary on Herodotus Book 6* (Boston: Brill, 2005), 601 note 13; Krentz, *Battle of Marathon*, 121.
46. Van der Veer, 307.
47. G.B. Grundy, *The Great Persian War and Its Preliminaries; A Study of the Evidence, Literary and Topographical* (London: John Murray, 1901), 164.
48. Hammond, "Campaign," 26; Grundy, *The Great Persian War and Its Preliminaries*, 163.
49. Grundy, *The Great Persian War and Its Preliminaries*, 165.
50. Hdt. 6.102.
51. Bury, "Battle of Marathon," 96.
52. J.F. Lazenby, *The Defence of Greece, 490–479* (Warminster: Aris and Phillips, 1993), 50.
53. J.A.R. Munro, "Some Observations on the Persian Wars," *Journal of Hellenic Studies* 19 (1899): 187.
54. How and Wells, II, 358.
55. Lazenby, *Defence*, 48; Munro, "Some Observations," 187–188; W.R. Loader, "Questions about Marathon," *Greece and Rome* 16, no. 46 (January 1947): 19.
56. Doenges, 3–4.
57. Lazenby, *Defence*, 48.
58. Scott, 606.
59. Munro, "Some Observations," 187; N.G.L. Hammond, "The Expedition of Datis and Artaphernes," in *The Cambridge Ancient History*, vol. 4, *Persia, Greece and the Western Mediterranean, c. 525–479 BCE*, ed. John Boardman et al. (New York: Cambridge University Press, 1988), 506.
60. Scott, 611; N. Whatley, "Marathon," *Proceedings of the Hellenic Traveler's Club* 129 (1929): 71.
61. Lacey, *First Clash*, 157.
62. Ibid., 156 note 4.
63. Krentz, *Battle of Marathon*, 133; Hammond, "Expedition," 507; Hammond, "Campaign," 33.
64. Pritchett, "Marathon," 158.
65. See Krentz, *Battle of Marathon*, 154, for a map based on Dunn's work.
66. Hammond, "Expedition," 506–507; Hignett, 67; Whatley, "Marathon," 71.
67. N. Whatley, "On the Possibility of Reconstructing Marathon and Other Ancient Battles," *Journal of Hellenic Studies* 84 (1964): 121–122. He adds two examples. He describes an experiment in which a fellow from his college had asked soldiers return from a patrol in World War I how many bombs they had thrown. The men's answers totaled 21, while only 7 had actually been thrown. The NCO and the officer were asked about how many shots they had fired. Their answers totaled 21, when actually only three had been fired. In another case the adjutant and the colonel were asked about a night working party. The adjutant described a bright moon while the colonel described a dark night.
68. Ibid.
69. Ibid., 127–128.
70. Hdt. 6. 95.1–2.
71. Hdt. 4.87.1, 6.9.1, 6.95.2; Richard A. Billows, *Marathon: How One Battle Changed Western Civilization* (New York: Overlook Duckworth, 2010), 198; George Cawkwell, *The Greek Wars* (Oxford: Oxford University Press, 2006), 88; Hans Delbruck, *History of the Art of War*, vol. 1, *Warfare in Antiquity*, trans. Walter J. Renfroe (Lincoln: University of Nebraska Press, 1975), 463; Lazenby, *Defence*, 46; Hammond, "Campaign," 32; Krentz, *Battle of Marathon*, 91; Ray, 60; A.R. Burn, *Persia and the Greeks: The Defence of the West, c. 546–478 BCE* 2nd Edition. (Stanford: Stanford University Press, 1984), 237; How and Wells, 103; J.A.R. Munro, "Marathon," in *The Cambridge Ancient History*, vol. 4, *The Persian Empire and the West*, ed. J.B. Bury, S.A. Cook, and F.E. Adcock (New York: Cambridge University Press, 1926), 234.
72. Whatley, "Reconstructing," 127; Grundy, *The Great Persian War and Its Preliminaries*, 160; Lazenby, *Defence*, 46; Lacey, *First Clash*, 152; Scott, 610; Marek Wozniak, "The Achaemenid Army at Marathon: The Army of All Nations," *Ancient Warfare, Special Issue 2011: The Battle of Marathon*, 78; George Grote, *Greece*, vol. 4 (New York: Peter Fenelon Collier and Son), 239.
73. Wallinga, *Ships and Sea-Power before the Great Persian War: The Ancestry of the Ancient Trireme* (Leiden: Brill, 1993), 138–139.
74. H.T. Wallinga, "The Trireme and Its Crew," in *Studies in Honour of H.L.W. Nelson*, ed. J. den Boeft and A.H.M. Kessels (Utrecht: Instituut voor Klassieke Talen, 1982), 465, 471. Professor Lionel Cassin in a letter to W.H. Jameson stated that triremes could operate with 100 men. W.H. Jameson, "The Provisions for Mobiliza-

tion in the Decree of Themistocles," *Historia: Zeitschrift fur Alte Geschichte* 12 (1963): 394.
75. Wallinga, *Ships and Sea-Power*, 139.
76. Munro, "Marathon," 234.
77. Doenges, 4–5.
78. Billows, 198–199.
79. Ray, 60–61.
80. Krentz, *Battle of Marathon*, 91.
81. Maurice, "Campaign," 18.
82. Hammond, "Campaign," 32.
83. Billows, 209; Wozniak, 78.
84. Ray, 60–61.
85. Doenges, 5–6.
86. Munro, "Marathon," 234.
87. Grundy, *The Great Persian War and Its Preliminaries*, 184–185.
88. Hignett, 59.
89. Whatley, "Marathon," 71.
90. Wozniak, 78.
91. Krentz, *Battle of Marathon*, 91–92.
92. Maurice, "Campaign," 18.
93. Scott, 611.
94. Hammond, "Campaign," 32.
95. Lazenby, *Defence*, 46–47.
96. Cawkwell, *The Greek Wars*, 88.
97. Christopher Tuplin, "Marathon: In Search of a Persian Dimension," in *Marathon: The Battle and the Ancient Deme*, ed. Kostas Buraselis-Katerina Meidani (Athens: Instutut Du Livre- A Kardamitsa, 2010), 265.
98. Lacey, *First Clash*, 152.
99. Tuplin, "Marathon," 265.
100. John J. Mearsheimer, "Assessing the Conventional Balance: The 3:1 Rule and its Critics," *International Security* 13, no. 4 (Spring 1989): 54.
101. Nepos, "Miltiades," V.
102. Justin 2.9.
103. Pausanias 4.25.5.
104. Grundy, *The Great Persian War and Its Preliminaries*, 184.
105. Whatley, "Reconstructing," 132.
106. Billows, 208.
107. Krentz, *Battle of Marathon*, 102.
108. Scott, 608.
109. Hignett, 59.
110. Glenn R. Bugh, *The Horsemen of Athens* (Princeton, NJ: Princeton University Press, 1988), 8.
111. Robert Gaebel, *Cavalry Operations in the Ancient Greek World* (Norman: University of Oklahoma Press, 2004), 67.
112. Hammond, "Campaign," 34.
113. Thomas Figueira, "Khalkis and Marathon," in *Marathon: The Battle and the Ancient Deme*, ed. Kostas-Buraselis Meidani (Athens: Institut Du Livre- A. Kardamitsa, 2010), 200–201.
114. Hammond, "Campaign," 507.
115. Rachel L. Sargent, "The Use of Slaves by Athenians in Warfare," *Classical Philology* 22, no. 2 (April 1927): 201–202.
116. Ibid., 203.
117. Peter Hunt, *Slaves, Warfare, and Ideology in the Greek Historians* (Cambridge: Cambridge University Press, 1998), 27.
118. Ray, 62.
119. Peter Green, *The Greco-Persian Wars* (Los Angeles: University of California Press, 1996), 31.
120. R.M. Berthold, "Which Way to Marathon?," *Revue des etudes anciennes* 78/79 (1976/77): 86.
121. F.E. Winter, *Greek Fortifications* (Toronto: University of Toronto Press, 1971), 63–64.
122. Scott, 602, 602 note 15.
123. Lazenby, *Defence*, 52.
124. David Franklin Graf, *Medism: Greek Collaboration with Achaemenid Persia. Ph.D. dissertation, University of Michigan, 1979*, 372.
125. P. Green, 188.
126. Lazenby, *Defence*, 52. He says, "Peisitratis' opponents had done so c. 546 (Hdt. 1.62.2), Hippias had done so against Anchimolios c. 513 (Hdt. 5.63.2), and the allies c. 506 (Hdt. 5.74-7). The only sieges of which we hear were when the defenders were few enough to congregate on the Acropolis—Kylon and his supporters (Hdt. 5.71, Thucydides 1.126.3), and Kleomenes and Isagoras and theirs (Hdt. 5.72.2)."
127. Hignett, 61 note 5.
128. Hammond, "Campaign," 34.
129. Lazenby, *Defence*, 52; Hammond, "Campaign," 37; Hignett, 61; Burn, *Persia and the Greeks*, 241; Doenges, 6; Billows, 206.
130. Munro, "Marathon," 239–240.
131. Burn, *Persia and the Greeks*, 242.
132. Grundy, *The Great Persian War and Its Preliminaries*, 164.
133. Hammond, "Campaign," 34. In his article on Marathon in the 1988 edition of the *Cambridge Ancient History*, vol. 4, 507, Hammond suggests that the 9,000-man Athenian army "probably used the two available routes, partly by daylight, and then during the night"; however, he does not give an explanation for his change of mind, nor does he explain why both routes were used.
134. Burn, *Persia and the Greeks*, 243, 243 note 14.
135. Doenges, 7–8.
136. Scott, 601 note 13; van der Veer, 296–297. Van der Veer points out that Burn has changed his location of the Herakleion from the Vrana to Vanderpool's location and feels that Vanderpool's location "is more satisfactory from a tactical point of view; the Athenian encampment is blocking the south end of the plain and the coast-road more directly than by threatening from one flank only." Krentz, *Battle of Marathon*, 121.
137. Berthold, 85. Berthold says that H. Delbruck, *Die Perserkriege und die Burgunderkriege* (Berlin, 1887), 59, believes the capture of the city without the defeat of the Athenian army would be pointless, but he does not consider that Persian control of the city would mean that the Persians could use the families of the hoplites as hostages. If the Athenians managed to escape, the Persians would still have control of the harbor, and the city could serve as a site from which the Persians could take operations against the Greeks after reinforcements arrived by sea.
138. P. Green, 32 note *.
139. Krentz, *Battle of Marathon*, 107.
140. Scott, 608.
141. Billows, 208.
142. Burn, *Persia and the Greeks*, 241.
143. Macan, *Fourth, Fifth and Sixth Books*, 360.

144. How and Wells, 107.
145. Burn, *Persia and the Greeks*, 239 note 7.
146. Frank J. Frost, *Politics and the Athenians* (Toronto: Edgar Kent, 2005), 192. Scott, while leaning toward Philippides, says the controversy continues and suggests reading the opposing views of Frost and Badian.
147. Hdt. 6.106.1.
148. Hdt. 105.2–3.
149. Scott, 371, 605.
150. Victor J. Matthews, "The Hemerodromoi: Ultra Long-Distance Running in Antiquity," *Classical World* 68, no. 3 (November 1974): 162.
151. Grote, 341.
152. Krentz, *Battle of Marathon*, 108; www.spartathlon.gr.
153. Billows, 207.
154. Scott, 370; Tom Holland, *Persian Fire: The First World Empire and the Fall of the West* (New York: Anchor, 2005), 189.
155. Krentz, *Battle of Marathon*, 109; Holland, 189.
156. P. Green, 31.
157. Scott, 369.
158. Ibid., 371–372.
159. Scott, 615; Macan, 362; How and Wells, 108.
160. Scott, 617; Holland, 108.
161. Holland, 188.
162. Ibid., 188–189.
163. M.D. Goodman and A.J. Holladay, "Religious Scruples in Ancient Warfare," *Classical Quarterly*, new series, 36, no. 1 (1986): 152–154.
164. Krentz, *Battle of Marathon*, 110; How and Wells, 109; Macan, 362. Macan adds, "This argument, of course, assumes the truth of the tradition and that the action or inaction of the Spartans has not been rationalized, or religionized by afterthought."
165. Billows, 206–207.
166. P. Green, 37.
167. Scott, 617; Lacey, *First Clash*, 58.
168. Holland, 189.
169. Plato, *Laws*, 3.698d–e.
170. Krentz, *Battle of Marathon*, 110.
171. Guy Dickins, "The Growth of Spartan Policy," *Journal of Hellenic Studies* 32 (1912): 131–132.
172. W.P. Wallace, "Kleomenes, Marathon, the Helots and Arkadia," *Journal of Hellenic Studies* 74 (1954): 34–35.
173. Krentz, *Battle of Marathon*, 110; L.H. Jeffery, "Comments on Some Greek Inscriptions," *Journal of Hellenic Studies* 69 (1949): 30.
174. Hunt, *Slaves*, 30; E.S.G. Robinson, "Rhegion, Zankle-Messana and the Samians," *Journal of Hellenic Studies* 66 (1946): 17–18.
175. Ibid., 31.
176. Duncan B. Campbell, "Meanwhile in Sparta," *Ancient Warfare, Special Issue 2011: The Battle of Marathon*, 52. Concerning the dating of the base, see L.H. Jeffery, "Comments on Some Greek Inscriptions," *Journal of Hellenic Society* 69 (1949): 30.
177. Ibid.
178. Hdt. 6.49.
179. How, "Arms, Tactics & Strategy in the Persian Wars," *Journal of Hellenic Studies* 43, pt. 2 (1923): 117; van der Veer, 299.

180. Louis Rawlings, *The Ancient Greeks at War* (Manchester: Manchester University Press, 2007), 182–183.
181. Rawlings, 184; Lacey, *First Clash*, 133–134; van der Veer, 301; Hammond, "Campaign," 35; Gordon Shrimpton, "The Persian Cavalry at Marathon," *Phoenix* 34 (1980): 134.
182. See Chapter 7 for discussion of the Athenian decision.
183. Bugh, 10; Hammond, "Marathon," 510.
184. Ray, 59; Ronald Ruiters, "Marathon Dawn," *Ancient Warfare, Special Issue 2011: The Battle of Marathon*, 32.
185. Scott, 612–615; Hammond, "Campaign," 35; Burn, *Persia and the Greeks*, 241.
186. See Hdt. 109.3 for Miltides' speech.
187. Hdt. 6.110.
188. Aristotle, *Constitution of Athens*, 22.2.
189. Scott, 379. See pages 378–379 for a full discussion of this issue. Macan, 365; How and Wells, 110; Kurt Von Fritz and Ernst Kapp, *Aristotle's Constitution of Athens and Related Texts* (New York: Hafner, 1950), 165, note 56.
190. Scott, 380.
191. Lacey, *First Clash*, 160. See Ron Gregg, "Schitzquie," in *War on Two Fronts: An Infantry Commander's War in Iraq and the Pentagon*, by Christopher P. Hughes (Philadelphia: Casemate, 2007), 80–86, for a description of the problems sanitation causes even in a modern army in the 21st century.
192. Graf, *Medism*, 371–372.
193. How and Wells, 359. They add, "In spite of the refusal of Athens to receive back Hippias at the bidding of Artaphernes (V.96), the Pisistratidae were not without friends in Athens, as shown by the election of the leader of their faction, Hipparchus, to the archonship in 496. May we not fairly suppose that just as the aristocratic party of the plain relied on Sparta, so the Alcmeonids looked to Persia for aid in the strife of factions?"
194. Hignett, 67.
195. Berthold, 93.
196. Hdt. 6.110.
197. Scott, 618.
198. How and Wells, 361.
199. Macan, 241. When he wrote his commentary he believed that the Herakleion was in the Avlona valley and wondered if the Persians thought they could pass unmolested as the Greeks took the northern route to reach Athens ahead of the Persians. Today, knowing that the location of the Herakleion was located in Valaria, there is no doubt but that the Persians would have had to fight the Greeks whose camp covered the coastal road. Knowing the correct location of the Greek camp might have caused him to reach a different conclusion.
200. Munro, "Some Observations," 189–193.
201. Munro, "Some Observations," 193; How and Wells, 361.
202. Grundy, *The Great Persian War and Its Preliminaries*, 185–186. Grundy places the Herakleion in the Avlona valley, so the Greek army would have taken the northern route back to Athens. We now know the Herakleion was located on the southern route to Athens. He also claims that the small number of cavalry would

have been ineffective even if the southern route was taken.

203. Munro, "Marathon," 234, 241–245.
204. Maurice, "Campaign," 31.
205. Burn, *Persia and the Greeks*, 246–247; P. Green, 30, 35; Nicholas Sekunda, *Marathon 490 BC: The first Persian invasion of* Greece (Oxford: Osprey Publishing, 2002), 52.
206. Gomme, "Herodotus," 82; P. Green, 34; Sekunda, *Marathon 490 BC*, 52.
207. Scott, 620; Gomme, "Herodotus," 83; M.O.B. Caspari, "Stray Notes on the Persian Wars," *Journal of Hellenic Studies* 31 (1911): 104–105; Burn, *Persia and the Greeks*, 247; Holland, 192 note 44.
208. Billows, 209.
209. Billows, 210.
210. Billows, 212.
211. Billows, 213.
212. Whatley, "Reconstructing," 135.
213. Ibid.
214. Krentz, *Battle of Marathon*, 140.
215. Ibid., 140–141. See Hignett, 66.
216. Whatley, "Reconstructing," 137–138 ; Krentz, *Marathon*, 140.
217. Hignett, 71.
218. Hammond, "Campaign," 41; Hammond, "Marathon," 511.
219. Harry C. Avery, "Herodotus 6.112.2," *Transactions and Proceedings of the American Philological Association* 103 (1972): 21–22.
220. Lazenby, *Defence*, 61–62.
221. Doenges, 11–12.
222. Ray, 62–63. Ray says that the building of an abatis was borrowed from Cleomenes, who cut down trees to help defeat Hippias' cavalry in 510. He thinks it ironic that the same tactic was used against Hippias 20 years later at Marathon. While it appears that Ray is unaware that the Herakleion where the Greeks camped was not in the Vrana as he states, but rather near Volaria, it really doesn't matter as Datis had to attack the Greeks wherever their camp was located.
223. Krentz, *Battle of Marathon*, 142–143. He points out that if each horse took five seconds passing the narrow opening by the spring, 600 Calvary would take 50 minutes. If each horse took 10 seconds, the time would increase to one hour and 40 minutes. If there were more than 600 cavalry, the time would be even longer.
224. Tuplin, "Marathon," 266–267.
225. Johan Henrik Schreiner, *Two Battles and Two Bills: Marathon and the Athenian Fleet* (Oslo: Norwegian Institute at Athens, 2004), 23–62.
226. Whatley, "Reconstructing," 127.
227. Peter Krentz, "How Did the Battle of Marathon Go Down?" *Ancient Warfare, Special Issue 2011: The Battle of Marathon*, 40.
228. Hdt. 6.111. How and Wells, 111, state that based upon Cleisthenes' order they would have been Erechtheis, Aegeis, Pandionis, Leontis, Acamantis, Oeneis, Cecropis, Hippothoontis, Aeantis, and Antiochis based upon inscriptions from the time of the Peloponnesian War. The arrangement of tribes is supported by Pausanias who observed the monument at Marathon and the stele of the tribe Erechtheis; however, Plutarch suggests a different order that may have been determined by lot. Also see Scott, 386–387, and Lazenby, *Defence*, 63.
229. Hdt. 6.113.1; Marek Wozniak, "The Achaemenid Army at Marathon: The Army of All Nations," *Ancient Warfare, Special Issue 2011: The Battle of Marathon*, 78–79.
230. Hdt. 6.11 2.1. The stade in ancient Greece equaled about 583 feet on the Attic standard or about 630 feet on the Olympic standard. Using the Attic standard, eight stades equals about .88 miles, while using the Olympic standard eight stades equals about .95 miles. Martin, 775.
231. Van der Veer, 310.
232. Ibid., 311–312; Leake (1848), Pritchett (1960), Hammond (1968), and Berthold (1976/1977) supported this viewpoint, although with some minor variations.
233. Van der Veer, 313.
234. Ibid., 313–315.
235. Ibid., 315–316.
236. Ibid., 317. While he chooses the third location, he does point out objections raised concerning this location. He says Hammond objects because the Greeks could be attacked by the cavalry if their camp was on the plain. Van der Veer responds that phalanxes were not helpless against cavalry and they could have built an abatis as Hammond had previously described such a barricade; R. M. Berthold, "Which Way to Marathon," *Revue des etudes anciennes* 78/79 (1976/77), 90 n. 46, does not think that the location would give enough space for 10,000 hoplites to deploy nor enough land for the Athenian center to be pursued inland. He thinks Vanderpool's reconstruction would not offer room enough for a battle position of 10,000 hoplites, nor allow the Athenian center to be pursued inland. Van der Veer responds that the Greeks could have set up their southern entrance to the plain which is similar to the situation at Vrana which Berthold accepts. And if Berthold accepts the Vrana position, why does he not accept a battle line in the southern entrance to the plain, which affords a comparable situation?
237. Hammond, "Marathon," 510, 513 map.
238. Ray, 63.
239. Billows, 208, 219 maps.
240. Krentz, *Battle of Marathon*, 121, 155 map.
241. Lacey, *First Clash*, 217 note 20.
242. Hdt. 6.111.3.
243. Macan, vol. 1, 369; Macan, vol. 2, 245.
244. How and Wells, 112.
245. Scott, 387.
246. Lazenby, *Defence*, 64. He adds that "it is possible that the soldier-servants, probably mostly slaves, who will have accompanied the hoplites, were deployed on either flank, though their military value was probably not very great."
247. Krentz, *Battle of Marathon*, 142.
248. Billows, 215.
249. Lacey, *First Clash*, 167.
250. Grote, IV, 349.
251. Macan, 370.
252. W. Watkis Lloyd, "The Battle of Marathon: 490 BC," *Journal of Hellenic Studies* 2 (1881): 387.

253. How and Wells, vol. 2, 112.
254. W.W. How, "On the Meaning of ΒΑΔΗΝ and ΔΡΟΜΩΙ in Greek Historians in the Fifth Century," *Classical Quarterly* 13, no. 1 (January 1919): 42.
255. Grundy, *The Great Persian War and Its Preliminaries*, 188.
256. Hans Delbruck, *History of the Art of War, Volume I Warfare in Antiquity* Translated by Walter J. Renfroe (Lincoln, Nebraska: University of Nebraska Press, 1990), 74–75.
257. Munro, "Marathon," 247.
258. N. Whatley, "Marathon," 73–74.
259. Maurice, "Campaign," 22.
260. Hignett, 62, 69.
261. Hammond, "Campaign," 28.
262. Walter Donlan and James Thompson, "The Charge at Marathon: Herodotus 6.112," *Classical World* 71, no. 4 (April–May 1976), 339–342. In the spring of 1978 Donlan and Thompson repeated the testing with 13 young men completing an 8.75-minute treadmill run at 7 mph, a distance of 565 feet. Results of the tests were similar, except the additional energy required to carry the shield chest high was 6.8 percent as opposed to 28 percent at the longer distance. J. Hodgson, associate professor of applied physiology at Penn State, analyzed the data. Based on his analysis, it was concluded that "given a total panoply weight of 50 to 70 pounds (including a hoplite shield of 15 pounds carried isometrically, a grade of approximately 2.5 percent which simulates uneven terrain), and a reduced rate of 5 mph for 1.5 minutes, well-conditioned men can traverse a distance of 220 yards with sufficient energy reserves to engage in combat. Donlan and Thompson, 419–420.
263. Hammond, "Marathon," 511. 140 m equals 153 yards.
264. Lazenby, *Defence*, 67.
265. Billows, 216.
266. Krentz, *Battle of Marathon*, 146–147.
267. Ibid., 147.
268. Ibid., 150–151.
269. Ibid., 151.
270. Lacey, *First Clash*, 182–183.
271. Ibid., 183.
272. Ibid., 183.
273. Avery, "Herodotus 6.112.2," 21–22.
274. Delbruck, *History of the Art of War*, 81; Cawkwell, *The Greek Wars*, 89.
275. Shrimpton, 27. Shrimpton estimates that it would take the Greek army about 19 minutes to cross 1,420 yards at 2.5 mph, and about 1.5 minutes to cover the final 220 yards at 5 mph.
276. Shrimpton, 29–36.
277. Arthur Ferrill, *The Origins of War from the Stone Age to Alexander the Great* (London: Thames and Hudson, 1985), 110.
278. Doenges, 14.
279. Gaebel, 68–70.
280. Lacey, *First Clash*, 179.
281. Hammond, "Marathon," 511.
282. Krentz, *Battle of Marathon*, 140–143.
283. Christopher Tuplin, "All the King's Horse: In Search of Achaemenid Persian Cavalry," *New Perspectives on Ancient Warfare*, ed. Garrett G. Fagan and Matthew Trundle (Boston: Leiden, 2010), 165, 181.
284. Tuplin, "Marathon," 267–271.
285. W. Kendrick Pritchett, *The Greek State at War, Part IV* (Los Angeles: University of California Press, 1985), 47, 51.
286. G.L. Cawkwell, "Orthodoxy and Hoplites," *Classical Quarterly*, new series, 39, no. 2 (1989): 376.
287. James P. Holoka, "Marathon and the Myth of the Same-Day March," *Greek, Roman and Byzantine Studies* 38, no. 4 (Winter 1997): 336–338. Scott, 625, quotes Hammond as proposing 5:30 a.m.–9:30 a.m. for the length of the battle.
288. Louis Rawlings, *The Ancient Greeks at War* (New York: Manchester University Press, 2007), 95.
289. Everett L. Wheeler, "Land Battles," in *The Cambridge History of Greek and Roman Warfare*, ed. Phillip Sabin, Hans van Wees, and Michael Whitby (Cambridge: Cambridge University Press, 2007), 212.
290. Adam Schwartz, *Reinstating the Hoplite: Arms, Armour and Phalanx Fighting in Archaic and Classical Greece* (Stuttgart: Franz Steiner Verlag, 2009), 202, 217–218.
291. Ibid., 219–220.
292. Ibid., 220–222. Schwartz adds that the German historian J.P. Franz has pointed out that the only battle in which Thucydides actually participated is described as short. Schwartz, 221 note 957.
293. Ibid., 208–215.
294. Ibid., 216.
295. See Chapter 3 for a discussion on the possible weight of a hoplite's shield.
296. Schwartz, 216.
297. Ibid., 229.
298. Pausanias 1.32.3.
299. Robert B. Strassler, ed., *The Landmark Herodotus*, trans. Andrea L. Purvis (New York: Pantheon, 2007), 75 note 6.117a.
300. If there were 40,000 troops, the casualty rate would be 16 percent, 35,000 = 18 percent, 25,000 = 25 percent, 15,000 = 42 percent.
301. Peter Krentz, "Casualties in Hoplite Battles," *Greek, Roman and Byzantine Studies* 26 (1985): 19.
302. Richard A. Gabriel and Karen S. Metz, *From Sumer to Rome: The Military Capabilities of Ancient Armies* (New York: Greenwood Press, 1991), 86.
303. Ray, 67.
304. Harry C. Avery, "The Number of Persian Dead at Marathon," *Historia: Zeitschrift für Alte Geschichte* 22, no. 4 (4th Qtr., 1973): 757.
305. William F. Wyatt, "Persian Dead at Marathon (Historia 22 1973, 756), 483. His conversion follows. He says that the proper formula displaying the relation between the numbers is: . This formula is simple, yields the correct result, and also reflects an operation which Herodotus actually performed elsewhere in his work. The formula itself, though, contains problems, for as a formula it is as unmotivated as is multiplication by 33.33. There are at least three ways in which Herodotus can have operated to arrive at the attested numerical relation.

A. $64 \times 3 = 192$, i.e., the Athenian dead. $64 \times 100 = 6400$, i.e., the Persian dead. Arithmetically this solution is the most simple and satisfying, but the number 64 is unattested and unmotivated. We must discard this solution.

B. This solution is better, since it assumes as basic (and correct) the number of Athenian dead, and we know that Herodotus was accustomed to such operations. In his calculations with Egyptian dynasties, however, there was a principled reason for his division by three. Here there is not, and this solution, too, must be discarded.

C. $192 \times 100 = 19,200$; . This is the least satisfactory solution arithmetically, since it posits two separate operations, but it seems the psychologically most likely.

306. Wyatt, 483.
307. Ibid., 484.
308. Pausanias 1.32.6.
309. Hdt. 6.113.
310. See Chapter 7.
311. Krentz, *Battle of Marathon*, 143.
312. Lazenby, *Defence*, 72.
313. Ibid., 16–17.
314. Hdt. 6.115, 6.124.
315. Grote, 852.
316. Macan, vol. 2, 168.
317. Bury, "Battle of Marathon," 97–98.
318. How and Wells, 361.
319. P.K. Baillie Reynolds, "The Shield Signal at Marathon," *Journal of Hellenic Studies* 49, pt. 1 (1929): 101–104.
320. Maurice, "Campaign," 17–18.
321. Harris Gary Hudson, "The Shield Signal at Marathon," *American Historical Review* 42, no. 3 (April 1937): 445–446, 452–453, 458.
322. Hammond, "Campaign," 36–37. Burn, *Persia*, 251, basically agrees with Hammond. A. Trevor Hodge and Luis A. Losada, "The Time of the Shield Signal at Marathon," *American Journal of Archaeology* 74, no. 1 (January 1970): 34, completely reject Hammond and Burn's attempt to set the time of the signal using the angle of the sun or to set the location of the signal. They point out that "if the sun is at any reasonable elevation it is possible for a man, with a little care, to reflect a flash through an angle of the full 360° surrounding him."
323. Lazenby, *Defence*, 72–73.
324. Evans, "Herodotus and the Battle," 288–289; Daniel Gillis, *Collaboration with the Persians* (Wiesbaden: Franz Steiner Verlag GMBH, 1979), 50. Gillis says that "it is odd that Herodotus never accuses the Athenian followers of Hippias of having given the shield signal, not even at that the end of his discussion (6.124)."
325. Holoka, 339.
326. A. Trevor Hodge, "Reflections on the Shield at Marathon," *Annual of the British School at Athens* 96 (2001): 238–239, 243–245. His mathematical explanation is included in an appendix, 256–259.
327. Hammond, "Campaign," 37.
328. Hodge, "Reflections," 245–246.
329. Scott, 626–627.
330. Billows, 228.
331. Krentz, *Battle of Marathon*, 161–163.
332. Frost, *Politics*, 191.
333. Franklin T. Baker, ed., *Browning's Shorter Poems* (New York: Macmillan, 1917), 38.
334. See Chapter 7 for a discussion concerning whether the name should be Pheidippides or Philippides.
335. Plutarch, *Moralia*, 347 E.
336. Frost, *Politics*, 195.
337. Ibid., 193.
338. Lacey, *First Clash*, 175–176.
339. Billows, 230–231.
340. Hdt. 16.115–6.116.
341. Plutarch, "Aristides," 5.5.
342. See Chapter 1.
343. Plutarch, "Aristides," 5.5; Plutarch, *Moralia*, 350 E; Krentz, *Battle of Marathon*, 165–166.
344. Macan, vol. 1, 372; Macan, vol. 2, 166–167; How and Wells, 113, 362.
345. Grote, 351–352.
346. Grundy, *The Great Persian War and Its Preliminaries,* 191–192.
347. Munro, "Marathon," 251–252.
348. Burn, *Persia*, 252; Hammond, "Campaign," 92–93; N.G.L. Hammond, *History of Greece* (Oxford: Clarendon Press, 1959), 216, note 2. Hammond says that he walked to Marathon over Mount Pentelicus in seven hours, and returned the same day in eight hours. He claims the battle started at 6 a.m. and the Athenians left between 9 and 10 a.m., as the shield signal could not have been later. They would have arrived at Phaleron between 6 and 7 p.m.
349. P. Green, 38.
350. Holland, 198.
351. Dusk appeared about 7:50 at that time of year.
352. Billows, 229–231.
353. Lacey, *First Clash*, 176.
354. Ibid., 186–187.
355. Lionel Casson, "Speed under Sail of Ancient Ships," *Transactions of the American Philological Association* 82 (1951): 137–143, 147–148. Even with the wind, Casson found one voyage with a speed of only 2.7 knots.
356. A. Trevo Hodge, "Marathon: The Persians' Voyage," *Transactions of the American Philological Association* 105 (1975): 156, note 4.
357. Ibid., 157–162.
358. Ibid., 164–166, 168.
359. A. Trevor Hodge, "Marathon to Phaleron," *Journal of Hellenic Studies* 95 (1975): 170–171.
360. Evans, "Herodotus and the Battle," 302.
361. Pritchett, "Marathon," 173. He writes that "accounts of the precipitous haste with which the victorious Athenians marched home in order to anticipate a Persian landing in the bay of Phaleron suggest the battle took place in the morning." Hammond, "Campaign," 210. Hammond writes, "If the march took eight or nine hours and the army reached Kynosarges in daylight, they started about 9 a.m. or 10 a.m.; for darkness fell soon after 6:30 p.m.... The shield signal was made before 9 a.m.... It follows that the battle started very close to dawn, i.e. very close to 5:30 a.m.
362. Holoka, 334–336.
363. Ibid., 337–338.
364. Ibid., 340–341.
365. See Chapter 3.
366. Holoka, 345–347. He adds that Napoleon's army averaged between 10 and 22 miles per day, and in the American Civil War, 2 mph was considered the top

rate. In World War I, troops were expected to march 12 to 15 miles in an eight-hour day, and he says current British and American military manuals recommend rates of 1.5 mph cross country.

367. Ibid., 348.
368. Krentz, *Battle of Marathon*, 164–165.
369. Plutarch, "Aristides," 5.5.
370. Krentz, *Battle of Marathon*, 169.
371. Ibid., 169.
372. Pausanius 32.3.
373. Grote, 358; Hammond, "Marathon," 513.
374. Van der Veer, 1; Eugene Vanderpool, "A Monument to the Battle of Marathon," *Hesperia: The Journal of the American School of Classical Studies at Athens* 35, no. 2 (April–June 1966): 101; Krentz, *Battle of Marathon*, 125.
375. Krentz, *Battle of Marathon*, 170–171.
376. Van der Veer, 301–302.
377. Pausanias 32.4.
378. Vanderpool, "Monument," 96–101; See Krentz, "How Did the Battle Go Down?," for a picture of Krentz standing next to a replica of the white marble trophy now standing at Marathon.
379. Krentz, *Battle of Marathon*, 171.
380. Grundy, *The Great Persian War and Its Preliminaries*, 193.
381. Grundy, *The Great Persian War and Its Preliminaries*, 193; Hammond, "Marathon," 514; Krentz, *Battle of Marathon*, 210.
382. Lacey, *First Clash*, 162–163, 176, 185. He implies that Callimachus had led the Athenian army to victories over the Thebans Chalcidians and the Aeginetans and claims that the Athenians would have turned to him when the Persians landed at Marathon. He also credits Callimachus with being "a first rate commander" who was willing to take advice from Miltiades, who had some experience in dealing with the Persians.
383. How, "Arms, Tactics," 1–2.
384. Tuplin, "All the King's Horse," 181.
385. Krentz, *Battle of Marathon*, 159; Shrimpton, 36; Ray, 69; Gaebel, 69.
386. Gabriel and Metz, *From Sumer*, 70–73. They add some interesting statistics stating that at 250 yards an experienced archer using a composite bow similar to that used by the Persians was able to place 100 percent of his shots within a 50- to 20-yard target box while a person firing 200 rounds from an 18th-century musket could only hit within the box 16 percent of the time.
387. Blyth, 43, 63, 112 table 4.7, 195.
388. Gabriel and Metz, *From Sumer*, 63 table 3.2.
389. Christopher Matthew, "Testing Herodotus: Using Re-Creation to Understand the Battle of Marathon," *Ancient Warfare* 5, no. 4 (2009): 44.

390. Lacey, *First Clash*, 134; Rawlinson, 173–177; Blyth, 128; Ferrill, 101; P. Green, 36; Matthew, "Testing," 46.
391. Edward Shepherd Creasy, *Decisive Battles of the World* (New York: D. Appleton, 1898), 29.
392. Hammond, "Marathon," 515.
393. P. Green, 36.
394. Lazenby, *Defence*, 79.
395. Krentz, *Battle of Marathon*, 169–17.

Chapter 8

1. Edward Shepherd Creasy, *Decisive Battles of the World* (New York: D. Appleton, 1898), 29.
2. Pierre Briant, *From Cyrus to Alexander: A History of The Persian People* (Winona, IN, Eisenbrauns, 2002), 160.
3. Hdt. 7.22–7.24, 7.37; J.M. Cook, "Early Greek Land Warfare as Symbolic Expression," *Past and Present* 119 (May 1988): 99–100; See B.S.J. Isserlin et al., "The Canal of Xerxes: Summary of Investigation 1991–2001," *Annual of the British School at Athens* 98 (2003): 381. The excavations have convinced Isserlin that the canal "was indeed a canal across the whole isthmus."
4. Grundy, 194; George Grote, *Greece*, vol. 4 (New York: Peter Fenelon Collier and Son, 1900), 355; W.W. How and J. Wells, *A Commentary on Herodotus* (Oxford: Clarendon Press, 1912), 362; Jim Lacey, *The First Clash: The Miraculous Greek Victory at Marathon and Its Impact on Western Civilization* (New York: Bantam, 2011), 188–189.
5. Grote, 356.
6. Tom Holland, *Persian Fire: The First World Empire and the Fall of the West* (New York: Anchor, 2007), 201.
7. Richard A. Billows, *Marathon: How One Battle Changed Western Civilization* (New York: Overlook Duckworth, 2010), 235; Peter Green, *The Greco-Persian Wars* (Los Angeles: University of California Press, 1996), 39.
8. Billows, 235, 248; How and Wells, vol. 2, 363; Macan, *Fourth, Fifth and Sixth Books*, vol. 2, 247.
9. Macan, vol. 2, 247. A. R. Burn, *Persia and the Greeks: The Defence of the West, c. 546–478 BC*, 2nd ed. (Stanford: Stanford University Press, 1984), 256, compares Athens' victory at Marathon to England's victory over the Spanish Armada.
10. Fred Eugene Ray, *The Land Battles in 5th Century BC Greece: A History and Analysis of 173 Engagements* (Jefferson, NC: McFarland, 2009), 68.
11. Lacey, *First Clash*, 189–190.
12. Billows, 261.

Bibliography

Adcock, F.E. *The Greek and Macedonian Art of War*. Los Angeles: University of California Press, 1962.

Ahlberg-Cornell, Gudron. *Fighting on Land and Sea in Greek Geometric Art*. Stockholm: Svenska Institutet I Athens, 1971.

Anderson, J.K. "Hoplites and Heresies: A Note." *Journal of Hellenic Studies* 104 (1984): 152.

_____. "Hoplite Weapons and Offensive Arms." In *Hoplites: The Classical Greek Battle Experience*, ed. Victor Davis Hanson. New York: Routledge, 1991.

_____. *Military Theory and Practice in the Age of Xenophon*. Los Angeles: University of California Press, 1970.

Andrews, A.A. *The Greek Tyrants*. New York: Harper Torchbooks, 1963.

Anglim, Simon, Phyllis G. Justice, Rob S. Rice, Scott M. Rusch, and John Serrati. *Fighting Techniques in the Ancient World: 3000 BCE to AD 500*. New York: St. Martin's, 2001.

Aristotle's Constitution of Athens and Related Texts. Trans. Kurt von Fritz and Ernst Kapp. New York: Hafner, 1950.

Armayor, O. Kimball. "Catalogues of the Persian Empire in the Light of the Monuments and the Greek Literary Tradition." *Transactions of the American Philological Association* 108 (1978): 1–9.

_____. "Did Herodotus Ever Go to the Black Sea?" *Harvard Studies in Classical Philology* 82 (1978): 45–62.

_____. *Herodotus' Autopsy of the Fayoum: Lake Moeris and the Labyrinth of Egypt*. Amsterdam: Gieben, 1985.

_____. *Herodotus' Great Army and Satrapy Lists of the Persian Empire*. Amsterdam: Gieben, 1986.

Asheri, David, Alan Lloyd, and Aldo Corcella. *A Commentary on Herodotus Books I–IV*. Trans. Barbara Graziosi, Matteo Rosetti, Carletta Dus, and Venessa Cazzato. Oxford: Oxford University Press, 2007.

Atkinson, D., and L. Morgan. "The Willingborough and Nijmegan Marches." In *Roman Military Equipment: The Accoutrements of War. Proceedings of the Third Roman Military Equipment Research Seminar*, ed. M. Dawson. Oxford: BAR International Series, 1987.

Austin, Michel, Jill Harries, and Christopher Smith. *Modus Operandi: Essays in Honor of Geoffrey Rickman*. London: Institute of Classical Studies, 1998.

Avery, Harry C. "Herodotus 6.112.2." *Transactions and Proceedings of the American Philological Association* 103 (1972): 15–22.

_____. "The Number of Persian Dead at Marathon." *Historia: Zeitschrift fur Alte Geschichte* 22, no. 4 (4th Qtr., 1973): 757.

Badian, E. "The Name of the Runner." *American Journal of Ancient History* 4 (1979): 163–166.

Baker, Franklin T., ed. *Browning's Shorter Poems*. 4th ed. New York: Macmillan, 1917.

Bakker, Egbert J., Hans Van Wees, and Irene J.F. de Jong. *Brill's Companion to Herodotus*. Leiden: Brill, 2002.

Balcer, Jack Martin. "The Persian Wars against Greece: A Reassessment." *Historia: Zeitschrift fur Alte Geschichte* 38, no. 2 (2nd Qtr., 1989): 127–143.

Baldwin, Barry. "How Credulous Was Herodotus?" *Greece and Rome* 11, no. 2 (October 1964), 166–177.

Bardunias, Paul. "The Aspis: Surviving Hoplite Battle." *Ancient Warfare* 1, no. 3 (October–November 2007): 11–14.

_____. "Storm of Spears and Press of Shields." *Ancient Warfare, Special Issue 2011: The Battle of Marathon*, 60–68.

Barrett, Anthony A., and Michael Vickers. "The Oxford Brygos Cup Reconsidered." *Journal of Hellenic Studies* 98 (1978), 17–24.

Bedford, Peter. "The Persian Near East." In *The Cambridge Economic History of the Greco-Roman World*, ed. Walter Scheidel, Ian Morris, and Richard P Saller. Cambridge: Cambridge University Press, 2007.

Bekker-Nielson, Tonnes, and Lise Hannestad, ed. *War as a Cultural and Social Force: Essays on Warfare in Antiquity*. Copenhagen: Det Kongelige Danske Videnskabernes Selskab, 2001.

Bergman, C.A., and McEwen, E. "Experimental Archery: Projectile Velocities & Comparison of Bow Performances." *Antiquity* 62 (1988): 658–670.

Berthold, R.M. "Which Way to Marathon?" *Revue des etudes anciennes* 78/79 (1976–1977): 84–94.

Bertosa, Brian. "The Supply of Hoplite Equipment by the Athenian State down to the Samian War." *Journal of Military History* 67, no. 2 (April 2003): 361–379.

Bigwood, J.M. "Ctesias as Historian of Persian Wars." *Phoenix* 32, no. 1 (Spring 1978): 19–41.

Billows, Richard A. *Marathon: How One Battle Changed Western Civilization.* New York: Overlook Duckworth, 2010.

Blamire, A. "Herodotus and Histiaeus." *Classical Quarterly*, new series, 9, no. 2 (November 1959): 142–154.

Blyth, P.H. "The Effectiveness of Greek Armour against Persian Arrows during the Persian Wars, 490–479." PhD diss., University of Reading, 1977.

Boardman, John, N.G.L. Hammond, D.M. Lewis, and M. Ostwald, ed. *The Cambridge Ancient History.* Vol. 4, *Persia, Greece and the Western Mediterranean.* Cambridge: Cambridge University Press, 1988.

Bowden, Hugh. Review of *Herodotus and His Sources: Citation, Invention and Narrative Art*, by D. Fehling. *Journal of Hellenic Studies* 112 (1992): 182–184.

———. Review of *The Liar School of Herodotus*, by W. Kendrick Pritchett. *Classical Review*, new series, 45, no. 1 (1995): 15–17.

Briant, Pierre. "The Achaemenid Empire." In *Warfare and Society in the Ancient and Medieval Worlds: Asia, Mediterranean, Europe and Mesoamerica*, ed. Kurt Raaflaub, and Nathan Rosenstein. Washington, DC: Center for Hellenic Studies Trustees for Howard University, 1999.

———. *From Cyrus to Alexander: A History of the Persian Empire.* Trans. Peter Daniels. Winona Lakes, IN: Eisenbrauns, 2002.

Bridges, Emma, Edith Hall, and P.J. Rhodes, eds. *Cultural Responses to the Persian Wars: Antiquity to the Third Millennium.* Oxford: Oxford University Press, 2007.

Bugh, Glenn Richard. *The Horsemen of Athens.* Princeton, NJ: Princeton University Press, 1988.

Burford, A. "Heavy Transport in Classical Antiquity." *Economic History Review*, new series, 13, no. 1 (1960): 1–18.

Burke, Edmund. "The Greeks at War in the Fifth & Fourth Centuries BCE." *Military Affairs* 42, no. 3 (October 1978): 142–143.

Burn, A.R. "Hammond on Marathon: A Few Notes." *Journal of Hellenic Studies* 89 (1969): 118–120.

———. *Persia and the Greeks: The Defence of the West, c. 546–478 BC* 2nd ed. Stanford, CA: Stanford University Press, 1984.

Bury, J.B. *The Ancient Greek Historians.* New York: Dover, 1958.

———. *A History of Greece.* New York: Modern Library, 1913.

———. "The Battle of Marathon." *Classical Review* 10 (1896): 95–98.

Bury, J.B., and Russell Meiggs. *A History of Greece to the Death of Alexander the Great.* 4th ed. New York: St. Martin's, 1975.

Camp, John. "A Spear Butt from the Lesbians." *Hesperia: The Journal of the American School of Classical Studies* 47, no. 2 (April–June 1978): 192–195.

Campbell, Duncan. "Meanwhile in Sparta." *Ancient Warfare, Special Issue 2011: The Battle of Marathon*, 49–52.

Cartledge, Paul. "Hoplites and Heroes: Sparta's Contribution to the Technique of Ancient Warfare." *Journal of Hellenic Studies* 97 (1977): 11–27.

Cary, M. *The Geographic Background of Greek and Roman History.* Westport, CT: Greenwood Press, 1949.

Caspari, M.O.B. "Stray Notes on the Persian Wars." *Journal of Hellenic Studies* 31 (1911): 100–109.

Cassin-Scott, Jack. *The Greek and Persian Wars, 500–323 BCE.* London: Osprey Publishing, 1977.

Casson, Lionel. *Ships and Seamanship in the Ancient World.* Princeton, NJ: Princeton University Press, 1971.

———. "Speed under Sail of Ancient Ships." *Transactions and Proceedings of the American Philological Association* 82 (1951): 136–148.

Casson, S. "Cornelius Nepos: Some Further Notes." *Journal of Hellenic Studies* 40, pt. 1 (1920): 43–46.

Cawkwell, George. *The Greek Wars: The Failure of Persia.* Oxford: Oxford University Press, 2004.

———. "Orthodoxy and Hoplites." *Classical Quarterly* 39, no. 2 (1989): 375–389.

Chapman, G.A.H. "Herodotus and Histiaeus' Role in the Ionian Revolt." *Historia: Zeitschrift fur Alte Geschichte* 21, no. 4 (4th Qtr., 1972): 546–568.

Clark, Michael. "Did Thucydides Invent the Battle Exhortation?" *Historia: Zeitschrift fur Alte Geschichte* 44, no. 3 (3rd Qtr., 1995): 375–376.

Coates, J.F. "Carrying Troops in Triremes." In *The Trireme Project: Operational Experience, 1987–1990*, ed. J.T. Shaw. Oxford: Oxbow Books, 1993.

Connolly, Peter. *Greece and Rome at War.* London: Greenhill Books, 1998.

Connor, W.R. "Early Greek Land Warfare as Symbolic Expression." *Past and Present* 119 (May 1988): 3–29.

Cook, J.M. *The Persian Empire.* New York: Schocken Books, 1983.

Corvisier, Andre, and John Childs. *A Dictionary of Military History and the Art of War.* Cambridge: Blackwell, 1994.

Creasy, Edward Shepherd. *Decisive Battles of the World.* New York: D. Appleton, 1898.

Curtius, J. *Ancient Persia.* London: British Museum Press, 2000.

Dawson, Doyne. *The Origins of Western Warfare:*

Militarism, and Morality in the Ancient World. Boulder, CO: Westview, 1996.

Dawson, M., ed. *Roman Military Equipment and Accoutrements of War: Proceedings of the Third Roman Military Equipment Research Seminar.* Oxford: BAR International Series, 1987.

De Selincourt, Aubrey. *The World of Herodotus.* Boston: Little, Brown, 1962.

De Souza, Phillip. *The Greek and Persian Wars.* Oxford: Osprey Publishing, 2003.

Delbruck, Hans. *History of the Art of War.* Vol. 1, *Warfare in Antiquity.* Trans. Walter J. Renfroe. Lincoln: University of Nebraska Press, 1990.

Den Boeft, J., and A.H.M. Kessels, eds. *Studies in Honor of H.L.W. Nelson.* Utrecht: Instituut voor Klassieke Talen, 1982.

Dewald, Carolyn, and John Marincola. *The Cambridge Companion to Herodotus.* Cambridge University Press, 2006.

Dickins, Guy. "The Growth of Spartan Policy." *Journal of Hellenic Studies* 32 (1912): 1–42.

Diodorus. *The Persian Wars to the Fall of Athens.* Trans. Peter Green. Austin: University of Texas Press, 2010.

Doenges, Norman A. "The Campaign and Battle of Marathon." *Historia: Zeitschrift fur Alte Geschichte* 47, no. 1 (1998): 1–17.

Donlan, W., and J. Thompson. "The Charge at Marathon: Herodotus 6.112." *Classical Journal* 71 (1976): 339–343.

_____. "The Charge at Marathon Again." *Classical World* 72, no. 7 (April–May, 1979): 419–420.

Dougherty, Martin J. *Warriors of the World: The Ancient Warrior.* New York: Thomas Dunne Books, 2010.

Drews, Robert. *The Greek Accounts of Eastern History.* Cambridge: Harvard University Press, 1973.

Du Picq, Ardant. *Battle Studies: Ancient and Modern Battles.* New York: Macmillan, 1921.

Ducrey, Pierre. *Warfare in Ancient Greece.* New York: Schocken Books, 1985.

Eckstein, Arthur M. "Persia and the Greeks: Failure of an Empire." *International History Review* 87, no. 4 (December 2005): 807–812.

Engels, Donald W. *Alexander the Great and the Logistics of the Macedonian Army.* Los Angeles: University of California Press, 1978.

Epps, Preston H. "Fear in Spartan Character." *Classical Philology* 28, no. 1 (January 1933): 12–29.

Evans, J.A.S. *The Beginnings of History: Herodotus and the Persian Wars.* Campbellville, ON: Edgar Kent, 2006.

_____. "Cavalry about the Time of the Persian Wars: A Speculative Essay." *Classical Journal* 82, no. 2 (December 1986–January 1987): 97–106.

_____. "Herodotus and the Battle of Marathon." *Historia: Zeitschrift fur Alte Geschichte* 42, no. 3 (1993): 279–307.

_____. "Herodotus and the Ionian Revolt." *Historia: Zeitschrift fur Alte Geschichte* 25, no. 1 (1st Qtr., 1976): 31–37.

_____. "Histiaeus and Aristagoras: Notes on the Ionian Revolt." *American Journal of Philology* 84, no. 2 (April 1963): 113–128.

_____. "The Settlement of Artaphernes." *Classical Philology* 71, no. 4 (October 1976): 344–348.

_____. "What Happened to Croesus?" *Classical Journal* 74, no. 1 (October–November 1978): 34–40.

Everson, Tim. *Warfare in Ancient Greece: Arms and Armour from the Heroes of Homer to Alexander the Great.* Stroud, UK: Sutton Publishing, 2004.

Farrokh, Kaveh. *Shadows in the Desert: Ancient Persia at War.* New York: Osprey Publishing, 2007.

Fehling, Detlev. *Herodotus and His "Sources": Citation, Invention and Narrative Art.* Leeds: Francis Cairns, 1990.

Ferrill, Arther. "Herodotus and the Strategy and Tactics of the Invasion of Xerxes." *American Historical Review* 72 (1966): 102–115.

_____. *The Origins of War from the Stone Age to Alexander the Great.* New York: Thames and Hudson, 1985.

Fields, Nic. *Ancient Greek Fortifications, 500–300 BCE.* New York: Osprey Publishing, 2006.

Figueira, Thomas J. *Athens and Aigina in the Age of Imperial Colonialism.* Baltimore, MD: Johns Hopkins University Press, 1991.

_____. "Khalkis and Marathon." In *Marathon: The Battle and the Ancient Deme,* ed. Kostas Buraselis-Katerina Meidani. Athens: Instutut Du Livre-A Kardamitsa, 2010.

Finley, M.I. "The Fifth Century Athenian Empire: A Balance Sheet." In *Imperialism in the Ancient World,* ed. Peter Garnsey and C.R. Whittaker. New York: Cambridge University Press, 1978.

Flower, Michael. "Herodotus and Persai." In *The Cambridge Companion to Herodotus,* ed. Carolyn Dewald and John Marincola. Cambridge: Cambridge University Press, 2006.

Forrest, W.G. "Herodotus and Athens." *Phoenix* 38, no. 1 (Spring 1984): 1–11.

_____. "Motivation in Herodotus: The Case of the Ionian Revolt." *International History Review* 1, no. 3 (July 1979): 311–322.

Fowler, Robert L. "Herodotus and His Contemporaries." *Journal of Hellenic Studies* 116 (1996): 62–87.

Francis, E.D., and Michael Vickers. "The Oenoe in the Stoa Poikile and Herodotus' Account of Marathon." *Annual of the British School of Athens* 80 (1985): 99–113.

Fraser, A.D. "The Myth of the Phalanx Scrimmage." *Classical Weekly* 36, no. 2 (October 12, 1942): 15–16.

French, A. "Topical Influences in Herodotus." *Mnemosyne*, 4th series, 25 (1972): 9–27.

Frost, Frank T. "The Athenian Military before Cleisthenes." *Historia: Zeitschrift für Alte Geshichte* 33 (3rd Qtr., 1984): 283–294.

_____. *Politics and Athenians: Essays on Athenian History and Historiography.* Toronto: Edgar Kent, 2003.

Gabriel, Richard A. *The Great Armies of Antiquity.* Westport, CT: Praeger, 2002.

_____. *Man and Wound in the Ancient World: A History of Military Medicine from Sumer to the Fall of Constantinople.* Washington, DC: Potomac Books, 2012.

_____. *No More Heroes: Madness and Psychiatry in War.* New York: Hill and Wang, 1987.

Gabriel, Richard A., and Karen S. Metz. *From Sumer to Rome: The Military Capabilities of Ancient Armies.* New York: Greenwood Press, 1991.

_____. *A History of Military Medicine from Ancient Times to the Middle Ages.* New York: Greenwood Press, 1992.

Gabriel, Richard A., and Donald W. Boose. *The Great Battles of Antiquity: A Strategic and Tactical Guide to Great Battles that Shaped the Development of War.* Westport, CT: Greenwood Press, 1994.

Gabrielson, Vincent. "Naval Warfare: Its Economic and Social Impact on Greek Cities." In *War as a Cultural and Social Force: Essays on Warfare in Antiquity*, ed. Tonnes Bekker-Nielson. Copenhagen: Det Kongelige Danske Videnskabernes Selskab, 2001.

Gaebel, Robert. *Cavalry Operations in the Ancient Greek World.* Norman: University of Oklahoma Press, 2004.

Gallant, Thomas W. *Risk and Survival in Ancient Greece.* Stanford, CA: Stanford University Press, 1991.

Georges, Pericles B. *Barbarian Asia and the Greek Experience from the Archaic Period to the Period of Xenophon.* Baltimore, MD: Johns Hopkins University Press, 1994.

_____. "Persian Ionia under Darius: The Revolt Reconsidered." *Historia: Zeitschrift für Alte Geschichte* 49 (1st Qtr., 2000): 1–39.

Gershevitch, Ily, ed. *The Cambridge History of Iran.* Vol. 2, *Median and Achaemenid Periods.* Cambridge: Cambridge University Press, 1985.

Gillis, Daniel. *Collaboration with the Persians.* Wiesbaden: Franz Steiner Verlag GMBH, 1979.

Goldhill, Simon. "Battle Narrative and Politics in Aeschylus' Persae." *Journal of Hellenic Studies* 108 (1988): 189–193.

Goldsworthy, Adrian K. "The Othismos, Myths and Heresies: The Nature of Hoplite Battle." *War in History* 4 (1997): 1–26.

Gomme, A.W. "Herodotus and Marathon." *Phoenix* 6, no. 3 (Autumn 1952): 77–83.

_____. *The Population of Athens in the Fifth and Fourth Centuries BCE.* Chicago: Argonaut, 1967.

Goodman, M.D., and A.J. Holladay. "Religious Scruples in Ancient Warfare." *Classical Quarterly* 36 (1986): 151–171.

Graf, David Frank. "Medism: Greek Collaboration with Achaemenid Persia." PhD diss., University of Michigan, 1979.

Graf, David F., et al. "Persia at the Crest." In *A Soaring Spirit Time Frame, 600–400 BCE.* Alexandria, VA: Time-Life Books, 1987.

Grant, John R. "Leonidas' Last Stand." *Phoenix* 15, no. 1 (Spring 1961): 14–27.

Grant, Michael, *A Guide to the Ancient World: A Dictionary of Classical Place Names.* New York: Barnes and Noble, 1986.

Gray, G. B., and M. Cary, "The Ionian Revolt." In *The Cambridge Ancient History*, vol. 4, ed. J.B. Bury, F.E. Adcock, and S.A. Cook. Cambridge: Cambridge University Press, 1960.

Green, J.R., and R.K. Sinclair. "Athenians in Eretria." *Historia: Zeitschrift für Alte Geschichte* 19, no. 5 (December 1970): 515–527.

Green, Peter. *The Greco-Persian Wars.* Los Angeles: University of California Press, 1996.

Griffiths, W.B. "Re-enactment as Research: Towards a Set of Guidelines for Re-enactors and Academics." *Journal of Roman Military Equipment Studies* 11 (2000): 135–138.

Grossman, Dave. *On Combat: The Psychology and Physiology of Deadly Combat in War and Peace.* Milstadt, IL: Warrior Science Publication, 2004.

Grote, George. *Greece.* Vol. 4. New York: Peter Fenelon Collier and Son, 1900.

Grundy, G.B. *The Great Persian War and Its Preliminaries: A Study of the Evidence, Literary and the Topographical.* New York: Scribner, 1901.

_____. *Thucydides and the History of His Age.* Oxford: Basil Blackwell, 1948.

Haas, Christopher J. "Athenian Naval Power before Themistocles." *Historia: Zeitschrift für Alte Geschichte* 34 (1st Qtr., 1985): 29–46.

Hackett, General Sir John, ed. *Warfare in the Ancient World.* New York: Facts on File, 1990.

Haines, Tim, Graham Sumner, and John Naylor. "Recreating the World of the Roman Soldier: The Work of the Ermin Street Guard." *Journal of Roman Military Equipment Studies* 11 (2000): 119–127.

Hale, John. *Lords of the Sea.* New York: Penguin, 2009.

Hammond, N.G.L. "The Campaign and Battle of Marathon." *Journal of Hellenic Studies* 88 (1968): 13–57.

_____. "Casualties and Reinforcement of Citizen Soldiers in Greece and Macedonia." *Journal of Hellenic Studies*, 109 (1989): 56–68.

_____. "The Expedition of Datis and Artaphernes."

In *The Cambridge Ancient History*, vol. 4, *Persia, Greece and the Western Mediterranean, c. 525–479 BCE*, 2nd ed., ed. John Boardman, N.G.L. Hammond, D.M. Lewis, and M. Ostwald. Cambridge: Cambridge University Press, 1988.

———. *History of Greece*. Oxford: Clarendon Press, 1959.

———. *Studies in Greek History*. New York: Oxford at the Clarendon Press, 1973.

Hansen, Mogens Herman. "The Battlefield Exhortation in Ancient Historiography: Fact or Fiction?" *Historia: Zeitschrift für Alte Geschichte* 42, no. 2 (1993): 161–180.

Hanson, Victor Davis. *Carnage and Culture: Landmark Battles in the Rise to Western Power*. New York: Anchor Books, 2001.

———. "Hoplite Technology in Phalanx Battle." In *Hoplites: The Classical Greek Battle Experience*, ed. Victor Davis Hanson. New York: Routledge, 1991.

———, ed. *Hoplites: The Classical Greek Battle Experience*. New York: Routledge, 1991.

———. *The Other Greeks: The Family Farm and the Agrarian Roots of Western Civilization*. Los Angeles: University of California Press, 1999.

———. Review of *The Greek State at War Part V*, by W. Kendrick Pritchett. *Classical Philology* 87, no. 3 (July 1992): 250–258.

———. "The Status of Ancient Military History: Traditional Work, Recent Research and On-Going Controversies." *Journal of Military History* 63, no. 2 (April 1999): 379–413.

———. *Warfare and Agriculture in Classical Greece*. Los Angeles: University of California Press, 1998.

———. *Wars of the Ancient Greeks*. Washington, DC: Smithsonian Books, 2004.

———. *The Western Way of War: Infantry Battle in Classical Greece*. New York: Oxford University Press, 1989.

Harris, George. *Ionia under Pericles, 547–477 BCE: A Political History*. PhD diss., Northwestern University, 1971.

Harrison, C.M. "Triremes at Rest: On the Beach or in the Water." *Journal of Hellenic Studies* 119 (1999): 168–171.

Harrison, Evelyn B. "The South Frieze of the Nike Temple and the Marathon Painting in the Painted Stoa." *American Journal of Archaeology* 76, no. 4 (October 1972): 353–378.

Hartog, F. *The Mirror of Herodotus: An Essay in the Interpretation of the Other*. Los Angeles: University of California Press, 1988.

Head, Duncan. *The Achaemenid Persian Army*. Stockport: Montvert Publications, 1992.

Henkelman, Wouter, and Amelie Kuhrt, eds. *A Persian Perspective: Essays in Memory of Heleen Sancisi-Weerderburg*. Leiden: Nederlands Instituut voor het Nabije Oosten, 2003.

Herman, Gabriel. *Ritualized Friendship and the Greek City*. New York: Cambridge University Press, 1987.

Hignett, C. *Xerxes' Invasion of Greece*. Oxford: Clarendon Press, 1963.

Hodge, A. Trevor. "Marathon: The Persians' Voyage." *Transactions of the American Philological Association* 105 (1975): 155–173.

Hodge, A. Trevor. "Marathon to Phaleron." *Journal of Hellenic Studies* 95 (1975): 169–171.

Hodge, A. Trevor. "Reflections on the Shield at Marathon." *Annual of the British School at Athens* 96 (2001): 237–259.

Hodge, A. Trevor, and Luis A. Losada. "The Time of the Shield Signal at Marathon." *American Journal of Archaeology* 74, no. 1 (January 1970): 31–36.

Holladay, A.J. "Hoplites and Heresies." *Journal of Hellenic Studies* 102 (1982): 94–103.

Holladay, James. "Medism in Athens, 508–480 BCE" *Greece and Rome*, 2nd series, 25, no. 2 (October 1978), 174–191.

Holland, Tom. *Persian Fire: The First World Empire and the Fall of the West*. New York: Anchor, 2007.

Holoka, James P. "Marathon and the Myth of the Same-Day March." *Greek and Byzantine Studies* 38, no. 4 (Winter 1997): 329–353.

Hornblower, S. "Greeks and Persians. West against East." In *War, Peace and World Orders in European History*, ed. B. Heuser. New York: Routledge, 2001.

How, W.W. "Arms, Tactics & Strategy in the Persian Wars." *Journal of Hellenic Studies* 43, pt. 2 (1923): 117–132.

———. "Cornelius Nepos on Marathon and Paros." *Journal of Hellenic Studies* 39 (1919): 48–59.

———. "On the Meaning of ΒΑΔΗΝ and ΔΡΟΜΩΙ in Greek Historians of the Fifth Century." *Classical Quarterly* 13, no. 1 (January 1919): 40–42.

How, W. W., and J. Wells. *A Commentary on Herodotus*. 2 vols. Oxford: Clarendon Press, 1912.

Hudson, Harris Gary. "The Shield Signal at Marathon." *American Historical Review* 42, no. 3 (April 1937): 443–459.

Hughes, Christopher P. *War on Two Fronts: An Infantry Commander's War in Iraq and the Pentagon*. Philadelphia: Casemet, 2007.

Hunt, Peter. "Military Forces." In *The Cambridge History of Greek and Roman Warfare*, ed. Phillip Sabin, Hans van Wees, and Michael Whitby. Cambridge: Cambridge University Press, 2007.

———. *Slaves, Warfare, and Ideology in the Greek Historians*. Cambridge: Cambridge University Press, 1998.

Hyland, Ann. *The Horse in the Ancient World*. Westport, CT: Praeger, 2003.

Isserlin, Bruce, R.E. Jones, V. Karastathis, S.P. Papamarinopoulos, G.E. Syrides, and J. Uren. "The Canal of Xerxes: Summary of the Investigation 1991-2001." *Annual of the British School at Athens* 98 (2003): 369-385.

Jackson, A.H. "Hoplites and the Gods: The Dedication of Captured Arms and Armour." In *Hoplites: The Classical Greek Battle Experience*, ed. Victor Davis Hanson. New York: Routledge, 1991.

Jameson, M.H. "The Provisions for Mobilization in the Decree of Themistocles." *Historia: Zeitschrift fur Alte Geschichte* 12 (1963): 385-404.

Jameson, Michael. "Sacrifice before Battles." In *Hoplites: The Classical Greek Battle Experience*, ed. Victor Davis Hanson. New York: Routledge, 1991.

Jarva, Eero. *Archaelogia on Archaic Greek Body Armour*. Rovanie mi: Pohjois-Soumen Societas Historica Septentrionaliis, 1995.

Jeffery, L.H. "Comments on Some Greek Inscriptions." *Journal of Hellenic Studies* 69 (1949): 25-38.

Jeskins, Patricia. *The Environment and the Classical World*. London: Bristol Classical Press, 1998.

Kagan, Kimberly. *The Eye of Command*. Ann Arbor: University of Michigan Press, 2006.

Keaveney, Arthur. "The Attack on Naxos: A Forgotten Cause of the Ionian Revolt." *The Classical Quarterly*, new series, 38, no. 1 (1988): 76-81.

Keen, Antony Graham. Review of *Ships and Sea-Power before the Great Persian Wars*, by H.T. Wallinga. *Scholia Reviews* 3 (1994): 5.

Khorasani, Marouchyehr Moshtagh. *Arms and Armor from Iran: The Bronze Age to the End of the Qajar Period*. Tubingen: Legat-Verlag, 2006.

Kuhrt, Amelie. *The Ancient Near East, 300-350 BCE*. 2 vols. London: Routledge, 1997.

_____. *The Persian Empire: A Corpus of Sources from the Achaemenid Period*. London: Routledge, 2007.

Krentz, Peter. "The Nature of Hoplite Battle." *Classical Antiquity* 4, no. 1 (April 1985): 50-61.

Krentz, Peter. *The Battle of Marathon*. New Haven, CT: Yale University Press, 2010.

_____. "Casualties in Hoplite Battles." *Greek, Roman and Byzantine Studies* 26 (1985): 13-20.

_____. "Continuing the *Othismos* on *Othismos*." *Ancient History Bulletin* 8 (1994): 45-49.

_____. "Fighting by the Rules: The Invention of the Hoplite Agon." *Hesperia: The Journal of the American School of Classical Studies at Athens* 71, no. 1 (January-March 2002): 23-39.

_____, "How Did the Battle Go Down?" *Ancient History, Special Issue 2011: Battle of Marathon*, 34-35.

_____. "The Salpinx in Greek Battle." In *Hoplites: The Greek Classical Battle Experience*, ed. Victor Davis Hanson. New York: Routledge, 1991.

_____. "War." In *The Cambridge History of Greek and Roman Warfare*, ed. Phillip Sabin, Hans van Wees, and Michael Whitby. Cambridge: Cambridge University Press, 2007.

Lacey, Jim. *The First Clash: The Miraculous Greek Victory at Marathon and Its Impact on Western Civilization*. New York: Bantam, 2011.

_____. "The Persian Fallacy." *Military History* 29, no. 2 (July 2012): 42-51.

Lang, Mabel. "Herodotus and the Ionian Revolt." *Historia: Zeitschrift fur Alte Geschichte* 17, no. 1 (January 1986): 24-36.

Larsen, Jakob A.O. "Sparta and the Ionian Revolt: A Study of Spartan Foreign Policy and the Genesis of the Peloponnesian League." *Classical Philology* 27, no. 2 (April 1932): 136-150.

Lateiner, Donald. "The Failure of the Ionian Revolt." *Historia: Zeitschrift fur Alte Geschichte* 9, no. 3 (August 1987): 438-455.

_____. Review of *Herodotus and His Sources: Citation, Invention and Narrative Art*, by Detlev Fehling. *Classical World* 84 (September-October 1990): 75-76.

Lazenby, J.F. *The Defence of Greece, 490-479*. Warminster: Aris and Phillips, 1993.

_____. "The *Diekplous*." *Greece and Rome* 34, no. 2 (October 1987): 169-177.

_____. "Essays and Reflections: Naval Warfare in the Ancient World: Myths and Realities." *International History Review* 9, no. 3 (August 1987): 438-455.

_____. "The Killing Zone." *Hoplites: The Greek Classical Battle Experience*, ed. Victor Davis Hanson. New York: Routledge, 1991.

_____. "The Strategy of the Greeks in the Opening Campaign in the Persian War." *Hermes* 92, no. 3 (1964): 264-284.

Lazenby, J.F., and David Whitehead. "The Myth of the Hoplite's Hoplon." *Classical Quarterly*, new series, 46, no. 1 (1996): 37-33.

Lewis, D.M. "Datis the Mede." *Journal of Hellenic Studies* 100 (1980): 194-195.

_____. "Persians in Herodotus." In *The Greek Historians, Literature and History: Papers Presented to A.E. Raubbitschek*. Stanford, CA: Stanford University Press, 1985.

Lloyd, Alan B., ed. *Battle in Antiquity*. London: Duckworth, 1996.

_____. "M. Basch on Triremes: Some Observations." *Journal of Hellenic Studies* 100 (1980): 195-198.

_____. *Marathon: The Crucial Battle That Created Western Democracy*. New York: Souvenir Press, 2004.

Lloyd, W. Watkiss. "The Battle of Marathon: 490 BC." *Journal of Hellenic Studies* 2 (1881): 388.

Loader, W.R. "Questions about Marathon." *Greece and Rome* 16, no. 46 (1947): 17-22.

_____. "Letter." *Greece and Rome* 16, no. 48 (October 1947): 134-136.

Lorimer, H.L. "The Hoplite Phalanx with Special Reference to the Poems of Archilochus & Tyrtaeus." *Annual of the British School at Athens* 42 (1947): 76–136.

Louraghi, N., ed. *The Historians Craft in the Age of Herodotus*. Oxford: Oxford University Press, 2001.

Luginbill, Robert D. "Othismos: The Importance of the Mass-Shove in Hoplite Warfare." *Phoenix* 48, no. 1 (Spring 1994): 51–61.

Macan, Reginald Walter. *Herodotus: The Fourth, Fifth and Sixth Books*. 2 vols. New York: Macmillan, 1895.

———. *Herodotus: The Seventh, Eighth and Ninth Books*. 2 vols. London: Macmillan, 1908.

Martin, Thomas. "Ancient Greek Units of Currency, Weight and Distance." In *The Landmark Herodotus*, ed. Robert B. Strassler. New York: Pantheon, 2007.

Manville, P.B. "Aristagoras and Histiaeus: The Leadership Struggle in the Ionian Revolt." *Classical Quarterly* 27, no. 1 (1977): 80–91.

Markle, Minor M. "The Macedonian Sarissa, Spear and Related Armor." *American Journal of Archaeology* 81, no. 3 (Summer 1977): 323–339.

Marshall, S.L.A. *Men against Fire*. Norman: Oklahoma University Press, 1947.

Matthew, Christopher. *A Storm of Spears: Understanding the Greek Hoplite at War*. Philadelphia: Casemet, 2012.

———. "Testing Herodotus: Using Re-creation to Understand the Battle of Marathon." *Ancient Warfare* 5, no. 4 (2011): 41–46.

———. "When Push Comes to Shove: What Was the Othismos of Hoplite Combat?" *Historia: Zeitschrift fur Alte Geschichte* 58, no. 4 (2009): 395–415.

Matthews, Victor J. "The 'Hemorodromoi': Ultra Long-Distance Running in Antiquity." *Classical World* 68, no. 3 (November 1974): 161–169.

Maurice, F. "The Campaign of Marathon." *Journal of Hellenic Studies* 52, pt. 1 (1932): 13–24.

———. "The Size of the Army of Xerxes in the Invasion of Greece 480 BCE." *Journal of Hellenic Studies* 50, pt. 2 (1930): 210–235.

McCullagh, C. Behan. "Bias in Historical Description, Interpretation and Explanation." *History and Theory* 39, no. 1 (February 2000): 39–66.

McGreer, Eric. *Sowing the Dragon's Teeth: Byzantine Warfare in the Tenth Century*. Washington, DC: Oaks Research Library and Collection, 1995.

McLeod, Wallace. "The Bowshot and Marathon." *Journal of Hellenic Studies* 90 (1970): 197–198.

———. "The Range of the Ancient Bow." *Phoenix* 19, no. 1 (Spring 1965): 1–14.

Mearsheimer, John J. "Assessing the Conventional Balance: The 3:1 Rule and Its Critics." *International Security* 13, no. 4 (Spring 1989): 54–89.

Meijer, F. *A History of Seafaring in the Classical World*. London: Palgrave Macmillan, 1986.

Milns, R.D. "Alexander's Pursuit of Darius through Iran." *Historia: Zeitschrift fur Alte Geschichte* 15, no. 2 (April 1966): 256.

Mitchell, B.M. "Herodotus and Samos." *Journal of Hellenic Studies* 5 (1975): 75–91.

Mitchell, Stephen. "Hoplite Warfare in Ancient Greece." In *Battle in Antiquity*, ed. Alan B. Lloyd. London: Duckworth, 1996.

Montagu, John Drago. *Greek and Roman Warfare: Battles, Tactics and Trickery*. London: Greenhill Books, 2006.

Morgan, Catherine. "Symbolic and Pragmatic Aspects of Warfare in the Greek World of the 8th to 6th Centuries BCE." In *War as a Cultural and Social Force: Essays on Warfare in Antiquity*, ed. Tonnes Bekker-Nielson and Lise Hannestad. Copenhagen: Det kongelige Danske Videnskabernes Selskab, 2001.

Morris, Ian. "Archaeology and Ancient Greek History." In *Current Issues and the Study of Ancient History*, ed. Stanley Burstein, Ian Morris, and Lawrence Trittle. Claremont: Regina Books, 2002.

Morris, Ian, and Walter Scheidel, ed. *The Dynamics of Ancient Empires: State Power from Assyria to Byzantium*. Oxford: Oxford University Press, 2009.

Morrison, J.S. Review of *Ships and Sea-Power before the Great Persian War: The Ancestry of the Ancient Trireme*, by H.T. Wallinga. *Journal of Hellenic Studies* 114 (1994): 206–208.

Morrison, J.S., and R.T. Williams. *Greek Oared Ships 900–322 BCE*. Cambridge: Cambridge University Press, 1969.

Muhly, J.D. Review of *The Greek Accounts of Eastern History*, by Robert Drews. *Journal of Near Eastern History* 35, no. 1 (January 1976): 41–43.

Munro, J.A.R. "Marathon." In *The Cambridge Ancient History*, vol. 4, *The Persian Empire and the West*, ed. J.B. Bury, S.A. Cook, and F.E. Adcock. Cambridge: Cambridge University Press, 1926.

———. "Some Observations on the Persian Wars." *Journal of Hellenic Studies* 19 (1899): 185–196.

———. "Some Observations on the Persian Wars (Continued)." *Journal of Hellenic Studies* 22 (1902): 294–332.

Murray, Oswyn. "Herodotus and Oral History." In *Achaemenid History II: The Greek Sources*, ed. Heleen Sancisi-Weerdenburg and Amelie Kuhrt. Leiden: Nederlands Instituut Voor Het Nabije Oosten, 1984.

———. "The Ionian Revolt." In *The Cambridge Ancient History*, vol. 4, ed. John Boardman, N.G.L. Hammond, D.M. Lewis, and M. Ostwald. New York: Cambridge University Press, 1988.

Myers, John L. *Geographical History in Greek Lands*. Westport, CT: Greenwood Press, 1953.

Neumann, C. "A Note on March Rates." *Historia:*

Zeitschrift fur Alte Geschichte 20, nos. 2/3 (2nd Qtr., 1971): 196–198.

Neville, J. "Was There an Ionian Revolt?" *Classical Quarterly*, new series, 29, no. 2 (1979): 268–275.

Notopoulos, James A. "The Slaves at the Battle of Marathon." *American Journal of Philology* 62, no. 3 (1941): 352–354.

Ober, Josiah. "Classical Greek Times." In *The Laws of War: Constraints on Warfare in Western Warfare*, ed. Michael Howard, George J. Andreopoulos, and Mark R. Shulman. New Haven, CT: Yale University Press, 195.

———. "Hoplites and Obstacles." In *Hoplites: The Greek Classical Battle Experience*, ed. Victor Davis Hanson. New York: Routledge, 1991.

———. "Edward Clark's Ancient Road to Marathon AD 1801." *Hesperia: The Journal of American Studies at Athens* 51, no. 4 (October–November 1982): 453–458.

Olmstead, A.T. *History of the Persian Empire*. Chicago: University of Chicago Press, 1948.

———. "Persia and the Greek Frontier Problem." *Classical Philology* 34, no. 4 (October 1939): 305–322.

Orlin, Louis C. "Athens and Persia, ca. 507 BCE: A Neglected Perspective." In *Michigan Oriental Studies in Honor of George C. Cameron*, ed. Louis Orlin. Ann Arbor: Dept. of Eastern Studies, University of Michigan, 1976.

Pavlopoulos, Kosmas, et al. "Palyrological Investigation of Holocene Palaeoenvironmental Changes in the Coastal Plain of Marathon (Attica, Greece)." *Geobios* 42 (2009): 43–51.

Payne, H.G.G. "Archaeology in Greece, 1933–34." *Journal of Hellenic Studies* 54, pt. 2 (1934): 185–200.

Plutarch. *De Malignitate Herodoti*. Trans. Anthony Bower. Warminster: Aris and Phillip, 1992.

Pritchett, W. Kendrick. *Essays in Greek History*. Amsterdam: J.C. Gieben, 1994.

———. *The Greek State at War, Part I*. Los Angeles: University of California Press, 1974.

———. *The Greek State at War, Part II*. Los Angeles: University of California Press, 1974.

———. *The Greek State at War, Part IV*. Berkley: University of California Press, 1985.

———. *The Greek State at War, Part V*. Los Angeles: University of California Press, 1991.

———. *The Liar School of Herodotus*. Amsterdam: J.C. Gieben Publisher, 1993.

———. *Marathon*. Berkeley: University of California Press, 1960.

———. *Studies in Ancient Greek Topography, Part II: Battlefields*. Los Angeles: University of California Press, 1969.

———. *Studies in Ancient Greece Topography, Part IV: Passes*. Los Angeles: University of California Press, 1982.

Raaflaub, Kurt A. *The Discovery of Freedom in Ancient Greece*. Chicago: University of Chicago Press, 2004.

———. "Greece." In *Ancient History: Recent Work and New Directions*, ed. Stanley Burstein, Ramsay MacMellen, Kurt A. Raaflaub, and Allen M. Ward. Clairmont: Regina Books, 1997.

———. "Herodotus, Marathon and the Historian's Choice." In *Marathon: The Battle and the Ancient Deme*, ed. Kostas Buraselis-Katerina Meidani. Athens: Institut Du Livre- A. Kardamitsa, 2010.

Raaflaub, K., and N. Rosenstein, eds. *War and Society in the Ancient Mediterranean, Europe and Mesoamerica*. Boston: Harvard University Press, 1999.

Rahe, Paul. "The Military Situation in Western Asia on the Eve of Cunaxa." *American Journal of Philology* 101, no. 1 (Spring 1980): 79–96.

Raubitschek, A.E. *The Greek Historians: Literature and History: Papers Presented to A. E. Raubitschek*. Palo Alto, CA: Stanford University Press, 1985.

———. "Two Monuments Erected after the Victory of Marathon." *American Journal of Archaeology* 44, no. 1 (January–March 1940): 53–59.

Rawlings, Louis. *The Ancient Greeks at War*. Manchester: Manchester University Press, 2007.

Rawlinson, George. *The Five Great Monarchies of the Ancient Eastern World*. New York: Dodd, Mead, 1881.

Ray, Fred Eugene. *The Land Battles in 5th Century BC Greece: A History and Analysis of 173 Engagements*. Jefferson, NC: McFarland, 2009.

Reynolds, P.K. Baillie. "The Shield Signal at the Battle of Marathon." *Journal of Hellenic Studies* 49 (1929): 100–105.

Rhodes, P.J. "The Impact of the Persian Wars on Classical Greece." In *Cultural Responses to the Persian Wars*, ed. Emma Bridges, Edith Hill, and P.J. Rhodes. New York: Oxford University Press, 2007.

Robinson, E.S.G. "Rhegion, Zankle-Messana and the Samians." *Journal of Hellenic Studies* 66 (1946): 13–20.

Roisman, Joseph. *Ancient Greece from Homer to Alexander: The Evidence*. Chichester, West Sussex: Wiley and Blackwell, 2011.

Rose, H.J. *A Commentary on the Surviving Plays of Aeschylus*. Vol. 1. Amsterdam: Noord-Hollandsche Uitgevers-maatschappij, 1957.

Ruiters, Ronald. "Marathon Dawn." *Ancient Warfare Special Issue 2011: Battle of Marathon*, 32.

Runciman, W.G. "Greek Hoplites, Warrior Culture and Indirect Bias." *Journal of the Royal Anthropological Institute* 4, no. 4 (December 1998): 731–751.

Sabin, Philip. *Lost Battles: Reconstructing the Great Clashes of the Ancient World*. New York: Hambledon Continuum, 2007.

Sabin, Philip, and Michael Whitby, eds. *The Cambridge History of Greek and Roman Warfare*. Vol. 1. New York: Cambridge University Press, 2007.

Sage, Michael M. *Warfare in Ancient Greece: A Sourcebook*. New York: Routledge, 1996.
Sancisi-Weerdenburg, Heleen, and Amelie Kuhrt, eds. *Achaemenid History I & II*. Leiden: Leiden University Press, 1987.
Santosuosso, A. *Soldiers, Citizens and the Symbols of War*. Boulder, CO: Westview Press, 1997.
Salmon, Paul. "Political Hoplites." *Journal of Hellenic Studies* 97 (1977): 84–101.
Sargent, Rachel L. *The Size of the Slave Population during the Fifth and Fourth Centuries before Christ*. University Studies in Social Sciences 7, no. 3. Urbana: University of Illinois Press, 1924.
_____. "The Use of Slaves by the Athenians in Warfare." *Classical Philology* 22, no. 2 (April 1927): 201–212.
_____. "The Use of Slaves by the Athenians in Warfare." *Classical Philology* 22, no. 3 (July 1927): 264–279.
Scheidel, Walter. "Demography." In *The Cambridge Economic History of the Greco-Roman World*, ed. Walter Scheidel, Ian Morris, and Richard P. Saller. Cambridge: Cambridge University Press, 2007.
Scheidel, Walter, Ian Morris, and Richard Saller. *The Cambridge Economic History of the Greco-Roman World*. New York: Cambridge University Press, 2007.
Schreiner, J.H. *Two Battles and Two Bills. Marathon and the Athenian Fleet*. The Norwegian Institute at Athens. Monographs, vol. 3. Oslo, University of Oslo, 2004.
Schwartz, Adam. *Reinstating the Hoplite: Arms, Armour and Phalanx Fighting in Archaic and Classical Greece*. Stuttgart: Franz Steiner Verlag, 2009.
Scott, Lionel. *A Historical Commentary on Herodotus Book 6*. Leiden: Brill, 2005.
Sealey, Raphael. "The Pit and the Well: The Persian Heralds of 491 BCE." *Classical Journal* 77 (1976): 13–20.
Sekunda, Nicholas. "The Achaemenid Military Terminology." *Archaeologische Mitteilungen aus Iran* 21 (1988): 69–77.
_____. *Greek Hoplite, 480–323*. New York: Osprey Publishing, 2000.
_____. *Marathon, 490 BCE: The First Persian Invasion of Greece*. New York: Osprey Publishing, 2002.
_____. *The Persian Army, 560–330 BC*. New York: Osprey Publishing, 1992.
_____. "The Persians." In *Warfare in the Ancient World*, ed. John Hackett. New York: Facts on File, 1989.
Shaw, Timothy, ed. *The Trireme Project: Operational Experience 1987–90, Lessons Learned*. Oxford: Oxbow, 1993.
Shay, Jonathan. *Achilles in Vietnam*. New York: Scribner, 1994.
_____. "Learning about Combat Stress from Homer's Iliad." *Journal of Traumatic Stress* 4, no. 4 (1991): 561–579.
Showalter, Dennis E. "Of Decisive Battles and Intellectual Fashions: Sir Edward Creasy Revisited." *Military Affairs* 52, no. 4 (October 1988): 206–208.
Shrimpton, Gordon. "The Persian Cavalry at Marathon." *Phoenix* 34 (1980): 20–37.
Sidnell, Phil. "Press Home the Charge." *Ancient Warfare* 6, no. 3 (2012).
Simpson, R. Hope. "Leonidas' Decision." *Phoenix* 26, no. 1 (Spring 1972): 1–11.
Snodgrass, A.M. *Arms and Amour of the Greeks*. Ithaca, NY: Cornell University Press, 1967.
_____. *Early Greek Armour and Weapons from the Bronze Age to 600 BCE*. Edinburgh: University Press, 1964.
_____. "The Hoplite Reform and History." *Journal of Hellenic Studies* 85 (1965): 110–122.
Stanier, R.S. "Letter." *Greece and Rome* 16, no. 48 (October 1947): 133–134.
Starr, C.G. "Why Did the Greeks Defeat the Persians?" In *Essays on Ancient History*, ed. A. Ferrill and T. Kelly. Leiden: Brill, 1979.
Strasser, Robert, ed. *The Landmark Herodotus: The Histories*. New York: Pantheon, 2007.
Tarn, W.W. "The Fleet of Xerxes." *Journal of Hellenic Studies* 28 (1908): 202–233.
Taylor, Jeremy G. "Oinoe and the Painted Stoa: Ancient and Modern Misunderstandings?" *American Journal of Philology* 119 (1978): 223–243.
Trittle, Lawrence A. *From Melos to Mylai*. New York: Routledge, 2000.
_____. "Warfare in Herodotus." In *The Cambridge Companion to Herodotus*, ed. Carolyn Diewald and John Marincola. Cambridge: Cambridge University Press, 2006.
Tuplin, Christopher. "All the King's Horse: In Search of Achaemenid Persian Cavalry." In *New Perspectives in Ancient Warfare*, ed. Garrett G. Fagan and Matthew Trundle. Boston: Brill, 2010.
_____. "Marathon: In Search of a Persian Dimension." In *Marathon: The Battle and the Ancient Deme*, ed. Kostas Buraselis-Katerina Meidani. Athens: Instutut Du Livre-A Kardamitsa, 2010.
_____. Review of *The Greek Wars. The Failure of Persia*, by George Cawkwell. *Journal of Hellenic Studies* 126 (2006): 170–171.
Van der Veer, J.A.G. "The Battle of Marathon: A Topographical Survey." *Mnemosyne* 35 (1982): 290–321.
Van Wees, Hans. "The Development of the Hoplite Phalanx: Iconography and Reality in the Seventh Century," in *War and Violence in Ancient Greece*, ed. Hans Van Wees. London: Duckworth, 2004.
_____. *Greek Warfare: Myths and Realities*. London: Duckworth, 2004.
_____. "The Myth of the Middle Class Army: Military and Social Class in Ancient Athens." In *War*

as a Cultural and Social Force: Essays on Warfare in Antiquity, ed. Tonnes Bekker-Nielson and Lise Hannestad. Copenhagen: Det Kongelige Danske Videnskabernes Selskab, 2001.
———, ed. *War and Violence in Ancient Greece*. London: Duckworth, 2000.
Vanderpool, Eugene. "An Archaic Inscribed Stele from Marathon." *Hesperia: The Journal of the American School of Classical Studies at Athens* 11, no. 4 (October–December 1942): 329–337.
———. "The Deme of Marathon and the Herakleion." *American Journal of Archaeology* 7, no. 4 (October 1966): 319–323.
———. "A Monument to the Battle of Marathon." *Hesperia: The Journal of the American School of Classical Studies at Athens* 35, no. 2 (1966): 93–106.
Vaughn, Pamela. "The Identification and Retrieval of the Hoplite Battle-Dead." In *Hoplites: The Greek Classical Battle Experience*, ed. Victor Davis Hanson. New York: Routledge, 1991.
Wade-Gery, H.T. *Essays on Greek History*. Oxford: Basil Blackwell, 1958.
———. "Miltiades." *Journal of Hellenic Studies* 71 (1951): 212–221.
Wallinga, H.T. "The Ancient Persian Navy & Its Predecessors." In *Achaemenid History I*, ed. Heleen Sancisi-Weerdenburg and Amelie Kuhrt. Leiden: Leiden University Press, 1987.
———. "The Ionian Revolt." *Mnemosyne*, 4th series, 37 (1984): 401–437.
———. *Ships and Sea-Power before the Great Persian War: The Ancestry of the Ancient Trireme*. Leiden: Brill, 1993.
———. "The Trireme and Its Crew." In *Studies in Honor of H.L.W. Nelson*, ed. J. den Boeft and A.H.M. Kessels. Utrecht: Instituut voor Klassieke Talen, 1982.
———. "The Unit of Capacity for Ancient Ships." *Mnemosyne* 17 (1964): 1–40.
———. *Xerxes' Great Adventure: The Naval Perspective*. Leiden: Brill, 2005.
Wardman, A.E. "Tactics and the Tradition of the Persian Wars." *Historia: Zeitschrift fur Alte Geschichte* 8 (1959): 49–60.
Waters, K.H. "Herodotus and the Ionian Revolt." *Historia: Zeitschrift fur Alte Geschichte* 49 (November 1970): 504–508.
———. *Herodotus the Historian*. London: Croom Helm, 1985.
Wells, J. "The Persian Friends of Herodotus." *Journal of Hellenic Studies* 27 (1907): 37–47.
West, Stephanie. "And It Came to Pass That Pharaoh Dreamed: Notes on Herodotus 2.139–141." *Classical Quarterly*, new series, 37, no. 2 (1987): 262–271.
West, Stephanie. "Herodotus' Epigraphical Interests." *Classical Quarterly*, new series, 35, no. 2 (1985): 278–305.
West, Stephanie. Review of *Herodotus' Autopsy of the Fayoum: Lake Morris and the Labyrinth*, by O. Kimball Armayor. *Classical Review* 37, no. 1 (1987): 8.
Whatley, N. "Marathon." *Proceedings of the Hellenic Traveler's Club* 129 (1927): 67–75.
Whatley, N. "On the Possibility of Reconstructing Marathon and Other Ancient Battles." *Journal of Hellenic Studies* 84 (1964): 119–139.
Wheeler, Everett. "The General as Hoplite." In *Hoplites: The Classical Greek Battle Experience*, ed. Victor Davis Hanson. New York: Routledge, 1991.
Wheeler, Everett L. "Greece: Mad Hatters and March Hares." In *Recent Directions in the Military History of the Ancient World*. Claremont: Regina Books, 2011.
Wheeler, Everett L. "Land Battles." In *The Cambridge History of Greek and Roman Warfare*, ed. Phillip Sabin, Hans van Wees, and Michael Whitby. Cambridge: Cambridge University Press, 2007.
Wheeler, Everett, and Barry Straus. "Battle." In *The Cambridge History of Greek and Roman Warfare*, ed. Phillip Sabin, Hans van Wees, and Michael Whitby. Cambridge: Cambridge University Press, 2007.
Whitehead, Ian. "What Constitutes a 'Better Sailing' Ship?" In *The Trireme Project: Operational Experience 1978–90, Lessons Learned*. Oxford: Oxbow Books.
Wiesehofer, Josef. "The Achaemenid Empire." In *The Dynamics of Ancient Empires: State Power from Assyria to Byzantium*, ed. Ian Morris and Walter Scheidel. New York: Oxford University Press, 2009.
Williams, Dyfri. "A Cup by the Antophon Painter and the Battle of Marathon." In *Studien zur Mythologie Und Vasenmalerei: Konrad Schauenburg zum 65. Geburtstag am 16 April 1986*. Mainz am Rhein: Verlag Philipp von Zabern, 1986.
Winter, F.E. *Greek Fortifications*. Toronto: University of Toronto Press, 1971.
Wozniak, Marek. "The Achaemenid Army at Marathon: The Army of All Nations." *Ancient Warfare*, Special Issue 2011: The Battle of Marathon, 80.
Wycherley, R.E. "The Painted Stoa. 'Sapiens Bracatis Inlita Medis Porticus.' Persius 3. 53–54." *Phoenix* 7, no. 1 (Spring 1953): 20–35.
Young, T.C. "The Consolidation of the Empire and the Limits of Its Growth under Darius and Xerxes." In *The Cambridge Ancient History*, vol. 4, *Persia, Greece and the Western Mediterranean c. 525–479 BCE*, 2nd ed., ed. John Boardman, N.G.L. Hammond, D.M. Lewis, and M. Ostwald. Cambridge: Cambridge University Press, 1988.
Zutterman, Christopher. "The Bow in the Ancient Near East: A Reevaluation of Archery from the Late 2nd Millennium to the End of the Achaemenid Empire." *Iranica Antiqua* 38 (2003): 119–165.

Index

Adcock, F.D. 10, 30
Aegina 90, 91, 110, 111, 141, 142, 160
Aeschylus 11, 22–24, 34, 168
Ageladas 141
agonal warfare 46, 53
Aiakes 81, 98, 106
Amasis 69, 70
amphibious landings 74, 125, 128, 130, 143, 149
antilabe 30–32
Apasthines 72
Apis 70–72
Aristagoras 79, 81, 85, 91–96, 100–104, 112
Aristides 182
Aristophanes 137, 138, 190
Aristotle 44, 135, 144, 180
Armayor, O. Kimball 4, 7–9
Artabazos 5
Artaphernes (co-leader at Marathon) 20, 129, 131, 135, 137, 147, 152, 176, 188
Artaphernes, Satrap of Sardis 80, 85, 91–92, 95–97, 101–107, 111, 112
aspis 32, 49
Assyrian Empire 62, 63, 69
Astyages 62, 63, 65, 142
Athens 5, 26, 44, 46, 52, 61, 77, 81, 89–91, 106, 109–117, 119, 122–125, 128, 129, 131, 133–153, 161, 164, 167, 169–184, 186–190
Attic helmet 41

Babylon 3–5, 16, 17, 62, 64–68, 70, 74, 86, 142, 188
baivarabam 14
battle casualties 57–59
battle of Artemisium 12, 24, 97, 118
battle of Lade 20, 22, 96–99, 104–106, 128
battle of Plataea 6, 12, 115, 119, 120, 132, 155
battle of Salamis 11, 12, 23, 24
battle of Sphacteria 164, 165
bell cuirass 37–38

Berossus 68
Berthold, R.M. 135, 136, 145
Billows, Richard A. 77, 120, 129, 133, 137, 140, 147, 153, 154, 157, 167, 173, 174, 177, 190
Blamire, A. 76, 88, 93, 101, 103–106
Blyth, P.H. 33–36, 39, 40, 185
Bowden, Hugh 9
Briant, Pierre 73, 74, 109, 188
Bugh, Glenn 133
Burdunias, Paul 35, 49
Burn, A.R. 23, 123, 136, 137, 138, 167, 176
Bury, J.B. 12, 22, 106, 118, 124, 170
butt-spike 34–37, 40, 54

Callimachus 116, 117, 135, 144, 146, 150–152, 154, 161, 168, 183, 187
Cambyses 9, 20, 23, 62, 67, 69–74, 88, 142
Campbell, Duncan 142
Caria 4, 70, 81, 83, 87, 93, 95–97
Carneia festival 140
Casson, Lionel 26, 178, 181
Cassons, S. 13
Cawkwell, George 4, 16, 23, 24, 57, 79, 81, 87, 89, 90, 103, 107, 129, 131, 161, 164–166
Charadra 121, 122, 123, 126, 149, 153
chiliachs 14
Cholcians 8
Cleomenes 89, 90, 140–142
cleruchs 113, 114, 133
Connolly, Peter 30
Cook, J.M. 4, 6, 9, 18, 21, 23, 73
Corinth 13, 30, 56, 90, 160
Corinthian helmet 38–41, 48, 180, 181, 184, 186
cost of creating Persian navy 25–26
Crecy, Edward 186, 188
Croesus 63–66, 68, 85
Ctesias 9, 11, 12, 65, 69, 112
Cyclades 82, 100, 110–112, 115, 120, 188

Cyprus and the Ionian revolt 94, 95
Cyropedia 12, 14, 44
Cyrus 11, 16, 17, 20, 62–70, 72, 73, 80, 88, 98, 100, 103, 142
Cyrus cylinder 68

Darius: claim to throne 74; reorganization of Empire 77, 78
dathabatis 14, 28
Datis 12, 20, 111–115, 129, 131, 132, 136, 137, 141, 146, 147, 149–152, 171–173, 176–179, 188
Daurises 95, 96
dekarchs 14, 28
delay before the battle 144, 145
Delbruk, Hans 22, 27, 47, 52, 155, 156, 150, 161
Delian League 25, 26, 189
Demaratus 141–142
Demokedes of Kroton 5
deployment of armies 152–154
Dickins, Guy 141
Didyma 85, 99, 100
diekplous 26, 98, 99
Diodorus Siculus 8, 12, 20, 21, 71, 164, 165
Dionysus of Phocaea 98, 99
Doenges, Norman A. 119, 124, 128, 130, 136, 150, 162
Donlan and Thompson 156–160
Ducrey, Pierre 61
Dunn, Richard 122, 126, 169
Du Picq, Colonel 51
duration of the battle 164–166

"earth and water" 75, 110, 111, 141
economy of Ionia 86, 87
education of Persian boys 15, 17
effectiveness of hoplite shield 33–34
Egypt, invasion of 70–71
Ephesus 81, 91–93, 97, 99
Ephorus 12
epic tradition 4, 11, 165, 166
Epizelus 117
Eretria 81, 91, 109–117, 120, 124, 125, 126, 128–131, 133, 135,

227

136, 138, 141, 143, 145, 148–150, 160, 175, 176, 178, 183, 188
Euboea 18, 82, 91, 113, 114, 124
Evans, J.A.S. 7, 8, 19, 65, 80, 84, 89, 102, 119, 120, 130, 148, 172, 179, 184

Farrokh, Dr. Kaveh 16
Fehling, Detlov 4, 6–10
Ferrill, Arthur 10, 11, 162
Figueira, Thomas 133
Flower, Michael 4
Forrest, W.G. 80, 84, 85
Fowler, Robert 10

Gabriel and Metz 36, 40, 57, 58, 167, 185
Gaebel, Robert 133, 162
Georges, Pericles B. 76, 84, 87, 92, 101–103, 107
Gobyras 67, 68, 72, 73
Goodman, M.D. 140
Gorgo 90
Graf, Donald Frank 89, 99, 111, 115, 135, 145
Gray and Cary 86, 92, 93, 107, 109, 114
great marsh 121, 122, 125, 126, 164, 168, 169, 180
Greek and Persian casualties 167–168
Greek and Persian triremes compared 21–22
Greek charge 154–160
Greek command structure 44–45
Greek sword 42–44, 54, 58, 186
Green, Peter 24, 123, 126, 135, 137, 139, 140, 147, 177, 187
Grote, George 13, 22, 139, 154–6, 169, 176, 182
Grundy, G.B. 84, 85, 91, 92, 96, 97, 100, 101, 104–106, 109, 110, 112, 114, 123, 128, 130, 132, 136, 146, 155, 176, 183

Hammond, N.G.L. 5, 27, 119–122, 125, 129, 131, 133, 136, 149, 150, 152, 153, 156, 157, 163, 171, 173, 176, 179, 180, 182, 184, 187
Hanson, Victor Davis 31, 40, 44, 52, 58
Harpagus 62, 63, 66, 103, 106
Harris, George 76, 84, 86–88, 92, 93, 96, 97, 99, 101, 104, 106, 107
hazarapatis 14
Head, Duncan 12, 16, 17, 26–28, 30
Hecataeus 80, 85
Hellespont 5, 7, 75, 82, 93, 104, 106, 109
helots 90, 139, 141, 142
hemerodromes 138

Herakleion 122, 125, 136, 151–154, 182
"heretical view" 49–50
Herodotus 3–15, 17, 18, 20–26, 28, 36, 47, 62, 63, 65, 66–74, 75–77, 79–85, 87, 90–107, 109–115, 117–122, 124–133, 134, 135, 138, 139, 142–165, 167–175, 181–184, 190; as military historian 10–11
Hignett, C. 10–12, 14, 23, 97, 110, 118, 130, 133, 135, 145, 149, 153, 156
Hippias 116, 117, 124, 125, 128, 131, 145–148, 161, 176, 189
Histiaeus 75, 76, 79, 82, 85, 87, 88, 93, 94, 96, 100–106
Histories 4, 6, 12, 80, 107
Hodge, A. Trevor 172, 173, 178, 179, 181
Holland, Tom 140, 141, 177
Holliday, James 140
Holoka, James 164, 172, 179, 180, 181
Homer 4, 47, 48, 49, 51, 58
hoplite 6, 10, 16, 19, 20, 28, 30, 31, 32–55, 57–61, 84, 113, 115, 117, 121, 125, 131–134, 152, 154–160, 162, 164–166, 173–173, 177, 178, 180, 181, 185, 186; battle described 53–55; panoply 30, 31, 34, 38, 39, 43–45, 48, 51, 52, 58, 156–160, 164, 166, 185; shield construction 31–32; spear 34–37
hoplon 30
horse transports 18, 21, 112, 114, 120, 128, 129, 131, 132, 160, 179
How and Wells 5, 22, 118, 124, 128, 137, 140, 145, 146, 152, 154, 155, 170, 176, 189
Hudson, Harris Gary 171
Hydarnes 72

iconography 19, 42, 43, 48–52
Immortals 14, 16, 27
importance of Ionian Revolt 107–108
Intaphrenes 72
Ionia 4, 7, 14, 16, 20, 20–23, 63–67, 75, 76, 79–81, 125, 127, 128, 129, 147, 149, 150, 161, 163, 183, 186; cities 65, 66, 76, 81, 86, 89, 97, 107
Ionian Revolt 79–110, 128, 130, 135, 143, 188

Jarva, Eero 37–39, 42–44

Keaveney, Arthur 83–84
Khurt, Amelie 71, 112
King Darius 3, 5, 8, 9, 14, 16, 17, 23, 25, 26, 67, 72–77, 83, 86, 87, 88, 91, 95, 96, 100, 101, 103–106, 109–111, 113, 115, 128, 143, 186, 188
Koes 75, 76
kopis 43
Krentz, Peter 13, 28, 32, 37–39, 44, 47, 48, 50, 52, 56, 57, 80, 87, 113, 115, 120–123, 129, 131, 133, 137, 139–141, 148–151, 153, 154, 157–160, 163, 167, 169, 173, 175, 181, 182, 184, 187
Kynosoura 121, 126, 168

Labyrinth 7, 192
Lacey, Jim 29, 57, 66, 67, 71, 74, 120, 125, 128, 132, 145, 153, 154, 158–160, 162, 174, 178
Lake Moeris 7–8
Lang, Mabel 81, 93, 100, 102–104
Larsen, Jacob A.O. 90
Lateiner, Donald Wayne 9, 81, 83, 91, 97, 98
Lazenby, J.F. 5, 9–11, 14, 26, 30, 124, 125, 128, 131, 135, 150, 154, 157, 172, 187
Leake, W.M. 119, 122, 123, 172, 182
Liar School of Herodotus 4, 6, 8, 9
light troops 46
Lloyd, W. Watkins 155
Lorimer, H. 30, 31, 42
Lydia 16, 17, 62–66, 69, 75, 86, 87, 91, 152; cavalry 17, 64

Macan, R.W. 5, 11–13, 22, 26, 93, 118, 137, 139–140, 146, 148, 154, 155, 170, 175
Macaria 122, 123, 125, 126, 149–151, 163, 169, 184
magus 72, 73
Manville, P.B. 93, 101, 102, 106
march back to Athens 175–181
Mardonius 14, 107, 109–113, 143
Marshall, S.L.A. 51
Matthew, Christopher 35–37, 50, 138, 139, 185
Maurice, General Frederick 121, 122, 129, 131, 147, 156, 171
Medes 17, 21, 22, 28, 62, 63, 103, 116–118, 130, 131, 142, 152, 153
Median Empire 62, 63, 67
Megabates 82–85, 889
Megabysos 72, 75, 76, 103
Megabyzus 5
Messenians 142
Miletus 21, 75, 76, 81, 82, 84–106, 114, 125, 135
Miltiades 12, 13, 56, 75, 102, 106, 116–119, 125, 134, 135, 137, 144–152, 154, 156, 161, 163, 175, 176, 179, 180, 183, 184, 187
Morrison, J.S. 21
Mt. Agrieliki 121, 122, 124, 152, 153

Mt. Athos 109, 110, 128, 143
Mt. Drakonera 121
Mt. Starokoraki 125, 150
Munro, J.A.R. 22, 124, 125, 127, 128, 130, 135, 146–149, 156, 164, 176
Murray, Oswyn 10, 79, 86, 87, 94, 95, 107, 109, 113–115
muscle cuirass 37
Myrcinus 75, 76, 95, 102, 105
myriarchs 14

Naxos campaign 82–85
Nepos, Cornelius 12, 13, 129, 132, 146, 148, 149, 151, 162
Neville, J. 80, 81
Nubia 70, 71

Oibares 9
Olmstead, A.T. 22, 80
Olympia 31, 32, 35, 39, 41–43, 53, 122
Oracle at Delphi 6, 31, 53, 63, 64, 99, 141, 187
Oroites 16, 74, 77, 78
Otanes 5, 72, 73, 95, 97
othismos 35, 49, 50, 55–57, 166

Pan 138, 139
Pausanias 118, 121, 132, 142, 148, 167, 168, 182
Peisistratus 124, 135
Peloponnesian league 90, 111
Penofsky, H. 6
penteconters 21, 83
Persia: cavalry 17–20, 27, 106, 118–120, 133, 136, 143–146; 149, 150, 155, 158–163, 170; navy 20–24, 70, 78, 97, 107, 109, 142, 176, 183; style of fighting 142–144; sword 26–27, 29, 186; weapons and armor 26–28
Persian bows 27–28
Persian Wars 3–6, 11–13, 23, 34, 49, 52, 111, 118, 135, 140, 185
phalanx 10, 30, 37, 40, 45, 46–60, 125, 144, 147, 156–159, 162, 164, 166, 167, 184, 186, 189
Phaleron 117, 124, 125, 131, 134, 146–149, 161, 170–172, 175–181, 190
Phanes 69, 70
Philippides 116, 137–140, 174
Phoenicians 20, 23, 24, 94, 113
Pindar 8, 11
Plataea 5, 56, 116, 117, 133, 134, 148, 152, 182
Plato 44, 128, 129, 141, 190
Plutarch 13, 91, 92, 130, 174, 175, 181, 182

polemarchon 47, 116–118, 152, 183
porpax 30–31
Prexaspes 70, 72
Pritchett, W. Kendrick 8, 9, 53, 61, 121, 122, 123, 126, 163, 164
Propontus 7, 86, 95
provisional levees 16
Psammenitos 70
pteryges 38
punishment of Miletus 106

quickstep 155

Raaflaub, Kurt 20
Rawlings, Louis 164
Ray, Fred Allen 121, 129, 130, 134, 150, 153, 167
Reynolds, P.K. Baillie 170, 171

Saka 28, 74, 117, 130, 152
Salman, John 30
Samos 5, 21, 81, 88, 90, 94, 97–99, 106, 107, 112, 143
Sardis 4, 16, 24, 25, 64–66, 75, 76, 81, 82, 89, 91, 92, 95, 96, 101, 102, 113
satapatis 14
sauroter 34–37, 40, 54
Sayce, A.H. 6
Schoenia 125, 126, 152, 168, 180, 186
Schreiner, John Henrik 13, 151
Schwartz, Adam 30, 34, 36, 39, 41–44, 49, 50, 57, 165, 166
Scott, Lionel 6, 10, 21, 113–115, 122, 123, 125, 131, 137, 135, 137–140, 144, 145, 154, 173
Scythia 4, 22, 27, 40, 67, 74–77, 86, 87, 89, 90, 197, 110, 128
Scythian campaign 22, 97, 110, 128
Sealey, Raphael 110, 111
Sekunda, Nicholas 12, 14, 16, 17, 33–36, 147
shield signal 169–173
Shrimpton, Gordon 18, 161, 184
Sidnell, Phil 19
Skylax 82–84
small marsh 122–124, 136, 153
Smerdis 70, 71, 72, 73, 74
Snodgrass, A.M. 30, 31, 33, 38, 39, 42
Soros 152, 153, 155, 164, 167, 182
Sounion 117, 175, 179
Spada 16
Sparta 4, 15, 34, 44, 49, 51, 64, 65, 77, 89–91, 110, 111, 115–117,

120, 131, 135, 137–142, 144–151, 161, 165, 166, 170, 171, 173, 174, 178, 189, 190; and the Ionian Revolt 89–90
spearhead of Greek spear 34–36
split force theory 146–150
Stoa Poikile 5, 162, 187
strategoi 118
Suda 147–151, 161, 163, 188
Syloson 5, 98

Tarn, W.W. 22
tattooed slave story 100–101
Thasos 105, 110
Themistocles 13, 21, 102, 190
Thucydides 10, 12, 46, 47, 48, 60, 79, 118, 155, 164–166, 190
Tomyris 68
tonarchs 14
topography of marathon 121–124
"traditional view" 21, 30, 48, 52, 56, 57, 78
triaconters 21
trireme 21–26, 83, 91, 97, 104, 122, 127, 132
Trojan War 4
Tuplin, Christopher 19, 131, 132, 151, 163, 164, 184
tyrants 6, 75, 76, 81, 82, 85, 87–89, 92–94, 96, 98, 101, 104, 106, 107, 116, 128, 131, 142, 186, 189
Tyrtaios 34, 45, 46, 49, 52

Vanderpool, Eugene 123, 136, 153, 154, 182
van der Veer, J.A.G. 122, 123, 143, 152, 153, 182
van Wees, Hans 30, 43, 44, 47, 49, 50, 52, 54, 56
Vrana valley 122, 123, 136, 137, 150–153, 155, 182

Wallace, W.P. 141
Wallinga, H.T. 20, 21, 23–26, 80, 83, 128
Wells, J. 4
West, Stephanie 4, 7–9
Whatley, Norman 126–130, 133, 148, 149, 156
Wheeler, Everett L. 46, 57, 165
Whitehead, David 30
Winter, F.E. 135
Wyatt, William F. 168

Xenophon 12, 14–16, 44, 63, 69, 155, 166, 188
Xerxes 4, 5, 6, 11, 12, 21–24, 26, 106, 112, 120, 127, 188–189

www.ingramcontent.com/pod-product-compliance
Lightning Source LLC
Chambersburg PA
CBHW081553300426
44116CB00015B/2865